Corbett Mack

Illustrations

Maps
(*following page 22*)
Map 1. Smith and Mason valleys, Nevada
Map 2. Walker River region

Plates
(*following page 80*)
1. Corbett Mack, ca. 1970
2. Paiutes in camp
3. Two views of Stewart Institute, ca. 1910
4. Stewart Institute students, ca. 1910

Acknowledgments

A book as long in the making as this requires many acknowledgments. Fieldwork in Yerington was originally funded by National Science Foundation grants: the Field Training Program in Anthropology, (Department of Anthropology, University of Nevada, 1965) and a Grant Supporting Doctoral Dissertation Work (GS-2007) in 1969. IN 1992 I received a grant from the Nevada Humanities Committee of the National Endowment for the Humanities (NHC 87-33), and I thank its executive director, Judy Winzeler, for support and friendship. Long Island University, where I have been employed since 1968, has supported me in countless ways, most recently with funding from a Title III Grant, and I take pleasure expressing my appreciation to its administrator, my good friend Darlene Kindermann.

Kathleen O'Connor brought cartons of raw data to my desk in the Leo J. Ryan Memorial Federal Archives Building, San Bruno, California, and also answered many questions. Phillip I. Earle, curator of history at the Nevada Historical Society in Reno, often hosted me. He (and staff members) directed me to state newspapers for data on opiates and to other invaluable sources. Susan Searcy, manuscript curator, and Linda Perry, library assistant—in fact, the entire staff at Special Collections at the University of Nevada Libraries, Reno—were also enormously helpful and always courteous. So, too, were the staffs at the Lyon County Courthouse and at the Municipal Library in Yerington, where I spent numerous research hours.

I also wish to thank the staff of the Inter-Tribal Council of Nevada and particularly an old friend, Shayne Del Cohen, for allowing me to copy material they retrieved from the National Archives, Washington, D.C., for use in the Notes section of this book. This material as yet has not been cataloged in San Bruno and is cited here as ITC Archives.

Most recently, Jeff Kintop at the Nevada State Archives building helped by guiding me through State Prison Records. There in Carson City I had the eerie experience of finally seeing the faces—albeit mug shots—of Smith and Mason Valley opiate addicts whom Corbett Mack so frequently had told me about. Over the years, too, my late uncle Bernard Bader of Walnut Creek, California, not only generously put me up in his home, but also lent me a second car to conduct this research. I will always miss him.

Most of my informants, regrettably, are also dead: Andy Dick, Nellie Emm, Brady Emm, Hazel Quinn, Rosie Brown, Richard "Switch" Brown, Henry Fredericks, Irene Thompson, Howard Rogers, Chester Smith, and, of course, the subject of this work, Corbett Mack. They fed me well and taught me everything I learned about Northern Paiutes apart from the books; I note in this regard the supplemental assistance received from Russell Dick and Corbett's three surviving nieces: Lena Rogers, Bernice Crutcher, and Elsie Sam Ausmus. They not only were most cooperative in remembering their beloved uncle for me, but Mrs. Crutcher also went through a family album and lent me several photographs. Kay Fowler was kind enough to allow me to quote from the handout on Northern Paiute prayer delivered at a convention; her friendship over the years and her knowledge have enriched me.

Lastly, Ida Mae Valdez, whom I call *beeya*, or mother, because since 1965 this remarkable human being opened her home and Paiute family and embracing heart to me, recently chided me for writing this book. "He's a nobody," she said. "Corbett Mack's just a plain ordinary Indian drunk." Dear Ida, that is precisely the point. And just as the English Puritans opposed bear baiting, not so much because it gave paint to the bear, but because it brought pleasure to the participants, so too have I delayed writing about this destructive and painful subject for similar reasons.

Note on Orthography

Trained though I was to transcribe Northern Paiute according to the IPA, I have adopted transcription changes that have resulted over the years primarily from the work of Arie Poldervaart, Wycliffe Bible translator. In writing the *Yerington Paiute Language Grammar* and *Paiute-English/English-Paiute Dictionary* for the Yerington Paiute Tribe, Poldervaart taught us how to simplify the writing of the language. For even greater simplification, I have modified his system as follows:

aa	long *a* as in *bait*
oo	long *o* as in *boot*
ee	long *e* as in *we*
^	*u* as in *but*
uu	barred *i* as in *"jist"*
rr	trill as in the spanish *burro*
'	glottal stop
dz	as in *rouge*
gh	Germanic guttural

Stress is frequently on the second syllable. Final vowels are frequently silent.

Introduction

Corbett Mack: The Life of a Northern Paiute is an as-told-by (rather than -to) life history or "Indian autobiography" of Corbett Mack (1892-1974), my primary Northern Paiute informant. A "contradiction in terms," as Arnold Krupat has recently defined this genre,

> Indian autobiographies are collaborative efforts jointly produced by some white who translates, transcribes, compiles, edits, interprets, polishes, and ultimately determines the "form" of the text in writing, and by an Indian who is its "subject" and whose "life" becomes the "content" of the "autobiography" whose title may bear his name. [in Swann 1983:272]

Another literary critic who has made important contributions to this longstanding field of interest to anthropologists (cf. Kluckhohn 1945; Langness 1965; Mandelbaum 1973) is H. David Brumble III. According to Brumble (1988:10), the Indian autobiographer "will try to elicit stories about his subject's childhood, because his literate, western audience expects autobiography to answer [these questions]." This results, Brumble writes, in texts in which it is "the Anglo editor, who decides, finally, what is to get the shape of his subject's 'autobiography'" (1988:11). Emphasizing what Krupat has termed their "bicultural composite authorship" (in Swann 1983:272), Brumble significantly also adds: "The editors of life-history materials almost always arrange things in chronological order (whatever may have been the sense of time implicit in the autobiographical tales themselves)" (1988:16).

By his count, more than 600 such narratives have thus far been published (Brumble 1988:76): 43 percent of them collected and edited by anthropologists, another 40 percent edited by (other) non-Native Americans. The life histories or Indian autobiographies of Sam Blowsnake, Winnebago (Radin [1920] 1963), Chona, the Papago woman (Underhill [1936] 1979), Don Talayesva, Orabi Hopi (Simmons [1942] 1971), and, of course, Nicholas Black Elk (Neihardt 1932; DeMallie 1984) immediately come to mind. Yet for the Great Basin, and Northern Paiutes particularly, only a handful of these exist: the Humboldt River Paiute "Princess" Sarah Winnemucca's "heavily edited" (by Mrs. Horace Mann, cf. Brumble 1988:37, 61) influential plaint (Hopkins [1882] 1969; Canfield 1983), factually, among the earliest of this genre; two (brief) life histories of the Owens Valley Paiutes Jake Stewart and Sam Newland, as collected and presented by Julian Steward in 1934; and that of Lovelock Paiute Annie Lowry (b. 1856), as told to Lalla Scott in 1936 (1966). More recently, autobiographical sketches of well-known Great Basin Indians have been admirably drawn by the Inter-Tribal Council of Nevada and published as *Life Stories of Our Native People*. This life history or Indian autobiography of Corbett Mack, then, fills an obvious void. Because I neither systematically collected this information nor ever even remotely thought of publishing the life story of Corbett Mack as such, the questions *how* and *why* this work came to be "transcribed, edited, polished, interpreted, [and] thoroughly mediated" (cf. Krupat in Swann 1983:272) by me can serve as a useful starting point.

To begin with, I first went—actually I was assigned by lots—among Corbett Mack's people, the *Tabooseedokado* or 'Grass Nut Eaters' of Smith and Mason valleys, Nevada (Stewart 1939:143), a federally recognized modern tribe of Northern Paiutes known today as the Yerington Paiute Tribe (Hittman 1984), in 1965, after being selected to participate in the Tri-Institute Field Training Project in Anthropology. This was a National Science Foundation summer program designed to train beginning graduate students in techniques of ethnographic field research. Located at the University of Nevada, Reno, a dozen of us were trained by Warren L. d'Azevedo, Don Fowler, Wick Miller, Wayne Suttles, and William Jacobson and were sent to different reservations and Indian colonies, mostly throughout Nevada, with Franz Boas's historic anthropological mission: to collect ethnographic data from elderly informants as a way of preserving what remained of traditional Great Basin people's cultures, that is, "salvage ethnography." On the 9.45-acre Yerington Indian Colony in Mason Valley, and on Campbell Ranch, its 1,400-acre companion reservation eight miles to the northeast, I, by the luck of the draw, or fate, was privileged to interview elderly Northern Paiute men and women about beliefs and practices appertaining to the collection and preparation of plant and animal foods, what I called foodlore (Hittman 1965). Having been preceded in the field by another student, I duly took note of the praise heaped upon Corbett Mack by Eileen Kane, University of Pittsburgh student. She called him "the most excellent and co-operative of my informants: his retention of detail, of ethnohistorical fact, and of dates, was impressive" (1964:58).

According to my diary, it was on 21 June 1965, when I stopped a borrowed car at Corbett Mack's nephew's house on Campbell Ranch to seek directions to Tribal Chairman Frank Quinn's house, that I met Corbett. He seemed friendly, I happily noted. Indeed, apart from age, Corbett was very much like me: short (five feet, six inches), slight (120 pounds), light-skinned, and blue-eyed, though otherwise a stiff-kneed, retired Paiute, who was dressed in a faded blue denim work shirt, jeans, and dress shoes, and whose neatly parted head full of brackish white hair also reminded me of my paternal grandfather. Because Corbett Mack, seated alone on a rickety bench underneath a grove of cottonwood trees rolling cigarettes, pragmatically and romantically struck me as the ideal informant (cf. Casagrande 1960), I returned five days later on a purchased bicycle, eager to interview him. He was then weeding an impressive garden. Corbett invited me to wait, and I played with his friendly Australian sheepdog Pinto, whose own cloudy blue eyes were so much like his owner's—an interaction more pleasant than the encounter I had just experienced with Corbett's neighbor's vicious dog! Upon completion of his task, Corbett Mack joined me in that shady place; he accepted my (nervous) half-sandwich offer without a "Thank you," followed by a cigarette, again with no thanks. Thus we sat in silence for quite some time, I a fledgling anthropologist, grappling with how to broach ponderously worded ethnographic questions, Corbett Mack an experienced informant, hunched over, elbows resting on his knees, staring down at the ground. I did begin my ethnographic work that day—two productive hours collecting what seemed like a wealth of data (a basic word list, kinship terms, and so forth), which I could hardly wait to get home to type. But because of my proximity to the Yerington Indian Colony, I did not return to interview Corbett Mack at Campbell Ranch until 30 June 1965, when I recorded the following in my diary: "Corbett looked up at me as if I were stupid for repeating the same question." "Nice man," I also wrote. "And all he wants—he won't take payment!—is Prince Albert pipe tobacco and brown Wheat Straw paper!" I also learned that day that because his eyes went bad as a young man, Corbett had not really hunted very much; still, he said he knew of taboos surrounding the procurement and preparation of both animal and plant foods, which he would be willing to share. More importantly for the genesis of this book, after relating the belief that hunters who "played with" animals (that is, tortured them or threw porcupine guts in the air) could cause winter storms, Corbett Mack illustrated with family fact that his stepfather had skinned a jackrabbit one day and let it loose, "then [Big Mack] got sick and he nearly died!"

I saw Corbett eight more times that summer, interviewing him on only four of those occasions:

7 July 1965: After having been generously given the use of a motor scooter by Ken Stevens, a Yerington neighbor, I found Corbett drunk and immediately left.

13 July 1965: Corbett was again drunk. He screamed at his dog when I arrived, then, pausing with mild irritation to inquire what it was I wanted, regained his composure and abruptly left to irrigate the garden.

26 July 1965: Corbett Mack, sobering up, told me about Owl and an unidentified hawk, *tabudzeeba*, whose cry similarly foretold personal misfortune; the predicted trouble could be averted if only a person would "talk to 'em," that is, say, "Go away! I don't wanna hear you no more!"

27 July 1965: Revealing an ironic sensibility, Corbett told me how whites used laugh at "them Indians" for painting their faces, whereas "now their own women paint theirs worse than us! Same as smokin'!" he also wryly observed.

4 August 1965: Corbett Mack was not home.

9 August 1965: Drunk again, and surly. Even so, he regained enough composure to allow me to begin an interview, which was abruptly ended when Corbett left to irrigate his garden.

10 August 1965: I entered his house to this friendly greeting: "Hello, Mike!" In fact, I had brought Corbett some requested groceries—a loaf of Wonderbread, a can of Spam, macaroni salad from the deli, and cigarette makings—in lieu of informant pay. After insisting on paying, he related the folktales I retell in sections 151–54, including several "dirty stories" about Trickster Coyote (e.g., the Northern Paiute creation story with its *vagina dentata* motif), which Corbett laughed while narrating.

13 August 1965: Having forgotten to bring promised groceries, I recorded a short session on foodlore.

21 August 1965: Not at home. I intended to say goodbye.

22 August 1965: Returned again to say goodbye. Since Corbett declined my offer of groceries, I gave him my favorite sweater as a memento.

Three years then passed, and upon completion of Ph.D. coursework at the University of New Mexico, I decided to return to Yerington. Armed with my dissertation proposal to test a model of caste on Northern Paiute-*taivo* (white) relations in Smith and Mason valleys, while glancing through back issues of the weekly newspaper—work on the proposal admittedly was going poorly—I chanced upon a shocking item: "We regret to say this city has a 'hop head' population that would put many larger localities to shame." This was reported in the *Yerington Times* on 4 January 1908. Glancing ahead, I saw that on 27 November 1909 the same newspaper wrote: "The degrading influence of opium is rapidly reducing the Indian squaws to prostitution and the buck to the vile employment of procurers." Opiate addiction, moreover, not only seemed widespread but proved to be long-lasting, as revealed by a comment in the rival newspaper, the *Mason Valley News*, on 29 March 1924:

> With the death of these 2 Indians the people are beginning to awaken to the fact that conditions are getting pretty rotten at the Indian camp (Yerington). At present 90% of the Indians in the valley are hop heads and the time is coming when some dope-crazed Indian is going to run amuck and kill a few citizens. . . . Now is a good time to call the attention of the government to the fact that the so-called reservation within the city limits of Yerington is nothing more or less than a clearing house for yen shee peddlers. The place is so damn rotten that it smells to heaven.

And, again, four years later, in this same source: "One by one Yerington's Indians are succumbing to the ravages of booze and dope. Before long the ranchers will be hard put for hay hands" (6 October 1928).

Native American opiate addiction? Unprepared for this finding by graduate school studies, and particularly by ethnographic readings on Northern Paiutes of the Great Basin during the aforementioned Field Training Project in Anthropology, I was doubly surprised to learn that some of my informants had been arrested and imprisoned on narcotics-related charges. Feeling, therefore, that this information demanded immediate scrutiny, I changed dissertation topics—in the field. And how well I recall that fateful letter written to Philip K. Bock, my advisor—from the field!

The historical context was the late 1960s. Knowing that Smith and Mason Valley Paiutes originated the 1890 Ghost Dance (Mooney 1896); surmising that they had participated in an earlier manifestation of the same, the 1870 Ghost Dance (Du Bois 1939), which erupted on the Walker River Reservation in adjacent Walker Valley; and belonging to a generation for whom drugs were very much part of the counterculture in which I participated, whose own illusory dreams regarding a charismatic leader had been dashed by the assassination of a president in Dallas (dreams and idealistic yearnings that would reignite and be extinguished twice more by bullets in King and in Bobby Kennedy)—a Woodstock to Altamount decade also contradictorily symbolized by the "two Camelots" (cf. Horowitz 1967)—the following hypothesis, then, seemed to literally construct itself: Like drug use in the 60s, Smith and Mason Valley Northern Paiute opiate addiction was symptomatic of disillusionment with prophecies that had failed, specifically Wovoka's 1 January 1889 Great Revelation. Enter, or reenter, Corbett Mack.

Between 1968 and 1972 I interviewed Corbett no less than fifty-five times; the interviews took about 165 hours, and I recorded some 30 additional hours on audio tape. Of course, Leo Simmons wrote his 460-page life story of Don Talayesva on the basis of 350 interview hours and 8,000 diary page entries (cf. Brumble 1988:185). Be that as it may, I asked Corbett one day about opiates, and with characteristic honesty he related habitually smoking yen-shee, the remains of "wet" opium—called *moohoo'oo* 'Owl' in Northern Paiute, for reasons explained in section 87. Moreover, he told of subsequent addiction to *toha moohoo'oo* 'white black stuff', or morphine, injected intravenously. Hoping to quantify the incidence of opiate addiction, I became drawn to Corbett Mack for another reason: Northern Paiutes' unwillingness to discuss the dead. "Oh, he's dead a long time!" was too frequently the response to genealogical questions. Corbett Mack, on the other hand, was willing not only to name names, but also to name names of the deceased.

"Did so-and-so use *moohoo'oo*, Corbett?" "Was he a heavy user?" "Did he also use that white stuff [morphine]?" "Arrested?" Systematically, thus, I worked him, eliciting the hard data on addiction and addicts for this relatively stable population of approximately 500 Northern Paiutes during their forty-year travail with opiates. These data I, of course, cross-checked with other informants and historical sources, including newspapers and arrest and prison records. Despite the tediousness of this line of inquiry, Corbett Mack—gratefully—never tired of answering me. Indeed, he seemed to look forward to my visits, if only because I owned a car, and he was not loath to ask me to drive him to a nearby liquor store for his favorite wine, Tavola Red, which I never did; he would then beg me instead to "Bring me a jug next time, partner!" something I confess to foolishly having done on occasion, that is, until Lena

Rogers, Corbett's niece, admonished me. (Mrs. Rogers subsequently revealed how she would watch for my black Volkswagen from her kitchen window, then would drive to her uncle's house after I had left, to determine whether or not I had broken that promise!) In any event, this work, as I say, progressed slowly, torturously, as Corbett Mack patiently, courteously, monosyllabically, answered my every (monotonous) query, opening up, expressing himself more freely on the subject, especially on his life, only after the notebook (or tape recorder) blessedly was closed.

Now, it probably is true that I would have learned what I learned from him without doing what I did. All the same, during my fourth season in the field, 1970, while I was (still) grilling Corbett Mack about opiates, we were seated outdoors on an orange vinyl luncheonette booth his nephew had retrieved from the dump. A hot August day's stifling dry heat was penetrated only by the sound of cicadas and a tractor's engine in the background (much as indoors, on cold days, it would be the ticking of an alarm clock beside Corbett Mack's bed), and those Khoisianlike clicks from this old man's near-toothless mouth that framed our common enterprise. Having acquired my informant's habit of rolling cigarettes, I added a twist that day, marijuana, a sign of those times. Corbett at some point asked, "What are you smokin', partner?" I answered, playfully offering a toke. "No, thanks!" he most emphatically demurred. "How come, Corbett?" "'Cause I drink now," he answered, "so, I don't wanna mix!" "Why's that, Corbett?" "'Cause you see why?" he explained. "They say you can lose your mind that way!"

By my risking self-disclosure (cf. Jourard 1964) our roles then temporarily reversed, inasmuch as Corbett Mack began interrogating *me* about drugs: How had I obtained marijuana? Where? Cost? Had I encountered difficulties with "them government bulls"? But perhaps even more important than the revelation that he and other Paiutes had sold opiates as well as using them, subsequent interviews with Corbett were imbued with new intimacy, as if I had gained passage into the "underworld of the hophead," the "dope fiend," the "junky" (cf. Becker 1964; Burroughs 1969)—a breakthrough in fieldwork discussed at the Great Basin Anthropological Society Meetings in a paper entitled "'Never Mix—Never Worry': The Heuristic Value of Offering a 'Joint' to an Informant," whose misleading newspaper coverage, notwithstanding the happier ethnographic outcome, caused worry, grief, and turmoil in this budding professional's life. In any case, Corbett Mack as a consequence proved more willing than ever to fully discuss with me his life, as an opiate addict and otherwise.

Alas, teaching and a variety of projects directed on behalf of the Yerington Paiute Tribe came to occupy many of those postdoctoral dissertation years. In truth, too, I resisted publishing data on Smith and Mason Valley opiate addiction because of an inability to resolve an ethical dilemma: did I wish to establish a reputation on the discovery of what had caused so much anguish, misery, and suffering for friends in a host community I not only felt attachment to but worked for? While I was directing a Title IV U.S. Indian Education Project for the Yerington Paiute Tribe in the early 1980s, however, when our editor precipitously quit, and I was thrust into his role, a frenetic search for materials to include in *Numu Ya Dua,* a tribal "newspaper" designed for use in an after-school tutoring center in Paiute culture and language (Hittman, ed., 1979–82), threw me back onto my ethnographic heels, so to speak. Since neither the Education Committee nor the Tribal Council objected to my devoting most of an entire issue to opiates (and peyote), I reestablished contact with my field notebooks and came to realize just how much about Corbett Mack's life I actually knew. Some glimmering of its book potential led me to publish autobiographical snippets from Corbett Mack's life in a featured column of our tribal newspaper entitled "Conversations with an Old-Timer," as well as to work up a draft of Corbett Mack's life story for a Nevada publisher. That was why on 17 October 1982 I thought to interview Amos Mencarini, the Italian-American potato grower on whose Smith Valley ranch Corbett and his wife Celia Mack lived and worked for nearly thirty years. More years needed to pass following rejection of the manuscript before I would again consider publishing Corbett Mack's life story (and the story of Paiute opiate addiction). And so it was that upon completion of the Wovoka Centennial Project (1986–89) for the Yerington Paiute Tribe, I once again began to feel strongly about these subjects. If Jack Wilson, whose biography I wrote for this tribe (Hittman 1990), was the Great Man, Corbett Mack, I came to realize, was the tribe's Everyman.

Organizationally, this book is very much inspired by Paul Radin's *Autobiography of a Winnebago Indian,* which Brumble rightly or wrongly writes "is generally credited with having ignited the interest in autobiography for ethnographic purposes" (1988:57). The 159 sections of *Corbett Mack: The Life of a Northern Paiute* are followed by endnotes numbered to match the section numbers. The endnotes include historical and explanatory data and commentary regarding culture. (Radin's 96-page volume, by contrast, had 351 footnotes.) "Most Indian autobiographies [do] contain a mixture of narrative and cultural essay," another literary critic (W. F. Smith 1975:238) has observed. Yet I do not agree with his assessment that the endnote or footnote "hamper[s] our ability here to read the autobiography as narrative" (W. F. Smith 1975:238), siding instead with Krupat and Brumble: Krupat's passionate call for "other voices" to replace "monologue" leads him to defend their incorporation into the very architecture of Indian autobiographies or "bicultural works" (Krupat 1989:132-201); and Brumble writes that such notes "allow some pretty good guesses about where the Indian leaves off and the Anglo begins" (Brumble 1988:12).

Corbett Mack was born in 1892, and we learn in chapter 1 ("Birth and Family (1892)," sections 1-15) that he was named for James J. Corbett, world heavyweight champion, by Annie Hoye, the Irish store owner and Smith Valley employer of both his mother and his grandmother. Corbett Mack's birth date was thirty years after the white settlement of Smith and Mason valleys and also coincided with the demise of the 1890 Ghost Dance religion, a redemptive social movement (cf. Aberle 1966; Kehoe 1989; Hittman 1992) in Nevada, whose prophet was exposed to the frontier brand of Presbyterianism practiced by David and Abigail Wilson, who were among the earliest settlers of Mason Valley. Also long past was the Paiute militancy that accompanied white contact in the Great Basin—the rise of mounted predatory bands (Steward 1938) and related wars, such as the Pyramid Lake War of 1860 (Wheeler 1967), in which Corbett's own maternal grandfather participated (cf. sec. 13; Stewart 1939:143). Indeed, *Poogooga'yoo* 'Horseman' in 1859 might even have been among those 200 or so *Tabooseedokado*, who, according to Timothy Smith, for whom that valley was named, "at first kept away from us," then sent a delegation of "thirty or forty . . . up to where we were and in no uncertain manner ordered us off their range" (1911-12:225). Through voluntary labor, many of these same indigenous people and rightful landowners aided the likes of Smith and N. H. A. (Hoc) Mason from Arkansas, for whom Mason Valley was named, to transform the two alluvial, sagebrush-covered, mountain-surrounded Great Basin desert floors into lucrative alfalfa and livestock holdings. Corbett's grandmother, we also learn in chapter 1, was a *Kootseebadokado* Mono Lake 'Brine Fly Pupae-Eater' (she emigrated to Smith Valley from Bridgeport, California, with his mother shortly after white settlement); his stepfather, Big Mack Wilson, a.k.a. Wheeler—from "Paps" Wheeler, early Mormon settler of Mason Valley—had emigrated (with two sisters and an aged mother) from the Walker River Reservation, home of the *Agaidokado* 'Trout-Eaters' (Stewart 1939:141-42) to adjoining Walker Lake Valley, before resettling in Smith Valley. If Corbett's grandparents belonged to that generation which encountered the initial brunt of expanding Euroamerican civilization—that is, the "Real Old-Timers," many of whom both fought and refused to work for the *taivo*—his parents were contemporaries of the 1890 Ghost Dance prophet, whose bicultural adaptation amazed James Mooney (1896:770), and whose vision reflected the Protestant work ethic (Hittman 1990, 1992). They, in fact, became the cooks and domestics (women), and ranch and farm hands (men) universally praised for such labors by white employers—as dramatically evidenced by a listing of these occupations (alongside their white names!) for nearly every single one of the 148 Paiutes reported in Mason Valley and the 57 listed in Smith Valley as early as the tenth federal census in June of 1880.

Corbett Mack was a *nomogweta* 'half-breed'; the word derives from *Nuumuu* 'Northern Paiute' and *-gweta* 'cutting something in half'. He was "stolen," perhaps the first Smith and Mason Valley half-breed to survive to maturity. An Indian agent writing about this area in the 1890 *Annual Report of the Commissioner of Indian Affairs (ARCIA)* ("Indians of the State of Nevada/Off Reservations," p. 395) stated:

> The Indians off reservations . . . maintain themselves . . . by working at odd jobs, such as cutting wood, hunting stock, and through general chores. . . . They drink whiskey, fight, gamble and steal. The half-breeds raised this way are the most dangerous class of persons, as well as the most useless. These Indians generally live in little clusters of tents outside of the towns.

Yet Corbett Mack was neither "dangerous" nor "useless." In fact, so culturally identifiable as Northern Paiute was he, that a former tribal chairman in 1993, in welcoming me back, characterized Corbett while discussing my research as "the only full-blooded blue-eyed Yerington Paiute we ever had." His life history also marks him as a very different subject from Annie Lowry:

> I am a half-breed. That means I live on the fringe of two races. My white friends think I am just a plain old Paiute, while the Indians say I think I am better than they because my father was a white man. When the time came to make a choice between the Indians and the white race, I made up my mind to be an Indian . . . but to the white teaching my mind was closed. [Scott 1966:2]

And whether it be rape or financial hardship that uniquely prompted his birth—for I do record in my genealogies an additional total of twenty-nine "stolen children" who reached maturity between 1892 and 1929, including the third and youngest daughter of Jack and Mary Wilson—Corbett Mack's illegitimacy was clearly perceived by him as pivotal, or what literary critics might term a turning point in his life. Despised by his stepfather, he narrates in chapter 1 what appears to have been a chronic state of marital tension between Big Mack and Mary Mack revolving around his birth that episodically erupted in domestic violence; it was resolved only following the death of both of Corbett's male siblings.

In chapter 2, "Boyhood (1892-1905)" (secs. 16-30), although most of the narration is acculturationally emplotted (e.g., sec. 16, "Them *Taivo*, They Come to Smith [and Mason] Valley!"), we hear fragments of a surviving traditional culture, for example, section 24, "*Naavey^ts* or Firstfruits: Male Puberty Rite." One leitmotif is the positive feeling Corbett experiences for his *moo'a* or maternal grandmother, as he tells of the plant foods she collected and prepared for him, that is, only after *taivo* employers gave *Tseehooka* permission to lay off work. We also glimpse the pleasure Corbett Mack derived from hunting and fishing with male siblings and from riding horses. A trauma in early childhood, a horse and wagon accident resulting in loss of the little toe on his left foot, further shows the importance shamanism would have, both in Corbett Mack's life and for members of his family.

At thirteen or fourteen, he seems to serendipitously wind up at Stewart Institute, the newly built federal boarding school in Carson City named for Nevada's powerful senator. Like the "Paiute Princess," Sarah Winnemucca, who claimed her "happiest life has been spent . . . at school and living among the whites" (Canfield 1983:65), Corbett Mack will also lead us to believe as much in chapter 3, "Boarding School, 1905-10" (secs. 31-46), where he depicts those four and a half years (1905-10) in a way not only discordant with other Native Americans' views of "civilization" in the repressive, if not abusive, environment of the Indian boarding school (cf. Simmons [1942] 1971), but also different from what fellow Smith and Mason Valley Paiutes have told me. Indeed, apart from a single instance of corporal punishment (see sec. 42), for which Corbett accepts full blame, the sole trauma during those years appears to have resulted from his ingenuous use of his white genitor's surname—a letter sent home signed "Douglass," the name of the local constable who fathered him and was apparently frightened out of Smith Valley by Big Mack. For what was tantamount to creed was Corbett Mack's belief that he did not really "know" anything until he went to school, and that he would have truly "learned something" had not his stepfather pulled him from fourth grade in midwinter, when he was eighteen and a half, Big Mack requiring his assistance in locating Mary Mack, who had fled from death threats. "I don't know nothin' till I been in school," was Corbett Mack's reply to an inquiry for the date of 1890 Ghost Dance ceremonies in Smith or Mason valleys. "'Cause you see why? Them Indian, they can't count the year. No, sir! Ain't [even] got that in their word. No, sir! Can't [even] name the month like white people do . . . like July."

Chapter 4 ("Work and Girls, 1912-23," secs. 47-66) recounts his life back home again in Smith Valley, with parents, a remarried grandmother, and a newly married sister, in an extended family form of social organization called by Don Fowler (1966) the "kin clique," persisting even today. Before Corbett assumes a lifetime of wage labor, however, he romps with cousin-brothers, catching mustangs in the mountains and chasing "them young City girl" in Mason Valley. Or rather, he chases horses and catches (and deflowers) young Paiute women—until his stepfather shames him into accepting day labor: "So, you can buy your own food and clothing that way," Big Mack reportedly says. With the latter's assistance, Corbett Mack initially works for a Smith Valley blacksmith, though his first "real" job is driving cattle as a *pakyera'a* or cowboy to and from summer pasture in Bridgeport Meadows, California, no doubt a higher-status Indian occupation than farmhand, if only because of the legacy of equestrianism associated with those predatory bands that defended home and territory from *taivo* encroachment. But in the main, our subject begins a lifetime of hard labor as ranch- or farmhand: irrigation ditch digger, planter, irrigator, haycutter, and haystacker.

The second decade of the twentieth century saw a radical transformation of the Walker River regional economy. To that trinity of livestock raising (cattle, then sheep), alfalfa (and wheat and barley) cultivation, and mining (Kersten 1964) was added row crop cultivation, as Italian migrants parlayed wages saved as ranch- and farmhands to purchase their own lands. They planted potatoes, garlic, and onions in Smith and Mason valleys, but especially potatoes. Men such as Amos Mencarini from Crusta Lucca, Italy, whose single-minded economania prompted the *Lyon County Monitor* on 17 August 1901 to call potatoes the "new industry in . . . Missouri Flat [Mason Valley] . . . ready producing 400-500 tons." According to the 1920 census, 219 acres of Nevada's 4,864 acres of cultivated land in 1910 came to be devoted to this new crop, Lyon County, in which these valleys are located, ranking number one throughout the state. Among the social by-products or waste of the migration of these "restless strangers" (cf. Shepperson 1970) was the availability of homemade wine; three glasses, a matter for the record, served with daily board during Prohibition to Northern Paiute laborers, whose Italian employers then deducted $.75 from per diem wages of $2.00. The employers also gained illegal profits by selling them pints and gallons at the end of the day and on weekends. But potato work also meant year-round employment, and year-round wages allowed opiate addiction. In chapter 5, "Italians, Potatoes, Homemade Wine (1923-58)" (secs. 67-82), Corbett Mack discusses his longtime employer and alcohol: How *heebee*, or homemade Italian wine, played a determinative role in his meeting his future wife; how he and Celia Mack in essence worked for wine on Amos Mencarini's Smith Valley ranch, that is, when they were not using opiates. Corbett and Celia—*Qobit* and *Seeya*—a childless couple, are self-portrayed as living amicably together for thirty-five years in a cabin too tiny to accommodate more than a stove—a marriage consistent with the Northern Paiute practice of brothers-in-law marrying each other's sisters (cf. D. Fowler 1964; C. S. Fowler 1986).

Yet a second emigrant group, the Chinese, was to impact on Smith and Mason Valley Paiutes. Brought in originally to dig irrigation canals, some remained in the valleys as ranch and hotel cooks and gardeners, others becoming owners of laundries and restaurants in Wellington (Smith Valley) and in the towns of Mason, Yerington, and Wabuska in Mason Valley (see map 1). As single men, Chinese were attracted to Northern Paiutes for women and because these minorities shared a passion for gambling. But with the Chinese came opiates, the subject of chapter 6 (secs. 83-117)—which is, I am certain, the major contribution of this book. So serious, in fact, was the social problem of opiates that Special Officer George O'Neill, following passage of the Harrison Narcotics Act in 1914, was reassigned from the liquor traffic in western Nevada to narcotics; that a grand jury (Eighth District) would issue a special report on 18 April 1929 entitled "Narcotics in Smith and Mason Valleys" (Appendix C); and that the Senate Committee on Indian Affairs would gather and publish relevant testimony in *Conditions of Indians in the United States* (1931-32). Corbett Mack thought Henry Clay in 1896 or 1897 had taught Paiute relatives the habit of smoking opium, which he had acquired from Chinese in the mining camp of Bodie (Cain 1956), and his reliability in this regard is proven, insofar as the very first newspaper article discussing Indian narcotics appears in the *Lyon County Times* on 2 May 1896, a report of a Chinese man arrested in Smith Valley for running an opium den for Paiutes (appendix A of the eighth district grand jury's special report). Corbett Mack, in any event, began experimenting with yen-shee in 1910, while working alongside his cousin-brother/brother-in-law, Henry Dick. "'Cause you see why?" Corbett required no time nor had to think hard before offering this rationale for generalized narcotic addiction: "Them *moohoo'oo* men, they always say, 'You work hard, that [opiates] can kill your tired!'" In my dissertation (Hittman 1973a), this instance of the sociological commonplace "retreat into drugs" (Merton 1957) was explained through the presentation of opiate incidence for three birth cohorts (cf. Ryder 1965) as follows:

(1) Paiutes belonging to the 1835-59 birth cohort (Corbett's grandparental generation) were too old to experiment with opiates, as I found only 1 of 28 surviving men and none of the 20 surviving women to be opiate addicts.

(2) Thirty of the 63 men and only 4 of the 50 women belonging to the 1860-84 birth cohort used opiates; these addicts, the members of Corbett's parents' generation, were born closer to the 1885-1909 birth cohort, in which the highest incidence of narcotics use was found.

(3) Sixty-one of the 126 men and 20 of the 95 women belonging to the 1885-1909 birth cohort were addicts. These were the men and women of Corbett Mack's generation: they attended boarding school and were more significantly acculturated. Lacking the paternalism characteristic of their parents' nascent attachments to whites, they performed the back-breaking drudgery of year-round potato work for psychologically distant Italian employers—from fall harvesting to winter work grading potatoes in dark cellars, to the following spring's planting, and so forth—and came to use *moohoo'oo* (opiates) as well as *heebee* (drink) as soporific.

Lowered infant mortality due to the appearance of contract physicians, hospitals, and medicine, moreover, resulted in a dramatic increase in the total size of the 1885-1909 birth cohort (n = 30 families: 1 family had 1 child who survived to maturity, 20 had 2 children each, 7 had 3 each, 4 had 4 each, 6 had 5 each, 1 had 6, and 1 had 7 children), resulting in a demographic transition (cf. Petersen 1969:11). In Durkheimian terms this meant "generation density," resulting in peer pressure, which facilitated diffusion of this (opiate) innovation (cf. Coleman, Katz, and Menzel 1957) among what was tantamount to a generation of marginal people. Finally, the large number of women addicts of the 1885-1909 cohort was largely explained through marriage (or relationship) to opiate addicts.

"Opium can kill your tired!" was, according to Corbett Mack, the emic or rallying cry of this birth cohort's attempt to ease the physical, if not the psychic, pains of wage labor. Corbett Mack notwithstanding, addicts either chose not to or could not always work to sustain substance abuse, and those long years, 1896-1931, saw much crime against property, *taivo,* Chinese, and Paiute alike, with ensuing arrests and prison sentences (cf. Appendix A). A vicious cycle of drugs, crime, and dysfunction, thus, was both cause and consequence of year-round labor in the potato fields. Moreover, as Corbett narrates in chapter 6, a remarkable pattern of Northern Paiute entrepreneurship followed the arrest of Chinese opiate sellers—including the story of that most remarkable seller of them all, Willy Muldoon (see secs. 97-98), who employed at least two others (besides Corbett) while operating a drug ring from his grocery story on the outskirts of the Yerington Indian Colony. Small wonder that even a hard-working individual like Corbett, who earned $117.45 for seasonal work as a ranch- or farmhand one year, would be willing to risk imprisonment for the lure of several hundred dollars earned on a Saturday night alone selling yen-shee! But we also experience the paranoia of the drug seller (sec. 100), which in Corbett's case, anyway, echoes Northern Paiute beliefs in *booha,* or supernatural power, and its correlative fears and suspiciousness regarding witches.

Chapter 7, "Some Real Old-Timers (1896-1940)" (secs. 118-39), I think of as a nativistic interlude, for it contains a potpourri of ethnographic-ethnohistorical data about Northern Paiutes belonging to Corbett Mack's parents' and grandparents' generations or birth cohorts: Wodziwob and Wovoka, for example, 1870 and 1890 Ghost Dance prophets, respectively, who became shamans after their influential religious movements had ended and doctored members of the Mack family, including Corbett; Ben Lancaster, or Chief Gray Horse (see secs. 137-38), whose peyote cult in the 1930s was rejected in Smith and Mason valleys not only because of the perceived pecuniary motives of its proselytizer (Stewart 1944, 1987), but because of these tragic years of opiate addiction (Hittman n.d.a). Yet a second leitmotif permeates this part of his life history, Corbett's near-obsessive fear of Tom Mitchell (see secs. 129-31). Indeed, the classic operation of witchcraft (cf. Evans-Pritchard 1937) is evidenced, with regard to Corbett's shoulder injury, in his simultaneous acceptance of a natural explanation (that it was incurred from years and years of lifting heavy sacks of potatoes and 200 pound hay bails) and of a shaman's diagnosis that it was caused by this shaman's nefarious deed. Tom Mitchell's supposed smearing of red paint *(pizzapee)* on the door frame of his gambling house in Yerington Indian Colony, thereby bewitching Corbett en route to his courtship of Mitchell's daughters, was rationalized by our subject as retaliation for his lack of intention to marry them (see sec. 132).

The final chapter, "Retirement Years (1954–74)" (secs. 140–58), begins with Corbett Mack quitting the Mencarini Ranch and moving to his nephew's ranch assignment on Campbell Ranch in adjoining Mason Valley. Age and increased mechanization of potato operations, however, were not the only factors—the relocation was prompted more by Celia Mack's death in 1958. Here again we see the traditional culture still in operation, this Northern Paiute's refusal to live in a house he was supposed to have burned following the death of a family member. Corbett, in any event, leaves Smith Valley for good, aiding his sister Janie's son, the widowed Eddie Mack, who was raising two sons by their mother's previous marriage. This new location was where, of course, I first met him in the summer of 1965, interviewing Corbett from February of 1968 through 1972—interviews, I might note, interrupted only by his work in the garden; for meals; to feed the litters of wild cats he cared for underneath his front porch; to urinate; by visits from his nephew and niece; and worse, by Indian winos, predictably whenever Corbett's Social Security and pension checks arrived, resulting in inebriation. In these sections are also Northern Paiute folktales Corbett narrated for me originally in 1965, but which I re-collected in subsequent seasons. Unlike Andy Dick, his brother-in-law and lifelong drinking companion, Corbett was not a trained teller of these animal teaching stories or *natoonuudweba;* that is, he had not been taught by a grandfather in that line-at-a-time recitation-repetition mnemonic manner of Northern Paiute instruction called *nuugweegeeyaka* 'designated repeater' (cf. Liljeblad 1986). Rather, he—for reasons entirely congruent with his identification as Northern Paiute—paid close enough attention to the oral literature so as to recount adventures of the demiurge Wolf and his marplot younger brother, Trickster, with dramaturgical flair and humor. Moreover, some of the folktales Corbett told me appear not only to echo themes in his life history, at least as I have forged it for him; they also speak of a crisis, if you will, in Northern Paiute culture history: the fact that the dead were not resurrected according to the 1870 Ghost Dance prophet's promise (Hittman 1973b). So when, at the end of chapter 8, Corbett, during a discussion of his own age-related infirmities, introduces Coyote's role in the establishment of old age, suffering, and death, it seems congruent with an important conversation Corbett related to me early on that he had had with Wodziwob at the end of the prophet's life (ca. 1910). He reported the 1870 Ghost Dance prophet's own seeming disillusionment regarding the paradisiacal Land of the Dead that

Wodziwob must have seen in his Great Revelation, but apparently had unsatisfactorily revisited in dream or trance afterward, or in response to a collapsed movement. "No More, He Comeback(s)?" as I have entitled section 157, then, is inspired by the idiosyncratic or culturally patterned disillusionment shared by my informant with a more famous ancestor.

The epilogue (sec. 159), a partial transcript of my last visit to Corbett Mack as ethnographer, which took place in late summer of 1973, is intended to harmonize with recent concerns about fieldwork in cultural anthropology (cf. Tedlock 1983; Clifford and Marcus 1986). It also brings closure and a symmetry to my account of initially meeting Corbett Mack. The dialogue itself more properly belongs to a study of Paiute pragmatics. Commenting on his 1892 New Year's Day interview with Wovoka, James Mooney, the great nineteenth-century ethnologist, wrote:

> His uncle [Josephus] entered into a detailed explanation, which stretched out to a preposterous length, owing to a peculiar conversational method of the Paiute. Each statement by the older man was repeated at its close, word for word and sentence by sentence, by the other, with the same monotonous inflection. This done, the first speaker signified by a grunt of approval that it had been correctly repeated, and then proceeded with the next statement, which was duly repeated in like manner. The first time I had heard two old men conversing together in this fashion on the reservation I had supposed they were reciting some sort of Indian litany, and it required several such experiences and some degree of patience to become used to it. [Mooney 1896:770-71]

Indeed, Ruth Underhill ([1936] 1979:4) would generalize that "Indian narrative style involves a repetition and a dwelling on unimportant details which confuse the white reader and made it hard for him to follow the story." Literary critics, too, have discussed this question: the warning by Brumble (1988:11), for example, that what "can be a feature of style, yet [can be] abhorrent to the Western editor." Repetition throughout the book, then, is a deliberate instantiation of "biculturalism": the Northern Paiute subject's conversational style, as forged by his "Indian autobiographer's" deliberate attempt to work a cultural linguistic fact into received text.

Frequent use of ellipses is another matter; they represents breaks in the narrative. Since information about Corbett's life, as already stated, was gained piecemeal, this text, as Brumble (1988:10) otherwise wrote, came only after "hours of transcription and the editing: the ordering, cutting, and sometimes the rephrasing and the additions." And while there were no "sut off the postles" for "shoot off the pistols," as Catherine Fowler (1978:40) described Sarah Winnemucca's English, Corbett's prose was inconsistent enough in the matter of *s*'s at the ends of words, for example, to warrant only a vigorously moderate strain for consistency in representation of his voice. Still, much was edited to improve the read: the male pronoun (sing.) for both genders, for example, or Corbett's use of *a* for *of,* as in "kinda" for "kind of." On the other hand, the frequent use of "so" at the start of paragraphs is, according to Arie Poldervaart's Northern Paiute Bible translations, anyway, consistent with the demonstrative pronoun *esoo.*

Beyond whatever "literary" questions this life history or Indian autobiography raises—a comparison of the "episodes" (cf. Brumble 1988:17) of Corbett Mack's life, say with that of Owens Valley Paiute Sam Newland (cf. hunting, dreaming as a source of power, witches, becoming a doctor, women and venereal disease, eternal life, a fight, marriage, the exchange of food, contact with whites, imprisonment, frequent trips to California, contact with Washoes)—important historical and cross-cultural questions are also begged. For example, more research into this hitherto unreported account of opiates among a Native American community might force us to add a new ethnic-narcotic association (cf. Morgan 1981:x) to the list (Asiatics and opium, Near Easterners and cannibis, African Americans and cocaine, Mexicans and marijuana). By the same token, the fact that Smith and Mason Valley Paiute drug usage climaxed after the turn of the twentieth century challenges the generalization by David T. Courtwright that "opiate addiction increased throughout the nineteenth century, peaked in the 1890s, and thereafter began a sustained decline" (1982:2). Nor do these data gathered with Corbett's primary assistance reflect the recognized shift in America from women addicts of the nineteenth century to middle-aged men in 1915-23, "native-born white . . . [men] predominantly from the South, who were leading morphine addicts" (Courtwright 1982:36-42). And what to make of laboring Northern Paiute opiate addicts such as Corbett Mack in light of the following generalization: "American laborers and factory operatives did not take to opium and morphine with the enthusiasm of their English counterparts" (Courtwright 1982:40)?

On the other hand, the well-documented conclusion of H. Wayne Morgan (1981:43) that there had been a nineteenth-century shift in opiate patterns from women and professionals, especially doctors and "favored classes," to lower segments of society, is certainly supported here. Similarly, the generalization by Courtwright: "The basis for opium's lasting popularity is not its curative power, but rather its analgesic properties. [For] No other naturally occurring drug can match it as an anodyne" (1982:43). Or, another, Kane's comment—"Financially, the habit has but one tendency viz., ruin, not so much from the money expended on the drug (from 50c to $3.00 per day) as from neglect of business and the impaired mental power brought to bear upon it for the short time that it receives any attention" (in Morgan 1981:51). Corbett's observation that *heebee* (alcohol) made men and women lazy, whereas opiates made them work hard, echoes that contrast made by famed opium eater De Quincy: "Opium ennobled, alcohol degraded" (in Courtwright 1982:56).

"They are not facts but memories, and memories distorted by the wishes and thoughts of the moment," Franz Boas (1943:311) wrote in a posthumously published piece deriding life histories. Arguing against them, claiming that "beyond very elementary points" they are "doubtful," if only because "they require long-continued personal relations between the observer and members of the group which he wishes to study" (Boas 1943:343), the founder of modern anthropology concluded:

> The interests of the present determine the selections of data and color the interpretation of the past. . . . In short the tricks that memory plays us are too important to allow us to accept autobiographies as reliable, factual data . . . particularly in the case of the North American Indian. [1943: 311]

And again,

> Autobiographies, on account of the restrictions just mentioned and of the difficulty of assembling a sufficient variety of individual records are of limited value for the particular purpose for which they are being collected. They are valuable rather as useful material for the study of the perversions of truth brought about by the play of memory with the past. [1943:335]

Boas's student Alfred A. Kroeber, in his introduction to a Yurok life history, nonetheless commented favorably on this extreme position taken by his mentor: "The specific problem of method is whether the autobiography will or will not contribute something that cannot be obtained from other approaches to the investigation of culture." The encyclopedic Kroeber then asked: "Is it more advantageous to have a thousand concrete exemplifications all related to the life of one individual, or to be scattered among many individuals?" (1952b:320).

If only because of his discussion of the neglected tragedy of opiates, the life history of Corbett Mack is vital for our understanding of recent Northern Paiute culture history. Of course, the sandy-brown-haired young man with side part who regularly wore a tall black Stetson and Levi's and ordered Cambridge work shirts from catalogues (cf. plate 1) no longer needs to be defended as a unique and valued human portrait. And while nowhere evidenced in these pages is the Corbett Mack who, while drinking in my presence, once exploded with "God damn!" then nervously self-corrected: "Maybe God will hit me in the head!"; or the Corbett Mack whom a younger informant, Russell Dick, said he was forced to chop wood for in repayment of a loan and a night's residency; or the Corbett Mack who upon request once sang a Mono Lake handgame song for me, no Smith or Mason Valley Paiute ever spoke ill of him in my presence.

"He was an easy-going person. Never loses his temper. A friendly person who believed in medicine men and Indians ways, but doesn't gamble," said Elsie Sam Ausmus (b. 16 Mar. 1923), Corbett's niece, about her uncle. "A friendly person, I don't think he ever said a bad thing about anybody!" The late Howard Rogers (b. 1905), a nephew through marriage, commented. "He's friendly, Uncle. Talks to everybody. Never cusses. He's not a mean man. But he never gives money to take care of Big Mack," said Lena Rogers (b. 1906), one of Corbett's three surviving nieces.

Bernice Crutcher (b. 1928), another niece, also recalled:

A real good cook—cooks stew all the time in his Dutch oven. And he used to read to me and my brother from the Bible. And he knows the Lord's Prayer real good, too. Which my brother used to make him tell whenever Uncle got drunk. Nice man, Uncle Corbett. . . . Never mean. Lives next door to us in a board house he built when he was married. And he never teases nobody. Always good to little kids, too. To my kids. . . . Talks to them nice. Buys my son candy after he gets Social Security. And he speaks better English than *Seeya* [Celia]. Uncle can correct her mistakes she makes.

Indeed, the trusted informant I knew was a quiet, thoughtful and kind, curious, whimsical man, someone whose traumatic beginnings and hard life might well have been the template of an entire generation. True, on occasion Corbett contradicted himself: he recalled one time an opiate addict named

Billy Schurz, who threatened to blow out the belly of the Fallon shaman cum Yerington Indian Colony policeman, Jack Dalton; but during another interview it was Billy Miller who threatened to "shoot Jack Dalton's ass off." However, his memory was sharp at the end of his life. Nor were there such glaring gaps and errors as Canfield (1983:31, 114) would remark about Sarah Winnemucca Hopkins, who not only neglected to mention her short-lived second marriage but also wrote about attending a school in San Jose in 1860, which she later changed to the Convent of Notre Dame in 1861, and then elsewhere named another school, which did not even exist at the time. Nor was Corbett guilty of un-Paiute-like boastings, either, such as Sarah Winnemucca's claim that she rode 223 miles to save the lives of her father and her people during the Bannock War (Hopkins [1882] 1969:164). No, sir! For Corbett Mack gave an honest interview, much in the way I am certain he gave each boss an honest day's work. And since he was (painfully) honest regarding the struggle with his pater, we should assume honesty regarding his love for his maternal grandmother and his siblings and honesty regarding the seeming pleasure he experienced in boarding school, if not honesty regarding sexual triumphs! Corbett's attachment to Northern Paiute culture, in any event, shone through each interview, as it hopefully does throughout the pages of this text. For like Sarah Winnemucca, he "retained an essentially tribal sense of self" (Brumble 1988:71). And most importantly for my work with him, Corbett always seemed honest in his discussion of opiates. "I gotta give you a little, partner"—his insistence that he pay me for groceries I bought in appreciation for services rendered as informant—still rings in my ear. "'Cause you're doin' all the buyin'!" An honesty, a fundamental human decency, albeit derivation of long, hard years as opiate addict and "drinkin' man."

According to Bernice Crutcher, her uncle took sick while he was eating, in the summer of 1973, or shortly after my last visit with him. His niece Lena Rogers said she found him in distress and put him in the Lyon County Public Hospital in Yerington. "They bring me for a checkup, now this is my home!" Crutcher recalled that comment made by Corbett during a visit to him in the Senior Citizens' Wing of the local hospital. "Still, he talked good," her sister characterized his affect. Elsie Sam Ausmus also recalled his inability to walk at the end and his eventual lapse into coma. Corbett Mack died on 23 March 1974. His burial in Yerington took place two days later, at ten in the morning. Each of these three close relatives individually related to me how curious it was that their uncle died the same day as his nephew, Stanley Rogers. "But we had Uncle's funeral first, then Lena's boy," commented Elsie Sam Ausmus.

And Freitas [mortician] does the funeral. We buried Uncle Corbett in a gray suit Freitas gave us in Yerington [the Indian cemetery], by our mother [Lizzie]. Then we bought him a tombstone and wrote on it, "Our Beloved Uncle." Uncle paid for his own casket. Paid a good long time for it, too. His money saved went to Lena, who had to add onto the cost of casket. And it was an open casket we had. We kept it open for one day, then the burial. But we didn't put any of Uncle's belongings in it.

Since the Lyon County Medical Center does not save medical records beyond ten years, I was unable to ascertain exactly what my informant died of.

My last encounter with Corbett Mack was in late December of 1973, a Christmas spent by my fiancée and me with our adopted Northern Paiute family in Yerington. Hearing that Corbett was in the hospital, we drove in from Campbell Ranch to see him. I went into his room alone. Corbett lay quite still in bed; he was having trouble breathing. I gathered up Corbett's makings and poorly rolled two Prince Albert aromatic pipe tobacco cigarettes in his brown, ungummed wheat straw paper. (He was permitted to smoke.) "You'll get well, partner," I said dishonestly, after helping Corbett light up. "'Cause I want to see you back home again, partner, so I can ask you some more questions."

"No, I don't think I'm gonna leave this hospital alive, partner," Corbett weakly replied after inhaling. He was being honest again. We had little else to say to each other, and we sat together in silence, much as our relationship almost ten years prior had begun. When it was time to leave, I shook his hand, repeating the previous falsehood. In the hospital staff kitchen, where Ida Mae Valdez, laundress, and Meryl Singer were awaiting me, I cried for the first time as a man. We cannot always know the impact another human being will have on us.

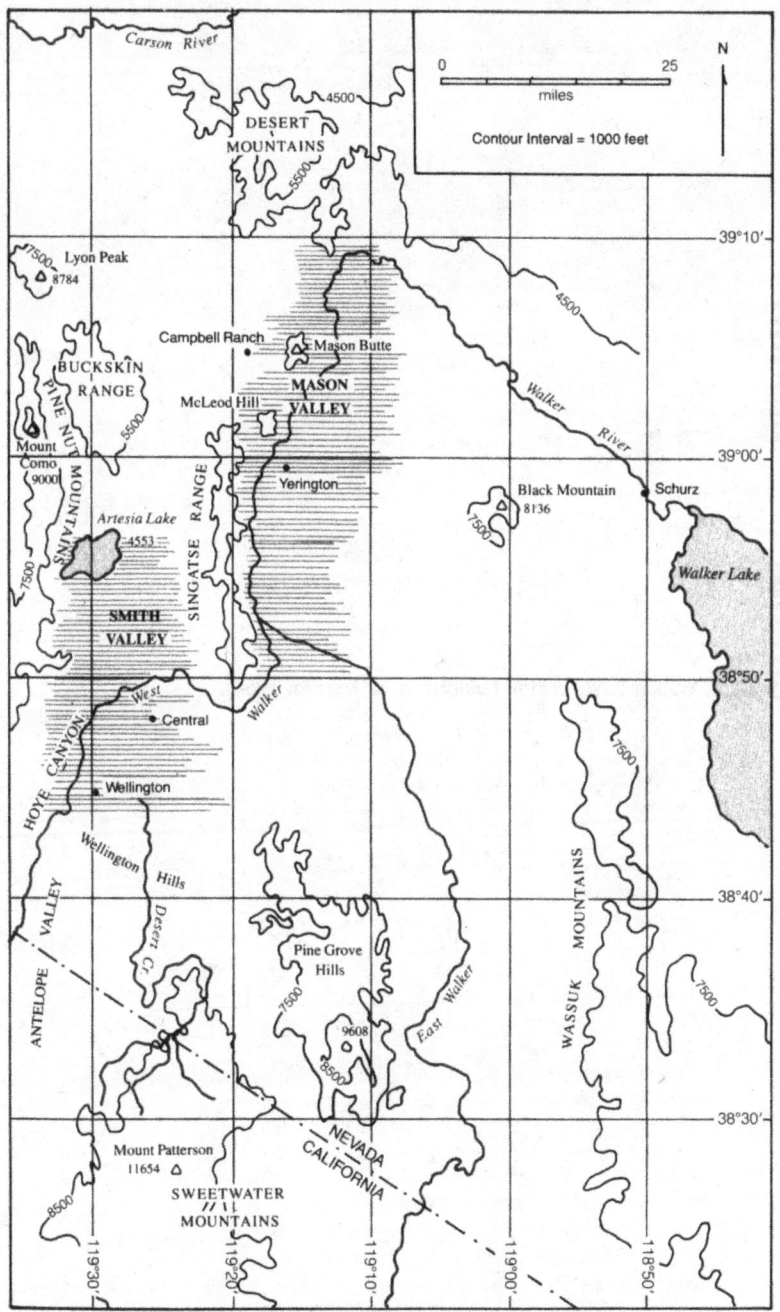

Map 1. Smith and Mason valleys, Nevada.

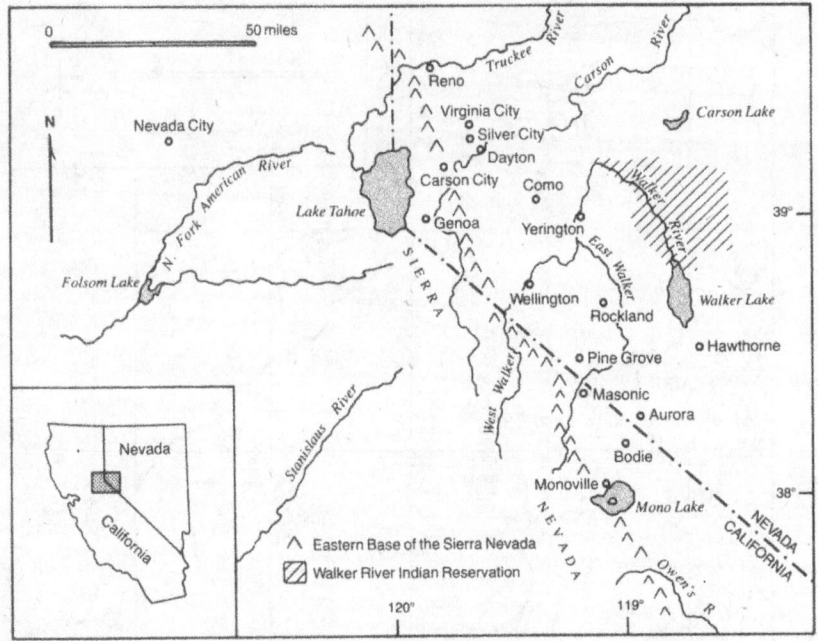

Map 2. Walker River region (adapted from Kersten 1964).

1

Birth and Family (1892)

1. A Stolen Child

The Old Man, he don't like me. 'Cause you know why? What my mom's doin'!

'Cause I'm stolen, you see . . . a *nomogwet* 'half-breed'. And you know why my mom's doin' that? 'Cause them Indian women, they like to have their own money; so they make them *taivo* pay for that [i.e., sex]. Yes, sir! 'Cause Big Mack, he don't make enough. So my mom, she do that.

Yes, sir! 'Cause them *taivo* [whites], they can pay three to five dollar: double what she make! And lotta them [*Nuumuu* women were] also doin' that, by God! My sister, Janie, Mamie Bob . . . yes, sir! 'Cause they [also] sneak with them *taivo* for money. Janie, she make Eddie [Mack] off Ed Purdy; Mamie make Howard [Rogers]. . . . And so, when Howard's born, they wanna put him in the ground [bury him]. But [Mamie's brother] Henry Bob, he won't let 'em. No, sir! Says, "You're just gonna look around for more *taivo*. He [Howard Rogers] can take care my horse!" What they're always doin' them days, anyway.

23

2. Sticks and Stones . . .

And so they make fun of me. . . . Call me *taivo*, you know. 'Cause maybe I'm the only one that time in Smith Valley? Old Man Wallace—they call him *Karoosee* Sam, he's a real old-timer—that's Mike Wallace's father—he call me *taivo natsee* 'white boy'. But not to my face. 'Cause I got light skin and blue eye, you know. But I don't get mad. . . . No, sir! Don't mind what he say, 'cause I already know I'm half *taivo*. And that old man, he always get mad at the Old Man [Corbett's pater]. Says Big Mack lied to him about somethin'. . . . Rabbit drive, maybe? Somethin', anyway. . . . But he's not related to us, neither, Old Man Wallace. No, sir! Wife's related to my grandma, so, maybe [if] he's related to me, that old man won't do that [i.e., ridicule his illegitimacy]?

Anyway, you see what they claim: them *nomogwet* get along better with their own family than full[-bloods]! But one thing I know I don't wanna be: *poohaghoom* [shaman]. No, sir! On account my blood!

3. A Name and a Birthdate

But you know who name me by that way? Old Lady [Annie] Hoye! Yes, sir! 'Cause she's the one give me that name Corbett. 'Cause my mom, and my grandma, both, they work for her: Old Lady Hoye own that general store in Smith Valley [Wellington Mercantile]; they clean house, iron, make the bed for her. . . . You know, that kind woman's work. Oh, and help Old Lady Hoye with her garden, too . . .

I'm born out in the brush, partner: in Wellington [Smith Valley]; across the [Nevada] highway [Alt 95] from that store. Born April 15, 1892. 'Cause you see what happen? My mom, she say Old Lady Hoye come to see me when I'm born. . . . Write that down. Then later, when I'm big, I go see her after I come to know somethin' and she tell me that [date]. . . . Same way, too, Old Lady Hoye name me by the ring [prize fight]. Yes, sir! Give me that real fancy name after that one boxer, Jim Corbett. And name my *wanga'a* [younger brother] by that other ring name, too: Sullivan. 'Cause I hear them two fight close by when I'm born; in Carson . . .

Yes, sir! 'Cause that's what all them *Nuumuu* are doin' that time, you know: don't go by their right name no more. *Karroo'oo* [no more]! They just take them *taivo* name.

4. My *Nuumuu* Name

But I get a real Indian name, too: *Todugwee'yoo*. 'Cause you see how I'm named by that way, partner? [I] pack a drunken woman on my back one time! And that's my wife's *hama'a,* her old[er] sister, Idie: Ida Bennett. Snow Ida, they call her; Dick Bennett's *barruu* [daughter]. 'Cause you see what happen? She's drinkin', and so, Ida pass out on the road. I'm walkin' along, find her there and pack her [home]. And so, my wife, she give me that name, *Todugwee'yoo*. . . . But nobody don't call me by that, neither. No, sir! 'Cause they always just say "Corbett." Or they can call me Corbett Douglass when I'm little—after my real father. Or Corbett Mack when I come back from Stewart [Carson Industrial School].

5. Another Name for Me

Same way, this one fellow around here, he always call me Corbett Macaroni. 'Cause you see why? I work for that same *Aytayay* [Italian] over thirty years, by God! Amos Macarini [Mencarini]. Yes, sir! Both I and my wife! 'Cause by real old-time way, you know, you're supposed to give somebody a name by what they're doin'.

6. Big Mack's Name(s)

"Big Mack," though, that's what everybody call my *na'a* [father]. 'Cause you see why? He's a big man! Jack Wilson's tall; Tom Mitchell, he's short and chunky. But Big Mack's real big! Wear size 12 shoe! Too big for potato work, I tell you, Mike! And even them *taivo,* they just call him that, too: Big Mack.

'Cause you see who he get that name from? "Mack" Wilson. 'Cause the Old Man used to work for that *taivo* a real long time ago . . . in Mason Valley, by Wilson Canyon, where his ranch is. Says, "When I'm a young guy, I see them covered wagon comin' through this [Mason] valley; then I go work for them *taivo* here. Make ten cents a day!" (Pretty tough wage, huh?) Then maybe next summer, they can raise him to twenty cents a day? 'Cause Mack Wilson, you know, his father [David Wilson] homestead Missouri Flat [southern end of Mason Valley]. And that's real early days ago, partner!

The Old Man's *na'a?* He always say his father's name's Tom, call himself Mack Tom. Says he's from Bridgeport, Mono Lake . . . down that way, anyway. . . . And that old-timer's got two wives.

Same way, Big Mack, he's [also] got two Indian name: call him *Nop^daka'a* and *Tsanorr^*, 'cause I hear he carry [rescues] this one girl off a real long time ago, too. Yes, sir! His own sister . . . cousin-sister, anyway. 'Cause you see what happen? Bunch them crazy Indian, they wanna gang [rape] that girl, so the Old Man, he do that: pack her on his back and run with her. 'Cause I know my mom, she's the one always tell that story. 'Cause that's what some them crazy Indian start doin' them days . . . drink, you know, then they wanna do that [gang rape].

Nop^daka'a . . . *Tsanorr^* . . . mean someone [who] run along with a pack on his back. But his right name's *Tsanorr^ Wasatsabeedoo*. Named by that seed, you know, *wasa*. 'Cause you see why? I guess when he's young, the Old Man's mom is grindin' *wasa*. She give him a little bit and so he get mad. Want more, you know; keep his hand out there like that . . . you know, till he get more. So, that's how come they name him by that way, *Wasatsabeedoo*, "Gimme me more and more *wasa* seed all the time." 'Cause that's what them old-timers are doin', you know. They name you by that way: [i.e.,] make you to stop what you're doin'.

7. Big Mack

And the Old Man, he belong to Schurz [Walker River Reservation]: *Aghaiduukuuduu* [Trout-Eater]. Says he's got land there, too, twenty acre. Only thing is, Big Mack don't never wanna work that land. No, sir! "*Ste'yoo!*" "No good land!" What he's always sayin'. "Ain't worth shit!" So that's why he come up to this valley, you know: to work for Mack Wilson; them other early day *taivo*, too. Then he go to Smith Valley. Gets marry to my mom there.

And I used to know my *hootsee*'s [paternal grandmother's] name, too. But I forget about her now. . . . Same way, too, the Old Man's got two sister: Sadie, she's older, she's get witched by Jack Wilson's father; his young sister, they call her *toosee* 'Little' Lucy. And you know what they're doin?' Marry the same man! Both 'em! 'Cause them days, you know, them old-timers can make a trade. Say I marry your sister, well, my sister can marry your brother. But when they're doin' that [sister exchange], them kids can't marry. No, sir! 'Cause they're already too close. "*Nanuumuuduu,*" they say. "That's your relation!" 'Cause I know Johnny Jones, he's my *ats* [mother's brother]. Him and Big Mack're cousin-brothers, so they can do that, you know: marry each other's sister. Same as what I'm doin' later on, partner. . . .'Cause after my own sister [Janie] marry Henry Dick, why, I marry Henry's sister! Anyway, my *pa'wa* [father's older sister, Sadie], she make only one kid with Johnny Jones. . . . Frank Jones; the other girl, the Old Man's *hama'a* [younger sister], she steal one kid from this *taivo*. Dies in the basket, though, then she die, too. Yes, sir! 'Cause Jack Wilson's *na'a* [father], he's the one doin' that to her. Kill Lucy by *Nuumuu pooharr^*, Indian witchin' way! Yes, sir! *Ste'yoo*, that one. No good! Not like his son [Jack Wilson or Wovoka], anyway. . . . 'Cause I know [when] we call him in to doctor her, she die. Anyway, both them sister are light, so the Old Man, he always say [tease?] they're different color from him [i.e., stolen?]. . . .

And so Big Mack, his mom, both sister, they leave Schurz for Missouri Flat. 'Cause pretty tough wage, them days, by God: ten cent a day! But the Old Man, he say he can do any them real old-time jobs: grubbin' sagebrush, irrigatin' work, harvestin' hay, stackin' job. . . . And once in a while, too, I guess he can be a milker. But main job when he's young is buckaroo.

'Cause he's a *pakyera'a* [vaquero or cowboy] that time. Yes, sir! Buckaroo for Old Man [Dan] Simpson when he move up to Smith Valley: catch wild horses and break 'em. 'Cause Big Mack says he's always ridin' horse when he's young. . . . Yes, sir! Both him and "Dutch" John Milton. (He's from Sweetwater, Dutch John. Real old-time *pakyera*. Wear chaps and a fancy cowboy outfit. But not the Old Man. No, sir! 'Cause you see why? Too big to fit! So he always has to wear work clothes. You know, blue denim shirt, blue jean. . . . 'Course them days, everythin' cost cheap, partner! Cost you only fifty cent for your shirt and a dollar for overall. And same way, too, Big Mack don't wear fancy cowboy boot, neither. No, sir! Can't! Foot's too big! Got his own saddle, though. . . .)

But you know what him and his cousin-brother [Buckaroo George Walker] are always doin? They can say: "Who's the best rider?" "Who can ride the toughest horse?" Act like little kid, you know. 'Cause Buckaroo George Walker, he's my *ats*. Work on cowhide all the time; make a hackamo, quirt . . . sell to them *taivo*. And they say Big Mack's [also] a good roper. [How] he can part cattle easy. . . . 'Cause I know one time I hear the Old Man and Addie Mason's *na'a*, they're gonna have a contest, in Fallon, where Big Mack go to get mudhen. Yes, sir! Say they're gonna race their horse and pick up a silver dollar on the ground. And so the Old Man, he wins. But that other fellow, maybe he don't wanna pay him? No, sir! So they just name him by that, you know, that old-timer: *Eshar^m* 'Liar All the Time'. (He's a *yogho* [sex] man, too, Addie Mason's father. Go from woman to woman. . . .) Same way I hear this Chinaman once [also] do that to [challenge] Big Mack. And the Old Man wins him, too.

Throws underhand when he rope them calf, the Old Man. . . . And Big Mack can make a Indian drum and Indian moccasin, too—them *moqo*. Real way, though, you say *Nuumuukwasee* 'Paiute shoe'. 'Cause I know Big Mack used to make 'em outta deer hide for my sister Janie's boy . . . when Eddie [Mack]'s small. But he don't make any for me. . . . 'Cause you see why? My real [white] *na'a* buy me that [shoes] when I'm young guy. And same way, too, that Old Man can make a *weega* [rabbit-skin blanket] outta jackrabbit skin. Oh, take, maybe, 100, 150 skin for a double [blanket]? 'Cause he's a real good hunter, Big Mack. Yes, sir! Told me before I'm born, there used to be lotta Indian these valleys; so they can bunch up and have a [jack]rabbit drive. Call that kind *kamuu tanu'a*—time when jackrabbit's got a different fur. And the Old Man, he's always gotta be *wanga'yoo*, you know, 'Rabbit boss'. 'Cause I know I used to go along when he's leadin' that kind [communal rabbit drives]. Fall [of] the year, right around about November; everybody just bunch up around that fire on the hill—till the Old Man wave his hands. Tell 'em when to speed up and slow down [on the drive]; where to put their net. . . . "Shoot straight!" What that Old Man's always sayin'. "Don't shoot any rabbit that's runnin' to[ward] another man!" Same way, he's usin' a shotgun them days. Me, I'm too small. I got a .22. Then we can pick up any rabbit they shoot; pack 'em, you know, on our horse. But he don't lead that kind [of rabbit drive] in Mason Valley. No, sir! 'Cause I never did hear that. Same way, I never did hear about any kind rabbit drive Big Mack leads in East Walker country, neither. But before I'm born, he say these Indian around here used to [also] go to Fallon to hunt jackrabbit. . . .

And same way, Big Mack can [also] lead that other kind drive in Smith Valley: them *sayya*, mudhen; at the Huniwell Ranch [northern end of Smith Valley], not that dry [Artemesia] lake up there. Yes, sir! Get permission from them *taivo* first. 'Cause he know how to do that, too, you see: cut them tules and tie 'em together to make that *sakee* [tule boat]. And that's also fall [of] year when they're doin' that. 'Cause them mudhen, they're fat then, can't fly; so these Indian, why, they paddle after 'em in that kind boat. Drive 'em better that way. . . . 'Cause I know him and George Decroy, they're always workin' that kind together: one's gotta paddle that *sayya,* the other can shoot in the water. Drive 'em to land, kill 'em there with boat paddle. And [if] they shoot, why, they gotta shoot sideway in that kind boat; 'cause otherwise, that can tip over.

He's got short hair, Big Mack; don't wear his hair long like women are doin'. No, sir! 'Cause the only one's doin' that any more is Jack Wilson. And I know I gotta cut Big Mack's hair all the time. Same way, too, he won't shave. No, sir! Just tweeze out his *moosoowee* [mustache or facial hairs] with his finger. Then taste 'em, so he knows they're out. . . .

But one thing I know I never did hear—that Old Man call me *doowa* [son]. No, sir! My mom, she call me that. My grandma, she call me *moo'a* [daughter's son]. Same way I call her that [self-reciprocal kinship term] back. But Big Mack, he just call me by my name, Corbett. Same way, too, I don't call him *na'a* 'father', neither. No, sir! Just mention his name, that's all. Call him Mack.

8. Big Mack's Final Name Change

Then you see what he's doin'? When he's already old and livin' here [Campbell Ranch, Mason Valley], right before he die, some government [social] worker come around and ask for his [sur]name, so the Old Man, he say "Wheeler." Yes, sir! Call himself "Mack Wheeler." Drop the "Big" and put himself down for his pension [Social Security] by that other name.

9. My Real Father

But you see who's my real father? Bill Douglass. 'Cause I know him, that *taivo:* used to be policeman in Wellington [Smith Valley], where we live. . . . Not marry, though, Bill Douglass, so my mom, she do that: sneak on him. And he's good to her, Bill Douglass. Good to me, too. . . . Always call me "son." Stay around [Smith Valley] till I get to be a pretty good size man, then leave. Maybe when I'm around about twelve years old?

And I don't think he ever marry, neither. No, sir! Go to Dayton after he leave this valley, and get a job in Carson City: guard in that [state] prison up there. Then he gamble a lot and lose his money; shoot himself. Drink too much, also.

10. Big Mack's Rage

Big Mack, he's kind of a mean guy: get mad, then he's always after his rifle. 'Cause he's that kind, you know: wanna kill my mom, on account what she's doin' [did]. Yes, sir! Scare us all the time. . . . Well, not all the time, some the time, anyway. . . . And Big Mack's not drunk, neither, when he's doin' that. No, sir! Just get that way, that's all: wanna kill me and my mom, 'cause what she's doin' with Bill Douglass.

Never swear or nothin', that Old Man. Just pick up his rifle like that and load 'em; then take them shell out and load 'em up again. Keep on doin' that, like that, you know, over and again; why we're afraid, partner. Afraid he might just leave some shell in there and pull on that trigger; so that's why we have to run outta our house; go hide someplace else. And sometime we have to stay outside there all night long! Then after a little while I guess he change his mind. Get to be good again, look around for us. . . . 'Cause them full-blood, you know, that's just the way they are: get mad at somebody [i.e., at a *nomogwet*] like that and wanna kill 'em! "You been goin' with some *taivo* and you made Corbett!" What he's always sayin' to my mom. And so I'm afraid of him all the time. Big fellow, you know, Big Mack; and he's handlin' a gun. I'm little, then. . . . But my grandma, she's not afraid of him. No, sir! Tell him to go ahead and shoot. 'Cause my grandma, she don't like Big Mack. No, sir! Don't talk to her *dogona'a* [son-in-law] too much, on account what he's doin' all the time.

Yes, sir! Bad Old Man, that one. But he won't be mean to them other *taivo*. No, sir! Only wanna kill my real father. And so my mom, she tell Bill Douglass what Big Mack's doin', sayin'. And that other fellow, he go to Dayton. Leave this valley and get that other job up there.

11. My Grandma, *Tseehooka*

My [maternal] grandma, she mostly raise me—when I'm big enough, anyway; off my mom['s breast]. 'Cause I sleep with her, then.

Taivo, they call her Maddy, but her Indian name's *Tseehooka*. (Sound pretty funny, ain't it?) *Tseehooka*, that mean some kind [of] leg. So, maybe my grandma's always showin' 'em off when she's young? Why they name her by that way? Anyway, she won't tell me her Indian name. No, sir! My wife, she's the one tell me that. . . .

And my grandma's from Bridgeport. 'Cause you see why? All her relation [are] from that way: Sweetwater Country, Antelope Valley, Mono Lake . . . back that way. Talk a little bit different than us, you know, my grandma. 'Cause them Bridgeport Indian, they're slow; we talk more fast, just like them Schurz Indian. And my grandma says she's a pretty good size girl when she first come into this [Smith] valley. But that's one thing I'd like to know: is my grandma marry yet? 'Cause she and my grandfather, they only get that one daughter between 'em, my mom.

Always workin' hard, that's my grandma! 'Cause she can work any kind job, you know. But you see what she really like is to work for Old Lady Hoye. Make a dollar a day, thirty dollar every month! Only thing is, my grandma, she's pretty tight. Yes, sir! Hide what everything she make! 'Cause all them old-timers, they're just that way, you know. 'Cause, one time, I know I ask my grandma for two bit to buy shell for my .22. "Where I'm gonna get that from, Corbett?" my grandma tell me. But she's got it, all right! So I tell her back: "*Moo'a* [mother's mother], how I'm gonna hunt for you? How I'm gonna put duck and jackrabbit on the table?" But you think my grandma's gonna listen? Hell, no! Won't even give me one cent! Not until I start to know somethin', anyway; then she can give me five cent. . . . And she don't even draw her pay every week. No, sir! Just by the month. Take me to work with her every mornin'; tell me to stay outside, you know . . . to play around. 'Cause that first boss [Annie Hoye] my Grandma work for, she don't have no kid; second one, though [Annie Fulstone], she has all them boys, so I play with 'em. Another *taivo* my grandma work for, her daughter like me; bring me cookies, candy, anythin' like that. Then somebody steal all my grandma's money!

'Cause you see what she's always doin'? Keep some in her dress, the rest my grandma hide. And I bet you my grandma's got over $2,000 saved! Yes, sir! $250 gold piece! Work for Johnny Rogers that time, then John O'Banion, when he [Rogers] sell: wash cans for them milk cow, and do house work—clothes, wash dish, make the bed; iron and do that garden work. . . . And my grandma don't like to gamble, neither. No, sir! Never wanna bunch up Sunday at Blind Bob's [Roberts's] place with the rest them Smith Valley Indian. No, sir! Not like my mom's always doin', anyway. Or the Old Man. 'Cause my grandma, she don't like spendin' what she earn! No, sir! [Rather] bury her money on the side the road, not too far from our camp—until somebody steal it! 'Cause you see what happen? Somebody must be watchin' all the time when she bury that money. On account one day, my grandma, she go there and it's all gone! *Karroo'oo,* no more! Nothin'! All gone! And gee, my grandma sure cry lots after that. Pretty near sound like somebody die. . . .

And you think she's [ever] gonna wear somethin' new? No, sir! My mom, she make [sews] dress for her, but my grandma [only] like to wear patched—just like a *wa'eetsee taivo* [literally 'old white man', i.e., 'hobo']. Same way, my grandma's always wearin' man's shoe: low cut, you know. 'Cause you see what she always say? "Woman's shoe fit too tight on my feet!" And she get them kind from that Porty-gese milker workin' for John O'Banion—before he sell to Old Lady Fulstone's son, George. Yes, sir! 'Cause he's the one always give my grandma his old shoe. And same way, too, my grandma [also] wear them old-time handkerchief all the time: to keep her hair down. But I don't know what's the matter with my grandma, either? 'Cause one time, I buy her a silk hanky, but you think she's gonna wear that? Hell, no! "People gonna make fun of me, Corbett." Won't even wear bloomer. 'Cause none them old-timers do that, by God! My mom, she's same way; sister Janie, too. . . . Not my wife, though. . . . So when they sit down on the ground, why, you can see their *soowee* [vagina]! So maybe that's why my grandma's always afraid of *taivo kweeda nobee* [white man's outhouse]? Won't go in there at all. Says, "Somethin's gonna crawl up my *tsaboo* [rectum]. Eat me inside out!" 'Cause that's what all them old-timers always [also] say. And say if you find that kind [lizard]'s egg, don't break 'em! No, sir! 'Cause that fellow can chase you just as far as you can go! Only kind lizard that's got teeth, you know, that black spotted lizard. Me, anyway, I'm not scared of that; I go to *taivo kweeda nobee* all the time. Then later on, when we work for Macarini, he give us one. . . .

English is not good, but my grandma, she always have to take off when them seed [i.e., traditional foods] are ripe. Yes, sir! Tell her boss, so he can let her lay off work. You know, to go out and get her own kind food. Like them *tuuba* [pine nuts] in the fall. Or *wuuyuupoowee* [buckberries] when they're ripe end of summer. Yes, sir! Fix them kind for me, and pray when I'm sick. 'Cause you see what she's [also] doin'? My grandma, she comb my hair with *sawabee* [sagebrush] when I don't feel good. Yes, sir! Dip 'em in water and talk [prays] to the Sun when he come up. 'Cause a person feel better when they do that to [for] you. . . .

"Don't steal and don't lie. Don't go into any *taivo* house!" That's what my grandma say. . . . And she's not mean to nobody, neither. No, sir! Feed me and put me to bed. . . . Never did bawl me out even once! 'Cause I know when I start bitin' my mom's tit, that's when I have to go to sleep under my grandma's *weega* [rabbit-skin blanket]: you know, to let my mom take care my *wanga'a* [younger brother]. And same way, too, my grandma has to do that to Lena [Rogers] when Eddie [Mack] finish that milk.

Never sick in her life, my grandma. No, sir! Never [even] once seen a *poohaghooma* [shaman]. Just get old and stiff and die. Always says [if] the white man don't reach us, we'd all be dead today. 'Cause that was a tough time, them early days ago, my grandma say. . . . Not enough food.

And I bet you my grandma's over 100 when she die!

12. My Mom

And same way, too, my mom: nice old lady, never once bawl me out. Never say anything rough to me. . . .

Her name's *To'dzeeqwuba'a*, but everybody's always callin' her Mary, Mary Mack. And you see what that Indian name mean? *To'dzeeqwuba'a*, that's some kind 'chapped face'. I kind of think my mom's born in Smith Valley—'cause she talk like us; don't drag her word like her mom, my grandma. Anyway, she stay there all that time. Don't go no other place to live, except for *Waseeyoo* [Washo] country when she's small girl: to Gardnerville . . . why my mom can talk their language so good. And stay up there one year, maybe two? 'Cause I know I got lotta them kind [Washo] relation, partner! Bill Sally's one. And them Snooks, too; they're also my grandma's relation. 'Cause I hear they [Snooks] wanna keep my mom. 'Cause you see why? They ain't got no family, only that one boy, George, so, I guess they wanna keep [i.e., marry him to] my mom. Then, later on, they try to get my sister, but Janie, she don't wanna marry that Washo guy they want her to marry. Won't even learn their language. No, sir!

Got no brother or sister, neither, my mom. Except I hear she's cousin-sister to Johnny Jones [husband of Big Mack's two sisters]. But that's one thing I wanna know is, How come my mom won't tell me about her early days? 'Cause that's just the way some old-timers are, you know: ask 'em a question, they don't say nothin'! 'Cause all my mom ever do is to work, work, work! Yes, sir! Just like my grandma, my mom: real hard-workin' woman! Work every God damn day, too! 'Cause them *taivo* lady, they [also] always want my mom on the job: you know, same kind work my grandma's always doin': washin' dish, clothes . . . them early day woman's job. 'Course, then, woman's gotta boil water before she can cook sheet, pajama, clothes . . .

[or] wash them dish that way, too. And same way, too, my mom [also] can iron everythin' neat for them *taivo*. . . . Likes to work for Old Lady Hoye best, my mom, 'cause you see why? She's got a roomin' house in Smith Valley, so lotta work there. . . . Can make her money. And same way, too, my mom can also work for Old Man Reading's wife. 'Cause that's another early days hotel job in Smith Valley, partner. Never quit workin', neither, my mom. No, sir! Work all the God damn time! Only time I ever seen my mom not workin' was after that accident on the buggy she had [sec. 122]. Doesn't work, then, for four or five years. . . . And my mom don't drink, neither. No, sir! Oh, sure, maybe every once in a while [when] the Old Man can go on a toot, he can force her to have a taste. But not really to drink, to get drunk, you know. 'Cause, like I say, all my mom like to do is to gamble.

And that's every Sunday, too, by God! 'Cause you see why? Only day them *taivo* let them Indian to do that. The Old Man, he's gonna get in there on that handgame once in a while. Not my mom, though. . . . 'Cause all she like doin' is that five card game. 'Cause Blind Bob [Roberts], he's the one doin' that: *Hoona* ['badger', i.e., casino owner], you know; always in charge of gamblin' in Wellington . . . over by Old Man Reading's hotel, by that highway curve. But he don't have a gamblin' house, Blind Bob. No, sir! Not like Tom Mitchell's doin' in this [Mason] valley, anyway [cf. secs. 129-32]. 'Cause they play outdoor only in Smith Valley. Blind Bob, he put one stick down after each [hand]game, then they're gonna have to pay him. Same way, he collect five to ten cents from each five card player—after every three hand. 'Cause you see why? Blind Bob's the one buyin' them playin' card. . . .

Yes, sir! [So] my mom work all week long to buy her grub, then she can gamble with them other Indian women on Sunday, . . . what them real old-timers like doin'. . . . But, me, I don't like to watch that woman's game much . . . just handgame. And they don't gamble in Wellington in winter. Too cold outdoor, partner! Just do that in the summer.

But my mom, she talk pretty good English . . . better than the Old Man, anyway. Better than her mom. 'Cause them real old people, pretty tough to learn to talk English, by God! Only thing is, she get headache all the time. So, you see what my mom's always doin'? Has to get up real early in the mornin'—before even the Sun—and dip that *sawabee* [sagebrush] in water; drip it on her head. "I wanna be like *sawabee*," she say to that one [the Sun]. "Feel new all the time, never get old." 'Cause that's on a prayer, you see. . . . What my grandma always say for me for when I'm *nuuma* [sick]. 'Cause you see why? Them old-timers, they say sagebrush never get old. And same way, too, they say to do that [prayer ritual] early in the mornin', 'cause *taba* [Sun], he can carry your sickness over the sky . . . to that water. So when you wake up next mornin', why, you feel better. But that's one thing I never seen: the Old Man do that. No, sir! A man can [pray], women, though, they do that mostly for you.

13. *Poogooga'yoo* ('Horseman')

Never did ask my grandma, though, or my mom, where my [other] grandfather's born. No, sir! Where he's from, anyway? And maybe I'm still in the basket when he die? One year old? Still, when I ask my grandma about my *togho'o* [mother's father], she won't tell me nothin'! No, sir! 'Cause them old-timers, they don't like doin' that [i.e., talking about the dead], you know. . . . But I find out, anyway. And you know who tell that? Winnemucca *natsee* [Young Winnemucca]. Says what my grandfather's doin', all right. . . .

Says he's a chief, been on that Churchill [1860 Pyramid Lake] War [sec. 17]. And Winnemucca *natsee* say no bullet can hurt my grandfather [i.e., bulletproof], neither. No, sir! Got his horse at Desert Creek—'cause there's plenty salt and pasture there. . . . Get [captures] 'em by that old way, too: puttin' out *ongabee* [salt]. But they're not real mustang he catch. No, sir! Some kind wild horse. . . . Small pony with short ear. . . . Different kind *poogoo* from what we got. . . . And same way, my grandfather, he teach Big Mack to ride, how to throw that rope underhand style. . . .

One time, someone steal my grandfather's horses. That's that Tom Ricci, you know: *taivo* [who] settle Antelope Valley. 'Cause you see what happen? My grandfather's horse are up there, and so Tom Ricci, he drive 'em to his own corral. Steal 'em by that way. . . . So the Old Man, he complain. But Big Mack can't make it. No, sir! 'Cause he can't talk good. Anyway, that's how my grandfather get his name . . . *Poogooga'yoo* 'Horseman'. On account him bein' a horse man.

And you see how he die? By his own gun! Yes, sir! His own grandson do that to him!

'Cause my grandfather, he lose his mind in that war—*khaishooname'yoo* 'not in his own head'. Don't doctor nobody right no more after that. No, sir! Not like he's supposed to be doin', anyway. . . . Witch everybody! Bad doctor! And so *A-peema'a*, he shoot him the back the head—with my grandfather's own gun! Then smash that old man's head with the butt. . . . Up in Wellington, where that happen. . . .

(Call *A-peema'a* Pat Hoye on the English side. He's grandson to *Poogooga'yoo*, but not by real [blood] way, by marriage.)

So you see what happen? His [Pat Hoye's] *beeya* [mother] get sick, and so *A-peema'a*, he call that old man to doctor her. But [since] my grandfather's not workin' that good kind no more, he work that other kind; that *nuumuu pooharr^* [witching way]. . . . So when she die, *A-peema'a*, he get mad.

"Gee, *togho*, that's a good gun!" What that other fellow [Pat Hoye] say to him. Yes, sir! Visit his grandfather, you know. To trick [kill] him. Talk good to him; even call him his *nanuud* 'relation'. And so *Poogooga'yoo*, he believe him, by God! Give him that gun to look at, too, and Pat Hoye, he make believe he's not aimin'; then he can shoot him in the back! Do that to him [bash in his skull] afterward!

And I hear *A-peema'a* run away from this country after he do that. . . . Go to Nixon [Pyramid Lake Reservation]; stay up there a good five year, maybe more? Then he go to California, work there as horseman [cowboy]. . . . And you see why he do that [runs away]? 'Cause Pat, he think that policeman in Smith Valley's gonna arrest him for what he's doin'. So my mom, she has to talk for *A-peema'a*. Yes, sir! Talk against her own father, by God! Tell that policeman what he's [Horseman] doin' all the time. . . . Says, "It's better now *Poogooga'yoo*'s gone. Supposed to be a *poohaghoom* [shaman], my father; not supposed to be witchin' his own family like that way!" And that's that Bill Douglass, you know: my real father. 'Cause he's still policeman [in] Smith Valley that time. Says how he's gonna put that other fellow [Pat Hoye] in jail; hang him. Only my mom, she won't let him. No, sir! "Leave him alone, Bill! No good doctor no more! *Ste'yoo!* Bad man! 'Cause he just witch everyone. Makes everyone to be afraid. Yes, sir! Good thing what my cousin-brother's done! 'Cause my own father's no good no more! Afraid him all the time! *Sa'ab* [witch]! Better to let my cousin-brother go!" Yes, sir! How my mom talk to that policeman that way. . . . 'Cause she know him, all right. . . . Know what her own father's doin'. And so that other fellow [Pat Hoye], he never go to prison for what he done.

He's my *pavee'ee*, *A-peema'a*—old[er] cousin-brother, on my grandma's side. Use *moohoo'oo* [opium] all the time when he come back to Smith Valley. . . . Hop head. . . .

14. Three Brothers and Two Sisters

And so I'm right in the middle my outfit. 'Cause Janie and Sullivan, they're both older; Willy, Herman, and Lizzie are younger. Lizzie, she's the baby: I name her by that way, "Lizzie," after I get to know somethin' [i.e., learned English]. But Willy and Herman, they just get their name from some *taivo*. Sullivan Mack, I already told you that, how he's named by Old Lady Hoye like me, on the ring. But that's one thing I never did find out, partner: who give my *hama'a* [older sister] that name "Janie"?

Real name's *Toyaba'a:* Janie's named for her *moo'a* [maternal grandmother]. And she's around about two years older than me? Marry Don "Coon" [Jones] on May 15, 1905—right after her cherry. 'Cause you see how I know that date? 'Cause that's right around the time I get back from Stewart that first time [i.e., end of school year]. . . . Anyway, his father's from Reno, Don Coon. Related to my mom; some kind *pavee'ee* [older brother] to her. *Kween'a hai'ee,* though, 'not too close'. And Don Coon, he [also] used to work for Old Man (Dan) Simpson them early days. . . . Then he can work for John O'Banion after Simpson sell out. Real old, too, that *Nuumuu* when he marry my sister. Too old, by God! So maybe that's why Janie's doin' that, you know? Steal them two kid! 'Cause [first] she steal Lena off that Portygese. (Name's Manual, he's always milkin' cows around Smith Valley that time. On account she wanna make [a] baby and Don Coon can't. No, sir! *Pash^pa* 'dry man', you know. . . . Lena, she's born 1906. But still he [Don "Coon" Jones] claim her. [Even] call her Lena Jones all the time!) And same way, too, my big sister steal Eddie [Mack] off that *taivo,* off Ed Purdy. 'Cause that one's [also] a policeman in Wellington. But he drink too much, so Ed Purdy, he get the snakes. Die in Sparks [insane asylum]. . . . 'Cause I know this one time, I hear him say to a store owner in Smith Valley, "How come you got that snake by that can?" So they have to do that to him, you know: send Ed Purdy there, to Sparks. 'Cause what that *heebee*'s [alcohol is] doin' to him. . . . Janie's supposed to get a saddle and bridle for sleepin' with that *taivo,* only Ed Purdy, he won't do it. No, sir! Can't! Can't make [afford] it!

Mean woman, though, my old[er] sister! Nobody can tell her what to do! Never [even] wanna take care them two baby she make, so that's why my grandma's always the one doin' that. Yes, sir! 'Cause I know my grandma raise both Lena and Eddie Mack. 'Cause you see why? Janie's usin' that black stuff [yen-shee] when she's marry to Don Coon. Yes, sir! 'Cause he's a *moohoo'oo* [opium] man, that guy. 'Cause I know him! Use that black stuff heavy. [He] live in a tent with my big sister for around about fifteen years, then Janie get stuck on Henry Dick; marry him. Yes, sir! Best partner I got, Henry Dick. 'Cause we used to chase girls together in Smith Valley. . . . Then later on, I marry his sister, too. . . . And my sister's too old to make babies when she's marry to Henry Dick. . . . 'Cause that's right around that First World War, partner. So Janie, after she leave Don Coon for Henry Dick, why, that other fellow [Jones], he come down here [Mason Valley] for her. . . . Beats Janie, give her a black eye, so she leave him. And both them [Janie and Henry Dick] die by that flu [influenza epidemic, 1918]. 'Cause they're livin' in Mason that time—with Henry Dick's father, Dick Bennett; *Pava'yoo* Dick, "Big Dick," they call him. He's a *poohaghoom* [shaman], you know. Boils *qaiva natusawabe* [mountain roots or medicine] to doctor them, but still they go out at night [for opiates?]. So they both die: Janie first, Henry Dick two years later. Bury by that white corral in Yerington [the Indian cemetery].

And gee, my sister can sure make pretty beaded belt! Yes, sir! Armband, too. Any kind design: butterfly, flower. . . . Call those kind *puuta wuupag^pa* [armbands] and *tsomeebee natuu* [beaded belts]. Sell 'em to them *taivo*. . . . And same way, too, Janie used to paint her face and cheek with *pijapee* [red paint]: paint long [horizontal] lines on her cheek, one [vertical] on her chin. Then when she's marry, she can take a needle and use that alfalfa juice to *naraqabo'o* [facial tatoo]. Pretty near like what I'm doin' in Stewart, you know: write my initial on my wrist. . . .

But my old[er] brother, he just get crippled up and die. Real name's *Poowee natsee* 'Eye Boy', 'Big Eye'. Pretty big when he dies, Sullivan. Maybe twenty, twenty-one? Never work, though. And he's tall, too. . . . Got a tall father, so maybe he's just that way? Sullivan, he get paralyzed quick like that, then die! Pretty hard to handle him when he can't walk no more, by God! 'Cause that's pretty tough when you can't walk, partner! Yes, sir! Suffer a good long time, too, my *pavee'ee*. . . . And never marry, neither. Same way, too, they try to operate on Sullivan. But he can't make it. No, sir! 'Cause you see why? Tom Mitchell! He doctor my brother but won't help him! No, sir! Bad man, Tom Mitchell, I tell you, Mike! *Sahab!* Witch! 'Cause he can witch a fellow he don't like pretty easy. . . . And I'm, maybe, nine when my big brother die [1901?]. Big Mack, he carry Sullivan to them hills back Colony District [northern Smith Valley] on his horse. Wrap him tight in his blanket and bury my *pavee'ee* under rock; just like real old-time way. 'Cause I know, afterward, I and Willy, we're both sittin' on the Old Man's knee, tryin' to look back to see where he bury our brother. But Big Mack, he won't let us. No, sir! Says, "*Ste'yoo!* Not good! Don't look at that place! Bad Place!" 'Cause them old-timers, you know, they got funny idea. Don't want you to know where they bury. . . . Afraid, maybe, they're [their ghosts are] gonna come back and bother a person! Not like today, though. 'Cause nowaday, *karroo'oo*. Nowaday, all these Indians bury in the cemetery and bring flower; decorate them grave and visit Memorial Day. Not scared no more. . . . Anyway, right after Sullivan die, the Old Man and my mom, and my grandma, they just sit home and cry. Cry, maybe, two-three week to a month? Don't eat much, neither. And after we lose my big brother, we just move away from there [Wellington]. 'Cause we're livin' back the Warner Garage that time—near Plymouth [irrigation] Ditch; so the Old Man, he make us to move about 200 yard away.

Willy, he come after me. And I always take my young brother to the [West] Walker River; fish with Willy up there. 'Cause gee, I sure like that [in] my young days, partner! Summertime, you know, we go up to that dam—above the Hoye store in Wellington—mouth the canyon; dam they call Simpson Dam, on account it's named for Old Man [Dan] Simpson. . . . Yes, sir! And fish pretty near every day! Stay up there all day long, too, by God! Fish for trout, catch great big one! 'Cause them little one, you gotta leave behind. And that time, used to be lotta trout in the [West Walker] river. . . . Then I can make fire, roast 'em on top that charcoal. Or, when we get hungry [and don't catch any], why, we can just roast minnow noontime. (Lotta minnow in the river!) And I bet you Willy's around about three that time: younger than me, but lots bigger! 'Cause, gee, I pretty near look like his young brother when we walk. And Willy's not sick at all when he die! No, sir! Maybe thirteen [1905]?. Die on that land the Old Man get from George Fulstone [sec. 55]. But nobody bring Tom Mitchell in to doctor my *wanga'a* [younger brother]! Still, they say he's doin' that to my young brother: witchin' him, you know! Me, though, I kind of think my young brother die on account what the Old Man's doin'. You know, scarin' us outta our tent like that 'cause my mom stole me. . . . 'Cause Big Mack, he's doin' that even in winter, that cold weather! You know, playin' with his shotgun; won't say nothin'; till we all get scared out. Makin' us [even] to stay outside our nice warm tule house all night long sometime. . . . 'Cause some kid, you know, they just don't like what their father's doin'. Worry too much, get sick pretty easy, and die. So maybe Willy's scared the Old Man might just do that? Pull that trigger? Maybe worry there's a shell inside there? Gonna hit somebody? Anyway, after he die, the Old Man and my mom, they [also] take Willy away. . . .

Herman Mack, he's around about two when he die. Die before Willy, right after Sullivan [ca. 1907?]. . . . So Tom Mitchell, he's the one can carry my young[est] brother away. Then my mom and my grandma, they cut their hair. 'Cause Herman, too, he just get sick like that and die—after that tent we bought [sec. 20] burn. . . . 'Cause you see what happen? Someone's foolin' with match. Anyway, my sister Janie, she rescue Herman. Only thing is, all our belonging burn in that fire! But [since] my mom and the Old Man, they're workin' for Old Lady Hoye, she give 'em a mattress. 'Cause same as my grandma, she get lots from Old Lady Rogers. Workin' for her that time. . . .

My young sister, Lizzie, she die way later—in 1958. Same year my wife die. Leg's no good, Lizzie get swollen up like that and die. She's forty-eight when that happen: Lizzie is buried right here in Yerington. . . . And she's the only one move outta these valleys: to Susanville [California]. Yes, sir! Live there a good many year, too. Marry to Harry Sam, but she quit him. 'Cause you see why? He don't take care her. No, sir! Peeyot [peyote] man, that one. 'Cause them kind, you know, they don't drink, but just as bad. And Harry Sam's [also] a "squaw man"—always after the woman! She make three kids with him, Lizzie: Bernice, Elsie, and "Crazy" Jackson Sam. And my young sister also make one baby with some *taivo:* Elizabeth. But she don't tell us about her. . . . No, sir! [Then] I hear she just drink with her husband, and Welfare take them kids away. Put 'em in foster home. . . . Anyway, my *nanagwa* [nephew Jackson Sam], he's done a lotta dirty work! Yes, sir! So they have to put him in prison. But then they let him out and he's gonna do wrong again, so they have to put him back! 'Cause I know him! Jackson Sam's always comin' around here to bum me. . . . One time he even steal from me. . . . [sec. 147]

15. Sibling Solidarity

So eight of us, in all . . . what they make. 'Cause one baby die in the basket. (Fit right between Willy and me.) But one thing I know we never do is fight! Oh, sure, maybe when I'm little, I and my sister and brother are doin' that. . . . But once I'm big enough to know better, *khai,* no such thing!

'Cause we just get along pretty good all the time, by God! Yes, sir! Go around together, make friend with each other. . . .

And so, after that last boy [Willy Mack] die, the Old Man, he quit botherin' me. No, sir! Start actin' good to me all the time. . . . You know, to make a friend [rapproachment]. Don't pick up his rifle no more and scare us outta our own house. Yes, sir! Stop actin' crazy like he's always doin'. . . . 'Cause maybe that's on account I'm the only one [son] he's got left? Anyway, I'm big already, so maybe Big Mack's afraid me?

2

Boyhood (1892–1905)

16. Them *Taivo,* They Come to Smith (and Mason) Valley!

My grandma, she's the one tell me that: how old man [Dan] Simpson and "Hike" [George] Fulstone make that early [first] settlement in Desert Creek [Smith Valley]. Say my grandfather, *Poogooga'yoo,* and Chief Joaquin, they wanna kill 'em. (Joaquin, that's Hazel Quinn's *togho'o* [maternal grandfather]; she's my wife's *oos^nabeeya* [sister-in-law], Blind Bob and Maggie's daughter.) 'Cause you see why they're mad? They don't want cattle feedin' on their food. No, sir! Same way, too, Old Man [Dan] Simpson, he don't want these Indian on his land. Say they can't cut [harvest] *mahaveeta* [sec. 17] no more. No, sir! Say that's his cow feed, so won't let them Bridgeport Indians do that [i.e., cultivate and harvest] that kind no more. And so they get mad. Wanna chase them first *taivo* outta Smith Valley. You know, to make a war. . . .

So Old Man [Dan] Simpson, he just make a friend with these Indian. Yes, sir! Hire 'em to work; give 'em plenty food to eat, too: flour, bacon . . . a knife to cut that bacon with. And same way, too, he give 'em gun powder. So they make a friend that way. Sign a treaty: we can let 'em stay in Smith Valley, live close by; them *taivo,* they have to give these Indian work. Yes, sir! To get along better that way. 'Cause them Simpson boy, they like these Indian. . . . Then later on, when Old Man [Dan] Simpson get marry—'cause

I hear he send to California for his wife—he's gotta invite all these Indians [in] the other [Smith] valley to that Big Time. . . .

And you know who's doin' all that talkin' [interpreting] for both [Dan Simpson and "Hike" Fulstone]? Blind Bob [Roberts]! Yes, sir! 'Cause you see why? [He's] been among them *taivo,* I hear, so Blind Bob, he know their lingo. Can talk their tongue real good. . . . Tell these [Smith Valley] Indians not to kill Old Man [Dan] Simpson and Hike. You know, to make a friend. 'Cause he's a real old-timer, Blind Bob. Older than my mom. Pretty near like my grandma, that old man. *Khai tabootaboowee* [blind], you know? 'Cause them early days ago, when *taivo* first start comin' into this valley, Blind Bob, he was grubbin' sagebrush for 'em: you know, so they can plant alfalfa. And you see what happen? Someone witch him! Yes, sir! Make him to have that accident that way: poke out his eye. And so Old Lady Simpson, she take Blind Bob to California. Stay two month. . . . But that don't help. No, sir! Can't make it! Eye all shot to hell! Both 'em! So maybe that's why my grandma's always sayin' that? How it's better with all them old-timers gone? 'Cause too many witch them days! my grandma says. *Ste'yoo!* Bad One! No good that kind!

17. World's War!

And when them early wagon start comin' through these valley, when them *taivo* start comin' through, we can watch 'em. . . . 'Cause I know Big Mack, he say they're headed to dry lake [Smith Valley] first, then Hudson, and over them mountain to California. Say he's only wearin' his "birthday suit" when them first *taivo* come through these valley. Hungry all the time, too, them days. Yes, sir! Afraid, too. Afraid maybe they're gonna grab him and run away with him. So you see what he do? Hide! 'Cause I hear they grab Tom Mitchell's brother and take him outta here. . . . 'Cause this one fellow, Brady [Emm], he go back to Utah; find him there. Say that other fellow's name's Charley Travis. . . . And same way, too, this one *taivo* and his wife, they're passin' through Wellington and nearly grab hold Eddie [Mack, Corbett's nephew]. . . . 'Cause Eddie's playin', you know. But he fight 'em off, all right; so they have to let go him. And so when we see 'em again, why, they're both ashamed.

But you see what them real old-time Indians are doin' when them covered wagon start comin' through these valley? They go over there and kill 'em! Yes, sir! 'Cause that's how they make trouble with *taivo*. And keep on doin' that, too, you know. . . . So [until] George Washington, he send troops to this country . . . that war I told you about, one my grandfather's in. Yes, sir! 'Cause that's how they start that battle.

And you know who tell me that? Winnemucca *natsee*. He's from Pyramid Lake, that old-timer: *Kooyuweeduukaduu* [Pyramid Lake Trout-Eater]. Short fellow . . . around about my grandma's age. Talk a lot, you know. Like he's a chief. Say them four doctor, they're in that war: Winnemucca *natsee*, Tom Joaquin, *Tabooseege'yoo*, and my grandfather, *Poogooga'yoo*. Say they all meet in Nixon. Tell everyone else to hide, or they'll get hurt. Tell how they're gonna fight George Washington's troop at Churchill, on account they're mad at us. 'Cause you see what happen? When them covered wagon start comin' through, why, we take gun from 'em. Yes, sir! And so Winnemucca *natsee*, he say [that's why] them soldier come.

Say they got horse, too, them *taivo* soldier. But we don't need any. No, sir! 'Cause you see why? They [four doctors] can go just as fast as any horse! Yes, sir! Winnemucca *natsee* say they can stay right up there with 'em, 'cause they're powerful! Say my grandfather can walk through their bullet! Tom Joaquin, he's from Bridgeport—some kind brother [also] to Tom Mitchell. And they say he [also] get stolen outta this country when he's young, but Tom Joaquin, he come back, all right. 'Cause I know I hear them soldier get mad at these Indian and wanna take 'em [relocate] outta here. . . . Yes, sir! [To] make a home for 'em someplace else. . . . Like what they done with Jack Wilson's *na'a* [sec. 123]. . . . Stole him from this country. 'Cause you see why? Too many Indian livin' here, so they're afraid!

And Trottin' Wijo, he's from this [Mason] valley. We call him *Tabooseege'yoo*, Trottin' Wijo: named for that *taboosee*, you know . . . old-time food we get [sec. 18]. Only one time, though, I seen him doctor Judy Joaquin in Wellington. Blind Bob—that's her son-in-law, he has to help that Indian doctor; repeat. . . . He's marry *Tabooseege'yoo;* got no children. . . . 'Cause I know I see 'em in Smith Valley . . . both. Real old-timers, they live in a tule house. . . . And last one in that world's war's my grandfather, *Poogooga'yoo*, Horseman. Yes, sir! So four doctor in all. And they can put their *booha* [power] together, you know: to take away George Washington soldiers' gun. Kill them *taivo* better that way. . . .

"Give me *nosee* [dream] to kill any man this world!" What Winnemucca *natsee* say he's doin'. Prayin' for, anyway. . . . 'Cause [he's] pretty powerful man, I tell you, by God! Winnemucca *natsee*, he can [even] cure that *qonoza*

[clap]! Spit that *wo'aba* [worm] out when he's finished [doctoring]. . . . Nickname's *tonada*. 'Cause I guess he always hit someone with his fist when he's a young guy. . . . And same way, too, Winnemucca *natsee* say, "No bullets can hurt me!" Yes, sir! Has [even] got more power than Jack Wilson!

"Them *taivo* are nothin'! *Karroo'oo!* [Their] guns too slow. 'Cause we can dive right in there and hit 'em left and right. And we got [only?] a hatchet. Their bullet feel just like hail!" What Winnemucca *natsee* say. . . .

And so they die, too, them *taivo*. "Gone just like a dead bird!" Winnemucca *natsee* say. "'Cause them *taivo*, they don't get up no more!"

He's related to my grandma, Winnemucca *natsee*. . . . Why he's always visitin' our camp. . . .

But [then] more on the *taivo* side keep comin', so Winnemucca *natsee*, he say my grandfather don't [even] care. No, sir! Call them new soldiers down . . . say, "You better fight!" Yes, sir! What *Poogooga'yoo* say to 'em! And so their leader, he blow a horn and wave 'em [forward]: you know, to fight better. . . . But Winnemucca *natsee* say their bullet can't knock my grandfather over. No, sir! 'Cause he's got too much *booha* [viz., bulletproof], that old man; same as them other [three] Indian doctor. 'Cause them soldiers' bullet, they don't even make a scratch on my grandfather! No, sir! And so they [finally] give up. But not that general [viz., George Washington]. . . . No, sir! Can't get him, 'cause you see why? Too tough! Just like them four doctor. . . . They try and shoot him, but can't make it! No, sir! [Even] take greasewood, ram that through his *tsaboo* [rectum]. But [since] he's on a horse, why, that don't work, neither. So Winnemucca *natsee*, he say he shoot [rifle?] at him. But that don't work, neither. Can't knock him off his horse, 'cause George Washington, he's got as much *booha* as them four [Indian doctors]!

But one bullet knock Winnemucca *natsee* in the knee. And so he falls down. Taste that, then; says it's not even lead. 'Cause they got steel bullet, them *taivo* soldier. . . . So Winnemucca *natsee*, he just spit on that bullet. Load powder to his gun [next], and shoot. And so when that don't work, why, he can just take hold *pozeeda*—use that to knock their leader in two!

So them [four] Indian doctor, they win that battle. . . . Get the best of 'em, all right. Then after that, we shake hand. Yes, sir! To make a better friend with *taivo* that way. . . . [Still] they take so many Indian away from here, you know. 'Cause afraid, you know. Afraid they're gonna start that war again. . . . What I hear, anyway. 'Cause that's a real long time ago, partner—them early days ago. But [when] I ask my grandma how my grandfather fight in that war? and about that treaty? she won't tell me nothin'! *Karroo'oo!* "Where's *Poogooga'yoo* buried, *mov'a?"* I ask my grandma. But you think she's gonna tell me somethin'? Hell, no! 'Cause Winnemucca *natsee,* he's the one always doin' that. And I'm pretty big myself that time. Yes, sir! Always comin' around to visit our camp in Smith Valley, Winemucca *natsee.* . . . Tell everybody about that World's War. . . . What these Indian are doin' them real early days ago. . . . When them *taivo* first start comin' here into America. . . .

Die by his own horse, too, Winnemucca *natsee:* war horse rear up, and so he fall.

18. *Tabooseedokado:* Smith (and Mason) Valley *Nuumuu*

And gee, there used to be lotta Indian in Smith Valley them days! Now, *karroo'oo:* not too many left up there. All dyin' off, you know. . . . Only one left's Irene [Thompson]. . . . But I know when I'm a little guy, there's eight, maybe nine camp [of Indians] in Wellington. . . . And same way, some at Smith. . . . Colony District. Over by Desert Creek, too. Yes, sir! *Karroo'oo,* no more Smith Valley Indian left, partner! Irene Thompson's pretty near last wild Indian left up there any more!

Call them Smith Valley Indian *Nuumuu,* you know: people. (Pretty near same word for your liver, partner!) And same name as down here, this [Mason] valley. . . . Or, they can call 'em both [Smith and Mason Valley Indians] *Tabooseedokado*—from that *taboosee,* what old-timers eat. 'Cause that one's just like a coconut, you know: grow by the river, and has got milk inside; hair on the shell. . . . Only *taboosee* is lot smaller [than a coconut]. 'Cause, gee, I know my grandma sure like that kind! Yes, sir! Always gettin' 'em, you know. Has to tell her boss when they're ripe, so she can leave her work. Then my grandma can get 'em; grind 'em up. And we eat that kind right off her *mata* [metate]. . . . But them Desert Creek [Smith Valley] people, they [also] got another name: call 'em *Pozeedagwe* (real old-time name). Or *Pozeeda naho*—after that *pozeeda,* you know: some kind clover grass they're after down there early days ago. Grow real tall, too, *pozeeda;* they can feed their horse on that kind grass; eat them green leaf themself. . . . But I never did see that kind, neither. No, sir! Anyway, they say *pozeeda* don't taste very strong. Not what I hear, anyway. Not like alfalfa. . . . 'Cause I know my grandma, she say her outfit used to come up here to harvest that kind from Bridgeport all the time. Yes, sir! Same like that Tom Mitchell's outfit. 'Cause they stay there all the time, too, when he's a boy, Desert Creek. And this one old-timer, they even call him *Pozeeda* Sam. (That's Sam Leon's father). 'Cause you see why? [They] own all Desert Creek. . . .

But same way, too, they have another name, them Desert Creek Indian—*Mahaveetaduukuuduu*. Never did see that kind, neither, but *mahaveeta,* that's a name for them kind root [also] growin' up there. 'Cause I hear them Bridgeport Indians, they're [also] comin' up for that kind. Only difference is, they plant that in Desert Creek. Yes, sir! Get that seed from Bridgeport and plant it there. Use an irrigation ditch on that kind; farm just like a *taivo!* Except them Indians, they been doin' that way before *taivo* start comin' to this country. . . . And you see who stop 'em from doin' that? Old Man [Dan] Simpson! Yes, sir! Don't like that. Say it's spoilin' his cow's feed. . . . Why them Desert Creek Indians don't try and grow *mahaveeta* no more. No, sir! But you know who them old-timers say [really] make that [irrigation] ditch? Two fish!

'Cause they're partner, you know, them two fish: one *pagwee* [fish], they call him *Aghaiboho*—got a great big head and small body; his partner, *Atsa Pagwee* [Red Fish], he's a little fellow that one. And so, that other [little] fellow, he wanna go through. Just like a ditcher, you know. But he can't make it! No, sir! Get down to the bottom that ditch and call back to his partner, "*Pai yahee.*" 'Water's dead!' 'Cause you see why? No water's comin' behind him. *Karroo'oo*! And so his partner—one with the big head—he go over there, all right. Yes, sir! 'Cause *Aghaiboho,* he's got a little horn on his head. (Some kind catfish, I figure . . . around about six inch long.) Hears his partner callin' for water and so *Aghaiboho,* he help out.

First he's gonna lay down, then he can pick up some pebble. Throw 'em, you know . . . to make a small hole everywhere with them kind rock. Then he's gonna belly whop through. Yes, sir! Plough that ditch that way, till that water can come right behind him. (Same way they say another fish up there [Desert Creek], that one's got no eye. Say if you take him out the water, it rain! Smaller than a minnow, that *pagwee* [fish]. 'Cause I know I'm always afraid to bother 'em. 'Cause one time somebody did and, gee, it sure hailed!) Anyway, that's what them real old-timers are always sayin'. On them *natoon˜udweba* [animal teachings. cf. sec. 151]. . . . How these animal real early days ago are makin' things good for these Indian. . . . You know [for example], so they can plant *mahaveeta*. . . .

Anyway, these [Mason Valley] *Nuumuu,* they used to be scattered all over this [Mason] valley—till the government give 'em a little piece land to put their house on [Yerington Indian Colony, 1917]. Yes, sir! Bunch 'em that way. 'Cause they used to live in this valley a little west of there—then move 'em there and line 'em up with that street in the center. You know, to live over by that old hospital; where the red light [whorehouse] was. . . . 'Cause lotta *wuuyuupoowee* back there then; they can put their tent behind buckberry brush, have that for a windbreak. . . . And same way, too, they live on ranch[es] down here: two or three camp in Missouri Flat [for example] . . . and out by the airport, that road goin' down to Schurz [Walker River Reservation] . . . and down by the [Walker] river, too, in Mason. 'Cause I know I always used to visit Fish Lake Joe [*Wodzeewob*, the 1870 Ghost Dance prophet] and *Soowee warr^b* my early days in Mason [sec. 122]. "You wanna eat?" what they always say to me. 'Cause your relation, you know, you gotta visit. And so they gotta be good to you, too.

19. One Real Old-Timer

Another real old-timer, Jim Wilson, he tell about *Nameedzweebwa* Jim. Say, "*Nameedzweebwa* Jim can put his head down, Storm start up; [then he] lift it up again, why, that kind clear!" Say he's askin' for land in Schurz, *Nameedzweebwa* Jim, only they don't wanna give him that. So he do that [i.e., causes a storm], you know. Say,

"You don't give me land, I'm gonna do that!"

And, well, so he do. . . . 'Cause *Nameedzweebwa* Jim, he can make it rain a good long time, too! And so afterward, he's lookin' for the best-lookin' girl. Line 'em all up . . . ride past that line on his horse. (Got a long white beard, *Nameedzweebwa* Jim; horse is white, too. No mane on that *poogoo*. . . .) And he can ride off with that one girl on that horse!

'Cause you see what [really] happen? After he call for land, *Nameedzweebwa* Jim ask for food. Only thing is, nobody don't understand him, so he get mad. Real mad! Then somebody try to give him meat, but [since] all he want is that land. . . .

Anyway, *Nameedzweebwa* Jim ride by that line, prettiest girl he like can get on his white horse; ride way up to the sky like that.

But nobody know where *Nameedzweebwa* Jim's from, neither. No, sir! Or, who that girl is? Same way, that kind horse, they say is not from around here. 'Cause it's bigger than ours. . . .

Nameedzweebwa, that's 'Comin' Outta the Canyon'.

20. Growing Up in Smith Valley: Our House

And we're still livin' in a wigwam when I'm born, partner! Yes, sir! That *kanee,* tule house.... 'Cause all them old-timers, they're still doin' that....

Build it back the Hoye Store in Wellington—where my mom and my grandma work. And that kind's nice and warm, too, by God! But still, we have to fix up our *kanee* when that north wind's blowin'. You know, cut up overall to cover the top with. And keep our fire goin' inside all the time, too. 'Cause, wintertime, that's *uudzuudzuu,* cold. And sometime, too, the Old Man [even] has to get pine nut wood from way up in the mountain for that fire. But that kind's *ste'yoo,* you know: no good! Hurt your eye too much.... And too heavy to carry with all that pitch on it.... Then everybody quit makin' them tule house—[because they] wanna live in a tent instead.

Call that kind *toha nobee* 'white house'. 'Cause that's not army tent, you know. No, sir! 'Cause that kind's green. What we're always buyin' is white.... Got a peaked roof on top.... And I know I'm around about seven when we get our first tent. Old Lady Hoye, she send [sells?] for it. Then we can slip four by fours underneath—for floorin'. Use our horses to pull [move] that tent whenever we move.... But like I say, gee, that wind sure blow through! And you can't do nothin' about that one, neither! Same way, too, you can't light no sagebrush [indoors] for your fire. No, sir! So, pretty cold, them canvas tent, I tell you, Mike! Need your *weega* [rabbitskin blanket] all the time to keep you warm....

Anyway, them days, we can set up anywhere—just so long as not in the [cultivated] fields. Or too close to your boss's house. Not like today, anyway. 'Cause, today, these *taivo* are different. Today, everythin's fenced, them days, not.... 'Cause back then, they want you livin' close to 'em. 'Cause you see why? Work! So you can pitch your tent close by; just so long as you're on the job and don't bother 'em too much, why, they don't bother you at all....

Then way later on, I know we buy our tent from John O'Banion. But that's way after we don't like Jack Wilson's lumber house no more.... Yes, sir! Just get tired that [tent], that's all... Buy that other kind house from Jack Wilson.

'Cause he's related to the Old Man, Jack: my *hai'ee* [father's brother]. Not real way, though, Jack Wilson's related by Indian way. 'Cause Big Mack's Jack Wilson's *pavee'ee* [older brother], you know—older than he is.... And so Jack, after he quit workin' for Old Man [Dan] Simpson that time, he wanna move to Mason town; why he sell us that lumber house. 'Cause that's when Mason's boomin', you know. Yes, sir! Lotta copper mine them days: Ludwig . . . Buckskin . . . Mason's [even] bigger than Yerington! Got hotel, restaurant. . . . And so Jack Wilson's wife, she can work in them hotels in Mason. Or maybe he wanna move back to this [Mason] valley, 'cause his mom and dad are livin' yet? You know, wanna live close by 'em? So anyway, [since] Jack Wilson's lumber house can't make that move, he sell to Big Mack. And by God, Jack Wilson's pretty near first *Nuumuu* to own his own lumber house in Smith Valley, too! Build it near Smith—on that hill by Macarini's ranch. Lot bigger than a tent, too, Jack Wilson's lumber house! Only thing is, don't have a floor inside, so we [still] have to make our bed on the ground. 'Cause I know I sleep on my grandma's *weega* [rabbitskin blanket] till she get a quilt. . . .

And you see why lumber house's better than a tent? Got a stove inside, partner! Quiet house, too: just as warm as *kanee*. . . . But you see how we lose Jack Wilson's [lumber] house? On account the Old Man! Yes, sir! Always changin' job, that old man! Keeps on movin' all the time. . . . Don't never work steady on any one job in Smith Valley. No, sir! 'Cause he's just that kind, Big Mack: has a job over here, then he's gonna get a different job, move over there. You know, to be closer. . . . 'Cause, gee, I don't know how many time we move! Movin' all over the godamn place all the godamn time! "We better move other there." Yes, sir! What that old man's always sayin'! And so we have to do that, move. [But we] never try to fix anything good, 'cause we move all the god damn time! Then when somebody in our family die, why, we have to move again. 'Cause them old-timers, you know, they got their own idea. 'Cause by old-time way, anyway, somebody die, you're supposed to burn that house. . . .

And so we keep on doin' that [moving], you know. . . . Until Jack Wilson's [lumber] house can't make it no more. Have to leave that behind in Smith, you know; after we move back to the Colony [District of Smith Valley]. But I don't see why Big Mack don't go back and get it. . . . 'Cause he [just] don't like tent very much. No, sir! 'Cause you see why? Big Mack don't like all that noise they're makin'. You know, canvas flappin' all the time. . . . Say it don't let him to sleep at night, so the Old Man, he put willows from the irrigation ditch in front: make some kind windbreak. And [he] put up a shade in front, too. Build a cellar, so we can go down there when there's that real bad wind. . . .

21. The Outfit

We're always campin' together, my family, you know: the Old Man and my mom, they got one tent; my grandma, she's got another, the one I stay in with her; my sister Janie, she's got another. 'Cause that time Janie's big, and still livin' with Don Coon. That's before she quit her husband and move in with my cousin-brother, Henry Dick; camp with him and Henry's father, Dick Bennett, in Mason. 'Cause it don't matter which way you're doin' that, you know. Say a woman wanna stay with her folk after they're marry, why, then that's what the man's got to do. But if he wanna move close by his folks, why, she can do that, too. . . . Still, by the right way, woman's supposed to stay with her mother, the man with his wife. . . . Then when I'm big, after I marry, why, I and my wife buy our own tent—from James Keno. Live close by the Old Man and my grandma, after my mom's dead. . . . 'Cause Old Man Keno, he don't like his house no more. . . . Why he's sellin'. "You wanna sell that tent to me, Jim?" I say to him. "O. K., Corbett," he say back. "You're my friend. I sell to you!" 'Cause you see why he's doin' that [i.e., selling and relocating]? Old Man Keno lose his boy! Why he has to do that [i.e., move away]. Sell that tent for forty-five dollars. . . .

22. Some Traditional (Plant) Foods

But mostly I eat Indian food when I'm a boy. You know, *paapee* [pine nut soup], *wuuyuupoowee* [buckberries], *kooha* . . . Them kind. 'Cause like I already told you, my grandma, she have to lay off work to get 'em. Yes, sir! All them different kind Indian food. . . . And she know how to fix 'em good, too. Work all the time, [then] get tired *taivo* food; so, when that other kind's ripe, she's gonna tell her boss, and he can let her lay off a couple or three days. . . .

Pine nut, you gotta go up into the mountain for. Yes, sir! And we're all lookin' for *tuuba* [pine nuts] all the time, too, by God! Go to Desert Creek to get 'em [for example]. . . . And Sweetwater. Sometimes we [even] have to go to Hawthorne. And we have to stay up in them mountain a good long time, too, pine nuttin', by God! Yes, sir! Maybe one month? Two? But early days ago, if they're starvin' they can go up there [mountains] real early—way before them [pine] cone are [even] ripe; hunt deer for their livin'. . . . And from the tree with their *goonoo'oo* [curved stick], then stack up them cone and cook 'em. Or they can climb them pine tree. . . . 'Cause men, they're the one always doin' that; them women have stay on the ground. . . . Do poundin' that way. 'Course, nowaday, they don't do that no more. No, sir! Nowaday, they just wait 'till them cone are ripe: [until they] fall from them pine tree. [Then] pick their pine nut that more easy way. . . . Yes, sir! Don't have to knock 'em from them cone with stick no more. . . . But pretty tough work, I tell you, by God! And we can bring down 500 pound. . . . Big Mack, he build *tuuba nobee* [pine nut house] outta lumber, so we can keep [preserve] 'em all winter long. . . . . And that's every fall, partner, when them pine nut are ripe. Gotta get lots, too, for winter use. . . . Work hard to grind *tuuba*, so we can dip our meat in that *papee* [pine nut soup]. . . . You know, to give a more better flavor that way. But no snow, there's not gonna be too many pine nut next fall. And so they starve. . . . Why they have that [pine nut] dance for 'em [sec. 23].

Buckberry, that's like a dessert. They get 'em from them kind bush at the end of summer. . . . With that same kind stick they're usin' for *tuuba*. Yes, sir! Knock 'em down, then press 'em through them tight [woven] basket. . . .

Kooha, they're easy. 'Cause I know my grandma can get a whole flour sack in three or four days! Yes, sir! 'Cause she just hit 'em inside that [flour] sack with that [crooked] stick like a fryin' pan, then pretty quick, my grandma's got a whole sack full! And she know how to fix *kooha* good, too, my grandma! Yes, sir! Fry 'em. . . . And, gee, they sure taste good!

Same way, too, my grandma can buy wheat: get that skin off and rub [grinds] that kind on her *mata* [grinding stone]; cook 'em with charcoal. Or she can mix that [wheat] with *pachee* [sunflower seed]: you know, grind 'em together and put water on top, lets us to eat off that stone. (Cook flour dough in a Dutch oven—make our own bread that way. . . .)

And by real old-time way, we only eat two meal every day . . . breakfast and supper. Sometime we can eat *kooha* for our breakfast and supper—both! Or we can eat *papee* with rabbit, deer meat for taste. . . . And them oldtimers, they just say *tuuka* 'eat', for their breakfast or dinner. Or they can say, "*Khai pazeeha?*" 'Aren't you hungry?'. Not me. That's not what I'm doin'. No, sir! 'Cause I know I like to eat three square meal every day: my breakfast, dinner, and my supper! 'Cause you see why? Always workin', so I'm used to the *taivo* side. . . . Eat bacon and egg, and potato, for my breakfast, spam and macaroni salad for my dinner; supper's my light meal. . . . But that's today, partner. 'Cause back then, they don't have egg in the store. No, sir! So pretty hard to come by. Same with your meat. . . . So you gotta buy on a ranch. Whoever butcher. . . .

And when I'm young, my grandma and my mom, they [mostly?] bring left-over from Old Lady Hoye, the Readings . . . whoever they work for. So only when we get sick of *taivo* food, that's when they go after that other [traditional] kind. And same way, too, I know I always go to work with my grandma all the time ever since I'm a little guy; so I always eat good! Yes, sir! 'Cause they got Chinaman cook where my grandma work; and you always eat good with them kind! But I never do go with my mom to work. No, sir! 'Cause you see why? My young sister always has to do that. 'Cause Lizzie's still on the breast. . . .

Already told you what my grandma's always sayin'? How she's glad the white man come. . . . 'Cause, otherwise, we might starve to death. . . .

23. *Tuubanuugwa* ('Pine Nut Dance')

Blind Bob, he's always *poweenabe,* good talker. Pray to them *tuuba* they're never gonna spoil. . . . You know, to be good always, so these Indian can have lotta food [i.e., pine nuts] always to eat. Yes, sir! *Pizza yarro'a,* Blind Bob. Good talker. 'Cause he know what to say. . . .

And same way, too, they have to have dance up there [Smith Valley] before they get that food. Yes, sir! Dance all night long, too. . . . Call that kind, *nuuga,* Circle Dance, *Tuubanuugwa,* Pine Nut Dance. Blind Bob, he's [also] in charge that kind. Say, "We're gonna have a *tuubanuugwa,* so you better go get some food so we can eat at night!" And people from all over pile up: from Smith Valley, Mason Valley, Schurz . . . whoever else wanna. . . . 'Cause you see what they're doin'? After he pray, and they dance, at midnight, why, they have to have a feed. Yes, sir! Men and women, they're gonna dance around that fire until midnight. Then after they eat, why, they can dance again, till mornin'. And when they're dancin' like that, somebody [else] has to sing. . . . Anybody [who] know them Circle Dance song[s]. . . . (Call that kind [singer] *hoobeeya.* He's got a drum and a stick. We call that drum *tuguveena.* . . .) Yes, sir! 'Cause that's around about the first of September when they're doin' that. . . .

But you can't really tell what Blind Bob say, neither. No, sir! 'Cause them real old-timers, they're [such] good talker, we don't know their word they're usin'.

24. *Naaveey^ts* ('Firstfruits'): Male Puberty Rite

Big Mack, he buy me a .22 when I'm small yet . . . to hunt. But I learn to shoot myself. Then after I grow up, I can use shotgun. 'Cause the Old Man, he always want me to hunt with him. Yes, sir! Take me out huntin' all the time: put me on the horse when we go after rabbit. . . . 'Cause we don't walk, and any rabbit, why, I have shoot 'em. But they say a man can't hunt when his wife's havin' a baby. No, sir! 'Cause you see why? That will hurt that baby! Can't hunt for six, seven days afterwards. . . . And same way, too, when you're just gettin' to be a man, why, they can say to you: "Don't eat that! That's your *naaveey^ts!*"

And that's just about every kind animal we eat, *naaveey^ts!* Say if you're fishin' first time, you gotta bring that home to your family. And it's gotta be a big fish, too: you know, them trout, catfish . . . not little one. 'Cause otherwise, Big Mack, he say them *pagwee* [fish] will know you! Won't like you at all. . . . No, sir! Won't let you to catch 'em no more, not if you're not doin' that. Have bad luck all the time. . . . And same way with deer, too. *Kamuu* [jackrabbit], *saya* [mudhen], *buuhuu* [duck]. 'Cause you gotta also give them kind to your folks, too; not supposed to be eatin' 'em [first hunts] at all! 'Cause I know Big Mack, he's always tellin' me [to do] that.

And same way, too, them girl, when they make their first cherry [period]. . . . 'Cause you see what my grandma's always doin' to my sister? Wake 'em up real early in the mornin' to run—before even Sun's come up. And gee, my grandma can run right alongside 'em, too! Yes, sir! [Runs] down to the [Walker] river, where she make 'em bathe. Then Janie and Lizzie, they gotta throw away their old clothes. And same way, too, they gotta carry firewood on their back while they're runnin'. (Use that sagebrush, you know, to make fire.) 'Cause my grandma, she [also] make 'em jump over that fire. Yes, sir! [Then] tell both [sisters] to stand on them ash: brush 'em both down with sagebrush and pray for 'em. . . . Tell 'em they should [also] keep runnin' all day long, so that way, they won't never be lazy. Always be lively that way.

Call that kind *namaraghai,* that first cherry. . . .

And same way, too, when you're young, and them old-timers tell you to do somethin', why, you gotta do that quick. Can't say, "Wait for later!" No, sir! 'Cause they say, "Do it now!" Say this will make you to be more healthy. . . .

Naaveey^ts, that mean to 'exchange'.

25. Hunting Proscriptions

And you see what else they say? After you kill *muuhuu* [porcupine], you're not supposed to toss them guts in the air. No, sir! 'Cause you see why? Make snow that way! 'Cause Coyote, you know, he's the one always doin' that. . . . And same way, too, them heart [of hunted animals], they say to throw that one away. . . . Them young boy, they're not supposed to eat that kind [e.g., mountain sheep, deer, rabbit] at all. No, sir! 'Cause you see why? Your own heart's gonna beat faster when you're doin' that [hunting], climbin' mountain; so when you're after somethin' [game], you're gonna get tired and wanna quit. And same way, too, you're not supposed to eat them *kamuu* [jackrabbit] gut. No, sir! 'Cause one time, Big Mack, he was mean to a rabbit. Skinned it and let it loose before he [it] died; and so that jackrabbit, he say: "Same thing's gonna happen to you!" Ran off and die, and, by God, Big Mack die after!

But no kind of story [viz., similar proscriptions] about them seed, root, plant. No, sir! 'Cause you see why? Them kind, they just grow by themself [viz., were not Indians in the beginning or "early days ago"].

26. Games and So Forth

But that's one thing I know I don't do too much when I'm a boy: go out and play. Sure like to swim with them girl, though, when I'm young guy! 'Cause you see why? I wanna see *tsaboo!* Yes, sir! 'Cause that's what I like! 'Cause we swim naked, you know. And, so, them girl, they take off their clothes and dive right in—don't hide their *soowee* [vaginas], either. . . . So I know I can take off mine—won't hide my *petho'o* [penis]. . . . But we don't swim in the [Walker] river, neither. No, sir! 'Cause you see why? Too deep! We like irrigation ditch. 'Cause that's our swimmin' hole, you know: Simpson Ditch, over by Wellington. . . . And that's Hazel [Quinn], her sister

Shirley [Quillici], Amy [Mitchell] I'm playin' [swimming] with. Yes, sir! 'Cause I'm around about seven, eight that time. So, gee, I sure used to have a helluva good time! Only when I get to be a man though [do] I swim in the [Walker] river. But then all I wanna do is to ride my horse.

'Cause even when I'm young guy, I can ride anywhere them days. Yes, sir! And ride all day long, too, by God! Never get tired, neither. . . . And same way, too, we're kids, we can tie a bunch them tule together: shoot arrow at 'em. 'Cause the Old Man, he make a bow and arrow for I and my brothers to play with—outta greasewood and rosebrush. And Big Mack, he use deer sinew for that rope [bowstring]. 'Cause I know I and Jack Wilson's young[er] brother, Pat, we [also] used to shoot them *taboo'o* [cottontail rabbits] with that kind all the time. Yes, sir! And same way, too, we can make a spear: to catch carp in the [Walker] river, you know. . . .

Take willow stick and shoot mud at each other, too. Call that *pazaghoba*. . . . 'Cause that's any kind mud, you know. And we can [also] make a horse, cow, sheep outta that mud ball: dry 'em in the sun and do that [i.e., play], you know. Or we can make *pazaghoba natsee*, mud boy. But we don't put head, eye, ear on 'em. No, sir! Don't carry 'em around, neither. Just play with 'em, leave 'em on the ground when we're through. Same way, too, we can make animal outta that red clay . . . that *atsa tuubeezupa*. But I kind of think that [form of] play we get from *taivo*. 'Cause you see why? None them real old-timers are doin' that. . . .

Women, they always like to play that stick game. (Call that kind *nazeetsaka*.) And you see what they're doin'? They can get a rag and braid it, then with a stick they bunch up and hit it. . . . Maggie Milton, she can run fast. . . . Men, though, they like to play football.

Different from *taivo* game, football. 'Cause these Indian, they kick that ball, don't throw it. Five to six on each side. . . . They bunch up and make some kind ball. . . . (Call that *wuutsuumoi*.) And that's a pretty rough game, too, football, by God! But you can't grab your partner [opponent] too easy on that kind, neither. No, sir! 'Cause you see why? Them old-timers, they play naked! Got a diaper to cover their *peetho'o* [penes], that's all; no shirt on. Play barefoot. . . . 'Cause I know Old [Big] Mack, he always like to be in on that football game. . . . First one in. And same way, too, Tom Mitchell, he sure like to play that. . . . His young day. . . . And Blind Bob, when he can see yet. But I never did see Jack Wilson play *paisee'i*, that football. No, sir. Me? I know I don't play yet. Too small!

27. *Pahmoo* ('Indian Tobacco')

[When I'm] too little to play *nayagwee* [handgame], so, for fun, too, we can roll cow *kweeda* [dung]—on a smoke. 'Cause that's in a paper bag, you know. . . . But that kind make too much smoke: hurt your eyes when you're smokin'. And, gee, some them old lady sure like to smoke! Yes, sir! "Roll me smoke! Roll me smoke!" 'Cause I know that's what I hear Blind Bob's wife always sayin'. . . . That Maggie Bob. 'Cause Blind Bob, he can't see, but still can roll 'em [cigarettes]. And same way, too, I know I seen lotta them real old-time lady buyin' chewin' tobacco in the store: chew some, then rub [away] their soreness. And they can [also] tie that on sore muscle. But they always have to talk [i.e., pray] before they do that. . . . Yes, sir! You know, say how that's gonna help, so they won't hurt next mornin'. . . . That kind, you know. And that [pray] before Sun comes up in the mornin' — just like any kind medicine, you know. . . . Like *tubiseeguna* [?], [which] clear up sinus! Or that stick they're also usin', that *moogoodoohoop*. . . . Little bush, you know; got a purple bloom on it. 'Cause they [also] boil that up and drink it when they get a cold. . . .

'Cause I know we can get that other kind [*tubiseeguna*] high up in them mountain—the other side a Smith Valley, over toward California. Yes, sir! 'Cause lots grow up there. . . . Here, though, you only see that other kind . . . that stick. Anyway, them real old-timers, they always got both on hand. Keep 'em dry all the time, you know, so they can boil 'em for [common] cold. . . . And you're [even] supposed to talk [pray] while that tea's boilin'. Yes, sir! Same way, too, they say you're supposed throw money down when you're collectin' 'em [medicinal plants]. Oh, five cents, maybe ten cents? 'Cause you see why? Just like with Indian doctor, them medicine, you gotta pay! 'Cause, otherwise, they don't help you. No, sir! Same way, too, these hot spring, you're supposed pray before you step in. "I need help, partner. . . . Leg's not too good. . . . *Tsopigee nuuma*, head's hurtin' me." 'Cause I know the Old Man, he's always doin' that: goin' to Hot Spring in Smith Valley when he don't feel right. . . .

But my grandma, she won't never try that [tobacco poultice]. No, sir! My mom, she smoke. Never inhale, though, so never get that habit that way. And the Old Man, too, he like to smoke. Yes, sir! 'Cause Big Mack get *Nuumuu pahmoo* [Indian tobacco] all the time. And we call that kind *wuura'a duuk^na* 'snowbrush'. Shiny leaf, white flower. . . . They say that kind's chipmunk's

Boyhood (1892-1905)

food: grow the other side Coleville, in Antelope Valley [California]. . . . 'Cause I know the Old Man, he used to get that kind in Leavitt Meadows [Bridgeport, California]—when I used to go with him on cattle drives for Joe Blackburn to Pickle Meadows. 'Cause we start in May, by fall that same year, we drive back. Then way later, I'm drivin' cattle there myself, and I know I used to bring snow brush back for the Old Man. But that's not the real kind Indian tobacco, neither. No, sir! 'Cause that other kind—they call that *poowee pahmoo*, blue-green growing smoke—grow way up in them mountain behind Colony District [Smith Valley]. 'Cause I know I [also] seen that kind. Yes, sir! 'Cause another time we work together—we're cuttin' cedar back of Dry Lake [Smith Valley], then: the Old Man, he cut 'em, I drag 'em down. . . . When I seen him smokin' that other kind Indian tobacco. Not too strong, though, *poowee pahmoo;* you can inhale. Not like Bull Durham, anyway. 'Cause the Old Man, he has to mix that with that *wuura'a duuk^na*, that snow brush; for taste, you know. And you know what some them crazy Indian are always callin' that kind [Bull Durham]? *Buleekweetanoo pahmoo* 'Bullshit tobacco'! On account that cow's sittin' on front!

So anyway, the Old Man, he like to mix Bull Durham with his *Nuumuu pahmoo*. Say it smoke better that way. And same way, too, he [also] buy Union Leader, Dixie Queen, in the store. But you think he care if they're for a pipe? Hell, no! Break 'em up, smokes 'em that way. . . . And he's got his own *poweeto'eeza*, too, that Old Man. . . . Pipe made outta that soft stone. 'Cause he can use *tsee'abbee*, rosewood, for his stem. . . .

And he don't carry smoke [tobacco] with him, neither. No, sir! 'Cause you see why? Only smoke in the evenin'—right after his supper. Yes, sir! 'Cause that's the only time that old man do that, by God! Say, smokin' in the daytime only make a fellow to be lazy. . . . 'Cause I know he never did ask me for a smoke when we're workin' together. No, sir! 'Cause, me, I smoke all the time when I'm grown! Yes, sir! Always carryin' that around with me, too: Union Leader, Dixie Queen . . . just like the Old Man. And Bull Durham, too, when I'm a young man—even though that kind make me cough in the mornin' when I wake up. Nowaday, I know I like Prince Albert. (So, maybe, you can bring me some tomorrow, Mike? Give you money. 'Cause my supply's pretty low, partner!) 'Cause that other kind [Bull Durham] hurt my throat too much. Yes, sir! Makes me to cough at night, so [my nephew] Eddie, he say he can't sleep. Make me to roll that other kind [Prince Albert] all the time, that pipe tobacco . . . just like the Old Man.

But I never did smoke when I'm a little guy! No, sir! Just that cow *kweeda*. Just wait to be a man before I start doin' that. Same way with *heebee*, drink, too.

28. My *Waseeyoo* ('Washo') Indian Relations

My grandma and Susie Snooks, they're cousin-sister. Related some way, you know. 'Cause we're good to them and they're good to us. Yes, sir! Come down here and bring acorn.... Then you see what we're gonna do? Give 'em pine nut back! Make better friend that way.... Give each other somethin' what they ain't got.... Don't fight each other no more. 'Cause I hear a long time ago, these Indian, they don't get along too good with them *Waseeyoo*.... That's early days ago, partner.... But not real fight. No, sir! Just kind of scare one another all the time, that's all. Not shootin' each other.

'Cause them *Waseeyoo*, you know, they start comin' around here when Bill Dressler bring 'em into Mason Valley; to ranch. Make friend that way.... And they sure like playin' handgame with us, them *Waseeyoo*! 'Cause, gee, I know I always used to see a bunch 'em comin' down to Smith Valley on Sunday to play. And they can sing their handgame song [in] their own language when we gamble, we sing ours. Talk a little English to each other.... Lazy, though, them *Waseeyoo* women. 'Cause they don't like to work at all! Not like these Paiute women around here, anyway....

29. I Lose My Little Toe

I'm a boy, so when I'm sick, they can call in *poohaghooma*, Indian doctor. But not Tom Mitchell! No, sir! [We] won't have Tom Mitchell to doctor me! 'Cause whatchamacallit, he always used to always doctor me... *Tuutseeyoo* Dick! Little Dick, not *Pavatyoo* [Big] Dick, Dick Bennett, my wife's father. *Tuutseeyoo* Dick, he's Nelson Charley's mother—one they call *Apee*, "Happy Hooligan." She stay with that old man all the time—till she marry Jimmy Charley and move down here to Nordyke [Mason Valley]. Yes, sir! So Little Dick, he can doctor me when I get sick.... Only thing I can't get is who's the *nuugweegeeyaka* [designated repeater]? Lemme see? Lemme see? I don't know who we get! Blind Bob, maybe? 'Cause he's pretty good talker that old-timer. Or the Old Man, he do that, too. And Andy Dick. . . . But I don't think Big Mack can [really] do [assist the shaman] that too good. 'Cause he ain't a very good talker. No, sir! 'Cause you gotta be a real good talker to follow them kind [shamans]. . . .

And I'm five, maybe six years old when I lose this [left little] toe, so the Old Man, he has to hire *poohaghooma*.

'Cause you see what happen? I'm fishin' with Johnny Mack's son . . . *Waseeyoo* . . . and our horse is on a spook. So I drop our fishin' gear and try to hold onto that wagon. But I can't make it! No, sir! Slide my foot and that wagon mash my toe! 'Cause you see why? Not wearin' shoe, partner! No, sir! 'Cause I'm a real wild Injun when I'm young! Don't even try to wear no kind *moko* [moccasins] then! (Maybe I have these boot [Wellingtons], I can make it?) And gee, I know I'm hurtin' bad . . . bleedin', cryin' real loud, you know. Till the old man hear me. . . .

And so, Big Mack, he go right away to get *Tutseeyoo* Dick. 'Cause *Tutseeyoo* Dick's some kind relation to me: I call him *ats* [uncle], so must be related on my grandma side? Anyway, [since] he live four miles away, *Tutseeyoo* Dick walks to our camp. And not blind yet, neither. No, sir! 'Cause Tom Mitchell, he don't do that to him yet. 'Cause he's always jealous that one [Tom Mitchell]. And so, after he's doin' that to him, why, I always take *Tutseeyoo* Dick fishin'. (Wife's always workin' and that old man—real old-timer!—he loves to fish: use worm on his bone hook, and string he makes from willow bark he roll on his leg. Same kind [string] they're usin' for that *waana*, that nettin'. . . .)

But *Tutseeyoo* Dick don't sing over me. No, sir! Just rub, that all [cf. secs. 127-28]. Yes, sir! Put chewin' tobacco on my toe every day, till that sore bust. Then he can quit. Make it to feel better that way, you know. And same way, too, *Tutseeyoo* Dick don't try to tell me who's doin' that [witchcraft] to me, neither. No, sir! 'Cause he can, you know. *Tutseeyoo* Dick, he's a real doctor. But he don't. Just put that on and rub, that's all. Yes, sir! Good old man, *Tutseeyoo* Dick. 'Cause I know I sure like him!

30. My Horse Brown

Like I already told you, when I'm little, I used to like to ride Indian pony all the time. 'Cause you see why? Big Mack, he's got horses: one's for ridin', the other's for his buggy, that wagon he buy from Old Lady Hoye to pull wood; that light wagon. . . . 'Cause that old man's a real buckaroo, by God! Just like my grandfather! Him and them other old-timers, they go out after mustang. And Big Mack can break any kind mustang! 'Cause them mustang, they don't buck much—not like ranch horse, anyway. Buck a little, then quit. . . . Then way later on, I and the old man, we had a few mustang. Go out after 'em ourself, you know: catch 'em back this way, over by sunrise. . . . Pretty hard to get, too, I tell you, Mike! 'Cause tough horse, them mustang! Gee, they sure can wear your horse out!

Indian *poogoo*, though, they're different from *taivo* horse: got short ear, short leg. . . . Same way, too, with dog: them ear on them Indian dog stand straight up—like Coyote! But I hear they both belong [originate] here, horse and dog. Cat [though], I hear we get 'em from Yosemite. . . .

So anyway, the Old Man, he lets me ride this one saddle horse he's got when I'm a little guy. 'Cause that one's just a *poogoo doowa'a*, baby horse. And we have to buy hay to feed our horses from them *taivo* rancher. Yes, sir! Can't feed 'em on wild hay, 'cause that kind's already *karroo'oo*. No more! Gone! Nothin' left in Smith Valley. . . . My best horse, though, Old Lady [Annie Fulstone] give me.

Little bit of a colt, that one. 'Cause his mother, she die, and so Annie tell her boys to give me him. 'Cause they're raisin' him with milk, you see, so I guess they get tired doin' that? Why they wanna give him to me. And I bet you I'm around about fifteen when I get that horse. Yes, sir! Keep him for my saddle horse. . . .

Call him "Brown" that colt. . . . 'Cause you see why? He's kind of brown, so I just name him by that. By old-time way, though, not supposed to name your horse. No, sir! Just say *poogoo* 'horse', that's all. But not me. I'm gonna name mine on the white way. . . . And Brown's a good [racing] horse, too, by God! Quarter mile race they have on the Fourth [of July], he can win against them *taivo* horse! Yes, sir! Clean up just about everybody else in Wellington! Pretty fast runner, by God, Brown: real light horse, small neck, small face, little leg, small body. . . . Built that way. [Even] looks like a race horse, you know. But I know I won't ride my horse in them races. No, sir! 'Cause you see why? Afraid! Afraid maybe I might just slip off Brown; so I always let my cousin-brother to ride him—Henry Quinn, the one they call *kwagee* 'Dog with His Tail in the Air'. Best partner I got them days, Henry Quinn! And Henry, he ride Brown bareback, too. Yes, sir! Hold on, beat 'em all. . . . Never lose!

'Cause you see what they're doin' them days? No one has a car, and [since] it takes one whole day to go up to Carson City, they have to make their own big times in these valley [e.g., Fourth of July].

But you see who ruin my best horse? The Old Man! Put[s] a harness on him when I go to Stewart [Boarding School, secs. 31-46]—fix Brown to that buggy like that, you know. 'Cause you see what he's doin'? Haulin' wood, usin' my horse for catchin' mustang. . . . So he spoil Brown's shoulder with that harness, so he can't win on the race no more! 'Cause that same horse we always win, he beat us next year! 'Cause I know when I come home from Stewart [1910], my horse ain't good no more. *Karroo'oo!* All gone to hell! 'Cause I and Andy Dick, we enter our horse[s] in a race, but Brown, he just can't make it! No, sir! Can't run fast no more: legs are gone, all shot to hell. 'Cause I know I ride him that time—I ride Brown and Andy ride his; and we're way behind that winner. So I just sell him.

3

Boarding School (1905–10)

31. Stewart Institute

And I don't see why they don't let me go to school sooner! 'Cause them old-timers, you know, they got funny idea.... Won't let us go to school to learn to read and to write ... to get to know somethin' better that way.

'Cause none my brother and sister do that, you know. 'Cause that time, Indian can't go into the public school. No, sir! Don't let 'em to mix with them *taivo*.... 'Cause you see why? They say we *nuuma* got some kind sickness, so they don't let us into their school. Yes, sir! Have to build a special school [for us consequently].... How some them Indian boy go up there to Stewart [the Carson Indian School] that time.... Then way later on, this public school start up in Colony [District, Smith Valley]—at Simpson Ranch. The other one, in Wellington, that's too far away for us to go.... But you think my folks gonna let Eddie [Mack] and my sister [Lizzie] go? Hell, no! Only Lena [Rogers] go to that other [Colony District] school....

Anyway, me, I know I always wanna go. Yes, sir! 'Cause I'm always thinkin' maybe I can learn somethin' better on the white way? You know, by book.... So don't have to be so dumb all the time! 'Cause I'm too wild back then, partner. Yes, sir! Don't even know my age! My right name! *Karroo'oo!* Too dumb! Don't know nothin' when I'm a boy! 'Cause you see why? Never get too much acquainted with *taivo natsee* [white boys] in my own valley, so I never [even] learn their language before I go to Stewart. . . .

And I'm around fifteen, sixteen when I go up there first time [ca. 1905]. Too big for that kindergarten school. . . . Anyway, that don't look too good, so I have to go to grammar school. And you see who's doin' that [i.e., transporting kids], that time? Tom Mitchell! Yes, sir! 'Cause he's workin' for the government! He get a badge, you know; they give him horse and buggy and he come around the start every school year: catch them kid who don't wanna go; take 'em to Carson City in that wagon like that. But you see who take me? My uncles. . . .

And that's Buckaroo George [Walker] and Johnny Jones. Yes, sir! 'Cause they're the one take me up there first time. . . . 'Cause Buckaroo George—he work for Dan Simpson with the Old Man—he wanna see his own kid. . . . On a visit, you know. 'Cause he's got two son [Martinez and Buckaroo George, Jr.] and one daughter [Elizabeth] up there. . . . Wants me to go along with him. And so I do, too. 'Cause I wanna learn somethin'. Yes, sir! The Old Man, he don't wanna take me, so they do.

And that's fall the year, too, partner: September when that school start . . . same as *taivo* school. Ride take, oh, pretty near half-a-day to get to Carson City. . . . 'Cause you see why? Ain't got no car. No, sir! Have to go up there by buggy. . . .

"Corbett, you stay here. Your cousin-brother are here; cousin-sister, too. So, you not gonna feel too bad!"

Yes, sir! What Buckaroo George's sayin' to me. And so, by God, I do! Stay! But he's not my real *hai'ee* [father's brother], Buckaroo George. . . . Just by Indian [i.e., classificatory] way. And that one boy he's got up there, Buckaroo George Walker, Jr., he's way older than me. He's the one teach me English, you know; that Buckaroo George Walker, Jr. Never did marry, though. . . . And same way, too, he don't work too much. No, sir! Die in Wellington of weak heart: cough all the time, blood come outta his mouth, so he die. 'Cause Buckaroo George Walker, Jr., he always look like a sick guy. Small, you know; skinny. Cough so much, he fall down. . . .

And so, when that superintendent say to me, "How old am I?" "What's my tribe?" "What name he's gonna give me?" I can't say nothin'! *Karroo'oo!* No, sir! Can't even say, "*Khaisoobitagwatoo!* I don't know nothin'!" Cause you see why? I'm too dumb! Don't know nothin' yet. Can't [even] say, "My name's Corbett Mack. I'm born in 1892. I'm a *Nuumuu*." No, sir! 'Cause I can't speak a word English yet! And Buckaroo George Walker, Sr., he's a real old-timer, you know. Don't talk English too good, so he can't help me, neither.

32. Why I Change My Name?

'Cause you know what I think when I first go to Stewart? I think my right name's *Corbett Douglass*. 'Cause you see why? Buckaroo George Walker, he tell that superintendent that. And so the Old Man, he get mad.

'Cause we have to write letters home—You know, "How we're makin' out? Food's good. . . ." Letter like that kind. Copy 'em off the board from that school teacher . . . one who's learnin' us how to sign our name. You know, till we can write our own letter. . . . And you see what we call that kind? Matron. 'Cause they're not marry. No, sir! Never did see any them [even] walkin' with a man. . . . So anyway, when Big Mack find out I'm usin' "Corbett Douglass," why, he get mad at my mom. Wanna kill her!

"Go to that *taivo* if you like him that much!" What he tell my mom. Tell her to live with Bill Douglass if she like him better!

'Cause Old Man Readin' [Smith Valley hotel owner-employer], he's the one read that letter I write home to my mom. And so, after Big Mack do [says] that, she tell him to write me back. Say I better change my name. . . . "Put down 'Mack' whenever I'm writin' home," my mom say. Or else the Old Man'll kill her! And so I do, by God! Do that!

And ever since, I'm always "Corbett Mack." Yes, sir! Don't use my right name no more. Change that, you know. . . . Tell my cousin-brother [George Walker, Jr.] to write to my mom: tell her what I'm doin' [i.e., name change].

33. Readin' and Writin' and 'Rithmetic

And them matron, they teach you all right. 'Cause it take pretty near one whole year to learn to write your letter by that way. Yes, sir! And after you do learn to read, why, they can give you a book. . . . You're stuck, why, you just raise your hand: you know, to ask 'em how you can pronounce that word? And they tell you that, too, by God! 'Cause them matron, they're not mean. No, sir! Just so long as you mind, they won't slap you. . . . No, sir! Won't give you whippin' if you mind. . . .

But that first year up there, you don't do too much. No, sir! Second year, you can do a little 'rithmetic work. And third year, they give you another book to study on: geography . . . language, too. And lemme see what else they give you? What that other book is? Ah, God, I forget. . . . 'Cause that one's hard, you know. . . . [You] gotta get them answer outta your own head. Yes, sir! Can't get 'em from that book! 'Cause there's only question in there, that book. . . . What-in-the-hell's the name that other one?

34. Books and Grades

Physiology! That's that goddamn name I'm tryin' to get! 'Cause that's what they're doin' in fourth grade in Stewart. . . . Name that book they're givin' you to read then. . . . 'Cause you gotta study that one, all right! Lotta question in it. . . . Same way, too, I know I go to night school [study hall?] fourth year in Stewart. Yes, sir! 'Cause that's one hour after your supper. . . . And next day, why, I gotta write down that answer on paper. . . .

So many question, too, on physiology. . . . [If] you write 'em right, why, that'll be "A"; you miss, you don't put your word down right on that answer, why, they can give you "C."

35. Christopher Columbus

And [in] what they call geography, we learn about Christopher Columbus. 'Cause you see what happen? When he's a small boy, Christopher Columbus, he dream about this land called "America." 'Cause that angel come to him, you know. . . . Tell Christopher Columbus that. [He] was stayin' where they park them boat, and so that angel, he say to Christopher Columbus:

"There's a beautiful land someplace else called America; way back east. You better go find that place!"

And so, Christopher Columbus, he believe that! Yes, sir! Believe in his dream! Believe what that angel tell him! 'Cause I know I seen that in Stewart . . . in that geography book. Seen that angel standin' on top Christopher Columbus's bed. So that must be his *booha* [supernatural power], ain't it?

36. Civilization

We go to school work in the mornin', do other kind work [manual labor] every afternoon. Some, though, they work in the mornin' and go to school in the afternoon. . . .

First job I have in Stewart is to sweep them [dorm?] rooms. Yes, sir! And sometime, too, I wash window and them floor. But you see what they're doin' up there? They don't use a mop in Stewart. No, sir! Only a broom. 'Cause you see why? They got different kind floor there; not like this kind [linoleum], you know. So, we gotta scrub it hard. . . .

And that's one thing I wanna know. . . . Why I never did get a good job up there! No, sir! 'Cause I'm always on a woman's job in Stewart! And you see what kind work I'm mostly gettin'? Laundry job! Never put me on a man's job. . . . Never did get that shoemaker job . . . carpenter . . . plumber job. No, sir! 'Cause I'm just always on a woman's job! And they can change your job, too, every month; so that way, you learn a different job. But not me. No, sir! 'Cause I kind of think maybe I'm too small? Why they never give me no kind man's job? 'Cause I'm a man, all right, only I look like a little man. So maybe that's how come they always do that to me, you know? Puttin' me on that woman's job always!

And [it] take three boys in that laundry to work them heavy roller. 'Cause you see what we're doin'?' First we throw them dirty clothes in that rinser . . . for them girls to hang for dryin'. 'Cause you see why? Otherwise, they [girls] don't get taught nothin'! No, sir! Just lay around in the bed all the time. . . . But, still, I like my laundry job. 'Cause you see why? That's only time a fellow get to feel them girls' *tsaboo* [asses]! You know, when they bend over to pack it out and hang that wash. . . . Yes, sir! Only chance I know get on that in Stewart, by God!

And same way, too, I never did get to work in that garden they put, neither . . . like them farm boy do. 'Cause some boys are puttin' in potato. . . . And they got a horse barn up there; cow barn, too. 'Cause they got milk cow in Stewart, too. . . . So I don't see why I never get assigned to that kind work, neither?

37. Meals and Order

That great big bell on that [main] buildin', that's the one wake us up every mornin'. 'Cause you gotta get up when that first bell rings. Yes, sir! "Get up and fix your bed!" What them matron always sayin'. . . . You're lazy, why, she's gonna pull you outta bed! Tell you to go wash up. . . . 'Cause they're always lookin' in on you, them matron: you know, to make sure you wash and get ready for breakfast. . . . So you can't be lazy there. Then, after you wash, second bell, that one's for roll call. Make you to line up, you know. . . . See if anybody's missin'. 'Cause they have roll call all the time, by God! 'Cause you see why? Lotta them Indian boy, they don't wanna learn somethin' good in Stewart. No, sir! Don't wanna stay up there, so they run away. . . . Not me, though. . . . And do that [roll call] three time every day. . . . before every meal. Then after that bell, before you march into the dinin' room, that guard says, "Left face!" "Drop out!" "Halt!" "Turn around!" "Drop out!" And everybody has got to mind. . . . Gee, we sure line up lot in Stewart! Just like a sergeant [i.e., in the army]! And only them Indian boy on that kind job [guard]. . . .

Put you in line by size, too: big boy in front, small in the back. . . . So I know that's why I'm always in back. 'Cause even though I'm older, I'm a little man. . . .

So, after they line you up by that way, march you down to that dinin' room, why, you gotta keep your hand on the table when you eat. Yes, sir! Breakfast, we get bacon and potato; drink cocoa most the time. . . . But no egg in Stewart! No, sir! 'Cause that's pretty hard to get egg up there, I tell you, Mike! And same way, too, nobody don't serve you, neither. No, sir! 'Cause you see why? They got that food already on the table. And don't let you stay [remain at the table] too long, neither. No, sir! 'Cause they only let you to stay about half an hour. (Feel like only fifteen minutes you get to eat, though, by God!) So you gotta eat pretty fast! 'Cause [when] they tap on that table, you gotta take your hand off [finish]. Then they're gonna ring that bell again, you gotta get up. Get up and march back outside to line up . . . to go to school. Or, those workin', they have to go out on their job. So even [if] you're hungry, you can miss your meal that way [i.e., by eating too slowly].

But you see why you gotta keep your hand on that table when you eat? 'Cause they're afraid. Afraid maybe some them big boy are gonna put food inside their coat . . . that long coat they're givin' out. Real heavy coat, you know. . . . Call that kind corduroy. But they're missin' pocket, that kind, so, nobody can sneak food outta that dinin' room. 'Cause them big boy, that's what they're always doin' all the time. (Tryin' to do, anyway.) You know, to put somethin' in their pocket to take outta that dinin' room: meat, bread ... anythin' like that on sneak. So that's why they like to set the table, 'cause that way, they can grab what they can see. . . . 'Cause, I know, if I get that chance, I do that, too, by God! Yes, sir! 'Cause that's another kind job I'm always gettin' in Stewart—settin' them table. You know, set 'em, then wait when they need more bread, boiled meat. . . . So I just gotta take that plate then and go back into the kitchen. . . . Get some more. 'Cause it don't take too long to run out [of food]. . . . But, still, I don't see why I don't get to be a guard? Anyway, them matron, they're always watchin' you good. . . .

And your noon meal, why, you can get meat, potato, beans. Yes, sir! Same meal pretty near all the time, noon and supper! 'Cause cow meat's main meat they serve in Stewart. Yes, sir! Serve it boiled, you know. . . . Never fry that kind up there. 'Cause you see why? Fuel cost, maybe, I figure? Too many kid to feed! But that's mostly all what they give you in Stewart, beans! Same way, too, I hear they're givin' beans mostly for commodity food in Yerington nowaday. . . . Oh, and everybody has got to keep quiet, too, in that dinin' room. Yes, sir! Nobody can talk at that table, so that's all you hear is them dish. 'Cause they don't use plate that break in Stewart. No, sir! Use only metal plate and cup. . . . [Then] line up after that noon meal and play around till one o'clock. . . . [Then] whoever go to school's gotta go there, whoever's got a little job, why, he can go to that job. . . .

Oh, food taste pretty fair in Stewart, I'd say. . . . Only thing is, they don't let to you to eat enough. Always rushin' you, like I say. . . . 'Cause you don't finish in time, why, you just gotta leave that food there.

38. End of the Day

Four o'clock, that's [really] the end the day, partner! 'Cause they come outta school that time. Same way [if] you're workin'. . . . And so them boy, when they're done, well, somebody can just say, "Let's play football!"

'Cause you see what we're doin'? Around about ten to twelve boy playin' that game—six on one side. . . . And we can make a ball outta cotton sock, then throw it. 'Cause you can't kick that kind. No, sir! Then they fight over that. Pretty rough game, too, by God! Like that game my tribe always play. . . . Man's game, *paiseehee'ee*, that football. . . . But in Stewart they don't braid that rope. No, sir! Same as we don't kick it, neither. Just throw it like that and fight over it. . . .

Pretty rough game, football. . . . 'Cause no down in it, no stoppin'. . . . So, you just gotta keep fightin' for that ball all the time. And when you're down, if you got hold that ball, why, you give it to your partner reachin', and he can take off. 'Cause everybody just pile on when you're down. . . . Yes, sir! But not much baseball when I'm there. . . . 'Cause that's all they like to play in Stewart is football. . . .

Oh, and they got [gymnastic] rings also—rings big enough you can stick your leg through. Swing through that kind. . . . Another game we like playin' is high jump. 'Cause you see what they're doin'? They can make some kind plank [horizontal cross bar], then take that big long pole and try jumpin' over it. Just don't knock her off, though, when you bend that pole and jump over that other one [cross bar]. No, sir! Then if you can make it, why, they can raise that. Keep on tryin' that higher and higher, you know, till they knock that stick down across. Then pretty soon you can't make it over, so they quit raising that other one. . . . Stick [vaulting pole] sound pretty near like what that woman's doin' early days ago, ain't it? You know, to get away from *Paheezoho*, Giant Cannibal [sec. 153]?

So we can play football [or] do that high jump till that supper bell ring; then have to wash up. 'Cause after supper, you can't do very much in Stewart. No, sir! Can't, 'cause it's dark, then, so we just walk around a little after we come outta that dinin' hall. Then some can go to that night school for one hour. . . . The rest, why, they just stay in the sittin' room. . . . Don't go outside no more. 'Cause you see why? All gotta go to sleep same time! And that's around about nine 'o clock, partner: bedtime, when they ring that bell last time. . . . 'Cause them guard, they call out your name then. So you gotta say, "Yup!" 'Cause that way, they can see you're still there. Yes, sir! Know you haven't run away. 'Cause like I already told you, some boy are always doin' that. . . . Don't like it in Stewart, so they have to run away. . . . And same way, too, every night before you go to bed, you gotta line up. Them guard, they can call your name, and you answer last time [of day]. Say, "Yup!" so that way, they know you ain't run away yet. . . .

39. My Stewart Nickname

That kind football we're playin' in Stewart—that's how I get my nickname.... 'Cause you see what I'm always sayin'? "I can fly over you guys when I get the ball! Fly high, just like a duck!" So that's what they call me that up there, you know: "Duck!" In English, not my own language. Yes, sir! 'Cause what I'm always sayin' in Stewart.... Braggin' that way, you know....

40. Stewart Girls

But you see what's wrong up there? Won't let you to get close to them girl! No, sir! See you talkin', so them matron, they say, "Get away!" Think you're makin' up to meet them girl? 'Cause they don't wanna see a man get close to his girl in Stewart....

And they're in same class as us boy, them girl. Eat in the dinin' room, too.... But you think they're gonna let you to mix together? Hell, no! Nothin' like a public school that Indian school. No, sir! Divide you in Stewart all the time, you know: girls on one line, boys the other.... Same way in them dorm, too. Yes, sir! So, you just can't get too close to 'em no place there.

Them girls, they do housework: you know, wash window.... And some, too, they work in the laundry with me. 'Cause like I already told you, we sure like to play around with them laundry girl.... before that matron come.... But the rest the time, I guess they [Stewart girls] have to stay inside their own buildin' [dorm]. You know, just lay around....

One girl, though, she bother me all the time—that night watchman's daughter. *Waseyoo* girl, that one ... Dick Bender's daughter. 'Cause I know I always hug her when she bother me. 'Cause you see what she's doin'? [She] play with me! Yes, sir! Like to see my *peetho'o* [penis] hard, so, I let her feel....

And same way, too, I know I [also] used to have one girlfriend when I'm up there—Edith Powell. Half-breed girl, Edith; Pit River Indian and *taivo* ... But she can talk my language real good! Only thing is, Edith Powell's a girlfriend "long way".... You know, can't get too close to her, so, have to send a kiss. Or write a letter, give it to another girl to give to Edith.... So, only when they're havin' a dance can I can get close to Edith Powell. 'Cause otherwise, I only wave when I see her. . . . Send kiss by that way, too . . .

So, that's what I wanna know: why they don't let you to get in there with them girl? Yes, sir! Why always wanna keep you away from 'em all the time in Stewart? 'Cause you just try and talk to 'em, and them matron, they see you, they say, "Get away from there!" 'Cause, maybe, they [matrons] got some kind funny idea? Think, maybe, you're tryin' to make up after supper. . . . You know, to meet? Sneak out in the brush that way?

41. Parties in Stewart

So that's one thing they should have more [of] in Stewart—dance! 'Cause, by God, only once in a while they're havin' that. . . . Not like on the white way, neither. No, sir! 'Cause I know them Smith Valley *taivo*, they're always doin' it all the time when I'm young—pretty near every Saturday night, too. . . . And them holiday, too. . . . 'Cause they should learn them boys how to dance in Stewart. . . . Only time you can hug your girl!

But they [do] have a party in Stewart. . . . Only thing is they're not free! No, sir! You ain't got money, why, you can't eat! Not unless somebody else treat you. . . .

Thanksgiving, Christmas, New Year's . . . them kind. And I go every once in a while—when I got money. 'Cause my grandma, she always send me five dollar. But she won't send me ten dollar! No, sir! 'Cause I know I'm always writin' her to send me a little [more] money. 'Cause they [also] got a store up there, so when you're hungry, you can buy cracker, salmon. . . . Then you [might] bring your partner along on a treat—that's if you got money. But you think my grandma's gonna do that? Hell, no!

42. The Disciplinarian: Punishment and Jail

And same way, too, they got a jail in Stewart, you know. Pretty tough lookin' place, partner, by God! Look like a dark shell in there! Yes, sir! Small house, no window, no light—make you to wonder how it look when they close that door, by God? Dark, like night! And that jail, that one's [also] got partition in the middle. Only one bed in that room, so you ain't got too much space in there to walk around, neither!

'Cause I know one time, I and my partner, we went over there to look. Disciplinarian, he was [then] givin' this one guy somethin' to eat. 'Cause them big boy, you know, they're the one [usually] put in jail—for fightin' mostly. And sometime, too, they [even] have to hold [pull?] that rail [railroad tie]: pack it to dinner when they don't mind. . . . Yes, sir! But, me, I know I always mind. Yes, sir! 'Cause you mind them matron, why, they leave you alone. 'Cause I know I'm in Stewart four and one-half year, partner, never went to jail once. No, sir! One time, though, we get a good whippin'. . . .

'Cause you see what happen? We was riding calf down in the cow barn and get caught! And gee, that grass rope sure sting! 'Cause them matron, they can hit you on the wrist with that rod, but disciplinarian, he hit you right here where your shirt [back] is! Yes, sir! Won't hit you on your overall [backside?]. And they double that grass rope, too! Stiff one, that grass rope, I tell you, Mike! Sting! Same way, too, you gotta make some kind hollar when they hit you, then that disciplinarian can quit. 'Cause otherwise, he won't!

'Cause he's the one doin' that to you when you do somethin' wrong. . . . A man, *taivo*. . . . And I know I sure try and stand it that time that disciplinarian whip us. Yes, sir! Won't [even] say nothin' right off, just try to tough it out. But that disciplinarian, he won't quit, neither; so finally, I gotta make some kind hollar. You know, say, "Owwww!" Then he's gonna quit. But my partner, he don't do that [cry out], neither. No, sir! So that's why we get whippin' lot. . . . Only time I do get whippin' in Stewart, anyway. . . .

But he's not mean man, neither, that disciplinarian. No, sir! Just tryin' to learn you how to be good. Doin' that to you with that grass rope, you know, so maybe next time you'll mind!

43. That Jesus Business . . .

And every Sunday, too, you gotta go to church in Stewart.

'Cause I know I first hear about that Jesus business in Smith Valley: some preacher come around, woman. . . . Yes, sir! First one to tell us about that Jesus business. . . . But, me, I don't pay too much attention that time. 'Cause you see why? Too little. . . .

And that's every Sunday mornin' church in Stewart: from nine to eleven. 'Cause Sunday afternoon, we can go ice skatin' [on] that great big wide pond they got up there. . . . Only thing is, I don't know the name that church. Anyway, we gotta put a uniform on: blue shirt, no tie, jacket and blue pant.... Jacket's got button with an eagle on it.... And you can't sit down with them girl inside church in Stewart, neither. No, sir! Them boy on their side, girls on theirs. 'Cause maybe they think you're gonna make too much noise in that place? You know, by talkin' to them girl?

Preacher, he's a *taivo*—from Carson City. Name's Mr. Pike, and he's a *moosoowee* [facial hair] man just like you, Mike! Yes, sir! Let this one [sideburn] to grow way down his cheek real long [mutton chops].... Pretty good talker that preacher, I tell you, by God! Talk about "The Lord" and "Jesus" ... and "God." 'Cause that's what he's always sayin'.... And I can understand him, all right, 'cause he talk plain. You know, always tellin' us to be a good man, not a bad man. And don't swear.... Don't try to fight somebody.... You know, that kind preachin'....

'Cause in Stewart, they don't let you to fight or swear. No, sir! 'Cause [if] you do, why, them matron are gonna give you a slap in the mouth! Tell you not to use that word, you know.... 'Cause them big[ger] boy, you know, they can say, "SON-A-BITCH!" So if they hear that, why, them matron are gonna give 'em a slap in the mug! And they got a ruler, too. About a foot long. Hit you on the wrist with that if you're doin' that. Or if you fight.... Put you in that jail, too.

Mr. Pike, he can [also] sing once in a while, too. Yes, sir! Has a wine glass with a red snake painted on it, says to us: "You, boy, drink, this what's gonna happen to you!" Tryin' to [also] scare the hell outta person!

And you see what we're doin' before church? They got a flag on Sunday they raise.... Just like a soldier. Band's playin', you know, and so, them guard, they tell us what to do: "Left!" "Right!" "Halt!" March us just like a soldier to church. Only them boy, though.... Only thing is, we ain't got no gun! Then when you come outta that church at eleven, why, you take your uniform off and put back on your old clothes.... Wait for dinner. 'Cause you can't keep them good ones [on] on Sunday.

But we don't pray with our meal at Stewart. No, sir! Pray every night before bed, though. 'Cause that time, we gotta pray to Jesus: you know, to ask the Lord to help us out.... And we can pray downstair, too ... in that sitting room [chapel?]. 'Cause them matron, they're the one [also] leadin' that kind prayer....

But one thing I know I sure used to like—that Bible book! Yes, sir! Carry it around with me all the time after I get outta Stewart; read from it a lot! Till my eye go bad on me.... Around about 1914 when that happen.... Can't hunt no more, then.... *Karroo'oo*, nothin'! Can't get into that other

World's War on account my eye, so I just quit that Bible readin' [as well]. Quit 'cause I can't see it good no more.

But I don't get nothin' outta that Jesus business. No, sir! 'Cause you see why? Jesus, he don't help me! 'Cause that's what that prayer mean, you know. . . . And, so, [if] a fellow don't get somethin' outta somethin' else, how can he keep on [believing]? No matter even how much he pray! 'Cause, then, it's *karroo'oo*, nothin'. But maybe I don't get nothin' outta that 'cause I'm a bad man already. *Ste'yoo*, you know; no good. . . . So maybe that's why Jesus won't listen to me? 'Cause if you believe in somethin' first, well, then, that's different.

44. Saturdays in Carson City

Saturday, they let you go downtown to Carson City—that's if you got money. . . . 'Cause you see why? [If] you get hungry, why, you gotta eat, and [if] you ain't got no money, well, you can't make it!

And that's the only time they're lettin' you to do that, you know [i.e., leave the grounds of Stewart Institute]. Let you stay all day long, too. . . . But you gotta be back before four o'clock, before your supper. 'Cause [if] you stay later, why, that [municipal] policeman's gonna tell you, "You're late! You boys better go back to your own place!" Yes, sir! 'Cause I know I used to like to go to Carson City all the time. . . .

But not too many Indian livin' there [Carson City Indian Colony] that time. . . . Just a few. Look like they're never home, neither. So, must be always workin'? Anyway, we [boys] always go downtown together. 'Cause you see why? Can't go with them Indian girl from Stewart. No, sir! On account they always have to go with that chaperon . . . matron [who] lead 'em around in the street. 'Cause them Stewart girl, they can't scatter. No, sir! Have to go behind that matron all the time. But they should go any place they want! Yes, sir! They should just turn 'em loose in town, like we boys. 'Cause we can go anywhere. . . . Ain't got no boss Saturday. . . . And same way, too, them matron, they don't watch us on Saturday in Carson City. No, sir! Just watch them girl. And they [girls] get to ride to town in a wagon, too. Not us! We gotta walk. Both ways, too. So I don't see why they don't just let us go with our girlfriend in Carson City Saturday? Anyway, they don't, so we just fool around by ourself.

'Cause after we visit that Indian camp—'cause that time, you know, they live way down [south] below Carson City; in the brush, you know; by the town dump. 'Cause that's before they [also] make a reservation over there for them.... Like Yerington. So, after we go over there to talk our own language, why, we like to go to Chinatown.

'Cause they [also] got a Chinatown in Carson, you know. Yes, sir! Not like here [Smith and Mason valleys]. 'Cause here, they just live out on the ranch where they cook.... in town [Mason, Yerington, and Wabuska], too. 'Cause you see what we're doin' in that Chinatown? We like to go "see" them two [Chinese] whores! Yes, sir! 'Cause for two bit, they let you see their *suk-suk!* And for a dollar, why, you can just crawl right in! 'Cause, me, I know I used to like to do that when I got somethin' [change] in my pocket, partner.... Yes, sir! Only thing is, nobody don't wanna get that *qonoza*... that clap. So anyway, that's what we like to do Saturday in Carson City.... Go straightaway to Chinatown to see them whore. Yes, sir! Fool around there like that way....

But one thing you can't do in Carson City is to buy smoke [cigarettes]. No, sir! Not unless you're twenty-one, anyway. So I have to tell them big[ger] boy to buy for me. 'Cause, gee, I know I sure want my Bull Durham already then.

45. Why I Leave Stewart?

May fifteenth's when school's out.... 'Cause that's when my family come after me.... You know, to take me back to Smith Valley. And we always go [home] in the Old Man's buggy, 'cause no cars yet that time.... But you see how [why] I'm leavin' Stewart that last time? On account the Old Man, he wanna marry another woman!

And that's Roy Higgens's mother. She's from Fallon, you know. Not a single woman, neither.... Big Mack, he's workin' with her—at Colony District—and so my mom, she get mad at that other woman. Try to kill her.... Then she tell the Old Man, "Go ahead and marry her!" And you see who Roy Higgens's mother's marry to that time? Buckaroo George Walker! Big Mack's [own] cousin-brother! His *norr^gwa* [wife] he wanna marry! But they don't fight, neither. No, sir! 'Cause Buckaroo George, he just walk away from that woman. "Let him have her, if that's what he want!" All what he [Buckaroo George Walker] say.... Yes, sir! Walk away from her....

'Cause they was workin' for Frank Simpson that time. . . . And so, when my mom run away, the Old Man, he come after me.

I'm in fourth grade . . . just ready to go into fifth. And Big Mack, he fool that superintendent, too. Yes, sir! Tell him he [just] wanna take me downtown: you know, to buy me clothes in Carson City. . . . Or maybe he can say:

"Corbett can read and write his own name. [He] wanna be with his mom!"

Fool him, you know, by that other way. . . .

And that's December, partner. 'Cause, gee, I know I pretty near freeze to death comin' through them mountain! Hands are frozen; feet, too. . . . Big Mack, he bring an extra saddle horse with him. . . . Tell me he want me to help him to find my mom. . . .

But you see who help me find her? Blind Bob! Yes, sir! 'Cause they're both hidin', you know: my mom, and young sister Lizzie; both are hidin' at Annie Fulstone's house. . . . 'Cause I go straightaway to Old Lady Hoye's store in Wellington when I get back. 'Cause you see why? Blind Bob, he's always there; so I can just ask him where they're hidin'?' And he tell me, all right! Says [also] what Old Lady Fulstone's doin' for my mom. 'Cause she's the one always doin' that, you know . . . hidin' 'em. . . . And same way, too, Blind Bob say my grandma's [also] hidin' with them. 'Cause them blind people, you know, they got somethin', maybe? Some kind *booha* to help 'em out a little? 'Cause Blind Bob, he can hear your voice once and he alway knows you! Yes, sir! Poke around with his stick every day to that store in Wellington. . . . Never get lost, neither. And same way, too, I seen this other blind guy in Yerington . . . *taivo* . . . same thing . . . never bump into nobody! [He] even used to play [music] for them whore in that red light [Yerington]. . . .

So anyway, Blind Bob, he help me to find my mom. But I won't tell the Old Man where she's hidin', neither. No, sir! So he get mad. Take off again with that other woman. . . . But one week later, Big Mack, he come back again. Talk good to my mom. . . . Act real nice to everybody. . . . You know, just like he's happy bein' home. Say he's workin' for Old Man Readin'—clearin' brush. . . .

And so, after that, no more trouble. 'Cause you see why? Big Mack's afraid, maybe? Afraid, 'cause I'm already big when I come from Stewart? Or maybe the Old Man stop makin' that kind trouble on account all my brothers are dead and I'm the only one [son] he's got left?

46. *Nuumuu skooruunobee* ('Indian School House'): Stewart Reprise

Yeah, I like it up there. . . . Pretty good place for these Indian, Stewart, by God! Nothin' to worry about. . . . 'Cause there's lotta boy in Stewart, so we have fun. And same way, too, they got other kind [tribes of] Indian up there. . . . Food's all right, too. Get a lotta exercise. . . . Yes, sir! Nothin' don't make me to feel bad [miss] about home, neither. Don't even think once about home when I'm up there in school. . . . And they can [also] teach you to play [musical] instrument in Stewart. 'Cause some them boy, why, they can get in that band. . . . And give you your clothes, too, up there. Teach you to raise a garden. . . . So that's pretty good place, you know—to learn somethin' good. Like how to read and write on the *taivo* way . . . thing like that. . . . 'Cause, otherwise, you don't know nothin'. A fellow be dumb all the time! So even my grandma, she get to like that place after a while. . . .

Still, I don't see why the Old Man has to do that to me? 'Cause I never did graduate from Stewart! No, sir! Eighth grade's when you're supposed to graduate from that grammar school. . . . So maybe I should have said somethin' to that superintendent? But he just ask if I can read my ABC's, and I tell him I can [also] write my own name. So he let me go. 'Cause otherwise, I might know somethin'!

Plate 1. Corbett Mack. Photograph by Michael Hittman, ca. 1970.

Plate 2. Paiutes in camp. Photograph courtesy Nevada Historical Society (no. 319).

Plate 3. Two views of the Stewart Institute, Carson City, Nevada, ca. 1910. Photographs courtesy Nevada Historical Society (*top*, no. 782; *bottom*, no. 790).

Plate 4. Stewart Institute students, ca. 1910. Individual on bottom step may be Corbett Mack. Photograph courtesy Nevada Historical Society (no. 791).

4

Work and Girls (1912–23)

47. Back Home Again in Smith Valley

And ever since 1912, I been workin' steady!
'Cause that's around about two year after I first get outta Stewart, you know... Yes, sir! 'Cause you know how a kid is: just wanna ride around the mountain all the time, chase them mustang ... fool around that way. So [from 1910 to 1912], I never did go to work yet. No, sir! But [then] the Old Man, he give me hell:
"You're old enough to work, Corbett. Lotta job around here.... And [if] you work, you can have enough money to buy your own clothes; your grub...."
And so I tell him back:
"Then you find me a job, Mack! I'm gonna work!"
'Cause you see what happen? My cousin-brother, he make me lazy! Yes, sir! And that that's Jimmy Burbank, best partner I got! 'Cause you see what we're doin'? I and Jimmy, we chase mustang. Don't get any, though. No, sir! 'Cause don't know how to run after 'em, you know.... Not like my grandfather, anyway. Or Big Mack.... And oh, sure, we find a few. 'Cause there's lotta mustang in them mountain back Smith Valley them days, partner: over by Dry Lake.... But still, we can chase 'em. Yes, sir! Get close to 'em, too, that way.... Keep drivin' em toward home, the two of us.

'Cause one of us can ride low, the other high.... Keep on doin' that, you know, till maybe they're gonna hit that [barbed] fence, and that wire can knock 'em down? And so, when they fall, we can get 'em! 'Cause you can break mustang pretty quick, you know: you pat 'em, they get tame pretty easy. Too bad, though, I don't know how to throw that rope far enough to catch 'em.... Then Jimmy Burbank go to jail for that rape.

But that woman, she lie. Yes, sir! 'Cause Jimmy, he start workin' for this one *Aytayay* [Italian] in Smith Valley, and so his wife, she scratch her leg with a fork.... Say he [Jimmy Burbank]'s tryin' to do that [i.e., rape] to her. 'Cause some women, you know, they're just that way. Then when Jimmy comes outta jail, he freeze to death. Yes, sir! All-around man, Jimmy Burbank: first he use that *moohoo'oo* [opium], then drink. Die in Hawthorne on a drunk.... Run outta gas and try to walk home. And that's wintertime, too, by God! Pass out on that Schurz road, freeze to death....

"Leave your *wanga'a* [younger cousin-brother] alone, Corbett!" So Big Mack, he [also] tell me that. "Spoilin' your good horse that way!"

'Cause we're only wearin' out our horse[s] that way [i.e., chasing mustangs]. Yes, sir! And so, after I'm through foolin' around that way, I go to work. And work ever since 1912, by God! Ranch work, mostly....

48. First Job

That first job, though, I'm workin' for that blacksmith in Smith Valley....

'Cause that's spring that year [1912], partner.... The Old Man, he find me a job. Ask Frank Simpson, 'cause Frank's foreman—they call him Sawyer, he's from Coleville: blacksmith on the Old Simpson Ranch—he need help. So, [Sawyer] give me that kind job. Say he need help, so I can work for him: you know, fixin' them old-time mowin' equipment, them buck rake, dump rake, sock rake, mowing rake ... sickle, scythe ... changin' them guard on them old-time mowin' machine.... Yes, sir! Any kind blacksmith job like that, why, I can help him do that.... You know, like puttin' new teeth and pullin' old ones outta them kind old-time rake, changin' bolts....

So you see what I'm doin'? I can work for that fellow [blacksmith] every mornin', then check [for] stray cattle for Frank Simpson on my saddle horse in the afternoon. Yes, sir! And I'm also on that cattle drive with the Old Man.... But that one's all summer long job, that cattle drive.... Start in May, and I work every day till October on that kind. Make dollar and a half a day—same as what them other *taivo* pay.... 'Cause that's cheapest wage, by God! All they pay them days.... But everythin' is cheap them days—sack flour only cost you dollar and a half.... And them old-timers, why, they can make bread outta it—bread and biscuit. Cook it in a Dutch oven, 'cause we don't have no kind stove [yet] them days. No, sir! Move around too much.... Anyway, I'm workin', so I can earn my own money. You know, to buy my own grub and my clothes that way.... And have to help out my family, too: you know, buyin' grub.... And some [e.g., Corbett's sister Janie], they're already usin' that *moohoo'oo* [opiates], so, that's pretty tough, by God! But me, I don't bother that yet. No, sir! Only sometime [I] drink....

And so, after that first [blacksmith] job, I never quit [working]! No, sir! Never lazy, neither—not like some guy. Never try to hide away from my job.... Never walk from it, neither. Not like a lotta these young guy, nowaday. No, sir! Just work, work, work! Work all the time ever since I start!

49. Ranch Work

Big Mack, he learn me everythin': you know, how to irrigate, stack hay.... Then after I get older, why, I can do it myself. And call that *tuuvaroi'ee*, that irrigatin' work....

'Cause the Old Man, he take care the beddin', and can [also] cook on them cattle drive we go on for Frank Simpson. Cook as good as any woman, too, by God! Yes, sir! Same way, too, after Old Man [Dan] Simpson's boy [Frank] cut up that ranch, he can feed cattle in the winter. 'Cause that's the only kind job there is in Smith Valley wintertime ... before them *Aytayay* come. Yes, sir! Feed cattle for Al Trielof.... 'Cause them rancher, you know, they're always askin' for him [Big Mack] to work....

And so that's what I [also] do: help Frank Simpson on that cattle drive to Leavitt Meadow every summer. Then feed 'em all winter.... Then no more cattle, when Simpson sell out, I can irrigate and stack hay. 'Cause that time, lotta hay, by God! And no bail, neither. Stack! 'Cause I know I can build up mine [stack] high as that boom, by God! Yes, sir! Raise that [hay] on top that pile all by myself! 'Cause you don't wanna leave it flat. No, sir! 'Cause [of] rain! 'Cause rain, you know, that can hurt that hay. Use a pitchfork on that kind job.... And same pay, too.... Dollar and a half a day! So you don't earn very much that way. Just enough, anyway, to buy your own grub, your overall, shoe.... And that's eleven-hour work, partner! Frank Simpson, he have to hire a big crew: Indian and *taivo*. But they don't mix. . . . No, sir! Got a Chinaman doin' the cookin' and workin' his garden. . . .

Then, way later, you can get more pay on stackin' job: seven dollars a day. Plus board. Yes, sir! Stackin' hay in Colony [District], first kind ranch work in Smith Valley I do for them *taivo*. . . . Hardest job I get till potato work. . . .

50. Some Other Early Jobs

And so, after I'm done stackin', I know Frank Simpson and his brother can hire me to cut cedar post.

'Cause that's winter work: Frank, he want a thousand post; his brother-in-law want five hundred more. . . . And so I take Big Mack's wagon: go up into them mountain with that. 'Cause that's a light wagon, you know. Not like spring wagon, anyway. No, sir! Pony can pull that other [light] kind . . . Yes, sir! We're usin' that wagon—that one the Old Man saw parked by that store in Wellington . . . when I'm only five or six . . . before I have that accident and lose my little toe. . . . Yes, sir! 'Cause the Old Man, he sure like that kind. So he buy it. And gee, our horse sure afraid that jackass: that bell on them. . . . Anyway, so Big Mack, he buy it; use that for his wood wagon. Give that light wagon to me, so I and Henry Quinn, we [can] go to work for Frank Simpson that winter. . . . You know, cuttin' them cedar post.

'Cause we figure we're gonna make a lotta money, by God! 'Cause you see why? One *waapee* [cedar tree], why, that can get you eight to nine post. Yes, sir! And we get twenty-five cent for every seven-foot gate post. (Corner post get you fifty cent.) But we have to sneak 'em down to them foothill in that wagon; Frank Simpson, he cart 'em the rest the way home. . . . And Pat Wilson—Pat's Jack Wilson's *wanga'a* [younger brother]—he's also up there. Also doin' that kind work. . . . And [since] that's around about October, I have my twelve gauge pump shotgun to hunt. (Eye ain't bad yet that time. . . .) But I know I always have to get [manage] our money: you know write down how much my partner's usin', so when he's paid, Henry Quinn, he can pay me back. Yes, sir! 'Cause Henry, he's usin' that *moohoo'oo* then; so when that check come to me, I always have to be the one to cash it. 'Cause we just split that cost [groceries] and buy our hay from Frank Simpson; Henry, what he's got left, why, he can buy that *moohoo'oo*. Yes, sir! We have to come down from them mountain for that. . . . So, lucky thing I learn my countin' in Stewart, ain't it?

Oh, and we stay up in them mountain pretty near all through November . . . December, too! Live in a canvas house that time. . . . Yes, sir! 'Cause we make a low house outta that kind [canvas], you know: use rock and wood to hold it down. . . . One time, so much snow, why, come mornin', that roof sag down on top us, so we have a helluva time to get out! And same way, too, we have to shoe our horse for that kind work. 'Cause even if they're mustang, they can get tenderfooted. . . .

But I know one kind [of] wood we don't want—that pine nut wood! No, sir! 'Cause they're too green [wet], that kind. And same way, too, that kind can't be hauled, neither. No, sir! Too heavy, got pitch on 'em, so, they have to stand [dry] all winter before you can use 'em. . . . Why we always go for that other kind, you know . . . that *waapee,* cedar. Yes, sir! Cut that tree and roll 'em down the mountain in big section; then cord in pile of twenty.

'Cause by old time way, anyway, Coyote, he make all them *waapee.* Yes, sir! His brother [Wolf], he want him to spit them pine nuts they're stealin' from the north; but you know Coyote—always doin' somethin' [i.e., bad]! Swallow that *tuuba* [pine nuts] instead of sprayin' these mountain with that seed, so that's how come it's so hard before *taivo* start comin' around here. . . . Why there's all these cedar instead *tuuba* [piñon pines]. 'Cause Coyote, he don't listen to his *pavee'ee!* No, sir! Not doin' what his older brother's tellin' him what to do, anyway!

And I [also] can trap before *Aytayay* start comin' into these valley. 'Cause that's winter work, you know. Trap *poneeda* [skunk, for example], 'cause that kind's *khaishooname'yoo:* don't know nothin'! So you just lead 'em to water and drown 'em, so that way, they don't stink. And same way, too, I can trap *eeza'a* [coyote]. That other fellow [skunk], he only get you two or three dollar for his skin, but coyote, you can get eight or nine dollar. . . . Pretty hard to catch, though, *eeza'a,* by God! Smart! And you see who teach me how to make that kind trap? The Old Man! Yes, sir! Show me how to make that kind trap to grab coyote by the leg. Then you can kill him by hittin' him on the nose or chokin' him with rope. . . .

51. Yet Another Early Job

Another [early] job I have is for Mike Sava. . . .

'Cause he run that Hot Spring in Smith Valley, you know. . . . Used to be Charley Hinds had that one, so the Old Man and my mom, they both work there . . . so we move close by. 'Cause them Smith Valley *taivo,* you know, they like to swim in that Saturday night; Sunday, too. . . . 'Cause them days, they're just as bad as these Indian: don't have no hot water in their house, so [they] have to swim in Hot Springs! And they can make a dance there on Saturday night, too. . . . Yes, sir! Hinds Hot Springs, that's [also] where my mom learn to drink. . . . 'Cause them *taivo,* they [also] like to do that, you know: drink at that bar. . . . And you see how my mom learn that? The Old Man! Yes, sir! 'Cause Big Mack, he does hay work for Charley Hinds. . . . Me, my job's to drain that water there; then clean *payoghoba* [algae] from that pool. . . . And you see what I like doin'? Swimmin' while I'm doin' that! Yes, sir! Same way, too, I can do a little alfalfa work for Mike Sava. On account he's got a couple or three acre in Smith Valley. . . .

52. Workin' for the Man

Best kind boss, though, them *taivo!* Yes, sir! 'Cause you see why? They just give you your water [for irrigation] and leave you alone! Not like them *Aytayay,* anyway. . . . No, sir! Don't bother you at all, them *taivo.* . . . Just leave you alone all the time to do your own work. And pay you better wage, too! 'Cause ranchin' job, that's the most I'm ever makin': $117.45. And I only draw some that money early: you know, to buy clothes. . . . Same way, too, them *taivo,* they feed three meal every day—that's on the board. 'Cause no matter even it's Sunday, they feed you, too. . . . Not like them *Aytayay.* . . . 'Cause you gotta buy your own food for Sunday when you work for 'em. . . .

Start work [for whites] at 7:30 a.m. . . . Get your breakfast at 7:00 a.m., then work half-past the hour. . . . And work till half past eleven. (That's pretty near five hour, ain't it?) Then you gotta quit. 'Cause they're gonna give you a noon meal. Real meal, too, noontime . . . good. And same way, too, suppertime. . . . And you can rest your noon meal till 1:00 p.m., then go back to your job—work till half past five, quittin' time. Time for your supper. . . .

'Cause I know Old Man Scieroni, he say them Indian are best worker! Yes, sir! And he's *Aytayay!* Say them *taivo* worker, they talk too much! 'Cause I know I used to work with this one *taivo* at Simpson's Ranch. . . .

[He] say to hide till the boss come, then we can do our work. . . . But I know I sure get tired that. . . .

53. Jobs I Don't Like

One year, I work for this dairyman in Smith Valley. . . . But I don't do milkin' job. . . . No, sir! 'Cause my boss, you know, he's the one doin' that. Yes, sir! Workin' that machine on them tit! So, that's all I get to do: clean the barn and fill up that hay. But [I] don't do much work. . . . Just stand around lot. Still, I get more pay than Macarini give me when I start workin' for him . . . five dollar a day! But one job I know I [really] don't like, that's herdin' sheep! No, sir! 'Cause that's pretty tough job, partner! Yes, sir! 'Cause, I have that kind two time . . . before I marry . . .

First time, I'm workin' for this one fellow's named Aw [Art?] Jones; he's got a band sheep in this [Smith] valley, Aw Jones, and no feed; so he's gotta move 'em to Pine Grove. But no feed up there, neither, so Aw Jones's band is havin' a helluva time! Why he's gotta hire lots to watch 'em. . . . 'Cause you see why? No feed, them sheep run away. . . . Why he lose lotta them that time. . . . And that other fellow [sheep herd owner] I'm workin' for, I can't get his name. . . .

These Indian, they just call sheep same way: "sheep." Goat, same way, too . . . *Shavoo*, why, that's your shovel. . . . Cattle drive they call *kootsoo mahuu*. . . . And potato plantin' they call potato *masug*. *Dohon*, that's when they dig 'em up. . . .

And I don't work too long for Aw [Art] Jones, neither. No, sir! 'Cause half the time, anyway, I must be lookin' for lost sheep! [If I] find 'em, why, I just bring 'em back to that band. . . . But [since] they're always hungry and don't wanna camp at night, they're too hard to find, by God! And too many canyon, too! So a fellow can't hardly take off his clothes to go to bed at night! No, sir! Can't take his shoe off even! And too much damn noise, too, them sheep are makin'! "Baaaaaa. Baaaaaa." 'Cause soon as they do that, why, you gotta put back your shoe on and tell your dog, "Go on!" 'Cause he's gonna have to try and chase 'em back into that band. . . . And same with them bell they're always wearin'. . . . 'Cause you hear that kind all the time, and so that sound, why, even when you're away from it, well, that, too, can stay in your ear! Yes, sir! Drive a fellow crazy that way. . . . Same like that "baaaa."

But that's not hard work, sheep work. No, sir! Just walkin' around, you know; [the] kind job that kind herdin' is. . . . Pay you four dollars a day. . . .

And so, that's how come them Basqo, they gotta do that work. Yes, sir! 'Cause they don't mind it, you see. No, sir! Only one [who] can take care them sheep pretty good, I tell you, Mike! And same way, too, they make pretty good soup, them Basqo! 'Cause I know I eat that! But one thing you won't never see: no Basqo woman! No, sir! 'Cause not too many around, you know. . . . Only Basqo's got a wife is Joe Asp [?]. 'Cause that fellow, he's got his own ranch, you know, over toward Wellington. Basqo wife and a boy and a girl. . . . Anyway, that's one thing I still wanna know is: where them Basqo belong [i.e., originate]?

So anyway, I quit Aw Jones—even though he's a good friend mine. Still, I know I don't like my boss. . . . No, sir! 'Cause you see why? [If] I can't find them sheep, why, I miss my meal! 'Cause I'm out there after them all the time, you know, and Aw Jones, he move that band. Don't even tell me where to, neither, so I come back and can't find him! And [he] don't [even] say, "Better take your lunch with you, Corbett." No, sir! So I just quit Aw Jones. Then Joe Yeager want me to work for him.

'Cause that's his name, you know: Joe Yeager, [the] other sheep man I work for. And I help him, oh, one week, maybe two? In Pine Grove. . . . Pretty good friend mine, too, I tell you, by God! 'Cause I know I sure [also] like Joe Yeager! Feed you real good! But I don't last on that job, neither. No, sir! 'Cause I don't wanna do that kind work no more. 'Cause like I say, you just have to walk behind them sheep all the time—till they get their breakfast. Then around 4:00 P.M., why, they wanna feed some more; so you just gotta let 'em out again. Keep on watchin' 'em all the goddamn time, too! Till 10:00 P.M., when they don't go around no more in that hot weather. . . . No feed, so they just break off. . . .

Same way, too, another kind job I know I don't like is that minin' job. 'Cause you see why? Afraid to go inside there, partner! Afraid they might just cave in on me! 'Cause I never did see no Indian work in the mine, neither. No, sir! Too scared, maybe, to go into them cave? 'Cause [maybe] that's where them *poohaghooma* [Indian doctors] have to go to get their *booha*, you know—cave near Wabuska [for example]. . . . Got white patch [on the side of its mountain] they [also] get *ebe* [white paint] from. . . . 'Cause them Indian doctor, they have to make a [facial] mark when they doctor you: pass out that white paint, same as that other kind when they doctor, that *pizzapee:* [red paint which] come from them Buckskin Mountain.... And same way, too, they can go to McCloud Hill in this [Mason] valley. 'Cause a fellow can get handgame [gambling] *booha* from there. 'Cause you see what them old-timers say? [If] you throw money down that hole and take [a] pebble home with you, why, you're gonna win all the time! And so this one time—that's around about 1935, 1936?—I guess this one *taivo* find out about all that money that's up there on McCloud Hill. 'Cause somebody tell him, I guess, what all them Indian are always doin' up there, and so he blast for it. Must have been a lotta money up there, too, by God! Anyway, nowaday, *karroo'oo!* Nothin'! No more left! All fenced off, too, so nobody can go there no more....

And more cave back [Fort] Churchill.... 'Cause that place they call *muhuuna*. (Sound pretty like "moon," ain't it. *Muuhuu?*) 'Cause to me, anyway, them cave look like apartment.... And I know I also hear [that] lotta them Indian doctor can go to that place, too. (Same place Wolf tells them animals to meet: before they go north to steal them pine nut for this country.) And they say if you go into that cave alone, and lay down in a hole, why, you can ask Rattlesnake for *booha* to suck [cure]. Yes, sir! So, pretty soon after that, you'll get your own [curing] song! And same way, too, they say them "People" will be jumpin' all over a person.... [How] *Pahwa*, Bear, he can walk over your body. Or, some kind boulder's gonna roll down over you.... But [if] you're afraid, then you're not gonna get your *booha* [supernatural power] you're askin' for. No, sir! 'Cause same way, too, they say [if] you make one mistake, [if] you don't mind what you're supposed to, they say that Medicine can kill you! And them Churchill cave are real high, too.... But them kind [shamanic noviates], they can just jump down when they're finished! And don't get hurt, neither! No, sir! So, after they do that [i.e., return with spirit helpers], why, that's when they have to get ready what they're gonna need to doctor....

'Cause I know Wesley Keno, he go up to them Churchill caves for *booha*.... Ask for *booha*, to soldier, you know, Wesley, only, Coyote, he butt in. Trick him, by God! 'Cause you see what he's doin'? Start in to talkin' that other [contrary or deceptive] way, you know. 'Cause you see what he's [Coyote's] always doin'? Wanna make Wesley Keno a *tuduhun*, thief, only he don't want that. No, sir! So, he say he just come down from there. Give up, you know. Say, "I don't want 'em!"

54. One Boss I Especially Like

One boss I know I sure like working for is Charley Day. Yes, sir! 'Cause can't never get away from him. . . . No, sir! And that's also summer work, you know. 'Cause I do all that irrigatin' work for Charley Day. Can't work for nobody else when I work for him! Do hayin' work, too. . . . Hayin' time, though, Charley Day, he has to hire lotta them *taivo*, by God! Yes, sir! So they work right alongside these Indian: you know, cuttin' alfalfa and doin' rakin' work. . . . But I'm mostly on the irrigatin' side, partner. 'Cause you see why? The Old Man, he [originally] used to work for Charley Day, so I get to work right alongside him. And pay's good, too. Charley Day, he pay three dollar a day. Feed you [also] on Sunday. Not hard work, neither. . . . Seem like he pay a fellow just to walk around all day long. You know, [to] carry your shovel like that. . . . So that's hardly no work at all!

Pretty good man, Charley Day. Too bad he ain't got no cattle, though. 'Cause he's a[nother] sheep man: has to hire them Basqo to do that . . . to take care 'em. . . . 'Cause [if] Charley Day has got cattle, then maybe I can work all winter long for him?

55. Ownin' Land

'Cause, nowaday, we don't own nothin'! *Karroo'oo!* But before them *taivo* start comin' into our country, we do. . . . 'Cause I know my grandma, she always used to say: "*Nuuga deeva deeweeba!*" 'That's my pine nut land.' Say she used to own [pine nut range] from this one canyon in Smith Valley over toward Big Mountain [Mt. Grant]—where she get *tuuba* [pine nuts] all the time. Even name that place, too: call it *o-baha* 'Rocky Spring'. On account there's water comin' up from under that cave. (It's on the road from Wellington to Sweetwater.) And same way, too, Jack Wilson's wife say she own. . . . And Jim Wilson and his wife, they [also] used to say they own part this country—wife he marry before he marry Big Mack's mother. . . . So maybe all them old-timers own [piñon pine groves]? But I never tell you how *tuuba* [pine nut] get here? 'Cause that's on a story, partner: them *natoonadweba* . . . animal teachin'.

'Cause them real old-timers, they say "*Moo'esa*" . . . 'early days ago'. Tell how Coyote, he smell that kind . . . that *papee*, pine nut soup. And so he go up there, all right: to North Country. 'Cause that fellow, he always like to brag. Can brag, you see, how he's gonna bring that food back to his own [this] country [for example]. . . . Only *Ang* [Pine Nut Bird] won't let him. No, sir! 'Cause you see why? That kind [of bird] know Coyote! Gonna make that [pine nut] soup too watery, so when that other fellow [Coyote] try to steal it, why, he can't! No, sir! 'Cause it's only gonna leak through his *weega* [rabbitskin blanket]! And so Coyote, he came back home again [i.e., with empty mouth]. . . . Tell his *pavee'ee* [older brother] what they're doin' up there, and so Wolf, he tell all them animals to make a council. Yes, sir! Say to meet at Churchill. . . . Same place where them *poohaghooma* supposed to go for their *booha;* same place them four doctor have that World's War with George Washington's soldiers I [also] tell you about! 'Cause Wolf, you know, he [also] wanna bring that food to this country. Yes, sir! To plant 'em here, so these Indian can have somethin' good to eat all winter long . . . his *Nuumuu* [Paiute] children. Only Coyote, he don't listen to his brother. No, sir! 'Cause after they steal that—'cause you see what he's doin'? First, Coyote can put *Ang* to sleep, then he send *poongatsee* [mouse] to them roof beam where they're hidin' *tuuba* . . . in that bow . . . to steal 'em! So after they're done carryin' *tuuba* back here, escape from North Country, why, Coyote, he just swallow 'em! Yes, sir! Don't listen to his older brother! So wherever Coyote spit, that's where them *waapee* [cedar trees instead] grow!

'Cause you see why he's doin' that? 'Cause that's his winter food, them juniper berry! Why Coyote don't listen to his *pavee'ee* [older brother]. . . . 'Cause, otherwise, there'd be piñon pine tree everywhere [in] this country, by God! Yes, sir! Lotta food for these hungry Indian to eat!

But that's a real long time ago, partner. . . . And so, after Old Man [Dan] Simpson settle [Desert Creek Ranch, Smith Valley], he take away our land. Yes, sir! 'Cause the Old Man, he say he seen that. . . . And same way, Big Mack [also] say he seen [T. B.] Smith and "Doc" Hutson on that Wild Hay Ranch [Smith Valley] start up. 'Cause that's them pioneer days! 'Cause Big Mack, he say he cut *wahaba* [wild hay] with a scythe for 'em. 'Cause them days, you know, they're not puttin' in alfafa yet. No, sir! And say he [also] works for pretty near all them real *taivo* old-timers. . . . And so I guess the Old Man, he [consequently] makes a partner[ship] with George Fulstone.

'Cause Hike, you know, he give Big Mack five acre. All brush land, though, pretty rough. . . . Anyway, the Old Man, he plough up that land himself. And we can help him, too: you know, burn that brush. . . . 'Cause he use a walkin' plough, the Old Man. (Call that kind *tuudzizoguno;* to loosen up ground.) Yes, sir! 'Cause I know I and my brother Willy, we help him.

And Big Mack, he can hire Indian women, too, on that land: you know, to cut that wheat. 'Cause they're doin' that old-time way, you know—with knife! Yes, sir! Just cut the head and throw it in a bundle, thrash that wheat's piled up. . . . Only thing is, that [Scieroni irrigation] ditch ain't done [dug] yet, so it's hard to grow somethin' what's good on that land George Fulstone give him. . . .

Five acre, that's a pretty good piece land them days, partner! 'Cause the Old Man, he say how he's gonna haul that wheat down to Nordyke [Mill in Mason Valley]: make flour outta it . . . then pay them *Nuumuu* women who help him that way. Or maybe he can just give 'em a couple sack that flour? Or potato from that garden he [also] always put him? You know, instead of pay . . . to help 'em out with their grub for workin' for him. . . . Yes, sir! 'Cause that's what that old man's [also] doin', you know: puttin' in a vegetable garden every year. . . .

And so Big Mack, he tell Little Dick's wife: "Maybe I can give you potato [if] you gonna help me?" But you see what I'm thinkin'? He's only bullshittin' her? 'Cause you see why? Maybe he just wanna lay down with her? Make a baby off that girl! Anyway, that's what he's doin': pay them workin' women with that kind [flour or vegetables], 'cause he ain't got no money! And, by God, too, they're satisfied! "*Peeza'yoo!* Good!" they say. "Pretty good to get somethin' to eat!" 'Cause the Old Man, he put in that garden twice. . . .

But you see what happen? George Fulstone, he cheat Big Mack! Yes, sir! Say two-third that profit is for him, Big Mack's supposed to only be gettin' one-third. . . . Say how he'll keep the barley, Big Mack can get the wheat. . . . So, too bad we ain't got paper on that land! Should have signed paper on it, ain't it? What I'm thinkin', anyway. 'Cause, pretty quick, they start fightin' over it, and Hike, he kick us off our land! And [since] that's his ranch, we hardly can't say nothin' at all about it. No, sir! *Karroo'oo!* Nothin' at all!

And you see why they fightin'? 'Cause the Old Man, he went [prospecting] after gold, and so Hike, he say he's supposed to be payin' him for that [i.e., discovered vein]. Yes, sir! Why he get mad and kick that Old Man off his own land! Say, "You don't have no paper on that land, Mack!"

So [he] can win us easy. . . . But that time, my young[er] brother [Willy] die, so we just quit our ranch. Yes, sir! 'Cause Big Mack, he say how he don't wanna stay there no more. No, sir! Get mad and just quit. Say he's gonna go [back] to work for them regular wage. . . . Yes, sir! Give back that piece land to Hike Fulstone. . . . So, too bad nothin' come of that, ain't it?

56. My Grandma Remarries

Then way later, my grandma say she want somebody to talk to. . . . Is all alone, you know, and [since] there's this one old-timer livin' in Smith Valley, my grandma, she do that [i.e., marries him].

'Cause I'm big then, you know. Already start to work. . . . And his name's Bridgeport Joe [whom] she marry. . . . 'Cause he's from Bridgeport, where my grandma belong. . . . Lost his wife, and do any kind light work for them Smith Valley *taivo*, Bridgeport Joe. And he's the only one makin' a sweathouse around here, too. Yes, sir! Call that kind *namoosa eeno*. 'Course, nowaday [ca. 1972], I hear this one [Death Valley] Shoshone guy livin' across the way is also doin' that [Ivan Hanson]. . . . But when I'm a young guy, none these Indian do that. No, sir! None except Bridgeport Joe. . . .

'Cause you see why? They can swim in that [Smith Valley] hot spring all they want. Or [the one] over at Wabuska when they wanna sweat. . . . Anyway, I know I used to hear lotta story about them Bishop Indian comin' into Bridgeport to gang [rape] women in their sweathouse! And [then] have to pay [indemnity] with a string of *tsomeebee* [bird bone beads] after. . . . Yes, sir! Pay 'em with them big bead, too. . . . Around the size a marble! 'Cause they can string 'em together, you know, them Bishop Indian: make a necklace outta them kind bead.

Anyway, I know I seen that sweathouse Bridgeport Joe make: make it outta willow post. . . . And he lace 'em together, too; cover it with dirt. . . . Pretty big, too, that sweathouse, I tell you, Mike! Big enough, anyway, for two to three people inside. . . . And got a fire inside: hole dug in the center that floor where Bridgeport Joe put them hot rocks he's cookin'. . . . Then when he's finished, why, he can dive right in that [irrigation] ditch above Smith. Yes, sir! Sweat any time, too, Bridgeport Joe. But I don't think I ever seen him in there wintertime. . . . No, sir! Anyway, only one time I stick my head inside. . . . But too damn hot, partner! Yes, sir! So, that's why I won't go near there no more. No, sir!

So, anyway, that old-timer, he marry my grandma. Only thing is, Bridgeport Joe, he don't like Eddie [Mack]! Too mean to him. . . . 'Cause I know one time, he bawl out Eddie, and so my grandma, she get mad. Walk all the way from Wellington to Colony [District]. . . .

So, then when Bridgeport Joe die, she get over it real quick. No more *namoosa eno*, neither. . . . And nobody bother that sweathouse [structure], neither. No, sir! They just leave it alone and it [eventually] cave in!

57. Coyote Dreamin'

My grandma, she always [also] has to help me on my dream. Yes, sir! 'Cause you see what them old-timers say? [If] you have *nosee* [dream] about a woman, why, that's on account Coyote! 'Cause he's a *yogho* [fornicating] man, that one, by God! Yes, sir! Can't stop thinkin' about *mochotnee* [woman]! No, sir! So they say Coyote's the one puttin' that kind in your dream! 'Cause I know on that one *nosee* I'm always havin', I'm goin' with this one girl, but bothered by another. So I tell my grandma, and she know what to do, all right . . . how to help me out. . . .

Wake me real early in the mornin', and we climb mountain. And that's right before sunup, partner. . . . Yes, sir! 'Cause that has to be real early in the mornin' when you're doin' that. . . . Anyway, my grandma, she take hold *sawabee*—dip sagebrush in water and comb my hair with it. Then pray for me. . . . Yes, sir! Tell that one [Coyote] to go away: "Don't bother my *moo'a* [grandson] no more!" she tell him, all right! And so Coyote, he listen. Has to listen, you know. 'Cause my grandma, she's a pretty tough old lady!

58. Girlfriend(s)

See, 'cause after I start workin', if I'm not tired Saturday night, so I can just saddle my horse and ride over them Singatse [Mountains] to this [Mason] valley—for them young girl! Yes, sir! 'Cause around about fifteen, sixteen year old, that's how [young] I like 'em. 'Cause I know I don't want them old one. . . . No, sir! 'Cause you see why? They drink, so I'm afraid I just might get a dose [i.e., venereal disease]! But not them young one. . . . No, sir! 'Cause they don't drink. "Oh, no," [but] they can say. "You might give me drink, Corbett. Then leave me." Afraid, you see, somebody's goin' to gang [rape] 'em! Yes, sir! What they're always sayin', them young girl. . . . So [they] don't wanna get drunk and pass out. . . .

And it take only one hour, one and a half hour to come down here to Yerington, you know. . . . 'Cause not too many young girl in Smith Valley, I tell you, Mike! No, sir! 'Cause you see why? This valley's got lot more [small] ranch—[so] more hay cuttin' job. Only a few [big] ranches in Smith Valley them days, so not too many different jobs up there that time. . . . Why I like comin' down here. . . . Beside, I'm [also] too close[ly related] to them Smith Valley girl. Yes, sir! So all I know is, I wanna come down here to Mason . . . to Yerington. . . .

And that's before they line 'em up [i.e., before the 1917 purchase of the Yerington Indian Colony], too. . . . So you can get *soowee* [vagina, i.e., sex] pretty easy with them young girl, I tell you, Mike! Yes, sir! Just talk to 'em good, that's all. Say, "Where you goin', honey? Let's take a walk!" Like that way, you know. . . . 'Cause they all like that, them young girl, you know. . . . Don't drink, don't wanna get marry, neither. . . . And so what I know I like to do is get 'em under the buckberry brush. Yes, sir! Go to 'em right there! And I can stay with one girl all day long, too, partner! Sunday. . . . Then in the evenin', why, that's when I start thinkin' about my job. . . . Wanna go back home. . . . 'Cause them days, lotta *wa'eets taivo* [hobos], and so your boss, he can always put that kind on your job. And me, I know I don't want nobody to take my job away from me! No, sir! Only thing is, my grandma, she always want me to marry. Yes, sir! Tell me, "Don't just go with *haitsee* [girlfriend] all the time, Corbett. Live [i.e., marry] with someone! 'Cause that's better that way!"

Same way, too, my mom, she's also sayin' that to me. . . . Say, "Behave yourself, Corbett. Settle down with one woman. Get a *norr^gwa* [wife]. So, you can] have a better life that way!"

But they can't say which one, neither. No, sir! "Any girl you like, Corbett—" Tell me that. "Just so long [as] she's not too close. Yes, sir! And bring your *norr^gwa* home, so she can cook for you, wash clothes. . . ." What my grandma and my mom's alway sayin' to me to do . . . both! But I know they don't want me to marry no *wawa'a* [stranger]. No, sir! 'Cause [they] say to me, "Marry your cousin-sister, Corbett! Better that way [if] you know her. Have a better life that way!"

And you see who start me off on that [sex] business? Steve Johnson's daughter. Yes, sir! First one doin' that to me, by God! 'Cause I know I bust Edie Johnson's cherry! Yes, sir! Get her first. . . . 'Cause I'm around about thirty-nine [*sic*] and she's fifteen that time. . . . Edie Johnson, she stay in Mason all the time: live with her aunt [*Apee* or "Happy" Hooligan], near Jack

Wilson. 'Cause Edie, she don't like her mother. . . . No, sir! Say to me, "I don't like my mom, Corbett. Too bossy!" 'Cause I know I visit Edie there all the time. . . . And gee, I sure like her! Only thing is, she won't marry me. No, sir! Then later on, she marry Howard Remus.

Rosie Conway, she's also my girlfriend. That's Happy Jack Conway's girl, Rosie—from Sweetwater [California]. Father's related to my grandma, you know, so whenever he visit, Happy Jack bring *kootsabee* [Mono Lake brine fly larvae, *Ephyadra hians*]. And same way, too, my grandma, she can give him pine nut back. 'Cause that's on a trade, you know. . . . *Quuavee*, that's what they call Rosie Conway . . . eighteen, nineteen, maybe, that time? And you see how we get together? Pete Penrose! Yes, sir! 'Cause Pete, he's my *ats:* Pete Penrose and the Old Man are cousin-brother. Anyway, Pete, he hire me. Say, "Corbett, we need two men for hayin' job!" 'Cause that's in East Walker country: Charley Perry Ranch. I'm stayin' down here in Yerington that time: you know, foolin' around with them young girl. . . . 'Cause Pete Penrose, he's got a house there [Yerington Indian Colony]. . . . So I [agree to] go there . . . Pete's camp in East Walker . . . to work.

And so Pete Penrose, he ask for my blanket. . . . [Then] he tell me: "There's a man sleepin' in it, Corbett. Go ahead and bunk down next to him!" And so I say to him back, "Well, I don't care!" and just lay down next to him. . . . But [when] I find that's a woman there, why, I jump up quick! Yes, sir! Touch her hair [accidentally], you know, then light my match. Find out who she is that way. . . . And so I and Rosie Conway, we work together that time in East Walker country. But that's flu time, partner—1918, 1919. . . . Lotta these Indian dyin' on that one. . . . 'Cause I know I and Rosie Conway, we both also get sick. . . .

And you see how I lose her? 'Cause I gotta go back to my own family— to take 'em pine nuttin'. And so when I don't come back soon enough, Rosie, she miss me and go crazy. Start in drinkin' heavy. . . . And I hear her older sister try to catch her by the hair, but can't. . . . That Lucy Penrose, [who is] marry to my Uncle Pete. Then way later, when I come back to Yerington, Pete Penrose, he tell me what Rosie been doin': "Corbett, your wife went haywire! Been foolin' around too much!"

And so I don't bother her no more. No, sir! 'Cause that's the kind you gotta watch out for, you know: hard drinkin' woman! 'Cause they can pass out, and them Indian men *habee:* lay down with 'em! And so you can get that *qonoza* that way . . . that "dose." Anyway, way later on, Rosie Conway, she

Work and Girls (1912-23)

marry Tom Mitchell's boy, Doud . . . [who] run that gamblin' house after his father die. . . .

But you see who can fix [cure] that kind [venereal disease]? Winnemucca *natsee!* 'Cause I know one time, he come down here from Nixon [Pyramid Lake Reservation] to doctor somebody on that. . . . And same way, too, they say Rosie Quartz can. 'Cause I hear she doctor Mike Pete for *qonoza*. Only thing is, Mike Pete's too far gone, and so he die. But they say Rosie Quartz is supposed to sing; to sing and suck [out] that poison. 'Cause that's the real way to get out that *wo'aba* [worm, i.e., poison], you know. Only thing is, she don't. No, sir! Just rub his belly, and so Mike Pete, he die. . . . Rosie Quartz, she's from Schurz [Walker River Reservation]. Real old-timer. . . . They call her *akuudzee*.

And you see what else's wrong with Rosie Conway? Why I don't [really] want her? Too close! 'Cause she's my *hama'a* [younger sister] by Indian way! But Pete Penrose, he say that don't matter. "Close on top, closer on the bottom!" Pete say. Still, I feel too much ashamed. Ashamed my grandma, and my mom, can bawl me out. Both! 'Cause all them old-timers are that way, you know: worry [if] you're too close. "Go take her, Corbett! She won't hurt you!" Pete Penrose say to me. And he's another old-timer!

'Cause you see how we're related: Pete's *wanga'a* to the Old Man. Anyway, I know I used to see Rosie Conway in town [Yerington] afterward. But I don't talk to her too much then. . . . No, sir! But she must be after me, 'cause Rosie Conway, she spoil my best girl! Yes, sir! And that's that Mary Mason.

Way younger than I am, Mary Mason. . . . 'Cause I'm, maybe, fifteen years older? Maybe more! Pretty young girl, too, when I'm first acquainted with her, Mary Mason, by God! 'Cause she [also] live at that Indian camp [Yerington Indian Colony]—before her family move to Wabuska. And gee, she sure is nice girl! But you see what Rosie Conway's doin'? Say to her, "I'm Corbett's *norr^gwa!*" Yes, sir! Try to tell Mary Mason how I'm her husband. . . . You know, to take my best girl away from me! "Corbett's mine!" And keep on sayin' that to Mary Mason, you know. 'Cause she know I wanna marry her! And so that other girl [Mary Mason], she give me back my ring! Real solid gold ring, too, that one! Cost me pretty near thirty-five dollar! And gee, it sure take a fellow a good long time to make that much money! Yes, sir! Got a diamond in the center, I carve [engrave] my initial in it. . . . Still, Mary Mason give me that ring back. . . . And I know I don't wanna take it back, neither. No, sir! But I do. And so, after that, Mary Mason, she don't wanna marry me no more. No, sir! Say to me, "I wanna go back to school, Corbett! To learn somethin'!" On account what Rosie Conway's doin'.... And so she do that, too, by God! Go to Stewart....

Yes, sir! Rosie Conway, she spoil my best girl!

59. Them City Girl(s)!

And same way, too, I like Mary Charley. 'Cause that's Jimmy Charley's sister, Mary.... Way younger than I am, Mary Charley. [But] she [also] wanna marry me.... And so you see what happen? Her mother [Maggie Wright] don't like me! No, sir! Say we're too close—just like a brother and sister. 'Cause I know I used to play with Mary Charley in Smith Valley when we're both young: you know, [we] take off our clothes, and swim together and go fishin' in the [West Walker] river.... Same way, I [also] like to swim [naked] with Bessie Wright and Steve Moose's daughter when I'm a young guy, partner.... So anyway, you see what we're doin?' Have to sneak off together durin' potato time—to make *yogho*.... And you see who else I'm with, then? Tom Mitchell's girl[s]!

"Come on, Corbett: Let's walk to the brush! We won't tell on you!" Yes, sir! 'Cause that's what them girl are always sayin' to me ... both! And that's that Daisy and Carrie Mitchell! 'Cause they [even] look alike, them two Mitchell girl. Laugh alike, too. Yes, sir! 'Cause I know I pretty near went through all them Tom Mitchell girl, partner! Daisy Mitchell, Carrie Mitchell, Nellie Mitchell, Minnie Mitchell.... All except for that old[est] one [Sadie].... And they're all virgin.... But when I wanna marry Minnie—'cause, gee, I know I sure like her best—I'm sure afraid! Afraid, you know, on account her father. 'Cause you know what he's doin', that Tom Mitchell—witchin' way!

But still, that one's pretty tough, I tell you Mike: to marry them city girl[s]. Yes, sir! 'Cause you see why? They don't wanna come to the country where I'm livin'! No, sir! Say they don't like to try to make a home out in the brush no more. 'Cause town, you know, that's what they say they always like. 'Cause you see why? Where they can buy their *heebee* [drink] more easy!

And another one them city girl[s] I like, her name's Alvina [Reymers]. But everyone call her "$100 Beauty!" 'Cause you see why? Her *na'a* [father], he was gamblin' in Tom Mitchell's gamblin' house [at Yerington Indian Colony] one time and won $100. So that old man, he say to everybody: "Anybody wanna marry my daughter, I can give him $100!" And so that's how that name stick. . . . 'Cause I know that girl! Yes, sir! But we never try to get marry, though. 'Cause you see why? Alvina, she like town too much. . . .

Edie Johnson . . . Rosie Conway . . . Mary Mason . . . all them Mitchell girls . . . well, most them, anyway. . . . And same way, too, I know I like Judy Dyer. . . . Not real dark, Judy. . . . No, sir! 'Cause none them Dyer girl are: Judy, Agnes, Sadie. Only their brother [Gus Brann]. . . . So [they] look pretty near like *nomogwet*, them three Dyer girl; so must belong to that *taivo*, Bob Dyer? 'Cause he always go after these Indian, that one. Yes, sir! What he like best! Anyway, Judy Dyer, she work for them *yogho moghotnee* [whores] in Yerington . . . over by the old hospital in town; by that Indian camp. . . . 'Cause you see what kind work she's doin'? Washin' them whore clothes. Has a lumber house behind them buckberry bush over there—by that upper bridge goin' into Yerington. . . . Where Judy Dyer live with her mother and that old lady's second husband, *Parroogarrig*. (Real short guy. Name's 'Hanging on the Edge'. Like some kind stick over the water. . . . And he gamble all the time; that five card game with women.) 'Cause Sunday, that's when I come down here to see Judy Dyer. . . . And I know I have to buy somethin' what she like. 'Cause, otherwise, Judy won't like me no more. No, sir! Here I'm only makin' nine dollar a week—that ain't hardly no money at all!—still, I have to buy present. . . . And them whore, they sure like these Indian. Yes, sir! But police, they don't let 'em go in there. No, sir! Kick 'em right out! 'Cause you see why? Afraid! Afraid maybe they're gonna ask for drink. 'Cause that time, you know, Indian can't drink. No, sir! Not allowed in the bar yet; and them whore Judy Dyer work for, why, they always gotta keep a drink inside. And [since] there's always a bull close by—you know, watchin', always watchin'—so they're afraid. Afraid maybe some crazy Indian's gonna get in there and raise hell!

60. Waseeyoo Girls

And same way, too, lotta time, I know I like goin' to Gardnerville—for them *Waseeyoo* girl!

'Cause I and Henry Quinn, we go there on a buggy. 'Cause my partner, you know, he's got that [opiate] habit; me, I only use *moohoo'oo* [yen-shee] once in a while then. . . . 'Cause not yet on a habit. And so Henry, he go to buy [opiates]; me, I go for them *Waseeyoo* girl. . . . And stay overnight, too. 'Cause you can't come back from Gardnerville same day. No, sir! 'Cause that's a long ride back on your horse, partner! So, bring grub when I go up there. . . .

'Cause I know I sure like them half-breed [Washo-Dutch] girl! Yes, sir! 'Cause nice-lookin', them kind *nomogwet*, I tell you, Mike! For change off. . . . Why I go there. . . . And you see what they're always sayin' to me: "*Mookoos skee'*"

So all I can say is "Hello" back. 'Cause I don't know what that means. No, sir! And so they laugh when I say that. So I have to ask my *Waseeyoo* grandma what that mean. And she tell me, all right. Say, "'I got big *mookoo'!*"

'Cause them half-*Waseeyoo* girl, they also can say to me: "*Pa'leeyoo meho mookoos taleeyalee?*" Paiute: 'You got a big *peetho'o?*" And so, I have to say back, "*Waseeyoo salum teeveets!*" Washo girl: 'You got a big pussy!'

Make fun that way, you know. . . .

61. Ranch Work in Mason Valley

So when I start to go with them city girl[s], I just go crazy! Yes, sir! Don't even wanna go home when I come down here [Mason Valley] to work. . . .

No steady work down here, neither. Lotta small ranch in this [Mason] valley—not like Smith Valley where there's big ranch, steady work . . . like I already told you. Still, one year, I know I work pretty near all over this valley, partner! On them hayin' jobs, mostly. . . . You know, one week here, another there. . . . 'Cause you gotta keep lookin' for another job in this valley. Yes, sir! Keep on doin' that, and so maybe they can ask you to irrigate [if] they know you? 'Cause I'm even workin' right here [Campbell Ranch]—the old Miller-Lux Ranch. For them two Swede.

'Cause them two guy, they're workin' [leasing] Willy Penrose's place. But they're mean guy, them two! Yes, sir! Both! 'Cause you see why? Won't pay! No, sir! Say they ain't got money, then say they're gonna have to pay by check. And so, when I do ask for my money, why, one 'em say he's gonna cut my throat [if] I ask again! And so, Willy Penrose, he put up that money! Yes, sir! Tell 'em [Swedes] to pay him instead. And so, after that, I know I ain't gonna work for 'em no more. No, sir! [Even] seen 'em lookin' for men—for their second crop; but I won't go. Hell, no! [I] go to work for Willy Penrose instead. . . . Good man, Willy Penrose. . . . Then after Willy, I can work for George and Henry Keema . . . them two brother. 'Cause their ranch is the other side Scieroni [Ranch]. And same way, too, I know I can also work for Jim Lancester. . . .

'Cause you see what I'm doin'? I can start in Mason [town], work my way ranch to ranch in this valley till I get to Wabuska. . . . But the Old Man, he come lookin' for me—to bring me back home to Smith Valley. Say how my mom miss me too much. . . . So, want me to go back home. And so I do, too . . . go back home.

62. My Wife

And I'm around about thirty-five when I get marry. . . .

'Cause I know I try to get Florence Brown to marry me before that. But she say she won't marry no *taivo!* (Say she already's marry to my cousin-brother, Charley Brown, so she's my relation. . . . 'Cause Big Mack and Old Man Brown, they're cousin-brothers, you know. But me, I always say I don't care if Florence Brown's my cousin-sister. No, sir! 'Cause I wanna marry her!) And same way, too, I try to marry Addie Mason. But she honkey tonk with too many *taivo,* so I just quit her. 'Cause all her sister are [also] doin' that, too, by God! Even [if] they have a husband!

"*Ewa goomaga'yoo,* Addie!" what I'm always sayin' to Addie Mason: 'You got too many husbands!' 'Cause I'm afraid, you know. Afraid I might just get that [venereal disease if] I marry her. . . .

And you see how I'm first acquainted with my wife? Husband don't treat her good! No, sir! Always chasin' after women, that guy. Won't buy her no grub, so my wife, she [finally] quit him. Yes, sir! 'Cause that's all he want his money for: to buy *moohoo'oo* [yen-shee], and [to] treat them drinkin' women! And that's that Frank Jones, Big Mack's nephew: [His] father's marry to the Old Man's sister. . . . That Johnny Jones . . . [who] marry both them sister. . . . 'Cause I know him [Frank Jones]! We visit Frank and my wife all the time. . . . Marry to Irene Thompson's mother [Sadie Mitchell] after he leave my wife—make Clarence Brown with her. . . . Yes, sir! Bad fellow, that one! *Ste'yoo!*

And Frank Jones, he's maybe one year younger than my wife? Leave her at Mack Wilson's ranch in Mason all the time, so my wife's mad. 'Cause you see why? She has to take care Frank Jones's grandfather and grandmother. Both! Doin' that all the time [i.e., drinking and carousing], you know; then he can come home broke. And so, my wife, she [finally] leave him. Yes, sir! Get a hotel job in Mason; stay there with Gus Brann's sister, that Judy Dyer—after she leave the whore house in Yerington. 'Cause you see why? They're cousin-sister, my wife and Judy Dyer. Then my wife go to live [marries] with Teddy Pitts. . . . But he also die on that big flu [1917], so my wife get with Tom Mitchell's boy, Yankee. He's also a *moohoo'oo* man, Yankee Mitchell: same as Frank Jones. And so she quit him, too. 'Cause Yankee [also] only wanna spend his money on that dope business! They're livin' on Charley Perry's Ranch that time . . . in East Walker. And so, my wife, she go to live with her brother next: with Andy Dick, in Smith Valley.

Say, when she's a small girl, my wife come up from Sweetwater to Smith Valley to live. . . . Got the same father [Dick Bennett] and mother [Annie] like Andy Dick; different mother than Henry Dick, though. . . . 'Cause that old-timer [Dick Bennett], he's got two wife. . . .

And my wife's workin' for Macarini [Amos Mencarini] when I'm first acquainted with her. . . . Yes, sir! Weedin', sortin' potato . . . them kind job, anyway . . . in Mason Valley. 'Cause he's the first *Aytayay* to put potato in Smith Valley, by God! And so, Andy Dick's boy, Howard [Rogers], he say to me: "Uncle, you're gettin' old. Better get my *pahwa* [father's sister]! 'Cause pretty soon you won't be gettin' no more them young girl!"

And so, by God, I do that. Listen to him all right! Get tired them young girl after Rosie Conway spoil my best girl and go to Macarini's ranch to see her. . . . After my boss move to the other [Smith] valley.

'Cause you see what I'm doin' then? Have to buy my *heebee* [wine] from that *Aytayay*. Yes, sir! 'Cause that's Prohibition, partner: pretty tough to get drink them days! But them *Aytayay*, they can do that, you know. 'Cause you see why? Got special permit to bring their grape in from California. . . . To make that home brew. . . . And some, why, they sell to Indian. Yes, sir! Sell what they're supposed to be drinkin'! You know, to make more money that way! So anyway, after I buy my quart from Macarini, I tell him,

"Where's my *punee'ee*, Amos? Where's my old[er] sister?"

"Oh, she's workin', Corbett!"

And so I go over to see her. 'Cause I'm workin' at Charley Day's ranch that time . . . pretty close. . . . And so we get acquainted better that way. Yes, sir! 'Cause I know my wife a good long time before that: Janie, my sister, she marry my wife's brother, Henry [Dick]. . . . Anyway, I and my wife, we sure drink lot [then] together! Yes, sir! And sometime, too, why, I [even] stay overnight. 'Cause I'm always sayin' to her:

"I can sleep with you tonight?"

"No, Corbett," she say. "I'm too old!"

'Cause my wife, you see, she's way older than I am! Yes, sir! Maybe fifteen year? 'Cause she already know when I'm born, my wife. 'Cause when she's *nuumuurukai'i* [menstruation ceremony], that's when my wife say I'm born. And so that must make her fourteen, fifteen year older than I am, by God! But anyway, I stay with her at night. . .

'Cause you see how these Indian are [still] doin' that [marriage]: [if] you stay with your girl overnight, you're marry! Same way, too, [if] you wanna marry somebody, you're [also] supposed to give that girl's family somethin'. . . . But I know my grandma don't like what I'm doin'. No, sir! 'Cause you see why? [She's] cryin' all the time, 'cause my mom's already dead [after 1923]; so she miss her. Want me to bring my wife to her camp. . . .

"Where you sleep last night, Corbett?" what my grandma's always sayin' to me when I don't come home till next mornin'. Bawl me out good, too, you know!

"I sleep with this one woman who work for Macarini, *moo'a.*" So I can say back to her.

"Well, don't you know she's your wife, *moo'a?*" My grandma say right back. "Don't you know you're both my grandchildren? Marry her, Corbett; bring her here. That way, I can forget about my own *barruu* [daughter]."

Cryin' like that all the time, you know, 'cause she miss my mom. . . . And so I do: bring my wife home. 'Cause that's real old-time way to marry, you know . . . not on a license, just like a friend!

"You wanna make a home?" what I ask my wife. 'Cause you see why? She think my grandma don't like her. . . . Yes, sir! Why we have to sneak around. . . . 'Cause my wife's ashamed: think my grandma don't like her, on account she's way older than I am. Anyway, she [finally] say, "Yes!"

"Hello." Say that to my grandma, my wife. And so my grandma, she tell me:

"Now you don't have to be ashamed, Corbett!"

And quit cryin'. And so Big Mack, he give us his tent to live in. Yes, sir! Get work elsewhere.... And I and my wife, we been together ever since.

63. Celia Mack's Real Name

Three tent, that's how many we [extended family or "outfit"] got: my grandma and my young sister, they're in one; the Old Man, he got another; and I and my wife, we're in the third....

My wife, she never go to school. (Never go to church, neither.) No, sir! Don't talk too much English.... Don't explain her word [in English] too good.... But she's a real hard workin' woman, my wife, I tell you, Mike! Yes, sir! 'Cause no man can beat her on the job! Work just like a man! She can go out in the field and pitch hay, work any kind job, and beat the hell outta any man! 'Cause my wife, she [even] know how to handle a pitch fork.... And potato work, too, she can [even] help me to load them heavy sack—them 100 pound sack.... 'Cause that's the hardest job of all!

Seeya—what they call my wife.... Same way they call me *Qoobit*.... But you see how she's really named? "Cotton *porramoo*. Cotton Plum." Yes, sir! 'Cause, Hazel Quinn, she's the one tell me that. Never did tell, though, how my wife get that kind Indian name....

64. *Pash^p!* ('Childless!')

By old-time way, you know, you stay with a girl one year, why, you're gonna blow 'em up [impregnate her]; less, well, that don't count. And same way, too, they say your second kid, that one's not much work at all. No, sir! And say that the woman, when she got no more cherry [i.e., stops menstruating], that's when she's gotta quit [having sex]. 'Cause, otherwise, that baby's gonna come out dirty—all full that stuff [semen], you know. Same way, too, by old-time way, they don't [even] wait for that baby to come out. No, sir! Not like them *taivo* are doin', anyway.... 'Cause these Indian, they just push down on that belly! 'Cause I know when Margaret's [Corbett's stepdaughter is] gonna have that baby, I help my wife and *Apee*.... She's pullin', we're both pushin' ... put that cloth around Margaret's *natuu* [belly], then move that baby down.... And my wife, she [also] know how to cut and tie that *see* [umbilical cord], too. Yes, sir! Then we have to wait till that fall off: [either] throw it away afterward, or keep it for gamblin' luck. 'Cause [if] you're doin' that [i.e., saving it], you know, you have to hang it behind the baby's [cradleboard] hood. . . .

And gee, I know I sure wanna make a baby off my wife. But she don't wanna! Say to me,

"Corbett, maybe I'm a little younger, I can do that with you? But I'm afraid. Afraid, maybe, that baby won't pass out!"

'Cause you see why? When a woman's gettin' to be too old, why, that's pretty hard to do, partner. . . . You know, to push that baby out. . . . 'Cause I know Roy Sam, his mom's old already; so when he's born, why, they have to pull his head out. . . . Why he's not too smart. . . . 'Cause they pretty near pull Roy Sam's neck off when he's born, by God! Never seen him, Mike? Bald-headed guy: where your backbone and your neck is there's that lump. But not on Roy Sam. No, sir! 'Cause on him, it's way down! Yes, sir! Hollow guy. . . . *Khaishooname'yoo*. Don't know nothin'! Can't [even] learn nothin' in school! And he can't hear, neither. . . .

Anyway, my wife, she just make that one girl off Frank Jones, that's all—Margaret. Say she would have made more, too, [if] her husband treat her right. . . . 'Cause like I already told you, he's *ste'yoo*, that one: No good! Chase after women too much. . . . Why she don't wanna make no more baby! Quit it, you know, by Indian way. . . . Yes, sir! 'Cause you see what my wife's doin'? After Margaret's born, she can get *Atsa Hooweeda*, Red Ant. . . . 'Cause by old-time way, [if] a woman don't wanna make no more baby, why, she can just take that sack [amniotic sac] where the head pop out, put that upside down in their [Red Ant] house. (Call that sack *no'apoo*.) And same way, too, they say [if] you wanna make a baby after that [i.e., change your mind], you just have to talk to *Atsa Hooweeda*. . . . Yes, sir! Kill lotta them red ant; break off their *pigwuuda*, them stinger; then say to him: "I want another baby, *Atsa Hooweeda*. Help me!" And he listen all right! 'Cause by his *booha*, Red Ant can do that. . . . You know, to "open" that [buried] *noapoo!* Make you to have another baby. . . .

But you see what I think? I think her own father's doin' that [sterility magic] to my wife! That *Pavatyoo* Dick, Dick Bennett—call him *Tseyanamaqapa* by right name. . . . 'Cause you see why? After that first girl's born, my wife, she want a brother for Margaret; so she made a baby off this one *Aytayay* . . . Ambrose Quillici. . . . 'Cause he's that kind, you know, Ambrose: goes after them Indian women all the time. Sneak on 'em when they're workin'. 'Cause I know my wife, she always tell me that. Says when Ambrose Quillici's comin' along, woman's supposed to stand up that quick!

You know, to let him go by. . . . And Ambrose, he [also] make a baby off Judy Dyer—before she marry Henry Miller. . . . But that baby [also] die. So, anyway, my wife's father tell her,

"Don't make no more baby, 'cause you ain't even got no home!"

Not any good, that *poohaghooma* [Dick Bennett]! Don't even try to help a person. No, sir! 'Cause his own son tell me that. . . . Andy Dick. Say his father lose his *booha;* no good no more. So that baby Celia has with that *Aytayay,* he die in the cradle, and Dick Bennett carry him off. . . .

No'apoo, what we call them kind women—ones that make only one kid. 'Cause you see why? [We] always think they're doin' that [magic] with Red Ant. . . . And same way, too, I kind of think my mom fix my big sister that way; so Janie can't make no more baby! Same with my wife, too? 'Cause maybe she's workin' that kind on Margaret, too? 'Cause she's got four husband: Logan Williams, he's the first. He's drinkin' wine, Logan, and so, when he pass out and die pneumonia, Margaret, she marry Mike Pete. Then she can marry Leslie Quartz. Only thing is, that fellow drink all the time, too. Then, get into a fight in Yerington, and knock his head on the sidewalk; die, too. So, Margaret, she marry Jake Bypon. . . . And after that first baby she make, Margaret, she don't make no more for three year. . . . Then no more kid after them other three—that boy who never get marry; and Florence and Shirley. . . . Why I'm thinkin' maybe her own mother do that to her?

So maybe [if] my wife's a little younger she can do that with me? You know, talk to Red Ant. . . .

65. Marital Bliss

But that's one thing I know we never do is to fight! No, sir! 'Cause you see how some [couples] are? Always have to argue about somethin'! And especially when they're drinkin'. 'Cause I know I seen lotta them [married] people doin' that, that way: you know, sayin' how this one's goin' out with that woman. . . . Well, so then he can say how she's goin' out with that guy. . . . That way, you know, just to start thing up; then they can fight over that. And so, pretty quick, one's gettin' hurt. Yes, sir! Seen that lotta time. . . . But not us. 'Cause I and my wife, we're never doin' that. No, sir! No matter [even how much] we been drinkin' or usin' *moohoo'oo,* we always try to get along good. Yes, sir! Always talk good to each other all the time. You know, to get along better that way.

But I know one thing my wife don't like: me talkin' to Judy Dyer!

"*Yabbee meeyakwe*, Corbett! Come with me in a hurry!" what she always sayin' to me . . . whenever we come down here to Yerington on a visit. . . . Even though Judy's Henry Miller's wife that time. 'Cause she don't make no baby, Judy Dyer. No, sir! 'Cause can't! Went with too much big *peetho'o* when she's young, so, get that clap before she marry him or that other [second] husband. . . . One they call "Jack" [Brannigan], [whose] Indian name's 'Somethin' hanging on a stick on his back'. But he can't make nothin' with Judy, neither. No, sir! And gee, she sure is nice lookin' girl! All three Dyer girl. . . . Too bad I never fuck Judy, though. 'Cause I pretty near had a chance one time. . . .

'Cause you see what happen? Everybody's gone home for supper, and she's comin' up the road.

"What's the matter, Corbett? You don't like me?" Judy, she just call me that way. . . . Seen her on the highway near Macarini's place, and I know I sure want her. 'Cause that's the way she is, Judy: she can take any man! Same way, one time I'm with her sister and Judy want to join in. . . .

"What's the matter with mine, Corbett?" she tell me.

"But I like your *hama'a* [young sister Agnes, better], Judy," I say right back to her.

"But you gonna hurt my *hama'a*," she can [then] say. "Too small!" Yes, sir! Cause Judy Dyer wanna piece of me, partner! And take hold my *peetho'o*, too!

"No, I won't hurt her, Judy!" I say back. "Weenie's too small! Too small for you, too!" Only Judy can say right back:

"[Still] your weenie can tickle me!" Yes, sir! Always sayin' somethin' [nasty] to me when we come down here, you know. . . . So, gee, my wife, she sure get mad at that! Mad when I [even] talk to Judy Dyer!

66. Reflections on Bachelorhood

But I kind of think I don't get marry sooner on account I get mad too easy. Yes, sir! 'Cause you see why? [If] I see my girl with somebody else, I say:

"Go ahead! If that's what you like better!"

And just leave 'em alone!

5

Italians, Potatoes, Homemade Wine

(1923–58)

67. Them *Aytayay* ('Italians')!

'Cause there's no *Aytayay* in this country them early days ago, you know, just *taivo*, that's all. Yes, sir! And all kind, too: *D^tsaman* [Dutchmen]. . . . And so, after a while, them *Aytayay*, they also start comin' over here to America.

    'Cause I hear they come from Christopher Columbus country, them *Aytayay:* you know, after he discover this place called America. . . . 'Cause they're just like a Chinaman, them *Aytayay:* ain't got no woman! No, sir! And you see what they're doin'? They can work for somebody else, then pretty quick lease small place their own; then, by God, buy [land], and send back to their own country for *norr^gwa* [wife]! Yes, sir! Bring her over here to this country called America. . . .

    And before they come, too, no winter job these valleys, partner! No, sir! 'Cause that ranch work, that's only in the summer. Fellow can plow, plant, irrigate; cut and bail them three crop hay. And stack, too. . . . But no kind winter work at all! And same way with cattle drive . . . also [a] summer job. 'Cause short drive—that one's only four days. And none them old-timers like that other kind [long drive], neither. . . . No, sir! 'Cause they don't wanna stay away that long. . . . So anyway, when Charley Day quit, I know I go to work for his son [Harvey], [who] pay me three dollar a day and give me board, Harvey Day. But after that, no more ranch work, partner, so I start workin' for them *Aytayay*.

'Cause you see what they doin' all the time? Puttin' in row crop. Yes, sir! Potato, garlic, onion. . . . But mostly potato. And that's pretty steady work, potato work—all-year round job! *Tsopa*, how we call potato in our language. . . . And them *Aytayay*, they gotta hire bunch these Indian on that kind job. Yes, sir! Come around in their truck to hire. . . . Same way, too, Indian from Fallon can come up here for that kind work. But they don't hire no Mexican. No, sir! Don't [yet] take our work from us! But [even if] they do, we can't say nothin'. *Karroo'oo!* No, sir! Can't complain, 'cause you see why? They come here on contract work. . . . Same way with them Okie. . . . 'Cause they also work around here. Yes, sir! Come into these valley in old car, them Okie. Clothes all ragged, torn pants, torn shirt. . . . Look just about as bad as them *moohoo'oo* [opium] men! Yes, sir! Just like *toha wa'eets* [hobo]!

And potato work, why, it take ten to fifteen men three week to work forty acre. . . . Yes, sir! And that's six days every week, too, by God! 'Cause Sunday, you gotta rest. 'Cause you see why? Too tired! And them potato worker, they all get paid the same: two dollar a day. [That is] unless them *Aytayay* wanna get through quicker. . . . Then they can pay more. Or have to hire more Indian on that kind job. . . . Fall the year, that's harvest time. . . . Just startin' to get cold then. But you think they're gonna get some kind bunk house for them Indian? Hell, no! You gotta sleep outdoor! Bring along your own beddin'. . . .

Feed you three meal, them *Aytayay* . . . just like *taivo* [i.e., non-Italian alfalfa growers]. And feed you pretty good, too, by God! Especially [if] a Chinaman cook's workin' there. 'Cause then you eat best. But them *Aytayay* women, they don't like cookin'! No, sir! Not least what I seen, anyway. . . . So, always has to be a [Italian] man on that cookin' job, by God! But you think they're goin' to feed you Sunday? Hell, no! 'Cause Sunday, you gotta buy your own grub . . . even [if] you're workin' steady for 'em!

And so, after that harvest's done, well, them *Aytayay*, they can [also] hire you to grade potato. Yes, sir! 'Cause that's what I know I like, winter work! Been doin' that for Amos Macarini a good many year, partner. . . . Start soon as that buyer come around. . . . And same way, too, you gotta stay in them

Aytayay cellar on that kind job all winter long! Women, they sew them sack; the man has got to lift 'em onto that truck. 'Cause I know that's what I and my wife do for Macarini every winter.... Yes, sir! 'Cause take 350 sack to fill one [truck] load.... And that's pretty hard work, too, I'm tellin' you, Mike! Gee, your arm tired, leg get sore.... You can hardly stand afterward. And come springtime, why, that's when you have to do your plantin'. 'Cause by old-time way, we use six horse team on them potato: four on the inside, two the outside. Same way, too, we have to use that two-bottom plough. 'Cause that's pretty tough plowin'. 'Cause that's March, you know. Ground's still frozen. And them root, they get caught.... Make your blade to get dull. So I know I have to plow as deep as I can. Yes, sir! And add two more horse on the outside that team [as well].... Then after you're done plantin', why, that's when you can do irrigatin' work.

'Cause I know before I'm workin' for my boss, I irrigate for this other *Aytayay* all the time: Amos Quillici. [He's] got a *Nuumuu* wife [sic] cookin' for his potato crew, Amos. 'Cause he make a "friend" with Blind Bob's *barruu* [daughter], you know—that Shirley Bob: Hazel and Mamie Bob's young[er] sister. Afraid to talk her own language, though, Shirley ... 'Cause you see why? Left her own country for [Riverside] boarding school in California when she's young, so when Shirley come back, *karroo'oo!* Don't remember nothin'! 'Cause same thing happen to my wife's daughter—why my wife take Margaret outta Stewart.... Anyway, Amos Quillici, he come for me every day, to irrigate. And bring me home at night, too.

68. *Aytayay* Stinginess

And you see what I'm always doin'? After I'm finished hayin' work, I'm done stackin' that second crop for them Smith Valley *taivo* and come down to this [Mason] valley: work for them *Aytayay* ... where I meet my wife first time.... But [since] they don't pay much, them *Aytayay*, I know I [have to] fight like hell to get more from 'em! Why I like workin' for them *taivo* better....

'Cause I know I hear about this one *Aytayay* won't pay, so bunch them real old-timers, they grab hold his wagon and won't let go. No, sir! Say to him, "Better pay us!" And so he do, by God! Pay 'em in gold, too! And same way, too, them *Aytayay*, they're pretty tough boss! Yes, sir! Work you hard.... Too many hour; overtime, too. And don't pay too much, neither. . . . No, sir! Same way, too, they don't leave you alone. No, sir! Not like them *taivo* boss, anyway . . . [who] give you a job—your water for irrigation—then don't bother you at all. Not them *Aytayay,* though. . . . No, sir! 'Cause they always [also] wanna make you to do somethin' else. You know, to show you more work. . . . 'Cause you see why? They don't wanna see you standin' around. . . .

So, pretty tough boss, them *Aytayay,* I tell you, Mike! Work the hell outta man! And don't pay him right, neither! But [at least] they don't try to say nothin' rough to these Indian. No, sir! Can't! 'Cause they [we] can just walk away from that job. . . . Yes, sir! 'Cause these Indian, they're [also] pretty touchy: *Aytayay* get too rough, why, they gonna just strike. Leave that job and just walk away from it. . . . What I'm always doin', anyway. . . . And so, the boss, he can't say nothin' at all about it.

Yes, sir! Why these Indian don't like them *Aytayay* too much. No, sir! Why Big Mack won't work for 'em. . . .

But still, they're pretty good to 'em, them *Aytayay.* . . .

69. My Boss, Amos Macarini [Mencarini]

And I bet you I'm workin' for my boss over thirty year! And never miss a day's work, neither!

Already told you how I met him. . . . 'Cause Amos, he's the first *Aytayay* puttin' potato in Smith Valley! Yes, sir! Move up to Colony District from this [Mason] valley; lease Charley Hinds' Ranch . . . by that Hot Springs . . . thirty-five acre. 'Cause that's part the old [Frank] Simpson Ranch, you know. Amos Quillici, he try takin' that after my other boss [Hinds] quit. . . . ("One Gallon Too Many," that's what they call Amos Quillici. His own son give him that name!) So anyway, when he can't make it, my boss take over. And so, after Macarini's doin' good, Amos Quillici, he can rent Dr. Foster's [Smith Valley] land: start puttin' in potato there. And he do good there for around about ten years. . . .

But that's one thing I don't know: what year I go to work for Amos Macarini?

First ranch my boss is leasin' is the old Nordyke Place: Bill Wilson's place in Mason Valley, where Jack Wilson's raised. . . . 'Cause Bill and his brother Joe, they still run that [Nordyke] flour mill. And Macarini, he lease two, maybe three to four year in Mason Valley? Make a partner, you know, with his brother Colombo. . . . And so, one fall, I got no more ranchin' job in Smith Valley; hear about this one *Aytayay* in this [Mason] valley [who is] hirin' bunch them Indian for potato work. . . . So I come down here. Yes, sir! Go to work there for Macarini first time. . . .

'Cause I'm a young guy that time. . . . Way before I'm marry [pre-1923]. And when Macarini move up to Colony District, I don't work for him right away, neither. No, sir! 'Cause I rather work for them *taivo*. . . . So later on, that's when I do: start workin' for Amos Macarini up there first time . . . and get marry to my wife.

70. The Boss's Wife

I bet you my boss don't speak one word English when he's first startin' out! No, sir! Dumb, just like me before I went to Stewart, when I don't know nothin' yet. . . . And you see what he's doin'? Send his brother [back] to the Old Country for a wife. But Colombo, he's too much on the *yogho* [fornicating] side. Gets a dose that clap, so that woman, she marry Amos instead!

And you see what we call my boss's' wife? Name's "Paulina" by the right way, but we call her *Pava'yoo Tsaba'yoo* 'Big Ass'. Pretty lazy woman, too, that one, by God! Just wanna lay around in bed all the time when my boss first get her. And so, his brother Colombo, he's the one does all the cookin'. . . .

71. Working for Amos Mencarini

And that's one thing about my boss: you can't make him pay more higher! No, sir! 'Cause he's pretty cheap on the wage, I tell you, Mike! Like all them *Aytayay*. . . . Yes, sir! You just can't get nothin' [more] outta 'em [him]!

'Cause Macarini, he pay two dollar a day, that's all . . . twelve dollar a week. Same as the rest. . . . 'Cause that's wage, them days. And he pay by check, too . . . on Saturday night. Plowin', that's a long job. You gotta harrow in some place, disc when there's small rock. . . . But loadin' is the hardest job of all! 'Cause gee, you're sure sore after you're done on that. . . . Yes, sir! But that's the only way you can get your extra dollar, by God—on them hard job! Still, my boss is a tight son-of-a-gun. 'Cause you have to [practically] stick your finger up his *tsaboo* till he's gonna throw in that extra couple dollar more! And gee, I know I just about die when Macarini say,

"All right, Corbett. Make it four dollar a day!"

'Cause a fellow can get five dollar a day loadin' job for them *taivo* that time. . . . Yes, sir! And dependin' how many [hay] wagon you run, why, you can get more pay. Two wagon, maybe five dollar a day? But [if] you run three, well, then your worth is seven dollar a day. 'Cause me, I know I do that by myself . . . run three wagon. . . . Make more money that way. . . . But that's way later on. . . .

72. Life on the (Potato) Plantation

So that's all we're doin' all winter long is gradin' them potato. Yes, sir! 'Cause you gotta grade 'em pretty careful, you know—'cause [of] them eatin' worm in there. . . . Some kind worm with green head, anyway. . . . 'Cause them inspector, they're always watchin' for that kind. Don't want 'em, so you gotta watch for that kind. Yes, sir! Can't let 'em pass through. And so we put that kind [of potato] in different sack. . . . What they call number two [second grade]: sell that cheaper around here. 'Cause you see why? They can't ship no bad spud to California. No, sir! Inspector won't let 'em through. . . . Then my wife can sew up them sack and I load 'em for buyer. And same way, too, her daughter's there with us. . . . help us out . . . till Margaret marry. And sometime, too, my boss can hire two more to do that sortin' work.

But pretty heavy liftin' them sack, partner! Yes, sir! 'Cause 360 sack for one load! And you do that all day, pile 'em five high, so by evening, why, you walk like this. . . . Can't hardly straighten up at all! Feel pretty tired, I tell you, Mike! You know, from doin' that all the time. Every day, every day. . . . And don't [even] change [jobs] with nobody, neither! 'Cause [if there are] two Indian, well, they can do that [exchange jobs]: you know, one can work that fork—that's the woman job—the other can do the [actual] liftin'. But [if] that other fellow don't want no heavy work, why, you gonna do it all yourself. . . . And all winter long, too, by God! So pretty tired toward quittin' time . . . [at] half past five. . . .

And them *Aytayay* cellar, gee, pretty dark! Nowaday, they got light in 'em, back then, not. . . .

Italians, Potatoes, Homemade Wine (1923-58)

And you see what else we're doin'? Pick out them seed for plantin'. Yes, sir! Separate what's good from no good, put that kind out for their hog feed.... 'Cause some potato, you know, they got a little sprout. No good, so you gotta throw 'em away.... Know what's good or not by that sprout, you know.... How tall's that sprout.... 'Cause April tenth, that's plowin' time. Macarini, he want me to plow thirty-five acre, sometime forty.... 'Cause soon as that ground warm up, why, I can plow again....

One man job, plowin'.... I do that.... You gotta disc some place; some, you harum[-scarum] plant them potato seed and take care 'em all summer long.... Help also on what hay he's got.... Then after that third crop [of alfalfa], why, we can dig 'em up [potatoes]. And it takes two to three week—depend how many acre; how many Macarini hire in that crew.... Then I and my wife, we go out after pine nut. Stay up there, them mountain, one month ... till we call our boss; tell him to come get us. 'Cause we're usin' Warren Simpson's phone—Desert Creek Ranch. 'Cause [if] we get lotta pine nut, why, Macarini's gotta come haul us. You know, to start sortin' potato again; all winter long....

Pretty hard work, potato job, I tell you, Mike!

Already told you how my boss make his brother do all the cookin.... 'Cause, Paulina, she don't wanna do that. No, sir! Too damn lazy! Well, same way, too, Macarini, he's too cheap to hire Chinaman! 'Cause [if] they do hire Chinaman cook, why, you eat good! Anyway, breakfast, we get at 7:00 A.M.—so we can be out in the field by 7:30 A.M. And half past eleven, why, that's quittin' time for lunch. (Pretty near five hour, ain't it?) And they give you a real meal, noon meal, them *Aytayay*. Yes, sir! Then you can rest till 1:00 P.M.; 'cause then you're back on that [potato] job again—till half past five, partner. Till my boss say,

"Come on in for your supper!"

'Cause you see what we're doin'? I and my wife, we eat with 'em. Yes, sir! Three time every day! But not when they hire potato crew.... No, sir! 'Cause, then, we just gotta eat with the rest them Indian. Sunday, though, no board.... No, sir! Not even [if] it's just I and my wife. 'Cause then we gotta cook for ourself. But maybe Macarini can sell us somethin' on Sunday [if] we wanna buy? An egg? Somethin' like that, anyway.... Or my boss can take us to town to buy grub Sunday....

But that's one thing I know I sure don't like, that *Aytayay* food. No, sir! 'Cause you see why? Too greasy! 'Cause they're always puttin' too much that greasy stuff [olive oil] on their kind cookin'! Yes, sir! Same way, too, chicken, that's all what Macarini's always puttin' out for board! 'Cause I know I get so goddamn sick eatin' chicken, don't even wanna take another bite of one.... Why I bawl my boss's wife out....

'Cause she can speak our language, you know. Little bit, anyway. And that's on account my wife. 'Cause she teach her that, all right! Paulina can say, *"Hanoo heebee,* Corbett? Where's your drink?" Or say to me, "How *managwee tsopeegee nuuma?* 'How am I feelin'? [head hurts? i.e., hung over?]. 'Cause Sunday, you know, we drink all day long! And sometime, too, we see my boss's wife hung over.... So anyway, this one time, I tell my wife:

"Macarini can kill a hog! For sausage! 'Cause I'm sick of chicken!"

Yes, sir! What I say to my wife. And tell her, too:

"Let's go over to Amos and get bologna. Fry that [instead] to eat!"

And so, by God, that's what we do: go over to my boss's house, bother him by that way.... 'Cause that's on a Sunday morning, you know. No work that day.

"Wanna buy some sausage, Paulina!" Talk tough to her, you know.

"Still too new, Corbett; don't taste good yet. Too fresh. Not good time to eat that yet," she say back. "Eat chicken instead!"

"To hell with chicken, Paulina!" so I tell her. "Been eatin' that kind every day on the board! Too goddamn sick to take a bite! Even to look at chicken!"

Yes, sir! What I say to Paulina! And by God, she don't answer me back, neither. No, sir! Don't say nothin' to me, 'cause you see why? Can't! 'Cause don't know what to say!

"All right, Corbett, I can cut you a piece...."

And so, that's what she do, too, by God: cut a piece that [fresh] bologna [sausage] for us. 'Cause they're real good when they're fresh that kind.... 'Cause I know we like to fry that all the time....

73. One *Nuumuu* Death, One Bunkhouse

[But] come harvest time, my boss, he [ordinarily] has to hire a crew. Yes, sir! Go around in his Model T Ford and hire eight, maybe nine Indian that time.... Can't feed more than that, you see. And if not enough in the other [Smith] valley, why, Macarini come down to this one [Mason Valley]. Or he can go to Schurz [the Walker River Reservation].... You know, see who wanna work there? Same way, too, lotta them Indian, they already have a car them days; so they can [also] go around. You know, see who's lookin' to hire?

But you see what Macarini's doin'? Make 'em [those he hires] to sleep outside! Yes, sir! And that's fall the year, partner, pretty cold! Damp, too, sleepin' on that ground! 'Cause only way later my boss, he get a bunk house. Yes, sir! Buy that from this one *taivo* whose sellin'.... Move it right by that highway. And that one's [even] got separate room for them young girl.... But you see why Macarini buy that house? On account that one girl who die.

Name's Annie Dugan, and I hear she catch cold sleepin' way out in the brush like that. But still, she keep on workin'; never wanna quit. And so, finally, they have to take her to the hospital in this [Mason] valley. But she die, anyway.... Guess she can't afford no tent; and no time to make a tule house, neither. 'Cause Annie Dugan, she bring her own blanket for beddin'.... Use *sawabee* [sagebrush] to make a fire. But that's not enough.... No, sir! Should have had a tent....

Anyway, after that happen, we all stay in Macarini's barn [bunkhouse] potato time. Yes, sir! Pack us in to sleep just like a hog....

74. Our Own House to Live in

'Cause like I already told before, my wife, she work for Macarini a good many year before I do. You know, pullin' weed, and in on the harvest.... And sortin' potato on that electric grader every winter for him.... Yes, sir! All them kind potato job.... And she follow Macarini from this valley when he move to Colony [District of Smith Valley].... Gotta furnish her own house, though. 'Cause you see why? Them *Aytayay*, they won't do that. No, sir! Too cheap! Then we get together and wanna live in that [vacant] bunk house—instead of walkin' to his ranch every day from where we're livin'—so, Macarini, he won't let us! No, sir! 'Cause afraid, maybe, we're gonna burn that down. You know, get drunk, then one of us can pass out and start a fire that way.... So that's not until I quit him before my boss build that other house for us....

Never seen it, Mike? Not any bigger than this room [eight feet by ten feet]! No, sir! Got [only] one window in it, too.... Pretty small house, ain't it? Same size as that *kweeda nobee* [outhouse] Macarini [also] give us to use! Can't even fit this here spring bed in! Just enough room for two in that cabin.... And no insulation, neither.... So we pretty near freeze to death wintertime! Then way later, Macarini's daughter, she give us a bed.... double bed. But we already have small cookin' stove inside—one I bought off Mike Wallace: cast iron top, bottom's just tin, so we can cook on that kind—so there's no room for that bed. And so we just do it old-time Indian way. You know, put our mattress down on the floor near that stove; then we can have little more room to move around....

And Macarini, he don't charge rent, neither. No, sir! 'Cause you see why? [We] ain't [even] got no kind light in that house! No, sir! 'Cause [if] we want that, my boss, he say we gotta pay for that wire.... Pay for that post, too.

"Well, goddamn, Amos: you build that little cabin on the hill for us, why don't *you* run electricity?" I tell him. But you think he's gonna do that? Hell, no! Too tight! 'Cause that's the way them *Aytayay* are....

"Hell, that's your cabin, Corbett!" My boss, he tell me right back.

"Why I'm gonna put that electricity in for, Amos? [It's] your goddamn cabin!" So I can say right back to him.

"Well, you better do that, Corbett. [If] you want that!"

"Hell, you won't do that, Amos, [then] we can use lantern!" what I say back to my boss all the time. Hell, 'cause I don't even own it! And that house ain't too far from the boss's house, neither. No, sir! 'Cause you see why? No runnin' water inside; we have to pack our drinkin' water from there. [But] to wash them dish, our clothes, why, we get that [water] from the irrigation ditch. Still, we're not like them real old-time Indian.... No, sir! Don't take a *kweeda* [defecate] way out in the sagebrush, throw dirt at our *tsaboo* to clean ourself after! No sir! 'Cause like I say, we [also] got our own *kweeda nobee* [outhouse]!

75. The Real Deal

But you see what we're [really] doin?' I and my wife, we don't go by wage. No, sir! 'Cause we're always [getting paid] with *heebee* [wine]!

'Cause you see what them *Aytayay* like doin'? They can put that [Mason] jar down with every meal; serve you [wine] by the glass when you eat. And so, every time you do [drink] that, why, your boss, he's gonna write you down. Don't have to pay you by wage then.... No, sir! But still, you gotta call for that.... 'Cause, otherwise, they don't give you any *heebee*.

'Cause I know that's what my boss is always doin' to us. Yes, sir! And his wife, Paulina, she can write down every time we drink. We're only makin' two dollar a day, still they charge twenty-five cent by the glass. So that come to seventy-five cent a day, partner! Then in the evenin', we buy one quart from Mencarini.... Charge two dollar for that....

Yes, sir! What I and my wife are always doin'.... Why she work for Macàrini before me.... And so, after we're marry, I'm doin' the same! So we just earn enough to buy our own clothes ... and grub on Sunday ... my tobacco, too. 'Cause all that money's [only] for one thing: *heebee*. Unless we're usin' *moohoo'oo*.... 'Cause that way [i.e., opiate addiction], we're not gonna take that glass wine from Macarini. No, sir! Just workin' then to make money to buy dope [instead]! And [that's] how come I never did earn any [much] money from my boss.... No, sir! But I never did miss a Monday's work, neither! 'Cause even [if] I'm hung over, [I] always have to show [up] Monday mornin'! 'Cause otherwise, my boss, he can fire me!

76. Homemade *Aytayay* Wine

And pretty near all them *Aytayay* doin' that, you know: sellin' that homemade wine to these Indian. Yes, sir! 'Cause I know my boss do. And Amos and Angelo Quillici.... [Why,] even Fred Fulstone wanna get in on that wine business, but [his wife] Dr. Mary, she won't let him. No, sir! Make him to quit. 'Cause that's durin' Prohibition, you know: government let them *Aytayay* to do that [make homemade wine].... Why pretty near all these Indian around here [are] workin' for them kind. So they can buy their *heebee* from 'em! And same way, too, [if] you don't drink, [if] you're usin' that *moohoo'oo*, why, you still can work for them *Aytayay*, 'Cause you see why? They always keep cash on hand; [so you can] buy your dope more easy that way. 'Cause them Chinaman, they don't want check, and [if] you can't buy, why, you're just gonna have to tough it out.

And you see what else I'm doin'? Helpin' my boss on that *heebee* business....

'Cause Macarini, he's got a machine for that kind.... Two roller for makin' *heebee*. One person, he can turn it. And that stuff go into some kind big drum.... Big tank, he's got. Pretty near as big as this room! Over my head, anyway, that tank! You know, tank to ferment in. Then Mencarini, he put it in that wooden barrel he's [also] got—for storage, you know. And to buy them grape, why, he go over to California. Yes, sir! Buy by the ton with that special government permit he got . . . in Placerville. Then has to haul 'em back himself. . . . 'Cause that's where I hear they're growin' them kind grape, you know: California. . . . And [if] you haul 'em yourself, why, that's a whole lot cheaper! Same way, too, [if] they're gonna sell to these Indian around here, they're gonna have to bring back great big truckload!

And they don't sell that first grade, neither. No, sir! 'Cause them *Aytayay*, they keep that for themself. And don't throw away that mash, neither. . . . 'Cause that's what they're sellin' to these Indian. [So] just add sugar, you know; sugar and yeast to that mash; sell to these Indian. But you see what's wrong with that? Ain't got enough kick! No, sir! Can't [even hardly] get drunk on that! 'Cause not enough alcohol, partner. . . . Too mild that second grade. . . . Pretty near same as this kind wine [Tavola Red] I'm always drinkin'. . . . Call it "table wine." No kick like that first grade, anyway, 'cause I know it don't get me too drunk too easy, that *Aytayay* homemade wine. No, sir! Not [really] enough alcohol in it, that's why.

'Cause I know I drink one quart that first grade *Aytayay* wine, well, that's all it take! And we sure gotta cry around lot to get my boss to sell us that! Yes, sir! And sometime, too, Macarini, he mix both kind—that first with second grade; sell that instead. . . .

"Well, don't you know I'm payin' for it, Amos!" What I'm always sayin' to my boss. Bawl him out good, you know. Just to get that better kind. . . .

And gee, they sure make lot off these Indian, them *Aytayay*! Yes, sir! 'Cause what they're supposed to throw away, they put [serve] on the table. . . . But I hear in California, what cost two dollar a gallon here, cost you only sixty cent there. . . . So pretty cheap, them *Aytayay*. And not supposed to bootleg, neither. No, sir! But still they do. And drink their own wine, just like water. . . . But they don't drink with us. No, sir! Don't try to bunch up with these Indian and drink together. . . . And don't try to treat, neither. . . . Don't put no pitcher down on the table and say, "Come on Corbett, let's drink!" 'Cause they don't wanna throw away [even] one glass, by God! Jeez, they're sure tight by that wine! And them *Aytayay*, they don't try to get drunk, neither. No, sir! 'Cause only these Indian do: drink, you know, till they fall down. . . . 'Cause them *Aytayay*, they just drink that first grade to feel good. . . .

77. Bootleggin'

[And] only one *Aytayay* don't charge at all! Just set that pitcher down on the table, and whoever want some, why, he can take.... You know, to drink with when he eat.... Only one I see doin' that! 'Cause I know I used to work for that *Aytayay*—in Colony [District of Smith Valley]. All the rest, though, they do: charge you by the glass....

Or they can sell us that third grade wine, too; that brandy.... What they call "droppo." 'Cause you see what they're [also] doin'? Add lotta sugar and yeast and water to that mash, make that other kind that way ... what this one *Aytayay* at Colony [District] I used to work for is doin', anyway—one [who] don't charge at all ... [who] just serve you that other kind [droppo]. And however many glass you want, too....

Mike Sava and he bootleg, too. 'Cause Mike, he send for them dry grape to Hudson: soak 'em in water, then add sugar and yeast; boil it up and sell at that Hot Springs. 'Cause I know I used to go to Hudson to get them grape for him—Hudson, that's back of Nordyke, you know. And Mike Sava, he's got a cook at that Hot Spring. *Khaishooname'yoo!* 'Cause you see why? She drink lot, and so Mike, he's gotta watch her all the time. Yes, sir! Watch her, else she'll drink all that up! And so I know when I eat, Mike can watch her; then when he wanna eat, well, so I can watch. And they can sure fight, them two. Yes, sir! Fight [if] Mike don't give her drink! 'Cause if not, why, she drink lemon or vanilla extract. Yes, sir! Fight all the time, them two! 'Cause one time, they [even] fight in her room, and so that woman, she call me to help....

Same way, too, them bootlegger can [also] make wine from chokecherry.... From that *to'eeshaboowee*. And Mike Sava [also] make whiskey from *wuyoopoowee*, buckberry. Call that kind "jackass." Yes, sir! Keep his still way up in back Colony [District], Mike Sava—in the mountain. Bring that kind [jackass] down to that Hot Spring he's runnin' every Saturday night, and, by God, never get caught! 'Cause you see why? Mike Sava, he smart!

And same way, too, I know this other *taivo* [who] also make jackass all the time: Mac MacFarlane. Live way up in the mountains, Mac MacFarlane ... behind Colony District. (House at the end the canyon, near the spring.) But most the time, Mac MacFarlane, he [also] bring that *heebee* down to the Hot Spring on Saturday: you know, to sell to them *taivo*. But he can [also] sell to these Indian. Yes, sir! 'Cause I know him! I'm always up there, you know, gettin' wood for some *taivo*, and so I get [buy] glass jackass from Mac

MacFarlane. (Charge four bit, 'cause that's powerful stuff! You drink one glass, why, you feel like you're up in the air. Tiredness is all gone. . . .)

And them dry days [Prohibition], too, we can buy home brew [beer]. 'Cause that one they also bootleg. [They] use Blue Ribbon can for that kind. . . . 'Cause Amos Quillici, he do that—on this one white guy's ranch, Paul Regley. 'Cause Amos, he make both: home brew [beer] and that jackass. Yes, sir! And that's before he has his own ranch and is marry to Shirley Bob. . . . 'Cause he don't do anythin' but peddle then, Amos Quillici. No, sir! Just stay at that ranch and do that. . . . And so these Indian, why, they pile into his house to get some. 'Cause I know I always go. (Charge twenty-five cent on a pint.) The Old Man, though, he don't. 'Cause you see why? Stop drinkin' when my mom die. . . .

But you see what's different? In this [Mason] valley, these Indian can tell [inform] on who's sellin'; [in] Smith Valley, not! 'Cause you see why? Them government bull, they won't arrest there!

78. Indian Bootleggers

Only two Indian are doin' that [i.e., bootlegging] in Smith Valley, you know: Mike and Maddie Rube. . . . *Waseeyoo* [Washo Indians].

'Cause they live by that airport, them two: Maddie, she's half [Washo]. 'Cause her father's Ben Rube, from Coleville. And Mike and Curly Rube, they're sellin' *moohoo'oo* later on. . . . [They] wanna kill their uncle, Mike and Curley Rube, but kill their father instead! In Topaz. So both go to Folsom Prison. . . . Curley Rube, he's sheepherder; Mike work for Fred Fulstone. Went to Stewart and drink, then later on Mike get religion. . . . Eddie Mack's marry to their sister [Lucille Rube] for one year. . . . So anyway, Mike and Maddie Rube have a still. But make it most for their own use. . . . 'Cause Mike Rube, he's a heavy drinker. Yes, sir! Drink, and he never wanna quit! A drinkin' man, Mike Rube. But never mean. No, sir! Talk good all the time . . . laugh and joke a lot. . . . Nice man, Mike Rube. . . . 'Cause I know him! [I] used to buy beer from his wife—from Mattie Rube. From her and her other sister, Etta. Charge me twenty-five cent a pint. . . . Anyway, them days, Indian like whiskey better than that home brew or *Aytayay* wine. . . .

79. How I Learn to Drink?

Nowaday, though, too many drunkard in Yerington. . . . Yes, sir! Spoil everythin'. . . . 'Cause they get drunk, you know, and wanna fight. But I know when I'm young, hardly nobody's doin' that! No, sir! Just havin' fun, that's all: hunt, gamble, ride, dance. . . . 'Cause them days, they gamble on the weekend and don't drink. Nowaday, the opposite: just drink on the weekend, and don't gamble. Don't do nothin' else!

'Cause I know first time I see that [drunkenness], I sure get scared. Yes, sir! 'Cause Buckaroo George Walker and Old Man Keno, they're the one doin' that, by God! Drink, and get up on their horse; run through them gambler in Smith Valley. . . . Scare everyone out. 'Cause they're pretty rough, them two, I tell you, Mike! Yes, sir! Just like *pakyera* [cowboy]! And so, one time, Old Man Keno [even] ride his horse onto Reading's porch. . . . The Old Man, too, he get drunk and raise heck! Get on his horse and do fancy turn; ride through where people like to gamble and scatter 'em. . . . But I never seen Big Mack really drunk, though. You know, staggerin' around, fallin' down, can't stand up. . . . 'Cause he just drink to feel good, that's all.

And you see how I learn to drink? My boss on that cattle drive! Yes, sir! 'Cause he always let me to drink with him. . . . And that's that whiskey, you know, not homemade *Aytayay* wine. 'Cause that kind's pretty strong stuff, by God! Nobody can't drink too much [whiskey] without getting drunk! 'Cause my boss, you know, he buy by the case. And so, we drink all the way up to Leavitt Meadow. . . . Say to me,

"Drink some, Corbett! 'Cause you won't get tired on your horse!"

And so, by God, I do; try that. And gee, I sure like it! So when I come back, I let my mom to smell that kind. But she won't try it, neither. No, sir! 'Cause none them old-timers like that, you know. 'Cause I know my grandma, she never get drunk. Never even did try to drink once, my grandma! My mom, though, she drink some. . . . Like I already told you, just to feel good . . . try what the Old Man sometime drink . . . what they call "home brew," that jackass whiskey. . . . Yes, sir! And she can drink with Big Mack when he work at that Hot Spring in Smith Valley. . . . 'Cause I kind of think that's when the Old Man's doin' that, you know: start in to argue with my mom about thing long gone when he drink—"You been goin' with that *taivo*, that's how you make Corbett!" That kind, you know! But one thing I know, I never did get drunk with Big Mack. No, sir! 'Cause he drink alone! Anyway, I don't drink much them days, my early day. . . . No, sir! 'Cause you see why?

I'm single, so I work and bring my bottle home Saturday night. Drink all day Sunday, too....

80. Hard Drinkin'

Then when I [really] start drinkin', I can drink with Jess Reymers. 'Cause Jess, he's a real good partner that time.... Yes, sir! Been to that First German War, Jess, and so, when he come back, that's all he wanna do is to drink, drink, drink! 'Cause we're always buyin' a bottle together, I and Jess Reymers. "Let's get a drink, Corbett!" Yes, sir! what he always sayin' to me. And so, any kind Big Doin' that's goin' on ... Fourth of July, well, so we can always find each other and go out drinkin' together. 'Cause Jess, he throw away all his money after that, you know. Drunk all the time! (He's my cousin-brother, Jess Reymers: marry Tom Mitchell's daughter, Amy. And that's all they do is to drink!) And same way, too, Jess Reymers' boys, that's all they wanna do! All except Ed Reymers.... 'Cause they never even try to make their own house, them boys. No, sir! Just throw that away on that booze; just like their *na'a* [father].... And Jess Reymer's daughter, too ... Eva and Iva.... 'Cause Iva, she marry my *nanagwa* [nephew] Jackson [Sam]. [He] used to buck hay in Smith Valley, then they start drinkin' and fightin'; Jackson, he steal a car and go to prison; welfare has to take away them boys....

And my cousin-brother, Henry Quinn, he's same way.... Drink all the time! 'Cause, Henry, he work for Fred Fulstone. One time, Henry break into this one *Aytayay* cellar—for wine, you know; so he get one year [in jail] for that. Only thing is, [his] heart don't work right when he drink, so when Henry come out and start in to drink again, he get sick and can't breathe right; so he die. And same way, too, Hank Bender. 'Cause he's marry to Ida Wilson, Hank ... to Jack Wilson's daughter. Before she get with Pete Penrose. Real name's *Skeegee*, Hank Bender. (*Skeegee*, that's 'Guttin' a Rabbit'.) Older than I am, Hank Bender.... Drink and steal wheat from this one grocer and get caught.... Then Hank Bender do it again, by God! And you see how he die? Poisoned by this one *Aytayay* for what he done! Yes, sir! 'Cause you see what happen? Hank, he tell them government bull which one [Italian]'s sellin', so that one *Aytayay,* he get mad; poison his wine what Hank Bender's buyin' from him! Yes, sir! And same way, too, *Tsowee*—call him Old Man Pete; his wife's related to my grandma—he's another wino: drink, even though *Tsowee* is older than Big Mack! And every Saturday his wife's cryin' on the road. 'Cause you see why? She don't like her daughter. 'Cause that girl's stolen from *Aytayay* wine, you know! (Marry to Henry Quinn that time, and she drink with him and get poisoned; so her mother, she say to that *Aytayay:* "You killed my daughter, now, I wanna kill you!")

And so I'm drinkin', you know, before I start usin' that *moohoo'oo*....
And when I'm drinkin' steady, why, I can say to my mom:

"Give me money, so I can send [purchase alcohol] by *toha wa'eets* [hobo]!"

'Cause them hobo, you know, they start comin' around here, then. Always beggin': "We're hungry, partner. Got somethin' to eat?" And gee, they pretty near take our job from us! Anyway, [since] they can go to them bar, we do that: send by hobo.... Let them buy. 'Cause you see why? They [also] wanna make friend with us. And they got their own camp, too, them *toha wa'eets*—in Wellington. Yes, sir! Got a campfire to cook their soup. 'Cause they don't camp with us at all....

But you think my mom's gonna do that [provide money for drink]? Hell, no! Then after they open the bar for [to] these Indians [1953], I go there, all right; both I and my wife. Yes, sir! Go right up to that *taivo* bar [in Smith] and sit down; call for a drink. But you can't drink too fast in that bar. No, sir! 'Cause [if] you do, why, you're gonna get drunk! Anyway, that's not what I like. No, sir! 'Cause, me, I like to drink at home. Drink anytime I want to [at home].... And one right after another! 'Cause [at] that bar, you know, fellow's too much ashamed to stagger around like that.... Yes, sir! Same way, that bartender, he don't like that, neither. No, sir! [He] like to see you buy, but not doin' that.... [So] why I don't like goin' to that bar in Yerington, neither.... 'Cause too many wino botherin' a person there all the time....

And one time we're doin' that [drinking], you know, and Lilly Clay—she's my cousin-sister—Lilly tell me some girl's passed out by the slough in this [Mason] valley; I should go over there and make *yogho*. And so, by God, I do! Bust her cherry! Then you see what I'm doin'? Pack her to her house afterward! 'Cause that's that Mitchell girl, Minnie Mitchell.... And so, afterward, I tell her brother to put her to bed. But Lion [Gus Mitchell], he smell my breath. Say to me,

"You got a bottle, Corbett. Give me drink!"

'Cause you see what I'm doin'? After I'm finished workin' her over, why, I find bottle next to his sister: drink some, put the rest in my pants pocket. And so, when Lion find out, we both just drink the rest together. . . . But you see who's really doin' that to Tom Mitchell's daughter? Steve McCloud [Lilly Clay's brother]! Yes, sir! 'Cause he's the one doin' that to all them young girl in this valley. . . . You know, gettin' 'em drunk that way. 'Cause all them city girl, that's what they like doin' best, you know: drink and fly their dress around! Why Brady Emm's mother bawl out *Apee* one time. . . . Tell her,

"What kind *soowee* you got? Look what you done to your husbands!"

"Well, so they got no business marryin' me," *Apee* say back. "'Cause [if] they wanna die, they can marry me!"

'Cause I know my wife, she say some them drinkin' women are just that way—got somethin' in their pussy, and so they wanna give that to a man!

Anyway, that's one thing I know I don't want when I'm drunk: canned heat. No, sir! 'Cause one time, I seen this *toha wa'eets* [hobo] doin' that in Wellington: has a blanket on his back, and was shakin' bad after he drink that. . . . And same way, too, I won't go inside Tom Mitchell's gamblin' house when I'm drinkin'. No sir! 'Cause too much afraid that fellow. . . .

See, I and my wife, we never go crazy on drink. No, sir! 'Cause like I told you, my wife, she don't like passin' out like that. No, sir! Not like these crazy Indian women are doin'. . . . No, sir! Don't wanna do that, on account she don't want nobody to try and gang [rape] her. 'Cause that's what I'm afraid of, too, partner. . . . So [after I'm marry when], I see woman layin' out there in a ditch like that, I'm thinkin' she might just have that *qonoza* [clap]. Why I won't jump on [no more]. No, sir! 'Cause too much afraid them kind woman [then]. . . . So I and my wife, we just hold back on our drink. Same as we don't fight, neither, when we're drinkin'. No, sir! 'Cause like I already told you, we don't wanna put out no kind trouble. . . .

And so, that wine's [always] right there; so we can [always] buy from Macarini. Yes, sir! And don't have to ride around lookin' to buy, neither. Just buy from our own boss, that's all! And drink three time every day with our meal: breakfast, dinner, and supper. . . . What Macarini put out on the table. And night time, too, what we buy from our boss. . . . Same way, Saturday night, we buy from Macarini [also] . . . and drink all day Sunday. 'Cause lotta them wino, they come over and we bunch up. . . . Yes, sir! So, pretty much the same as that dope, that drinkin' business. . . . But that's way later on. . . .

Italians, Potatoes, Homemade Wine (1923-58)   127

81. One Time, Though . . .

One time, though, I and my wife, we kind of go wild by that [drink]!
    'Cause we're with Pete Penrose's daughter and her husband that time. . . . One they call *Soonoo* Ida, 'Snow' Ida. . . . And that's around about October . . . potato diggin' time. *Uudzuudzuu*, partner, cold; so we just have to build fire. And so, when we finish that [wine], well, somebody say: "Better buy some more!" And so, Gus Brann, he's with us; 'cause he's workin' for Francis Kinney, then, and so, Gus, he say we should go buy from him [Kinney]. 'Cause you see why? Macarini, he won't sell us no more. No, sir! But Francis Kinney's not sellin', so we remember who else is doin' that.
    "Better go to Amos Quillici's place!"
    Yes, sir! 'Cause somebody say that. Remember that, you know. . . . 'Cause he's got his own still, Amos—make home brew that way. And that's maybe four-five miles from where we're drinkin'. . . . And so we do that, too . . . buy from Amos. Then I and Gus Brann, after we finish that, why, we go to another *Aytayay* to buy . . . to Joe Vacini; to buy jackass from him. And so, after that, we go back to Macarini's—to look for can to divide up what we buy. But *Soonoo* Ida, she drink that all up! Yes, sir! My boss, he find out; chase us outta his barn. 'Cause we're makin' too much noise, he say. Say, [if] we drink there, we might just burn it up! So anyway, when we finish that, Ida, she pass out, and her husband, he pull off her dress: want us to gang her! But my wife say "No!" And so I have to pack her! Ida's naked, you know, but too heavy. So I leave Ida. And so, when I do, my wife, she bawl me out:
    "You kill my *hama'a!*" What my wife say . . . "Kill my younger sister!"
    Blamin' us, you know, 'cause *Soonoo* Ida won't wake up. And so I'm ashamed. . . . [I] go home to get my wife's daughter's husband—think Mike Pete can help me pack *Soonoo* Ida Penrose home. 'Cause, otherwise, she might catch pneumonia and die. Besides, she's got a weak heart. Still she drink all the time [too]. . . . 'Cause you see why? Don't care to live no more. No, sir! Just that kind woman, you know: made that one kid [Mike Wallace] off her first husband [Joe Brown], but that boy's grandfather, he raise him . . . that *Kuurrosee* Sam Wallace. 'Cause *Soonoo* Ida, she don't wanna take care that boy. No, sir! Always drinkin' and out lookin' for a man! Then she's marry to Mack Paddy—before Andrew Penrose take her away from him. . . . Crooked one, that guy, Andrew! Go to prison for murder. Always braggin', too: "I'm way older than my *norr^gwa* [wife]!" Even though he's way younger than *Soonoo* Ida! Anyway, she get Billy Schurz for her husband,

too.... Then Billy Miller's next.... 'Cause I know I and my wife, that's who we're drinkin' with that time: Billy Miller and *Soonoo* Ida.... So, anyway, my wife's daughter, she [also] bawl me out that time.... On account what we're doin'.

82. Why Indians Drink?

To feel good, happy ... why these Indian drink so much.... Only thing is, they go too crazy on that! Yes, sir! Grab hold that bottle and drink [guzzle] quick.... And don't let go too easy, neither.... No, sir! Then they can talk about anythin'! Don't even know what-the-hell they're talkin' about, though, when they drink.... Just bullshit, that's all.... Drink crazy and pass out.... Like Andy [Dick].... 'Cause he's always talkin' about that minin' business whenever he drink—how he's gonna go prospectin' some day. Yes, sir! Go up in them mountain to prospect and find gold....

See, 'cause them wino, they don't never wanna quit, neither. No, sir! Just keep on doin' that, you know, till their boss is gonna fire 'em! Not like them *moohoo'oo* men, anyway.... But me, I know I don't do that.... No, sir! 'Cause we just drink heavy on Saturday night.... And all day Sunday, too. But never miss Monday's work, though, by God!

6

Chinese Opium (1896–1931)

83. *'Oopeey^n* ('Opium')

'Cause even though I'm drinkin', I know I [also] start in to smokin' that *moohoo'oo* right after I'm back from Stewart. Yes, sir! But not heavy, you know. Just to try that out. And you see who start me out? Henry Quinn! My cousin-brother. Lives with us . . . his father's *Suunuuma'a*—related to my grandma. 'Cause Henry, he's usin' that *moohoo'oo* pretty heavy; so, shows me how to do that. . . .

Say to me:

"You can smoke a couple pills, Corbett, and you'll feel lively again. Make all your tired go straight outta you!"

And so I do, too. . . . Try that, you know. And by God, I don't feel lazy at all! No, sir! Feel lively again. . . . Don't feel my tired[ness] at all!

'Cause that's what everyone's doin', you see. . . . Sayin' that, anyway: how you use that, and you can do your work more easy. Don't feel tired at all! So a fellow wanna try that. . . . You know, to find out for himself. And so, when he does, why, his tired's all gone outta him! Yes, sir! [He] feel lively again. . . . 'Cause I know that's what [why] I'm doin' [that]. . . .

'Cause I'm workin' with my cousin-brother [Henry Quinn] that time: cuttin' cedar post for Frank Simpson and his brother-in-law; cordin' that wood, you know. . . . And [we] stay up there in them mountain all winter long, too, by God! Through January, anyway . . . like I already told you. . . . Come down once in a while [only] to buy our grub and hay for our horses; and when my partner run outta his *moohoo'oo*. . . . Only thing is, I don't wanna get that habit that time. No, sir! Not yet, anyway. 'Cause you see why? If you're usin' that heavy, why, a fellow can't buy his own clothes . . . grub . . . 'Cause you see why? [When] you're on a habit, you always gotta keep that *moohoo'oo* close by. Yes, sir! [So] work to feed your habit. . . .

And so that time, I use only a couple or three pills. Not too many. . . . 'Cause when you're just startin' out, too much can make you throw up. . . . So that's not really on a habit, you know. Oh, and sometimes, too, I drink, too. But not a lot. . . . [At least] *moohoo'oo* don't make you crazy like *heebee* [drink]. No, sir! Don't make you to act like a drunken man! 'Cause you act decent when you're usin' *moohoo'oo;* so, not so bad. . . . Only if you ain't got any. . . . 'Cause that's when a fellow really suffer. . . .

Yes, sir! Any kind work you're doin', why, you use that *moohoo'oo* and never feel tired! No matter how hard you work! 'Cause that's pretty near how everybody's startin' off to use that stuff around here, you know . . . what I hear, anyway. . . . What them Indians sayin' all the time, . . . And so I believe 'em, all right. Yes, sir! Believe what my cousin-brother's tellin' me. . . .

So, around about 1912 I start usin' *moohoo'oo* first time. . . . Fall the year. Right after the Old Man take me outta Stewart. . . .

84. Beginnings of Opiate Addiction in Smith (and Mason) Valley

But you see who really start everybody off with that? Henry Clay!

Tabooso'o, that's his real name. But everybody just call him *hoguud tabadzee'ee* 'Don't Like Hog'! 'Cause you see why? Always sayin' he don't like hogs 'cause they eat people! Anyway, Henry Clay's first one doin' that in Smith Valley, by God! Yes, sir! [Even] start off my cousin-brother, Henry Quinn. . . . 'Cause that time, hardly nobody else's usin' that. . . .

I'm fifteen or sixteen [ca. 1905–6] when he first come up here to work in Smith Valley. 'Cause Henry Clay, he's from Sweetwater Country . . . from Bodie . . . down that way, anyway. So, must be he learn about *moohoo'oo* when he's workin' there? 'Cause I hear Henry Clay work in them [Bodie] gold mines. Lots them Chinaman down there. . . . And he's related, too, some way to my grandma, Henry Clay. 'Cause I know I call his father's sister *pahwa,* so she must be some kind cousin-sister to my grandma? Same way, too, I call Henry Clay's father *ats,* mother's brother. (Father's name is *Sad^ba'a* 'Pullin' Somethin' outta the River'. Or *Wata'nee* 'Number Four in Deck of Cards'. Some kind Bridgeport Indian, anyway. From Mono Lake, maybe? 'Cause Henry Clay's mother's from there, too.)

Anyway, he move down to Missouri Flat with his parents [from Smith Valley], Henry Clay; where he die . . . single man, too, when he first come into Smith Valley: lives in a tent with his brother *No'amin* . . . crippled guy, [who] rides sideway on a horse, just like a woman. Walks holdin' both knees always and dies way later in Sweetwater: see, 'cause his brother [Henry Clay] put him on a buckin' horse; throws him. . . . Anyway, Henry, he stay with us for three years when he first come up from Sweetwater, from Bodie country. . . . Then later on, he can marry Annie Dugan.

But Henry Clay don't smoke raw opium like Johnny Mack [sec. 85]. . . . No, sir! Just *moohoo'oo* [scrapings from raw or gum opium—"enshi" or yen-shee in Chinese]. . . . Least what I see, anyway. . . .

85. Alternative Origin

Or maybe Johnny Mack's first one doin' that around here?

'Cause he smoke *'oopeey^n* [raw opium], that guy. . . . 'Cause one time, Johnny Mack, he send me to Colony [District] to buy [a] can that wet stuff. And I'm only six or seven, that time. . . . We're still livin' in Wellington. . . . See, 'cause that's just like gum, that wet stuff: more stronger than the dry stuff, that *moohoo'oo.* 'Cause later on, I know I smoke some [raw opium]. . . . And you see what they're doin' with that kind? Fellow has got to hold it over the fire to cook. Keep it turnin' on that needle, you know, till it cooks good; till it don't drop too far. Yes, sir! Cook it good, then roll it around till it's hard. Stick 'em in that [pipe] hole and [Corbett produced a loud sucking sound] pull in hard!

But gee, that wet stuff sure costs! Cost you, maybe, six to eight dollar by the can, by God! 'Cause I know that one time I try it, I'm in Carson [City]; tryin' to buy *moohoo'oo* from this one Chinaman who sell, and so he sell me that wet stuff. . . . Inside a lemon. 'Cause that's how them Chinaman ship that, you know. . . . And all cleaned out, too, that lemon. Got no "meat" in it; plug on one end. . . And, by God, that [raw opium] taste just that same way [i.e., like a lemon]! Even [if] it come in that square tin!

Half-*Waseeyoo,* half-*Nuumuu,* Johnny Mack. . . . 'Cause I know him! Real old-timer. . . . Can speak our language real good, too. Yes, sir! So, only old-timer usin' that dope, I tell you, Mike! Smokin' that wet stuff, anyway. . . . Then you see what happen to Johnny Mack? Had a rupture buckin' his hay bail, and so they have to take him to Schurz [Public Hospital]. Die there. . . .

And you see who Johnny Mack learn [to smoke] that wet stuff from? Laundryman in Wellington! Yes, sir! Chinaman, that kind. . . . 'Cause he just make a friend with them Chinaman this valley, Johnny Mack. Learn to smoke with [from] 'em. . . . So Johnny Mack's [probably] first one in Wellington usin' that [raw] stuff. . . . Teaches Sam Leon what to do. . . .

86. The Chinese Connection

'Cause them Chinaman, you know, they sell to anyone. . . . Just so long [as] you got money. . . .

All over these valley when I first come to know somethin', them Chinaman. . . . So I guess they come from oversea. Do laundry work, ditch work on them big ranch. . . . And they can cook, too. 'Cause I know them Chinaman cook in Smith Valley: on them big ranch, you know. Also in them four restaurant in Mason. . . . Ah Wee, Ah Bui, Charley . . . named by that way. . . . But not like in Carson [City] around here. . . . No, sir! 'Cause too much scattered here. There, they live like Indian: all bunched up in shack[s] one place. . . .

Louie Bovard he's another one. . . . Haul slop from them Mason restaurant for hogs at the slaughterhouse . . . where *Wodzeewob* and *Soowee warr^b* live. . . . But we call him Louie Chinaman, Louie Bovard. Got his own house, but he don't sell [opiates]. No, sir! Not like Ah Sam, Ah Gee. . . . But you see what happen? I hear Ah Gee and this other Chinaman, they get killed by bunch them Fallon Indian. . . .

Yes, sir! [I] hear they first come into these valley on them irrigation ditch work, them Chinaman. Build both ditch in Smith Valley: Scieroni Ditch—that one's from Hoye Canyon clear down to Wellington—and Simpson or Colony Ditch. 'Cause Big Mack, he's the one tell me that. . . . Says they're all lined up that time, usin' pick and shovel and horse on that kind job. . . . And that's pretty tough work, I tell you, Mike! Yes, sir! 'Cause that Scieroni Ditch, why, that one go a long way. . . . Then after that steam shovel come in, why, they can [even] extend it from Wellington to Sweetwater.... But still, that's one thing I wanna know: [if] them Chinaman dig these Mason Valley [MacGowen and Campbell] ditch? 'Cause that's my early days ago, partner....

Anyway, not too many Chinaman smokin' [opium]. No, sir! Least what I see, anyway.... 'Cause they're mainly on the sell, them Chinamen. Oh, and maybe some might eat that, too? 'Cause I know this one's workin' for Frank Simpson; he does that: eats that. Don't smoke *moohoo'oo*.... And put whiskey on top that, too. Yes, sir! Got a garden, sell [yen-shee] to these Indian around here.... 'Cause you can get that eatin' habit [opium], too. Just the same as smokin'! And same way, too, them two Chinaman [who] cook up at Topaz Ranch [Antelope Valley], they're [also] both sellin'. 'Cause I know one time, I and Henry Quinn go on a buggy to Coleville ... to that Topaz Ranch....

But you see what some these crazy Indians doin'? They can go into any restaurant and put their money down to buy coffee; stuff that *moohoo'oo* in their shirt! Yes, sir! 'Cause we make friend with them Chinaman, you know.... 'Cause they like to gamble.... Like to play card with us.... And same way, too, they like [want] to make "friend" with our women. 'Cause you see why? They're just like *Aytayay*, them Chinamen: come over to this country without woman, so they wanna make a "friend" with Indian.... And some, they even learn our language.... See, 'cause ours has only got a few word; theirs is harder to learn.... Like Ah Sam.... He can talk our language pretty good.... Marry Gertie Green—she's from Fallon—then Ah Sam sell his laundry in Wabuska, go to Gardnerville, own a restaurant there. And after that, his wife die and he goes someplace else.... Maybe here?

And one time, this Indian woman wrestle Louie Bovard to the ground; cut off his queue. 'Cause maybe he drink with 'em, and so they "feel good" [i.e., are drunk]? Why she's doin' that to that Chinaman? 'Cause some them Chinamen are always doin' that, you know: buyin' whiskey for a woman. "You come to my house, we make a good livin'!" Yes, sir! What they always sayin'....

So they're sellin', all right, them Chinaman.... But when they try to grow it in America, why, them *taivo*, they poison it! Yes, sir! And so, them Chinaman, they always have to send [for opium supplies] oversea. 'Cause I know that *moohoo'oo* used to come by the mail.... And they don't mail that kind down here from Carson [City], but Reno, too. And some Chinaman, they [even] buy from Chinatown in them big city: Reno, Placerville, Sacramento. ... Yes, sir! Go over the mountain to buy.

But real funny people, them Chinaman: sometime you see them, they hide. Peek at you, don't be friendly. . . .

Only one Chinaman I used to see drink, though—one used to cook for Frank Simpson. Yes, sir! 'Cause first he use that dope, then he can drink: put *moohoo'oo* in his mouth and chew that, then put drink on top. "Warm that up good," he tell me. "So you feel good!" But he don't never wanna give me drink, neither. "No, Corbett. 'Cause you got bad eye," he always tell me. 'Cause I go in his room after he finish cookin', you know, talk with him all the time. Good Chinaman, though. Sometimes he leave over some pie, biscuit for us. . . . "Bring it home to your grandma," he tell me. . . . Never seen no mean Chinaman yet. 'Cause they're good to these Indian around here, I tell you, Mike!

87. *Moohoo'oo* ('Yen-Shee')

See, 'cause them Chinaman, they don't [ever] try to sell you that *'o peey^n* . . . that wet stuff [raw opium]. No, sir! Just *moohoo'oo* [yen-shee], that's all . . . second smokin'. Or we can [also] call that kind *Tsainamin pahmoo* 'Chinaman smoke'. And that black stuff's lot cheaper, too. . . . Cost you only one dollar on the bindle. The other kind, that wet stuff [raw opium], that's maybe four dollar? five dollar? six dollar? And for one tin. . . . One year, why, that's even costin' ten to fifteen dollar a tin!

And you see what that mean, *moohoo'oo?* 'Owl'! 'Cause by old-time way, they say Owl bring bad news [i.e., death], so you're supposed to throw rock when you hear one. Yes, sir! And talk to him. Tell him, "*Moohoo'oo,* don't bother me no more. Go away! 'Cause I don't wanna hear what you gotta say!" And so, by God, you're doin' that, that fellow's gotta listen to you. . . . But you see why they call that black stuff [yen-shee] same name as Owl? *Moohoo'oo?* 'Cause them hophead, they can climb a tree and hoot like one! [Laughs] Yes, sir! 'Cause that's what this one Indian always say. . . . Rip [Rupert Pitts]. Make a joke outta that kind, you know. . . . 'Cause by right way, anyway, they call that black stuff *moohoo'oo*, on account pine nut.

'Cause my grandma, after she cook *tuuba* [pine nut seeds], she can tell us [children] to clean that [grinding] stone. You know, rub that [off] with flour. Lets us kids to play with that kind [residue]. . . . And so, we can make different animal with that. . . . Yes, sir! Take a rock, put that in there for eye. Or use a twig for his nose. . . . And we call that black stuff *moohoo'oo*. . . .

Same way, [when] we're rollin' that other kind [yen-shee]. . . . 'Cause we have to make same ball outta *moohoo'oo,* you know? Before cookin' it over fire. . . . You know, before we're smokin' *moohoo'oo.* . . .

88. Your Own Outfit

So when you're usin', you gotta have your own pipe. Yes, sir! [But the] only one I ever seen with that real layout, though, was Johnny Mack. Both Johnny Mack and Willy Muldoon! 'Cause everybody else, you see what they do? Buy any kind [bottled] cough syrup, and drill into that glass. . . . Make their own *to'eesa* [pipe] outta that kind. . . . 'Cause them drug store them days, they're all sellin' that kind [i.e., opiate-based cough syrups], you know . . . [until] later on, [when] they find out that medicine has got a kick to it, so they have to quit. . . . And we can use a hacksaw blade, three-corner file, to drill into that bottle: to fit stem in there. Or they can use bailin' wire for that—after they sharpen it first. But you see what we make that stem with? *Tseeyabee,* that rosewood bush. . . . Same one they're usin' to make pipe. . . . 'Cause them old-timers, they say when they're [rosewood berries] ripe, that's when them pine nut are comin' in good. Or they can use *moomoogoopa,* locust tree, for that stem. 'Cause they got lotta stick on it. . . . And same way, too, we gotta use bailin' wire to cook that *moohoo'oo:* you know, after we put a little water on that black stuff [yen-shee] . . . to roll it . . . make a ball outta that, that way . . . cookin' it, you know, before we suck on it. . . . And I know I buy Sterno for my cookin' fire. . . . 'Cause a fellow need some kind tin can for his stove. . . .

But you always gotta leave your outfit at home. . . . Yes, sir! 'Cause you see why? [A] fellow don't wanna carry it with him, 'cause afraid, maybe, he's gonna break it. And same way, too, these Indian always bunch up when they're smokin'. 'Cause lotta time, somebody don't have his outfit, so [he] has to use somebody else's. 'Cause I know that's what we're always doin'. Yes, sir! 'Cause I always got pipe on hand. . . . And so, lotta them [other] hophead, why, they're always comin' to our cabin . . . to smoke together.

But you can't smoke that *moohoo'oo* [yen-shee] again. No, sir! 'Cause you see why? Won't stick together! So they just boil it and drink it. . . . Same way, if you wanna make it last, you can just eat it. 'Cause [if] you're smokin', you use lot. Anyway, they call that other kind [twice-smoked opium] sanalow.

89. The Life of the *Nuumuu* Addict

Smoke, smoke, smoke! All I'm doin' once I get that habit. . . . What I'm after all the time. . . . 'Cause you see what that *moohoo'oo* is doin' to you? "Come on! Come on!" Yes, sir! Feel pretty near like somebody's callin' you all the time! And won't let you alone, neither. No, sir! Keep on callin' you that way, all the time. . . .

'Cause you're usin' that, you gotta smoke three time every day: mornin', you gotta get up early to smoke *moohoo'oo*. Yes, sir! Get up before work. . . . 'Cause feel like you got a tough feelin' when you first get that habit, partner. . . . And that don't take long to fix your pipe, neither. No, sir! Four, five, maybe six pill before you feel all right. . . . So, you're doin' that at 6:00 A.M., you can eat your breakfast at half past six, maybe 7:00 A.M.? Then lunch time, you gotta smoke second time. 'Cause half-past eleven's quittin' time, so twelve o'clock, you eat again; then, after your noon meal, why, you can smoke second time. Little bit, though, not lot. . . . Oh, one pill, maybe? Two? 'Cause you see why? Your boss, he don't give you too much time for lunch. No, sir! Anyway, you don't wanna be too lazy on that job, 'cause they can fire you that quick! And third time you're usin' is after supper: 'cause then you can smoke lot! 'Cause half-past five, well, that's quittin' time. . . . And I don't even know how many pill we smoke then? Fall asleep on that pipe, then pretty soon you wake up again, put another on. . . .

'Cause I know sometime, I don't [even] wanna get up next mornin'! No, sir! Just wanna stay down all day long, you know. 'Cause *pahmoodayp* 'all doped up on smoke'! 'Cause that *moohoo'oo*, that make you to sleep, all right! And gee, you sure sleep good when you hit that pipe at night, partner! Don't even remember your dream! 'Cause I bet you I don't [even] go chasin' no more spring chicken once I'm usin' that black stuff heavy. No, sir! 'Cause that's all I'm doin' [then], you know: Smoke, smoke, smoke! And Sunday, no work, so you can just lay around all day long and smoke! Yes, sir! Leave that alone for a little while, then you lay down some more. . . . Oh, and maybe eat some [food]? Not lot, though. . . . 'Cause once you're usin' that dope pretty heavy, you just gotta keep on doin' that, you know: get up, get back on that pipe; smoke another pill. . . .

But [still] it make you happier than hell! Never get tired, nohow! No matter what you do, no matter how hard you work, why, you don't feel tired at all! Yes, sir! 'Cause that's how them fellow get that habit. . . . 'Cause no matter how hard a job you take, you're usin' *moohoo'oo*, you don't get tired at all! No, sir! 'Cause you're so damn tired . . . all your muscle ache. . . . But [then] you smoke some, why, you don't feel tired at all . . . how that dope work. . . . Why a fellow don't wanna get away from that stuff nohow. 'Cause *moohoo'oo* give you a better feelin' than [even] whiskey. [If you] use that, you feel so damn lazy—lazy like hell. And sleepy, too, 'specially when that liquor run outta you. But not *moohoo'oo*. . . .

And so, after I finish work with my cousin-brother [Henry Quinn], you see who start me out again? Don Jones—my brother-in-law! Yes, sir! 'Cause I get a job with him. . . . Irrigatin'. And he give me a couple pill. . . . And so, I keep on doin' that, you know: take a couple or three pill, then I take some more. . . . Keep on like that, you know, goin' up, till pretty quick, I have to buy off Chinaman! Then [when] I'm usin', why, I have to treat him back. . . . 'Cause Don Jones, that's my old-sister's husband . . .

And that's around about 1914 when I first start to smoke pretty heavy, partner. 'Cause them days, all these Indian do that—smoke three times every day. . . . Don't use it no other way. . . . 'Cause Don Jones, he [even] get [sister] Janie to use that. . . . Same as my wife, she [also] smoke before me, but not much. 'Cause you see why? She like that *heebee* [drinking] business better! And cost you around about a dollar a bindle for yen-shee. . . . You're only makin' two dollar a day, so a fellow can't make much that way. No, sir! Make twelve dollar a week; money can go to buyin' his dope. . . . 'Cause that's what I'm doin', you know: smokin' that *moohoo'oo* [yen-shee]. . . . 'Cause only two time I smoke that other kind. . . . that *'oopeey^n*, wet stuff. Yes, sir! Cost too much. . . .

Oh, and it can take around about one year before you get that habit. Yes, sir! You're only usin' one month, why, you can quit easy. 'Cause all them young people then, that's what they do: smoke that black stuff. Not old people, though. 'Cause them old-timers, they don't pay no attention to that kind [opiates]. No, sir! And nobody don't say nothin' to you about that, neither. No, sir! 'Cause your old people, they don't bother a person. Just so long you earn your own keep, and you buy your grub, and your clothes, they don't say nothin' at all. *Karroo'oo!* Oh, sure, maybe [if] I'm usin' their money, my mom or my grandma can try to bawl me out: "No good that, Corbett. *Ste'yoo!* Bad!" But they don't [really] say nothin' to me. 'Cause you see why? I'm not botherin' 'em that way. Work for my own money. . . . Buy grub, clothin' . . . so they just leave me alone. . . . And same way, too, your boss, he don't say nothin' to what a fellow's doin'. No, sir! Just do your own work, nobody bother you at all.

But you always gotta watch your supply when you're smokin' *moohoo'oo*. . . . 'Cause you see why? Them hophead, they can steal! Yes, sir! Steal potato from them *Aytayay* cellar [for example]. . . . Steal anythin'! 'Cause they hardly bring home [enough] grub for their family. . . . 'Cause that's all they want, you know, that *moohoo'oo*. Yes, sir! 'Cause all what money they make, spend for that! Go around chasin' after that, where[ever] them Chinaman sellin'. And pretty tough when they ain't got no winter work, partner! 'Cause ain't got a penny in their pockets. . . . All that money's goin' to that peddler. . . .

So [that's why] they wanna work for them *Aytayay*, you know: where they can get their money from. . . . To make their livin'. Cause them *taivo*, [if] you bother them every night for cash, they can say: "What-in-the-hell you doin' with that money?" Have to write check, you know. Not them *Aytayay*. . . . No, sir! 'Cause *Aytayay*, they keep cash all the time! Yes, sir! With them *taivo*, you [feel] ashamed to ask 'em for your money every night. You know, to buy [dope]. . . .

90. Buyin' *Moohoo'oo*

You're usin' [opiates] and workin', so you buy once a week. Yes, sir! 'Cause too hard to buy every day. . . . Not unless you're workin' close to a Chinaman. . . . 'Cause one Chinaman, he work for Frank Simpson, and I hear they mail that black stuff to him. . . . Or we can come down here to Mason [town] from Smith Valley. 'Cause Mason's got them four Chinese restaurant them days, you know. And pretty near all them Chinaman are usin' that dope. . . . But that time, anyway, they don't wanna sell. No, sir! None them Chinaman! "Don't got nothin'! Don't got nothin'! *Karroo'oo!* No more! No more! Policee here! Policee here!" Yes, sir! What they tell us. . . . Won't sell to us, so we go [on] to Wabuska to buy: to see Ah Sam. 'Cause I hear he's cookin' in that restaurant in Wabuska. . . . 'Cause Wabuska's big that time. . . . Got that hotel and roomin' house. Restaurant, too. . . .

Another time, too, we're buyin', we're stopped [searched] by them government bull. . . . Yes, sir! And that's I and my cousin-brother, Henry Quinn. 'Cause you see why they're doin' that? On a tip! 'Cause Adam Dixon and Bob Muldoon, they tell on us! Adam, he's from Fallon; Bob Muldoon's the brother of Bill; they're both from Bodie. . . . Anyway, Adam and Bob

Muldoon are both usin' that dope, so when they get caught, why, they can make friend with them government bull. You know, tell who's buyin' *moohoo'oo* from who? Make it better for them, that way. . . . We're on a horse and light buggy that time, and so I call 'em down.

"Not Indian, I'm Irish!"

Yes, sir! Tell them government bull that. . . . So they have to leave me alone. But you see why [else] I'm goin' there [Wabuska]? 'Cause I wanna see my girl friend, Addie Mason! And she's the one tells who's sellin' there . . . tells about Ah Sam. So we go over there to buy from him. Already told you about Ah Sam? How he make friend with these Indians? 'Cause Ah Sam, he marry two them Indian girl: first wife's named *Pozeewa'a;* second's Gertie Green, from Fallon. . . . 'Cause Ah Sam, he like to gamble with them Indians. . . . Yes, sir! 'Cause he's the one bet Big Mack he can't pick up that silver dollar on the ground [on horseback] and the Old Man wins! Ah Sin, he's another Chinaman also sells in Wabuska. . . . Anyway, when Ah Sam get arrested, his wife [Gertie Green], she can pay that fine to get him outta jail. Then Ah Sam go to Mina with her; run a restaurant there. And way later, he's got another one in Reno; on Main Street. Same as I hear Ah Sam's also in Gardnerville and Bridgeport or Bishop. Yes, sir! So, all over man, Ah Sam. 'Cause I know him! Speak our own language, his wife Gertie Green's sister marry this one *taivo* before she get with [Corbett's nephew] Eddie, [who] raise both them kids at that Indian camp at Bridgeport, then later on down here at Campbell Ranch. . . . when I come to help him. . . .

So anyway, when Ah Sam get scared outta Wabuska, we have to go to Carson to buy. . . . And we can go right over these [Desert] mountain back here. . . . 'Cause through Wabuska, that's the long way. And I know one time, I got to Carson City to buy but have a helluva hard time to cash my check! Yes, sir! Lucky I find a witness who know my (white) boss, though. . . . How I [finally] cash that check. . . . And same way, too, I know Ah Hip. 'Cause he's [also] from Carson. So [I also] go up there to buy from him. But you see what happen? After Ah Hip get arrested, them other Chinaman hide when they see you comin'. Yes, sir! Won't [even] stop to say, "Hello!" Close their door on you; see a fellow comin' from a long way and go inside their house. Look out at you just like a gopher! 'Cause you see why? They savvy. Think maybe you're workin' with them government bull. . . .

Time we go to Mina to buy, we come down to this [Mason] valley at night. 'Cause I'm through Yerington at four in the mornin', partner; then [by] noontime, we're home again. 'Cause no more Chinaman in either valley, so

Addie, she wanna see Ah Sam. Addie's marry to Johnny Williams then, but she monkey around with this one *taivo;* so I know I don't wanna marry her no more. . . . Anyway, when we get there [Mina], Addie, she has to buy [dope] from Ah Sam. Too bad I don't know no Chinaman in Hawthorne, though? Lot closer. . . . 'Cause never did hear nobody talkin' about any Chinaman there. . . . And you see how we get to Mina? We go to Schurz, Addie, she get free train pass. 'Cause you have to go wherever you hear them Chinaman sellin', you know: Mason, Wabuska, Carson City, Reno, Mina. . . .

But you see what some these Indian are doin'? They get mad at Chinaman and try to beat [cheat] 'em! Yes, sir! 'Cause I know my wife's brother [Andy Dick], he change [denomination of] that bill. Yes, sir! Buys India ink and make that one dollar into a ten dollar. Rob that Chinaman [Jim Sing, 1923] that way. . . . And same way, too, *Yungaree* [Jimmy Bob], he kill a Chinaman from Fallon and rob him. . . .

91. Other "Celestial" Connections

But you see who else is sellin' [opiates]? Them Japs!

Yes, sir! 'Cause one Jap—he own Austin's Grocery in Yerington—and he's [also] doin' that. Yes, sir! [The] one who get caught as a spy in San Francisco—ready to sail home and they find all kind picture Hawthorne [munitions base]. . . . And same way, too, them Japs leasin' land over toward Wabuska are sellin'. [They] raise potato there, you know. Just like them *Aytayay.*

First one's named Joe Yama. And we call his wife *Maatha* [Martha]. They live closer to Yerington, Joe Yama and his wife. Other's named *Yoqamoto'o;* don't have no wife. His partner, we call him *Tazupa pacha'a* [?]. And both can talk our language pretty good! Yes, sir! Same way, too, that woman can. 'Cause she tell me: *"Karroo'oo doowa'a peetho ya'eepa"* 'Use dope, penis dead'. But that's one thing about them Japs: they don't pay very much! No, sir! $2.50 a day. 'Cause pretty cheap wage them [i.e., they pay], I tell you, by God! Same pay as them *Aytayay* are givin'. . . . So you're workin' all week, and don't have much to show for that. Just enough left over to buy your grub. . . . Anyway, you see what they're [also] doin', them Japs? Sell *moohoo'oo!* Yes, sir! Or they can give you that instead of them wage. . . . Mark that down in their book. . . . Why all these Indian around here like workin' for them Japs! Like John Brown and his wife [for example].... 'Cause they both use pretty heavy all the time....

But you see why I don't like workin' for 'em? Too many *wopongo* [mosquitos] that [northern] end this [Mason] valley! Yes, sir! 'Cause thick up there with Mr. Mosquito, partner! Yes, sir! 'Cause that's all I'm doin' when I work for them Japs—fight *wopongo!* And so I quit. Go to work for Willy Penrose, hayin' work. Then go back up to Colony District, where no more mosquito. Anyway, that's the time the Old Man come after me . . . before I'm marry.... [When he] says my mom want me to come back home, on account she miss me. And so, I do. Go home....

Tough little fellows, them Japs. . . . Yes, sir! These Indian women sure like 'em!

92. No More Chinaman!

But [mostly] we buy *moohoo'oo* from them Chinaman. . . . And pretty smart: 'cause they know how to get the money! Never get caught, neither! 'Cause you see why? These Indian, they tell 'em when government bull's around. So watch out for 'em all the time, you see.... Still they chase 'em all out! Every last one 'em.... Yes, sir! Send 'em back to their own country....

'Cause last one left is Amy Wallace's husband. But he goes away, too, so there's no more Chinaman left in Smith Valley . . . Mason Valley. . . . And so we're sufferin', by God! So my cousin-brother, Henry Quinn, he say he know this one Chinaman up in Sweetwater. So we go up there. 'Cause that take only half a day to Sweetwater, you know . . . on horse.

"Better not go inside with me, Corbett," Henry Quinn, he tell me. "'Cause you see why? [If] he see you, maybe he's gonna think we're workin' for them government bull?"

And so that's what we do. My partner, he go inside there—alone—to see that Chinaman; I can stay outside. 'Cause he's a cook on the Atchison Ranch, that Chinaman. Keeps his best stuff [hidden] in tomato can. But you see what that Chinaman's doin'? He sell that third smokin'! What they call sanalow! Bad stuff, you know. Juice [is] all gone outta that. . . . Too dry to add water to and smoke. . . . And sell for only fifty cent, too. So *ste'yoo*, that kind. No good! He cheat us! 'Cause we try and roll that kind after we buy; find that's no good....

And so Henry, he wanna go back. And so, by God, we do! Then he can steal that good kind from him! That *moohoo'oo!* Then later on, we stop. 'Cause you see why? We wanna try that good kind! And so we do, too. But you see what happen? We go at that like a goddamn cat in a potato patch! Never even try to watch what we're smokin', neither. No, sir! Just lay down and smoke, smoke, smoke! 'Cause a fellow's workin', he's gotta quit. But not us. No, sir! We're not workin', so we can just lay down all day long and smoke, smoke, smoke!

But we get scared that time. 'Cause you see why? We're smokin', and so this other fellow, he show up: Johnny Rogers! 'Cause he [also] buy some that bad kind from that Chinaman in Sweetwater—that sanalow, you know. And so [initially], we never tell him what we done. But Johnny Rogers, he finds out, all right. . . . Yes, sir! So we let him have some. And so the three of us, we just go crazy on that tomato can! Yes, sir! Smoke up all that *moohoo'oo* that time. Even [if] I wanna save some to pay back Don Jones, never do!

93. An Unlikely Connection!

Two times, my boss, he [even] buy for me!

'Cause that first time, Macarini can go [directly] to them Chinaman to buy *moohoo'oo*. 'Cause you see why? We're workin' for him already, I and my wife, so he just put that down in his book. You know, whenever we buy *moohoo'oo* from him—instead of payin' us wage [and wine]. But that other time, Macarini just put up the money: gives me thirty or forty or fifty dollar; tells me to go and buy that *moohoo'oo*, then I have to let him handle that black stuff for us. You know, gives it to us when we need it. . . . Pay him back by workin' for him that way. . . .

Oh, and maybe my boss can make a little money on that, too? But you see what's wrong? Macarini, he don't know how to load package like a Chinaman. No, sir! Tries to make it stretch a little more, but he can't make it! 'Cause I know how big them bindle are supposed to be! But still a fellow can't say nothin'. No, sir! 'Cause just so long you can get your *moohoo'oo*, why, you can't say nothin' at all to your boss. . . . Not about what he's doin', anyway. . . .

And same way, Angelo Quillici . . . [who] has a ranch in Colony [District]. Amos's brother, he pay Johnny Sam with *moohoo'oo*. Has to, you know, 'cause otherwise Johnny won't work for him. No, sir! Don't have no horse to go after that, and Johnny Sam's usin' pretty heavy. . . . *Wahee* Johnny, that's what we call him: 'Fox' Johnny. Pretty mean guy, too. . . .

But you see why my boss quits handlin'? 'Cause somebody bawl him out! Yes, sir! Gives Macarini hell, by God! And that's that Willy Wallace! (They talk funny, him and his brother, Doud. Tongue can't find their words too quick [stutter?].) And you see why Willy Wallace is doin' that? Bawl out my boss that way? On account his wife, Amy, she don't wanna go home! No, sir! Won't go where her husband's workin', on account she's workin' for Macarini, and he's sellin' Amy wine! So Pumpkin, he bawl out my boss. Yes, sir! Bawl the shit outta Macarini! Make him to quit handlin' our *moohoo'oo* that way!

94. A Meeting with My Real Father

I'm usin', I hear my real father's in Dayton, so I ride up there on my horse. 'Cause you see why? I wanna ask him for money—to buy *moohoo'oo*. . . . Sufferin' real bad, partner. . . .

'Cause when I'm little, can't talk English yet, so I can't talk to my real father. No, sir! Only when I'm big. . . . Already told you why he move outta Smith Valley? 'Cause the Old Man's gonna kill him? On account what Bill Douglass is doin' with my mom? So my real father, he have to leave this country. . . . Afraid the Old Man, you know. 'Cause Big Mack's a big man, and my real father's like me, real short guy. . . .

First time I visit him. He give me fifty, fifty-five dollar. . . . But that second time I go, I'm doin' that, and *karroo'oo!* Nothin' at all!

"Gee, Corbett, maybe [if] I have money in the bank, I can give you a little? But I'm broke, partner. . . ."

'Cause I hear he like to gamble and drink too much. . . . Ain't got no money at all! And I don't think my real father ever marry? 'Cause too Godamn crazy! Same as I hear he don't live much longer after that, neither. No, sir! 'Cause after Bill Douglass leave this valley, he go up to Gardnerville. . . . Was Sheriff there. Then after that, he's livin' in Dayton: guard in state prison [Carson City]. Loses all his money [gambling] and goes crazy. Shoot himself! 'Cause he don't wanna live no more!

95. The Indian Connection

And so, after they divide all them big ranch, they stop hirin' Chinaman for cook in Smith Valley. For raisin' a garden, too. . . . Yes, sir! 'Cause no more Simpson Ranch, John O'Banion. . . . And so that's when George Orange start in to sell.

'Cause he's marry to Maddie Rube that time. *Waseeyoo* guy, George Orange. Way older than his [second] wife, Maddie Rube. 'Cause he's around about fifty, fifty-one, when I'm a young guy, George Orange. Same age as Andy Dick. . . . And he don't sell in Mason Valley, neither, George Orange. No, sir! Stay up in Smith Valley all the time; work for Hans Crosby, that *D^tsiman* [Dutchman who] runs the dairy up there. . . . 'Cause hardly any government bull that time, by God, so them *moohoo'oo* users, they're not afraid to buy from George. No, sir! Go to his tent in Wellington, where George Orange lives with Maddie, any time. . . . And he make lotta profit, too, by God! 'Cause you see why? Neither use! No, sir! They just sell. And I don't see where George Orange buys from, neither? He's got a car, so maybe he travel to Carson? Reno? 'Cause I don't think he go to Placerville or Sacramento. . . . But we don't know for sure. . . . But you see what's wrong? George Orange, he don't wanna sell too much to a person. No, sir! 'Cause I know I'm not marry that time. [I] go over to their place to buy *moohoo'oo* lots. . . . But lotta time he don't have. 'Cause George Orange, he don't buy enough! No, sir! And don't sell [for] very long, neither. Oh, maybe one year? Get scared out and he quit. Go back to his *Waseeyoo* wife in Gardnerville and them kid. . . . On account Maddie Rube's *pash^p* 'dry woman'. Don't make no baby. . . . Then Curly Rube and Joe Bob start up.

Got a tent, them two. . . . Livin' way back up there in Wellington. 'Cause you see what they're doin'? Curley Rube and Joe Bob, they find a Chinaman in Carson City who sell; buy from him. And same way, too, they don't go from house to house. No, sir! Just stay in one place all the time; let everybody come to them. . . . Like George Orange is doin'. 'Cause Joe Bob, he does ranch work—feed livestock Macarini keeps across the highway from where that sheep corral shed is. You know, close to where they live. . . . So Joe Bob's partner, Curley, he's the one gotta stay home all the time; you know, sellin' that *moohoo'oo* that way. Older than me, Curley Rube, but not much. Pretty near same age as Joe Bob. . . . Younger than Andy Dick, though. . . . And you see what happen? They don't make good money sellin'. No, sir! 'Cause both are usin', that's why. 'Cause gee, you sure smoke lot when you got lotta that *moohoo'oo* on hand! Yes, sir! [You] just don't feel like lettin' go that! No, sir! And so you can smoke up your profit real quick that way. . . . [They're] sellin' in Smith Valley for one year, maybe, Curley Rube and Joe Bob? 'Cause I don't think there's seller in Mason Valley yet. . . . None before Henry Greely start up, anyway. . . . But that's way later, when no more Chinaman in Mason. . . .

And same way, too, Grover Pitts, he also sell in Smith Valley. 'Cause Grover, he's marry to Hazel [Bob] that time: sister to my wife. . . . Hazel, she don't suck on that pipe. . . . And Grover's another *Waseeyoo* guy [who] can understand our language real good—like all them Rubes. . . . Won't talk it, though. No, sir! 'Cause he always answer you in English. . . . Anyway, Grover, he can go to Sacramento to buy. . . . 'Cause he's got a Ford, you know. And funny tootin' horn on that car, by God! Like a whistle! So when he come around soundin' that, why, everybody say: "Here come Grover!" 'Cause that's what he's doin', you know, Grover Pitts: don't sell from his home. No, sir! Come around every night to where you're livin' after work. . . . And he make money pretty fast, too, I tell you, Mike! How he buy that Ford. . . . Yes, sir! 'Cause Grover Pitts can make a couple hundred in one night! Saturday's worst. Make $300–$400! Even if he use heavy. . . . And Grover, he sell in newspapers. Yes, sir! Got his *moohoo'oo* [bindles] wrapped in that kind, and so we all just pile up like that in my place after he come around: smoke, bullshit together; make better friend that way. 'Cause it's a seven-mile walk from Wellington to Colony District where we're livin', partner. But one thing I don't see is: what Grover Pitts does with his money? 'Cause after he die—was gettin' darker and darker, Grover; 'cause somethin' in his blood; so finally he go to that sanitorium in Stewart; die there—and nobody ever did find Grover Pitts' money! No, sir! [But] all-around man, Grover Pitts: uses everythin'! 'Cause when that dope business is outta here, why, Grover, he start to drink. 'Cause I know him! Always buy my *moohoo'oo* from Grover Pitts when I'm usin'. Yes, sir! And you see who really give him his start? Sullivan Tom.

'Cause he's just a little guy when I'm in Stewart, Sullivan Tom. . . . Eddie [Mack]'s age [b. 1905]. And I know him from Stewart, all right. 'Cause all them other [Mason Valley] seller go there when I'm there: Sullivan Tom, Dave Bobb, Henry Greely. . . . Sullivan Tom's wife, she's daughter to that [first] *Nuumuu* wife Ah Sam gets. . . . One they call *Pazeewa'a.* So maybe that's how come he know where to buy? 'Cause Sullivan, he buy lots! Gives it to Grover Pitts to sell for him, then when Grover quit—see, 'cause once Grover gets his start, wanna sell for himself—Sullivan Tom want me to sell for him. Says to me,

"You can get twenty-five cents on every dollar you make, Corbett."

Yes, sir! Tell me that same thing he's tellin' Grover Pitts. . . . How I can sell for him, he'll help me to get my own start. . . . 'Cause Sullivan, he say he can take me over into Sacramento, so I can buy my own there. You know, buy $30—that Chinaman ounce; sell for $300-$400. Make lotta money that way. . . . But I say, "No!" 'Cause you see why? I tell Sullivan Tom that's not enough profit. . . . But really I'm just sayin' that 'cause I'm afraid. 'Cause Dave Bobb, he got arrested that time—in Mason Valley. Keeps it in his pocket when them government bull search him, and so they catch Dave Bobb, all right. Get sent to the pen, and don't sell when he come out. . . . Was from Schurz, too, Dave Bobb. Sellin' *moohoo'oo* for Sullivan Tom in this [Mason] valley. . . . And you see why Sullivan Tom sells here [Mason Valley]? 'Cause not too many *moohoo'oo* men down there [Walker River Reservation]. And Sullivan, he use that, too, but not too much. . . .

Same way, too, Henry Greely, he's another seller. Works all alone, Henry. Younger than I am. But he's also from Schurz, that guy; live at the Yerington [Indian] Colony, though. . . . And I never did buy from Henry Greely. . . . 'Cause you see why? Henry, he don't sell for very long. No, sir! Back out quick after Dave Bobb get caught. . . . And same way, too, he's not usin', neither, Henry Greely. Just sell, that's all. . . . Has a car, so he can go to Sacramento to buy. . . .

Then Jimmy Summers start up to sell *moohoo'oo* in Smith Valley. . . . 'Cause I know I buy from him after Sullivan Tom quit. Yes, sir! And Jimmy Summers, he's from Coleville: A *nomogwet*. Father's a *taivo*. . . . Jimmy works for Ruby Terry all year long—[who] buys John O' Banion's ranch; so, Jimmy, he can feed Ruby Terry's cattle in the winter. And does hayin' work in the fall. . . . Sells [narcotics] from his house on that ranch, you know. . . . And I bet you Jimmy Summers sell for quite a few years, too! Would have made a lotta money, [if] he ain't afraid!

"I ain't got no more, Corbett."

Yes, sir! What he's always sayin'. And when Jimmy Summers does sell, he only give you small measure that *moohoo'oo*. Yes, sir! Why we don't like to go to him. . . . 'Cause them addicts, you know, they like to go to whoever's givin' a little more value. . . . And Jimmy Summers, he don't care how much sick a fellow is, neither. No, sir! Always says, "No credit!" Says, "I ain't got any, partner, so don't bother me. Anyway, I'm sick, too!" Yes, sir! 'Cause no matter how sick you are, Jimmy Summers, he won't treat! Not like Mike Rube, anyway. 'Cause he treat every once in a while. . . . 'Cause Jimmy Summers is like Jerry Keno: no trust! Don't give his *moohoo'oo* away. . . . And so, them hophead, they don't like to bother [beg from] Jimmy Summers.

'Cause you see why he's doin' that? Him and his wife [Daisy Nuna], they're both usin' that black stuff pretty heavy. So, don't wanna sell too much. . . . Then later on, they can sell that white stuff [morphine]—when there's no more *moohoo'oo*. . . . Smart fellow, though, Jimmy Summers, he don't get caught. No, sir! Quit only when James Keno gets caught [1928]. . . .

96. I Sell

And you see how I start up? When George Orange sell, I'm thinkin' to myself: "Maybe I can, too? Make lotta money that way!" So I borrow twenty-five dollar from my mom. (Ask the Old Man, too, but Big Mack, he say *"NO!"*) [But since] I got a horse—that's way before I marry—so I can ride over these [Desert] mountains to Carson City; buy from this one Chinaman there [Albert] Coffin introduce me to. . . . And so, by God, I do!

And gee, I make pretty near $100 that time, partner! 'Cause when I come back, everybody buy me out quick! But they catch my Chinaman friend, so nobody else up there won't sell to me no more. No, sir! Too scared, you know. Don't [even] know me. . . . So, [since] I can't find no other buyer, why, I have to quit. And I don't go around from camp to camp when I'm sellin' *moohoo'oo* for myself, neither. No, sir! Them addicts, they have to come to my camp to buy! But you see why I [really] don't have lots to sell? 'Cause I'm smokin' pretty heavy, by God! Yes, sir! And even [if] I try to save only a little for myself, that's pretty tough, partner. 'Cause too many people, they want that. 'Cause them days, pretty near everybody's smokin' *moohoo'oo*, and so, when they find out I got some, well, they can come to my house: to buy or bum.

And I can use thimble [for measurement] when I'm sellin'. Wrap that *moohoo'oo* in Prince Albert [pipe tobacco can] paper; sell for one dollar a package. . . . Have to hide that [also], you know; keep only a little amount on hand. . . . Then after I'm out, you see who get me started again? Sullivan Tom! Yes, sir! 'Cause he's the first one I work for! Start me out again after Grover Pitts go on his own.

"You work for me, Corbett, I can show you where to buy.... Start you on your own *moohoo'oo* business that way.... Take you to Sacramento, show you where I buy; then you can go yourself. Make better money that way...." Yes, sir! What Sullivan Tom say to me.... But he quit too soon, that fellow ... get scared out. Says to me, "I'm afraid, Corbett. [Because] my best partner got throwed in state prison!" And that's that Dave Bobb he's talkin' about.... So Sullivan Tom, he get scared out too quick. 'Cause he only brought me that black stuff one time.... Next time, Sullivan never show up.... But, gee, that money sure roll in when I'm workin' for Sullivan Tom. Must be I make around about $2,000! 'Cause, like I tell you, Mike, you're sellin' *moohoo'oo,* you can make around about $300-$400 Saturday night! 'Cause they don't go to Jimmy Summers when I'm sellin' for Sullivan Tom.... No, sir! All them hopheads go to me.... So anyway, after Sullivan Tom quit, Willy Muldoon jump right in.

97. Willy Muldoon's Base of Operations

Ask me to sell for him in Smith Valley, Willy, and so I say: "O.K., I can take a chance on it! 'Cause even if I get caught, why, that's all right, too!"

He's half-brother to Dave Bob, Willy Muldoon, you know: got same mother [Rena Bob], different father.... Same way, Willy Muldoon's related to my wife.... Kinda light[-skinned] guy—all them Muldoons are that way: George, Myra, Jimmy.... George Muldoon, he's not right in the head: *khaishooname'yoo,* don't think right, got funny idea.... Parents are from Hawthorne—that's Bill Muldoon and Jenny; stay in Schurz all the time. Bob Muldoon—that's Willy's *hai'ee* [father's brother]—he burn up from a cigarette in hand. Smokin' that way [drunk?] in Missouri Flat....

And Ida Rubens, that's Willy Muldoon's wife.... She's a well-to-do, Ida. *Nomogwet:* half *Waseeyoo,* half *taivo.* Only she's always sayin', "I'm not *Waseeyoo,* I'm white!" Won't [even] talk her own language, neither. No, sir! So anyway, she and Willy Muldoon, they live in Carson City. Nice house.... 'Cause all them Muldoons are livin' together in that one house that time.... But I can't say who's older, Willy Muldoon or Eddie [Mack, b. 1905]? So anyway, when Sullivan Tom quit, that's when Willy Muldoon take over....

He's workin' for Al Trielof, that time, Willy—that butcher from Coleville in this valley: bums [cash] from Dave Bob and Curley Rube, get his start that way. And so, later on, Curley Rube, he take twenty-five dollar outta what I'm supposed to be makin'. Yes, sir! Tells me that's what Willy still owe him! Anyway, Willy Muldoon, he buy that grocery store in this [Mason] valley—Austin's. You know, just outside the Yerington [Indian] Colony . . . east side. . . . 'Cause Frank Bovard, he [originally] own that. (Same as Frank own that land they build that Colony on). Small store, you know. No meat inside there. 'Cause they're just sellin' ten cent worth coffee, fifteen cent sugar to these Indian. . . . You know, them small amount. . . . And *moohoo'oo!* But Willy, he won't allow no kind credit [opiates? groceries?]!

And he use everythin', Willy Muldoon. 'Cause I know after a while he [even] start bringin' in that cocaine. . . . But not too much. . . . 'Cause we're makin' package [bindles] that *moohoo'oo* that night, you know, and so, Willy, he tell how to use that kind: "Just sniff it good, Corbett. Don't smoke or chew on it. And pretty quick you're tired's gonna go away!" 'Cause I'm sleepy when I'm workin' that. . . . 'Cause you see why? Them *moohoo'oo* men, they come all night long! Come on foot from Wellington clean up to Colony [District] any time night. . . . Yes, sir! Willy tell me how to use that cocaine. And by God, I do that. . . . Tiredness go all outta me! 'Cause you get to feel to be lively again when you sniff that kind. Yes, sir! Feel like your eyes open wide. Wake you up real quick! 'Cause Willy, he see, he's always usin' that kind to perk up. Puts it on a toothpick in his nose. . . . Only thing is, that [high] don't last very long. No, sir! And only one time I try to sell cocaine for Willy Muldoon, but you see what happen? He put too little in a package. . . . Too small for one dollar. . . . Still, I hear some them *moohoo'oo* men can mix that [cocaine] with that white stuff [morphine].

Willy, he talk to me in Indian [Northern Paiute] all the time. 'Cause you see why? My wife's English not too good, partner. Calls me Corbett, same as I call him Willy. But he only keep a little on hand in that grocery store; the rest, Willy has to hide in Weed Heights. . . . Yes, sir! Bury it in the ground. And same way, too, Willy, he won't sell to everybody. No, sir! Sell only to good friend. 'Cause you see why? He's got others handlin' for him. 'Cause I know I'm handlin' for Willy Muldoon in Smith Valley. . . . Billy Miller, he sell for Willy in Mason. (Younger than me, Billy Miller. He's from Schurz; live there [Mason], and at that [Yerington] Indian Colony.) Go around with Willy all the time to buy: to Carson City, Reno, Placerville, Sacramento. . . . Wherever them Chinaman live. . . .) Same as Willy's got Tommy Benjamin sellin' that *moohoo'oo* for him in Yerington. 'Cause Tommy, he's [also] got house in Mason and Yerington [Indian Colony], both. (Marry to Wakeen Brown's daughter, Tommy Benjamin). And same way, too, Dewey Norton can handle in this [Mason] valley for Willy Muldoon. (Used to be marry to Old Man Charley's daughter, Mary, Dewey Norton; his sister is Julia. And Dewey's younger than I am. Die young. Get sick, and that's all you hear, he's gone. 'Cause something's wrong with them young people, you know: die off too quick. And when Dewey Norton's marry to that Mary, he stays in this valley. 'Cause I know I used to see Dewey Norton in Stewart: half-breed guy.) [Also] go with Willy Muldoon once in a while to Sacramento, Dewey. . . . Act as his lookout—for them government bull. . . . (Same way, that other short, chunky guy from Schurz used to go around with Willy all the time: Corbett Williams.) And Dewey Norton, he also use that dope, that black one. But not Dewey's wife or sister. . . . One other Indian workin' for Willy Muldoon—they call him *Wannaveetsa* 'Ten Cents'! He handles in Virginia City and Dayton. Marry guy, related to them Virginia and Carson City outfits. . . .

Yes, sir! So, Willy Muldoon, has got lotta them Indian sellin' for him. 'Cause I know I work for him around about a year. Start in the fall, [I] go along that winter; then all that next summer, too. Yes, sir! So just about one year, I last. . . . 'Cause Willy, he can give you bag full to sell: 1,000 bindle. . . .

98. Sellin' for Willy Muldoon

And so, when I'm sellin' for Willy Muldoon, one ounce cost $35. We package that and can make $300! 'Cause I'm already marry when Willy want me to sell *moohoo'oo* to these Indians here [in Smith Valley]—after Grover Pitts and Sullivan Tom quit. We're workin' on the Charley Day Ranch then, and so Willy, he come and live with us; ask me to do that. And so I do, too; agree to sell for Willy Muldoon. . . .

'Cause you see what we're doin' when we're sellin' Willy's *moohoo'oo?* We just have to wait for them *moohoo'oo* men to come to our house to buy! Yes, sir! Can't go nowhere. . . . Just wait around in that all day long for that; in Colony [District], where we're livin'. And my boss[es], they don't bother me, neither. No, sir! 'Cause they know I'm too busy. . . . But you see what's wrong? I only get twenty-five cent on every one dollar bindle I'm sellin' for Willy Muldoon . . . twenty-five dollar outta that hundred dollar! Pretty cheap wage, ain't it, partner? Not for that poor chance I'm takin', anyway! 'Cause that's a pretty tough law, narcotic, by God! Fellow's gotta be watchin' for them government bull damn close all the time! Yes, sir! 'Cause they're always watchin' on the road who's comin'. . . . And, same way, too, you can't keep too much [dope] in your place. No, sir! You gotta hide it way out in the brush somewhere. . . . But I know sometime [when] I'm handlin' lots, maybe $1,000 worth, I gotta keep enough close by to sell. The rest, why, I can hide.

Willy, he make up them packages. Measure by a little cup, you know. Buy *moohoo'oo* for $3.75 an ounce—and that's a Chinaman ounce, partner! —then put that into that $1.00 package. . . . But you see what happen? Some them *moohoo'oo* men, they're askin' for [only] $.50 [worth]; so you have to divide that. 'Cause they don't have too much money. . . . And same way, too, lotta them poor guys usin' that, don't have no money at all, so they try to bum you.

"I'm pretty sick, Corbett. Ain't got no money. You can help me out?"

Yes, sir! What they're sayin'. But I'm not allowed to treat. 'Cause, Willy, he know [exactly] how much I got on hand. . . . So you see what I'm doin'? Both I and my wife, [since] we smoke lot ourself, I can give 'em that third smokin' . . . that sanalow. 'Cause that one's pretty weak, partner. Yes, sir! Give 'em that to help out when they're sufferin' bad. . . .

And my wife, she's not usin' too much. . . . Just enough to get a kick. 'Cause my wife like [prefers to] drink better. 'Cause you see what happen? I start her up again on opiates, after her first husband [Don Jones] start her on that *moohoo'oo*, that first time. . . . And my wife, she like it well enough, all right; but then she quit that when she quit him. Start to drinkin'. So I start her up again. . . . Yes, sir! 'Cause my wife can smoke right alongside me when I'm sellin' for Willy Muldoon. . . . Time my grandma's still livin'.

And so, by God, that's all we do is smoke, smoke, smoke! Smoke, and wait around for someone to buy! Maybe [if] I don't smoke so much Willy Muldoon's *moohoo'oo*, I can make some money on that? 'Cause what you're earnin' [left over] is yours. Same way, too, [if] you charge not enough, why, you still gotta straighten out with Willy! But a fellow don't wanna charge up a guy too much, on account he's gonna buy from somebody else. Yes, sir! 'Cause same way when I'm workin' for Sullivan Tom, I smoke too much. Don't hardly make no profit at all. . . .

And only one time I and Willy Muldoon fight. 'Cause you see what happen? Willy, he gets a new partner. . . . That's that Willy Astor. From Reno. Want him to handle. . . . But anyway, we make up. 'Cause Willy Muldoon, he come to my house that night to give me *moohoo'oo* to sell. And so we become partner again. . . .

But even [if] I run out, Grover Pitts can drive me in his Ford to that grocery store down here Willy's got.... 'Cause Grover, he get gas and oil from his boss. But them days are gettin' pretty tough, partner. Bunch these Indians are in the pen for that copper theft [1928], and so Willy Muldoon, he tell [warns] us to watch for 'em. Yes, sir! 'Cause they can tell them government bull on you, then they can find you out easy. So I'm always watchin' [for] government bull. And watchin' these Indians, too. 'Cause you [also] gotta watch your own people, I tell you, Mike! Yes, sir! So that's a pretty tough time sellin'.... Night time, that's about the only [safe] time you can go to your hidin' place....

99. Driving Mishap

Never [did] tell you yet about that accident I have? On the drive?

Willy, he's got a Dodge roadster; says he wanna sell to me for $150. Used car, you know. Real heavy, too, that one.... So anyway, I buy it. 'Cause you see why? I wanna see my wife! She's takin' care Willy's kid that time—in Carson City; 'cause Willy Muldoon's wife's makin' another baby in the hospital. And so I'm all alone in Colony [District]; miss my wife, why I wanna see her. So I do that: buy Willy Muldoon's roadster and go.

And you see how I have that accident? Only supposed to use [drive] in the daytime 'cause my eyes are bad. 'Cause I'm on the cataracts, then, partner. Yes, sir! Why I don't have no driver's license.... Why I can't hunt.... Can't go to that First German War, neither.... And you see how I went off that road? 'Cause that's night time, I'm a greenhorn driver: start out too late and run into rain.... And them old-time car, they ain't got no windshield wiper! And so that other driver's light, they blind me. So I miss the road.... Yes, sir! Slip off that grade the other side Gardnerville: by Carson River bridge.... Wreck up there....

And maybe [if] I can get a little more gasoline [acceleration], I can pull myself out? Anyway, I can't make it, so I just kill my motor. Wait there.... Lucky thing that other car stop, ain't it? And so that driver, he ask me:

"What's the matter with you? Fall asleep?"

"Hell, no!" I tell him. "You pretty near blind me with your light!"

"Well, you can't stay in there [the ditch] all night long," he say to me. And helps me out, too, by God! 'Cause you see what he's doin'? I can give a little gas, he can pull [tows] like hell. Use a heavy rope, pull that Dodge roadster back onto the highway. . . . So, must be pretty good people, ain't it?

So anyway, after that wreck, I know I don't wanna drive no more. . . . No, sir! Sell that roadster right back to Willy! 'Cause you see what I'm thinkin'? I kind think to myself, maybe Willy's hidin' from me? 'Cause he never show up like he's supposed to. No, sir! 'Cause I'm [also] all outta *moohoo'oo* then; don't have any that black stuff to sell no more. . . . So that's [also] why I'm goin' up there to Carson: 'cause I think Willy Muldoon's there, and I can buy. . . .

100. I Am Nearly Arrested

And, one time, by God, we're nearly caught!

'Cause that's around about 1:00 A.M. . . . And you see what happen? I and my wife, we're in bed. Somebody's knockin' on the door, two Indian [are] outside; so we get up; tell 'em to come in.

"Give us a dollar worth, Corbett," one of 'em, he say. "'Cause we're pretty sick, partner!"

And he put that one dollar bill down. . . . And they're also sniffin' around, you see. Sniffin' and wavin' their arm, just to show they're sufferin'. And outside is Jack Dalton and government bull!

He's a *Nuumuu*, Jack Dalton—from Fallon. Policeman at that Indian Colony in Yerington, where he's livin'; till Jack Dalton get a house right here [Campbell Ranch]. And he's [also] a *poohaghooma*, medicine man. . . . But I hear Jack Dalton don't bother nobody [i.e., addicts]. No, sir! Just leave you alone. Don't try to arrest nobody for *moohoo'oo*. Or on that drink. . . . So [if] you leave him alone, why, he's not gonna bother you. But [if] you bother him. . . . Like, one time, Billy Miller, he get mad at Jack and say:

"If Jack Dalton bother me, I'm gonna shoot out his *tsaboo* [rectum]!"

And so, by God, somebody tell him that! And Jack, he get mad. (Billy Miller's a cowboy for Miller Lux. Use *moohoo'oo*. . . .) Yes, sir! Don't like what Billy Miller's saying, and so Jack Dalton, he tell that government bull [George O'Neill] what that other fellow's sayin'. And so, by God, they arrest Billy Miller! But you see who I don't like? That other government bull, Andrew Vidovich! *Tovongo* [Shoshone], that one; Shoshone from Death Valley. Marry to Jack Wilson's young daughter, Alice . . . that *nomogwet*. . . .

'Cause you see what he [Andrew Vidovich]'s always doin'? Watchin' always for you [addicts and sellers]!

"Gee, we're pretty sick, partner. Maybe you can sell us some?"

'Cause Ray Sam, he's the one sayin' that. . . . Call him *Seeya Yano'o*, "Cry" Ray. Partner's Henry McCloud—Indians around here call him *Moibee* 'Fly'. And Ray Sam, he always bum me. . . . [We] would have done that, too: you know, sell 'em *moohoo'oo* that night. Only Willy Muldoon, he [previously] tell who's in jail. Yes, sir! [Ordinarily] comes up to Smith Valley day to tell that. . . . You know, who get arrested, so we won't sell to 'em. . . .

'Cause you see what they're [Ray Sam and Henry McCloud] doin'? In on that stealin' copper wire! Yes, sir! Bunch them crazy *moohoo'oo* men, they do that—seven in all! Take turn cuttin' up that wire; sellin' that copper to junk men in town [Yerington]. And so they get caught. . . . Tell on one another. . . . 'Cause them government bull, you see what they do? Promise to free who tell on who's doin' that [selling narcotics]! Charley Brown and Ed Reymers, they're also in on that. Andy Penrose, too. (He's a bad one, Andrew: kill somebody and go to the pen. Uses black and white *moohoo'oo* . . . both! But he don't sell, though. No, sir! And Andrew Penrose is marry to Dick Bennett's daughter, *Soonoo* Ida, after Pete Penrose; so she give him [Penrose] his start [narcotics addiction]. . . .)

So, lucky thing Willy Muldoon tell us to watch out for 'em, ain't it? Says them government bull let them two hophead outta jail early. How they can mark that money they're usin': you know, to try and trap us! And you see how I find that out? Grover Pitts! 'Cause he take me to see Willy [earlier] that day. And so Willy, he tell [warns] us about them two guys on the copper theft gettin' out. . . . To watch for 'em. . . .

Then after a while, them government bull, too, come inside our cabin. . . . And gee, sure make mess outta it! You know, lookin' everywhere for our *moohoo'oo*. . . . So, my wife, she [finally] bawl both Indian out. Yes, sir! Bawl the shit outta 'em! Talk to Jack Dalton [as well] in our own language, too:

"We thought you're a *Nuumuu*. But you're on the *taivo* side!" my wife say. And says to them government bull:

"Disturbed our bed, now you better make it again!"

Yes, sir! Can talk rough to 'em like that, my wife! Even though Jack Dalton, he call her his *meetho'o* [niece]!

"So, why you wake us up like this?" my wife [also] tell 'em. "'Cause we're hard-workin' Indian!"

She [even] tell [threatens] Jack Dalton how she's gonna kill him next time he do that. . . . Lucky thing we don't have nothin' on hand, though! 'Cause I'm always hidin' [opiates] in the brush! Yes, sir! 'Cause you see what I'm doin'? Hide mine inside Prince Albert [pipe tobacco] can. . . .

So we sure have a helluva scare that time! But you see what I'm [also] thinkin'? Maybe Willy Muldoon tell them government bull on me?

101. Willy, He Get Caught!

'Cause them days, you know, they don't arrest for smokin' [narcotics]. No, sir! Just for sellin', that's all. 'Cause I know Dave Bob, he go to prison for that. . . . Henry Quinn [though], he went for breakin' into somebody's cellar. 'Cause you see why he's doin' that? Henry, he can't get *moohoo'oo*, so, want some wine [instead]. And so them *Aytayay*, they're mad. Yes, sir! Report him. Same as Willy Muldoon: [who] get arrested in his own store for sellin' *moohoo'oo*. . . .

'Cause you see what happen? Him and Ida, they're usin' lotta that black stuff that time, and so they fall asleep. And them government bull are waitin' for him. . . . So, when they do that, why, they can rush him. Find lotta drug inside that store, too, by God! 'Cause Billy Miller's not handlin' for Willy no more, so he keep too much on hand. . . .

And I hear he go broke on that case, too. Yes, sir! Keep all his money in the Minden Bank—and so his lawyer, he use it all up! Get one to fourteen year, Willy Muldoon. . . . Should have just taken that sentence [instead of litigating]. . . . But [then] you see what happen when he's away? His brother goes crazy! That's that George Muldoon: he sleep with Willy's wife when he's in prison, kill both them kids before his brother come home. Yes, sir! Shoot 'em, then he wanna kill Ida. Only she jump through that window. And so Willy, when he find out, he get mad. Gets outta jail, and don't get along good with his brother no more. . . . George Muldoon, he's kinda dark guy. Not good lookin', neither. And he never talk right, neither. Younger than Willy, [who] pretty near look like a Jap , Willy Muldoon. . . .

Anyway, so after he get out, Willy open a garage in Carson City. Own a house and garage up there, both.

102. George Emm, Last of the Yen-Shee Sellers

So, George Emm, he's the last one sellin' *moohoo'oo* in this valley [Mason Valley].

Start around about 1928, George Emm . . . after I quit sellin' for Willy. Jimmy Summers, he's still doin' that; but a hard man, Jimmy, I tell you, Mike! Yes, sir! Don't care how sick a fellow is. . . . He won't give any. . . . Why them *moohoo'oo* men don't bother Jimmy Summers too much. . . . Anyway, *Waseeyoo,* George Emm—half, anyway. 'Cause he's from Topaz: part of that *Ungabee* ['Salt'] Sam outfit. But I hear George Emm's raised by some *taivo* in Coleville. Marry a *Nuumuu* [Emma] from these parts, and got all these kids around here: Brady, Howard Emm. . . . Same way, they say he's the father of Clarence Brown, too. . . . Anyway, George Emm, he use everythin': smoke that black stuff, then later on shoot *toha moohoo'oo* [morphine]. Sell both 'em, too!

'Cause I know, one time, I go with George Emm on a buy—to Reno. Not workin' for him, neither; I just go along to help George Emm out. 'Cause you see how? I can keep [hold] my hand on that *moohoo'oo* when we're comin' [driving] home, so [if] I see any government bull, why, I can just throw that some place [i.e., out the car window]. 'Cause he's takin' a poor [risky] chance, you know, George Emm. Yes, sir! Don't wanna go on them back road! 'Cause that's where them government bull are hidin', you know, main road. And George Emm, he has a Ford. . . .

And you see who we're lookin' for in Reno that time? Ah Sam! 'Cause he's got a restaurant. . . . And so we find him, too. Give that money to that Chinaman to buy *moohoo'oo* for us. Then we can come home. But you see what's wrong? George Emm don't sell for very long. No, sir! Six month, maybe? And sells from his own house, too. Yes, sir! So everybody's gotta go to George Emm's house in Colony District to buy. . . . But he give a good measure for your dollar, George Emm. Got caught only once—on that white stuff. . . .

103. Shootin' *Moohoo'oo*

Then you see what they're doin'? Everybody quit smokin' *moohoo'oo*, shoot that black stuff instead. . . .

And it don't hurt much, neither. No, sir! But comes right up, make you to feel good quick. [So that's why] I'm not afraid to do that. . . . 'Cause that needle's just like a mosquito bite! And you see who's the first one doin' that? Emory Dick! Yes, sir! He show me that. . . . How to work that needle down in your skin.

Says,

"That's the best way to do it, Corbett. You save lotta *moohoo'oo* that way. 'Cause [if] you smoke it, you waste [too much]."

Yes, sir! Learn me on that . . . when I'm workin' potato: both I and my wife. 'Cause that's winter time, that's when Emory Dick start [show] me how I'm doin' that, by God! And that black stuff, why, that go right through you that quick when you're shootin'. Yes, sir! So, you feel good right away. . . .

104. Shootin' *Moohoo'oo:* Alternative Version

Elbert Coffin, he's the first one doin' that. Railroad man from Schurz, Elbert: he live in Carson City, by them Chinaman. . . .

'Cause you see what he's doin'? Boil up that black stuff, then Elbert can use cotton to strain it; then shoot that *moohoo'oo* under his skin. 'Cause when you smoke, you know, you lose lot; you shoot, less. . . . What Elbert Coffin's always sayin'. . . . And same way, too, you feel that more quickly. . . . Yes, sir! 'Cause I know that's what everyone's doin'. Sayin' that time. . . .

Buy my first needle from Jerry Keno—that hypodermic needle. 'Cause Jerry, he's got lotta 'em; sell to these Indian. . . . But I don't know where he get 'em from, neither? Reno, I guess. . . . Or [if] a fellow ain't usin' that kind, he can use safety pin and eye dropper; you know, to squirt that in your arm. 'Cause you see how they're doin'? They can stick that [safety] pin under their skin, then squeeze eye dropper. And after a while, they can shoot that in the vein. . . 'Cause that's quickest way, partner. . . . Yes, sir! Go right through you in a minute—if you hit this big vein here. . . . And them kind [addicts], they [also] like get together when they shoot *moohoo'oo*. 'Cause you see why? Some ain't got no outfit. . . . But you gotta put a little paper around that dropper if you ain't usin' hypodermic needle—where that needle's goin' in. (Use Prince Albert [pipe tobacco] paper.) 'Cause otherwise, it's gonna leak out. . . .

And I know I start shootin' that black stuff before I work for Willy Muldoon—when I buy from George Emm. But we never did shoot that very long, neither. No, sir! 'Cause you see why? It [yen-shee] go outta this country when that other kind [morphine] come in.

105. Sanalow

But one thing I know I won't do: shoot sanalow in my vein. No, sir! 'Cause you see why? Too dirty! 'Cause that's that second smokin', you know. . . . What's left over [from] that *moohoo'oo* [yen-shee]. . . . So [if] I'm doin' that, I might just get pus under my skin. Get sick that way and die. . . .

106. *Toha Moohoo'oo* ('Morphine')

'Cause [when] there's no more *moohoo'oo,* so we just start in on that other kind . . . that white stuff.

'Cause that black stuff is *karroo'oo!* All gone! No more Chinaman sellin', you know. Too much afraid. And so Jimmy Summers, he go to Sacramento. But can't get *moohoo'oo* there, so he just buy that morphine. Bring that back here. . . .

Call that *toha moohoo'oo* [white yen-shee], you know, morphine. And that kind's strong, got more kick to it. . . . Work quick, too. Can [even] knock a fellow down! 'Cause I know one time, I seen this *Waseeyoo* usin'. And so he use too much, fall over. Yes, sir! Then we have to help him. . . . Why you gotta be careful usin' that *toha moohoo'oo* . . . that white stuff. . . . Why I know I don't try to use that too heavy right away. . . . No, sir! Just a little bit. . . .

Buy that *toha moohoo'oo* on the cube. . . . Must be over $100? But you see what them seller are doin'? They can sell that on the slice—charge you $2–$3 [per] slice; so that's why you [the addict] can't make too much when you're [also] usin' *toha moohoo'oo*. No, sir! 'Cause that other kind [morphine addiction], it don't [even] leave one cent in your pocket! No, sir! You gotta give all to your buyer. . . .

And you see how we're [also] doin' that? Buy a cube, and break off one slice; then boil it on a spoon. Strain that through cotton. . . . Shoot it. . . . So you always gotta carry spoon in your back pocket, partner—to cook that. 'Cause that's the way them [Reno?] *taivo* doin' that, you know. . . . And same way with that *moohoo'oo,* [we] use that hypodermic needle Jerry Keno sell. 'Cause I know I buy my first from him.... But mostly a fellow can use safety pin and eye dropper when they're shootin' *toha moohoo'oo*. 'Cause that kind don't leak. Then shoot that in their vein.... Get that feelin' real quick that way. Yes, sir!

'Cause I know, first time I'm usin' *toha moohoo'oo*, I'm workin' with my wife's daughter's husband's father—that Logan Williams. (Call him *Tsuveedee'ee* 'Pullin' Feathers outta Somethin''. He's from Schurz. Workin' for Virgil Canaan at Colony [District]: stacks hay.) And so Logan, he think I'm tired, tells me to try that other kind [morphine]. Says that can kill my tired.... And so, by God, I do! But you see what happen? I puke! Yes, sir! Feel dopey, all right, but [still] I puke. And I kind think Logan Williams is buyin' from Willy Muldoon....

But costs too much, *toha moohoo'oo*, I tell you, Mike! Yes, sir! 'Cause pretty expensive stuff.... And [I] don't know if them Chinaman ever use morphine, either? But not too many Indian women are usin'. No, sir! 'Cause more on the man side....

107. Sellin' Morphine

So that's one thing I know I never did try: to sell that *toha moohoo'oo*. No, sir! Jimmy Summers, George Emm, Louie Jones, Mike Rube, Jerry Keno, Billy Schurz... they're all doin' that.... But Jerry [Keno], he's main one [seller].

'Cause I know [even] before I'm workin' for Willy, I go up to Carson [City] with him. Fourth of July. But they're [yen-shee sellers] all closed down, so I and Jerry Keno, we have go to Reno. In his Model T Ford. And we find some [morphine], all right. Come back and make forty dollar that night! 'Cause that's my money, but [since] I have to pay gas, I give Jerry thirty package to start out. Sell for one dollar apiece....

'Cause Jerry Keno, he start out usin' *moohoo'oo* [yen-shee], then later on, that white stuff. Not Wesley [Keno], though. No, sir! 'Cause he don't use none that dope.... Just that *peeyot* business. Him and his brother [Jerry], they're both younger than me.... Anyway, crippled guy, Jerry Keno: has to go around on a crutch all the time. And I know another time, too, I ride with him to Carson City, and Jerry, he go into a grocery store to buy. But that's that *toha moo'oohoo*, that white stuff; to use, not sell. 'Cause when he sell that, you see what Jerry Keno's doin'? Let his mom and dad handle for him!

Yes, sir! In Smith Valley! [While] Jerry, he sell down here [Mason Valley]. Yes, sir! Says he can make lot more down here. . . . And Jerry Keno's [also] got a *Waseeyoo* wife. Yes, sir! Out buyin' *toha moohoo'oo* with her all the time. . . . Run around, so they can't catch him. . . . And he make so much money on that, Jerry can sell his Model T Ford for Buick. 'Cause I hear he buy that white stuff in Reno and Sacramento. . . . Anyway, we're always buyin' [morphine] from his mother—from Minnie Keno; call her *Tsavas*. . . . Buy that one dollar package from them. Little piece for one dollar. Get just a couple shot outta that. . . . Yes, sir! 'Cause we used to go to their place all the time. Minnie Keno, she don't use; James Keno can smoke a little that black stuff. . . . Jerry, he pack it up for 'em. . . .

One time, we went over to Old Man [James] Keno's place—to tell him about them government bull. But you see what happen? His wife won't believe us.

"You don't want somebody else make money!" Minnie Keno, she say. Mad, you know, 'cause these Indian around here are only callin' for one dollar [purchase]. So she don't wanna be bothered! No, sir! And so that's how come Jerry Keno got caught. Don't believe us! 'Cause Sarah Mason, she tell [informs] them government bulls on him. . . . And that's way up in Colony [District] where they get caught, partner. But Jerry's mom, she don't go to prison. . . . No, sir! 'Cause you see why? Husband does, James Keno. Yes, sir! He's the one goin' in for her . . . take her term. 'Cause they got a young girl that time, Nina, and so Minnie Keno, she's gotta stay home to take care her. Mae "Hash" [Benjamin], she's the one talkin' [interpreting] for Minnie Keno. Help her out at that trial, you know. . . .

Anyway, Jerry Keno, he sell for three or four year, maybe? And so, after he get scared out, George Emm and Jimmy Summers, they start up. . . . But you see what happen to Jerry? Get poisoned by this one *poohaghooma!* Yes, sir! 'Cause he was ridin' with this one *Waseeyoo* guy to Tahoe, and Jerry Keno's leg start to hurt. Dies by that same way. . . .

Then after Minnie and James Keno get arrested, I buy from Jimmy Summers. . . .

But like I say, he's a hard man, Jimmy Summers. 'Cause no matter how much you're sufferin', why, he can [still] always say: "I don't got any, partner! [Am] sufferin' myself!" Yes, sir! No matter even [if] he's got some on hand, Jimmy Summers won't hardly sell! Went up to Reno, I hear, that first time. On a buy that white stuff. . . . And same way, too, I hear he [also] goes over to Placerville. 'Cause one time, Jimmy Summers take his wife with him. 'Cause you see why? Daisy, she's got that girl on the cradleboard, so they figure they can hide that *toha moohoo'oo* inside there! But he's not buyin' in Reno from them Chinaman, though. No, sir! 'Cause them *taivo*, they're the ones workin' [selling] that kind there. . . . Anyway, Jimmy Summers don't last very long. . . . Get scared out that quick just like George Emm. . . . Quit. . . .

And same way, too, George Emm, he also buy in Reno. But he don't last very long, neither. No, sir! Oh, maybe six month on that *toha moohoo'oo*? No more. . . . 'Cause George Emm, he get caught at that weevil station—on Jack Wright Highway, a little above Simpson Ditch. . . . 'Cause you see what happen? Him and Sunday Sam's brother George, they're partners. Both are sellin' that white stuff, and so they take that main road back from California, when they should have used the back road. And so them government bull stop 'em: search George Emm's car and find that. . . . Arrest 'em both. And so they go to jail. . . . George Sam, he's from Topaz. . . .

Another one sellin' is Billy Schurz; sell in this [Mason] valley. Call him *Yaroogaz'a*, Billy Schurz: 'Always Laughing with His Mouth Wide Open'. And he use that kind, too. . . . Sell, oh, maybe one year? Then get caught and go to prison. . . . But I never did see Billy Schurz usin' that black stuff. . . . No, sir! Hear his wife rob somebody; help Billy to get this start that way. . . . But [I] never did buy from Billy Schurz, neither. No, sir!

Another time, I come down here, and Tom Benjamin wanna treat. 'Cause we're sufferin' pretty bad that time, partner; I and my wife. But he don't use any, Tom Benjamin; just drinks! So I kind of think Tom Benjamin's maybe handlin' Billy Schurz's stuff?

108. *Waseeyoo* Morphine Sellers

And you see who else is sellin' *toha moohoo'oo*? Them *Waseeyoo*!

'Cause I know Harry James, he use that white stuff. Yes, sir! His young[er] brother, Willy [though] don't. Anyway, they're partners: Willy James, he leave Harry in Smith Valley: to sell. 'Cause that time, Harry James live with us. And he sell some, all right; then when George Emm get caught, they both quit! And I hear Harry James and his son [subsequently] fight over a woman—in that gamblin' house in Dresslerville; and so his son throw a jug gasoline in the stove and it explode! Harry James, he's a[nother] *nomogwet*! Willy James, he's the *Waseeyoo* [who] wanna marry my wife's daughter,

Margaret.... Same way, too, Harry James, he's the one take that overdose.... Fall over that way, like he die; so we have to pour cold water on him. You know, to revive him from that overdose that way. O.K. afterwards.... 'Cause like I tell you, Mike, that *toha moohoo'oo*, that's pretty strong stuff.... Can knock a man over! And quick, too!

109. Mike Rube, Last of the Indian Sellers?

So pretty near all that dope's out that time.... Them government bull are watchin' everybody close.... Still, Mike Rube wanna try that [selling]. And his brother, Curley, he don't help him, neither. No, sir! 'Cause Mike Rube's got a different partner that time. Name's Eugene, he's from Sweetwater... Bridgeport... somewhere back that way.... Little fellow in Stewart when I'm up there, Mike Rube. Younger than I am. Sell *toha moohoo'oo* way up in Red Canyon—other side Sweetwater Ranch... where Mike Rube work.... Yes, sir! Start in around the time them *Waseeyoo* seller.... Anyway, his partner, he's the one always stayin' on top that mountain in Red Canyon: sells from up there....

But I hear Mike Rube borrow his brother Curley's car to get started. And he don't use that white stuff, neither. No, sir! Mike Rube just sell. But he won't tell nobody else where he's buyin' [morphine] from! No, sir! I kind of think Reno, 'cause Mike Rube, he's always comin' back [to Smith Valley] too quick? And sell for one year, maybe, that's all. Get scared out and quit. 'Cause one time, them government bull raid his cabin. But they don't find nothin', so just scare him, that's all. So then, you see what happen: after Mike Rube quit, his brother Curley come to our house.

"I'm pretty sick, partner. You can help me out?"

'Cause Curley Rube, he tell what happen: says some guys from Bishop were lookin' for his brother—Johnny Jack and another fellow; some kind Milton? Said they were usin' that white stuff and lookin' for Mike Rube to buy; only Mike's partner, Eugene, he tell 'em: "He ain't home!" And so Mike Rube, he get scared! Yes, sir! Run outta this country; go to Woodfords. 'Cause you see why? Mike Rube, he must think them Bishop fellow are workin' for them government bull! And so that's how come I and my wife, we went up there to his camp—after Mike Rube get scared out.

'Cause we're lookin' for his *toha moohoo'oo*, you know.... 'Cause we know he's hidin' that. And gee, lotta other Indian are [also] up there! You know, diggin' around, tryin' to find that white stuff. . . . What Mike Rube's hidin' before he get scared out. . . . 'Cause they're sick, too, partner. Same like we! Yes, sir! 'Cause everybody's havin' a helluva time, then. . . . So anyway, I and my wife, we find one whole can! And gee, we sure go crazy on Mike Rube's *toha moohoo'oo!* Yes, sir! Keep on usin' that all the time, you know. Don't even wanna sell any, neither. No, sir! And we don't [even] wanna help nobody else out. Not even my wife's brother! 'Cause Andy [Dick], he's back from prison, then [1924]. . . . Start usin' again. . . .

But anyway, we do; help him out. On a treat, though. Don't sell to him. And tell Andy, "Don't come back!" 'Cause you see why? We're afraid! Afraid maybe he's gonna start up heavy again, then everybody else will. So somebody might just call them government bull on us? Anyway, he don't— come back for more. . . .

But Mike Rube's *toha moohoo'oo* is not too strong. No, sir! Don't really have enough kick to it. . . . And so, by God, we finally run out. No more dope, and we have to go to Carson [City] for more. Go on the bus up there. . . . But we can't find any, neither. No, sir! 'Cause there's no more that white stuff that time, partner! *Karroo'oo!* All gone! No more *taivo* peddlers. . . . All scared out, you know. 'Cause I hear they put 'em in jail. Yes, sir! 'Cause them government bull, they get after 'em pretty hard that time. And them Chinaman what's left, they won't sell *moohoo'oo* no more, neither. 'Cause I know I and my wife, we [also] go lookin' for Mr. Sam Lowe. Think maybe he can tell us where to buy that other kind [morphine] in Carson? Or maybe Sam Lowe can give us somethin' to break that habit with [sec. 111]? But he's too scared, that Chinaman. Won't sell to no Indian. . . . So finally, we find one guy who can buy for us.

And he's another *Waseeyoo,* that fellow: belong to Carson City [Indian Colony]. . . . Why them Chinaman know him. Name's Long Henry, and he use, too; so we send him to buy. But Long Henry, he can't get any [morphine]. No, sir! Says that's all closed down, so he get us *moohoo'oo* [yenshee]. And so I and my wife, we shoot that. 'Cause that's really the last time, partner. . . . 'Cause after that, *karroo'oo!* No more nothin'! All that dope's gone outta this country for good! 'Cause I know we went up there a second time to buy [morphine]. But we can't find any. . . So, pretty tough time, that time, I tell you, Mike!

110. Withdrawal Symptoms

'Cause that's rough business when you got no more, partner. . . . Yes, sir! Be sicker than a dog! Bones achin', your arms, too. . . . Kick around . . . roll around on that ground. . . . And squeeze yourself, too, when you can't get no more *moohoo'oo*. Black or white! And same way, too, you don't feel like stayin' in any one place. No, sir! Don't feel like workin', neither. So when you got nothin', have a helluva time!

'Cause I know a couple time that happen to me. . . Once, when them Chinaman get scared outta Smith Valley, I come down here to Mason [town]. But *karroo'oo!* 'Cause that Chinaman, he say "No more!" And so, I go down to Wabuska. . . . See if Ah Sam's got any? But he's got another Chinaman peddlin' for him, 'cause Ah Sam don't handle no more. And so he say the same: "*Karroo'oo!* I ain't got nothin'! Policeman around. . . . Why I ain't got nothin' on hand!" And so I have to go clear to Sweetwater . . . with my cousin-brother, Henry Quinn. Yes, sir! We change horse at the [Yerington Indian] Colony; take a buggy ride up there. . . . 'Cause Carson [City]'s a little too far, and I'm feelin' pretty sick, partner. Yes, sir! And that's that time that Chinaman cook up there sell us that bad stuff . . . Sanalow. . . . Time we sneak back and find that good stuff and go at it like a hog in the potato patch! Sweetwater take you only half a day, and [if] you're sufferin' like that, why, you gotta look for that dope everywhere! Can't find any, then, you gotta just tough it out!

And same way, too, we're sufferin' real bad after we finish Mike Rube's *toha moohoo'oo;* so you see what we're doin'? Send by some *Waseeyoo!* 'Cause he live in Carson, that *Waseeyoo,* so we go up there after him that other time . . . after Long Henry. . . . But he can't get no morphine—just yen-shee. And so I buy that; use that up real quick. Shoot that black stuff. . . .

No, I go to Carson [City] twice when I'm sufferin'. . . . Yes, sir! Go up there again, and we get more [morphine?] from that *Waseeyoo.* . . . Then no more money, so we just make up our mind to quit.

111. What to Take for Withdrawal Symptoms?

And that first time I quit, I use "cake" whole summer. . . .

'Cause it's easy [to quit] with that one . . . that cake. Round pill, that one: brown, and taste pretty near like dirt. Come in a pack of seven: twelve [packs] in that small box. . . . Cost you $3.50 for one whole box. And you feel good when you take that cake. Same as that black one! Get that same feelin' outta that kind. . . .

'Cause first time I'm usin' cake, I know I take two: just to get used to that kind medicine. And if that work all right, well, I can break one in half, take one and a half. . . . So, keep on doin' that, you know, till pretty soon I get over it. . . . Yes, sir! You get over that habit quick with that kind. . . . And that's before I work for Sullivan Tom when I use that cake. . . . Before all these Indian are usin' that dope, too, by God!

And you see who's sellin' that cake? George Orange! But Mack Paddy, he's the one show me that. But you see what I'm doin'? I can buy that kind in Carson—to help people out [i.e., sell]. Cost $3.50 for that small box, so I can sell one roll for $2.00; make $14.00. . . . And so them *moohoo'oo* men, they buy me out. 'Cause I only buy three case in Carson City that time. . . . 'Cause that's around about that same time I lay off that black stuff. . . . Why I'm usin' cake all summer long. . . . 'Cause you see why? Edie [Johnson], she say to me: "Corbett, I'm not goin' to marry you, [if] you use! How we gonna make a family?" 'Cause Edie, she don't use none that dope; me, I'm spendin' all my money for that black stuff. . . . And so I wanna quit. . . . 'Cause them *moohoo'oo* men, they don't hardly take care their family. No, sir! And you're a family man, you're supposed do that. . . . But not if you're usin' either kind *moohoo'oo*. No, sir! 'Cause [then] what little money you got is for habit. Yes, sir! Have to spend everythin' what you got on that. . . .

And you see why I start smokin' again? After Edie Johnson and I break up. Then them Chinaman get over that; them government bull go away, and so they start in again. You know, sellin' that black stuff. Start up these Indian again, . . . And me, I start sellin' for Sullivan Tom. . . .

But same way, too, you can get over that [withdrawal symptoms] with red pill. . . . Call 'em *wuuyuupoowee* that kind: named for buckberry. 'Cause Sam Lowe, he's the one show me that first—Chinaman [who] live in Carson City. . . . Yes, sir! 'Cause them Chinaman, they're [also] the one sellin' *wuuyuupoowee*. Come in a little bottle, you know: 200-300 pill for two to three dollar. And they make you to feel happy, too, by God! 'Cause I know, one time, Stewart Mitchell is sick, and so I sell him one pill for two bit. Then he come back for more. Says, "Gee, I feel good, Corbett!" Buys some more from me. Then he can tell the rest, so they pile up on me. . . . But [subsequently] that Chinaman get caught, so everyone [else] close down. . . . Won't sell to me no more. . . .

112. Over-the-Counter Remedies

And same way, too, them *moohoo'oo* men, they keep that *chimoora'a* in their pocket. . . . Call that Chamberlain's by right name . . . by *taivo*. 'Cause even them old-timers who ain't usin', they keep it. Yes, sir! Not Big Mack, though. 'Cause he don't bother that kind stuff. Not Jack Wilson, neither. Or Jimmy Johnson, Old Man Benjamin . . . none them real old-timers. . . . And same way, too, I know my boss [Mencarini also] keep that in his pocket all the time. . . . Smell like a liniment, you know. Buy it in the drug store . . . that one drug store in Yerington. And that's got that writing on there, too: Says *"'Oopeey^n."* But I don't know how much percent is in that, only thing is, that one's got a kick to it! Yes, sir! Pretty near just the same as that dope, by God! So, I guess they quit sellin' that when they make a law [Harrison Narcotics Act]?. . . . But what I don't see is what kind kick outta Bromo Seltzer them hophead get? 'Cause they always carry that too, you know. . . . Put that in their hand, put that water on top it in their mouth. . . . So, must be some kind kick, ain't it? Anyway I keep that kind [Bromo Seltzer] all the time [i.e., at home]. 'Cause sometime, a fellow has a headache; don't feel good. . . . Take that to kill my pain!

113. Contract Physician

Used to be them government doctor in Yerington, you know . . . Magee, Leavitt, Knox, Rees. . . . Yes, sir! That's [some of] their name. . . . So we go up to 'em and say, "Well, I'm sick, give me somethin'!" And so they can say back, "I do that!" Give you that cough syrup they sell in drug store . . . whatever them Indian ask for. Yes, sir! But I don't know if them other *moohoo'oo* men ever do that [i.e., request shots]? 'Cause I know only one time we go down to Yerington to do that . . . to see that one *tota* [contract physician] . . . that Dr. Rees. 'Cause him and his wife, you see, they're helpin' these Indian at the [Yerington Indian] Colony: Dr. Rees, he can deliver baby and give flu shot; Mrs. Rees, she's nurse, distribute commodity food. . . . And gee, they sure work there a good many year. . . . After them other government doctor. . . . But Dr. Rees, he act funny: happy all the time. . . . Talk funny, too—tongue's always dry. And same way, he fall asleep all the time . . . like he's doped up all the time. *Paymoodayp* [Smoking dope]! So, make me to kind of think Dr. Rees is also usin' [opiates]! And you see what [else] these Indian always sayin' about him? That he give them Indian girl that "stuff" [venereal disease]! 'Cause you see why? If Dr. Rees see a woman on the street, he put his arm around her. . . . Same way, too, lotta these Indian down here [Yerington] don't like to use that medicine he give 'em when they're sick. 'Cause you see why? Some die, so their relation say how that ain't right. . . . Say that's wrong kind medicine Dr. Rees give 'em. . . . Poison 'em! Anyway, pretty good *tota*, Dr. Rees: die on a heart attack over by that Catholic church while he's drivin'. . . . But [since] Dr. Rees can give you that [morphine] shot inside his office [if] you're sufferin' [withdrawal symptoms], we go there. . . .

Yes, sir! And go when I'm sufferin' real bad . . . that one time we go down there to see him. 'Cause that's I and my wife, and Jerry Keno and Henry Quinn. "Maybe he can give you one or two pill for me?" I tell my wife. And so she do that, all right. . . . Go and get three pill off him for me. . . . Yes, sir! And [But] Dr. Rees don't give 'em any shot. . . . Then you see what happen? [I] never did get my shot that time!

'Cause we're travelin' [home] on the road, and Curley Rube—he's also with us—see them government bull; get scared they might just stop that car and arrest us, so Curly throw that away. 'Cause he's holdin' my pill outside that car window, you know. Think they're maybe gonna stop us. But they don't. . . .

114. Once More, Once

And so, after we [finally] quit usin', Macarini can let us go pine nuttin'. 'Cause that's after potato season, you know; fall the year. . . . We can make a few cent sellin' *tuuba* [pine nuts]. . . . And don't remember how much we gettin' for that, neither, but I know after I'm back from Stewart, Frank Simpson, he give us thirty-five cent a pound for raw pine nut. . . . Money to buy our own grub. . . . Anyway, I and my wife, we go up after them pine nut this side Sweetwater . . . over by Sulphur. . . . And you see who we meet there? Louie Jones and his wife. She's *Waseeyoo*, Louie Jones' wife; then later on, he marry one them Mitchell girl. . . . They're campin' up there, also pine nuttin'; and they're both usin', so, by God, they start us off again!

Louie, he's from Bishop; they call him Strawberry, on account his big nose. [He] sells that white stuff, all right, but not much. And not to everybody, neither. No, sir! Just whoever he want.... 'Cause I know I buy *toha moohoo'oo* from Louie Jones two time. And that time we're pine nuttin', we can't afford to buy, so we make a deal: we can trade our pine nut what we gather for morphine. Yes, sir! And so, by God, Louie Jones agree! ([Also has to] hire *Apee* Hooligan and George Sam to pick for him, 'cause they're [also] usin' morphine.) 'Cause Louie, he know where to buy that white stuff ... some place in Reno....

I and my wife, we can gather, oh, maybe, 100 pound every day? Then trade 50 pound *tuuba* for fifteen packet that white stuff to Louie Jones. Yes, sir! 'Cause that's four shot to every one packet, partner: a dollar a packet. 'Cause otherwise, we can sell our pine nut ... maybe for ten cent a pound? And so we do that, too, by God! Louie Jones, he then can take 'em to Reno ... 100 pound ... Come back with *toha moohoo'oo* for us.

But that [narcotic] don't last very long, neither. No, sir! Just about a couple or three month, maybe? 'Cause you see why? [He] get caught! 'Cause after we finish pine nuttin', Louie Jones and his wife, they come back down to stay with us—at our house on Macarini's ranch. And so that's [near] where he get caught. 'Cause you see how? Louie, he go to Carson [City] to get some more white stuff, and I guess they chase him from there ... catch him in Smith Valley.... 'Cause you see who's doin' that: Andy Vidovich! Yes, sir! Three Vidovich brother: Jerry, Marty, and Andy. *Tovongo* [Shoshones] from Death Valley.... Kind of dark lookin' guy, all them Vidovich.... Look pretty near like a *nuugatse* [Negro]! Anyway, Andy Vidovich, he's workin' down here.... And I hear his brother Jerry's in [law enforcement work in] Reno and Carson City. But none these Indian like him [Andy Vidovich]. No, sir! 'Cause what he's doin' all the time [i.e., making arrests]! Anyway, they can't say nothin'.... And so Andy Vidovich, he chase Louie Jones from Carson [Valley] to Smith Valley before he catch him; arrest him. But [he] never made much money, Louie Jones. No, sir! 'Cause he don't run very long. And Louie, he never went to prison, neither. They just lock him up for possession [?] when [really] it's his wife who's handlin' that white stuff [?].... Yes, sir! Call her Long Mary, she's from Schurz. Pretty tall woman, too, by God, Louie Jones's first wife.... But she don't use *toha mohoo'oo*. No, sir! 'Cause only Louie Jones is doin' that....

And so, that's the last round, by God! 'Cause nobody else is doin' that [selling narcotics] when Louie Jones get arrested.... *Karroo'oo!* Dope all gone outta here!

115. Geography of Addiction

And seem like just about every Indian down here [Smith and Mason Valleys] is usin' that stuff, by God! Both black and white *moohoo'oo* . . . man and woman . . . both! Yes, sir! 'Cause pretty near everyone smoke that black stuff. Then when they shoot that, why, everybody who's doin' that [smoking yen-shee], do that [injection], too. Except for them old-timers. . . . 'Cause they don't. . . . Only them young people. . . .

And same way, they're [also] usin' both kind in Sweetwater. . . . 'Cause Old Man Fredericks, he's got a Chinaman cook up there, and so them Indian workin' for him, they use *moohoo'oo*. . . . And [on] the Walker River Reservation, too. . . . Pretty near all them Carson City Indians [also] usin' that dope—before they get that Colony. . . . And Reno's the same. . . . But I don't think too many them *Kooyooweeyeedokado* [Pyramid Lake Indians were] doin' that. No, sir! Or Fallon, neither. Or them Coleville Indian. . . . 'Cause I know I go up there [Antelope Valley] all the time—on cattle drive. But don't see too many Indian doin' that there. No, sir! Only George and Sunday Sam, them two brother. . . . So, don't see why, neither, 'cause they got Chinaman cook up there?

And Bridgeport, my wife tell me they got Chinaman sellin' [opiates] up there—that black stuff. But me, [since I] don't go there too much, don't know if they Indian usin'. . . . And only some them Bishop Indian are doin' that [yen-shee] . . . like Louie Jones. . . . But Louie, he do that only when he come into Smith Valley, though. 'Cause he's a real heavy *toha moohoo'oo* user, Louie Jones. . . . And not too many *Waseeyoo* doin' that, neither. Just some . . . in Gardnerville. 'Cause I know I go up there lotta time to visit my relation once in a while, and one guy who's usin'—his wife's my grandma, Susie Snooks; her husband do that—they call him Long Nose Willy. Yes, sir! 'Cause he's got a pretty high nose, by God! But he don't smoke that *moohoo'oo*. . . . No, sir! Eat it! 'Cause I know when[ever] I go there, he alway bums me: "Gimme little piece, Corbett—I'm sick!" What he always say . . . and take my *moohoo'oo*, and away he go. Chew that like a chewin' gum! Old man, Long Nose Willy. [I] guess he's an old-timer. . . . But he don't drink, so he don't put whiskey on top that. Not like them Chinaman I used to see doin' that. . . . Anyway, not too many them *Waseeyoo* usin' [narcotics]. 'Cause you see why? All they wanna do is to drink! But never did go as far as Woodfords, so I can't tell you that. . . .

116. My Gripe

But you see what I'm [always] thinkin'? [That] Willy Muldoon beat me outta my money! Yes, sir! [That] he just bullshit me! 'Cause you see why? Never did show me where I can buy my own *moohoo'oo!* In Sacramento, you know.... 'Cause Willy, he don't show up for a good long time [after he gets Corbett started]. Hide around after they start arrestin' everyone—act just like he don't wanna know me! And same way, too, Sullivan Tom, what he's [also] doin' to me. "I can let you make a few hundred dollar, Corbett, then take you to Sacramento. Show you where to buy.... Then you can go over by yourself: make your own money that way!" What they two say to me.... Why I [originally] quit Sullivan Tom, you know.... But [then] I see how much Jimmy Summers makin', so I'm thinkin' to myself: "That's what I wanna do, too!" Yes, sir! 'Cause I know I also wanna have money in my pocket.... Why I go to work for Willy Muldoon....

So, real crooked fellow, Willy Muldoon! Yes, sir! Jew me down! [Why] I think Sullivan Tom's better partner than Willy Muldoon!

117. Opiates: Reprise

So I bet you I been usin' *moohoo'oo* for twenty years, partner! Yes, sir! And been drinkin' steady another twenty-five.... Ever since that dope business went outta here.... 'Cause [if] you're usin' [narcotics], a person don't even have a dollar in his pocket! No, sir! Give all to that peddler, you know. 'Cause you only make a couple dollar a day [if] you're workin'. And cost you twelve dollar a week on yen-shee.... 'Cause you're usin' three time every day: mornin', noon, and night. So you draw all your money to buy that, you know.... Got nothing left in your pocket....

'Cause all them addict sure got a tough time them days, by God! Clothes all ragged ... no food to eat ... can't [even] take care their family. 'Cause that's all they ever do is never think about nothin' else except that *moohoo'oo*.... Yes, sir! 'Cause always callin' them, you know.... "Come on! Come on!" Yes, sir! Won't hardly let you go.... And [if] they can't buy any, they're stealin' all the time, too, them *moohoo'oo* men: [especially] from them *Aytayay* cellar. You know, to sell to restaurant.... But mostly steal from each other, 'cause too scared to steal from them Yerington store ...

Mason. . . . Same way, too, they can steal wool from dead sheep. Yes, sir! Anythin' good, they look for that: to sell to them junk men. . . .

So, can't let go that pipe or needle when you're usin' *moohoo'oo*. . . . But you sleep pretty tight. Get up in the mornin' and you want a little pill, so you gotta light up again—before you go to work. . . . And Sunday, no work, why, you can do that all day long! Yes, sir! Don't have to quit till Monday mornin' when you gotta go to work again. . . . And you don't [even] hardly wanna eat. Don't want no kind woman to lay down with, neither. Be sick as a dog when you don't have any. . . . Yes, sir! Take me pretty near all winter long to get over it. . . . Till I can go back to work again. [So] I just go over to that *Aytayay* sellin' that jackass whiskey. . . . Buy. Drink that to get over my bad feelin'. . . . And some fellow, they can be mean when they're like that [withdrawal]. . . . Like Henry McCloud. . . .

But [at least] *moohoo'oo* don't make you to go outta your head like drink. No, sir! And same way, too, too much *heebee,* why, you just go to sleep! But *[toha moohoo'oo],* that one make you to be lively man. Happy, too. . . . 'Cause like I already told you, that kind [opiates] knock the tired right outta you! Yes, sir! 'Cause no matter how hard you're workin', no matter how tired you can get, why, you use that black or white stuff, and your tired's all gone. . . .

But even [if] I'm a drinkin' man now, that *toha moohoo'oo* is still callin' me. . . . Quit usin', but I know I'm damn stiff-handed when I quit usin' *moohoo'oo* that last time. . . .

7

Some Real Old-Timers (1896–1940)

118. Never Mix, Never Worry!

And so, no more *moohoo'oo*, everybody just start in on that *heebee* [wine]. . . .

Drinkin' that all the time, you know. . . . 'Cause I know I'm doin' that pretty near twenty-five years, partner. Yes, sir! Three time every day. . . . One glass with every meal. And I can buy that pint, half-gallon, gallon from my boss every night, too—depend on what I got left over. . . . 'Cause them *Aytayay*, you know, they don't pay too much. . . . No, sir! Pretty cheap on the wage! Same as on Saturday night, and [for] all day Sunday, too. . . . Yes, sir! 'Cause stay drunk all Sunday, too! 'Cause when you're usin' either kind *moohoo'oo*, a fellow don't wanna drink at all. No, sir! Don't like to use 'em both. . . . 'Cause you see why? They say, "[You will] lose your mind, [if] you mix!" 'Cause I know I'm that way. . . . [If] you offer a hophead a drink, why, he won't take it! No, sir! Anyway, I and my wife, we're drinkin' pretty steady after that *moohoo'oo* business go out of this country, partner. . . . Just so long [as] Macarini give us our wine!

Jackass, that home brew, and [especially] *Aytayay* homemade wine. . . . What[ever] they're sellin' to these Indian around here. . . . 'Cause [if] you don't buy from them *Aytayay*, why, you just gotta get some *wa'eets taivo* [hobo] to buy for you. 'Cause like I already told you, liquor's all closed down that time [Prohibition]; Indian can't drink. Still, you can always get somebody to buy for you. 'Cause I know one guy, Henry Fredericks—he's a *nomogwet;* from Sweetwater: father's a *taivo,* mother *is Nuumuu.* . . . But they always serve him in bar. When he's not drinkin', Henry Fredericks always sayin' how he's a *D^tsaman;* looked, though, like he's Indian—buy for us all the time. . . . And same way George Dick. . . . 'Cause he's also a light [-skinned, i.e., half-breed] guy, you know. Yes, sir! Look pretty near like he's Porty-gese, George Dick: the only light one outta that whole Dick outfit from Coleville. . . . Anyway, he can [also] buy *heebee,* George Dick. Help a sufferin' guy out. . . .

'Cause that's pretty near the same as with *moohoo'oo,* that drinkin' business. . . . Yes, sir! 'Cause them government bull, they're [also] always watchin'. Can give marked money to some crazy Indian, too—to find out by that way who's sellin' and not. . . . 'Cause I know that's what crazy Andrew Penrose is doin'. Yes, sir! Help 'em to clean them bootlegger outta these valley. . . .

Then, later on, they open up them bar to these Indian [1953], and some line up and go crazy! Not me. . . . 'Cause I know I'd rather drink Macarini's wine. Yes, sir! Stay home on my drunk; better that way. 'Cause when I'm home, I know I can drink as much as I want. Yes, sir! 'Cause [I] always have my own jug at home. . . . But that's one thing I [still] like to know: how come my boss never treat us? Sure is tight that Macarini—Never give I and my wife a treat! And same way, too, Amos don't drink with us, neither.

119. Another Time . . .

Another time, I and my wife, we're drinkin', and SS and Irene Thompson, they're with this Indian guy named Poncho. (He's related to Mike Rube, Poncho. Work for Fred Fulstone.) And so they're all drinkin,' walkin' hand-in-hand down the road; ask us for help. So I do; pack Irene Thompson's baby. . . . That young boy [Benny] she's got. . . . And so, when my wife pass out, why, I make *yogho* with them two girl! Yes, sir, fuck 'em both! And I tell 'em, too, "Don't tell my wife!" Then [when] I go back to my wife, find her with Poncho! Throw him off!

[Yet] another time, I'm fuckin' Catherine Bender . . . doggie-style. And she say, "Hurry up, Corbett!" But I can't. 'Cause you see why? I'm drunk!

So gee, we sure go crazy with that *heebee!*

120. I Am Arrested!

And only two times I'm arrested. . . . You know, drinkin' and get on a fight. . . .

'Cause that first time, I go to the [Yerington Indian] Colony; on a Saturday night. And that's I and Sam Leon and Steve Johnson. . . . We're at Daisy Brown's house, and so these two other guys from Schurz, they start raisin' hell with Steve Johnson's wife. 'Cause that's that Johnny Bob and John Brown. [They] get drunk and wanna jump on her, so we get into fight. Go to jail, too. . . . .

But that other time, I kill somebody!

'Cause you see what happen? Henry Frank, he try to get on my wife. But I won't let him. No, sir! So that fellow stab me, and so I stab him back! Why we make trouble that way, you know. . . . Why Macarini, he have to call that Smith Valley policeman . . . Henry Frank, he's from Bishop: *Pituunuugwet* [Bishop Paiutes], you know. From the south. . . . Mean guy, too. 'Cause we're afraid them.

And so, after that happen, we go [are taken] to that public hospital—at Schurz. Only thing is, Henry Frank can't make it. No, sir! Die there. And so that judge, [since] he's saloon keeper in Wellington, he know me: gives me twenty dollar or twenty day in jail. And so I call Macarini to help. But Big Mack, he's the one payin' that fine. Yes, sir! So I don't go to prison that time, 'cause that fellow from Schurz [superintendent?], he [also] help out. Smart man, out talk the Law!

121. One Real Old-Timer's Belief

Jim Wilson, he's from Schurz: some kind relation on the Old Man's side. . . . But he's not related to Jack Wilson. No, sir! Just named by that same way . . . after them [David] Wilsons [of Missouri Flat, Mason Valley, and Pine Grove]. . . . Anyway, I know him! 'Cause Jim Wilson's marry to Big Mack's mother. . . . But that's way later. . . .

Real name's *Ohugweedatoo* Jim, 'Bone' Jim. From Fallon? Or Pyramid Lake? And he's a real old-timer, too, by God! Used to live in Missouri Flat: bunch hay, do any kind light work for them early day *taivo*. . . . Same way, too, Bone Jim, he's the one tell that this world's goin' to tip some day. . . . 'Cause I know when I'm little, that's what pretty near all them old-timers are always sayin'. Believin', anyway. . . . 'Cause I know my grandma, she believe that. My mom, too. . . . But nobody know when that's gonna happen, neither. 'Cause you see what he say?

"Too many bad people on this world, that's why it's gotta tip."

Yes, sir! And so, when that happen, why, them dead people, they can come back. Come back and be young again. . . . And when that happen [i.e., during the apocalypse], you gotta hang onto sagebrush; [so when this world rights itself], why, you can be with your dead relation again. Yes, sir! Why I kind of figure that's why so many *sawabee* [sagebrush] in this world? You know, to hold on to! And you see what else them old-timers sayin'? *Taivo*, they're bad, so, they're gonna fall off this world when them dead people come back to be young again!

'Cause Mamie Dick—her husband Andy's my wife's *pavee'ee* [older brother]—she used to talk that way. Yes, sir! Talk like a preacher, you know, Mamie—*peeza'yoo*, good! 'Cause she's been there, you know, so Mamie already know that place . . . [can] talk about what she's seen. 'Cause when she's a little girl, Mamie [Bob b. 1885?] die, and so Blind Bob [her father], he get *Wodzeewob* to doctor her. 'Cause he's another old-timer, *Wodzeewob*: small thin guy, not real big, anyway, like Big Mack . . . [or] Jack Wilson . . . And so that's why he look kind of young. 'Cause I think *Wodzeewob* is [even] older than my Big Mack. . . . Well, maybe same age, anyway, as the Old Man? Dick Bennett? . . . Them real old-timers. . . . Only thing is, Jack Wilson's father's way older than *Wodzeewob*. 'Cause he's a real old-timer, that one!

Wodzeewob, that means 'Gray-Head'. 'Cause they say [if] you don't throw your hair in the river when you cut it, [if] you don't burn it, why, you turn gray before your time! And so maybe that's what that one mean, *Wodzee wobba* 'Gray Hair'? What he's doin'. . . . [But] Fish Lake Joe is his *taivo* name, so maybe he's from down that way? From Fish Lake Valley [California]? [So] they call him Hawthorne *Wodzeewob*, also. Wife's from Schurz, she's *Nuumuu;* why *Wodzeewob* stay there all the time. . . . 'Cause she's got [alloted] land there, you know. Stole that one boy, that *nomogwet*, Willy Frank, [who's] workin' that land now [1972]. . . . But never did hear her name, though. Just call her *Wodzeewob norr^gwa* [Wodziwob's wife]). . . .

Yes, sir! 'Cause I know that old-timer. . . . *Wodzeewob*, he move back and forth from Schurz to Mason and the [Yerington Indian] Colony. . . . 'Cause I always like to visit that old-timer when I come down to Mason . . . both him and that other real old-timer, *Soowee warr^b*. . . . [I] stay with

Wodzweewob all the time, 'cause his wife, she's my relation—on Big Mack's side. . . . And he don't work, neither, that old-timer. Oh, maybe when he's young *Wodzeewob* is doin' that? Not when I know him, anyway. 'Cause you see why? Too old; blind, that old-timer. . . . Same way, he don't say very much, *Wodzeewob*. No, sir! Don't tell about them early days ago. . . . Not like Jim Wilson's doin', anyway. Doctors my mom, though . . . [cf. sec. 122]. 'Cause you see what he can do? Send his *sunamee* [mind] to that other place [Land of Dead], bring that sick [comatose] person back!

And so, when he's doctorin' Mamie Bob [Dick], *Wodzeewob*, he put four feathers down: two by Mamie's head, other two by her feet. Say to everybody [assembled family members]: "When that feather start to move, that's when she's comin' back again!" And so, by God, that happen, too! 'Cause *Wodzeewob*, he lay down next to that girl, and pretty quick, feather start shakin' and Mamie wake up again. "Real pretty flower before me—" Tell what she's seen after. "'Cause I'm walkin' along, but pretty soon have to turn back. And so, when I do, there's lotta sagebrush . . . lotta sagebrush and one *Nuumuu*. He's standin' out in that field like that; got a shovel in his hand, he's diggin' potato!"

So *Wodzeewob*, he bring her back, all right! 'Cause all them real old-timers are always sayin' how that's a real pretty place; lotta flowers along that road. . . . 'Cause they say them dead people are all happy, you know: happy and dancin' *nuuga*, that Circle Dance. . . . 'Cause none are really very old there, neither. No, sir! 'Cause they say when you die, you'll turn into bein' young again. . . . What I hear, anyway. . . . What them real old-timers sayin'. Their belief, anyway. . . .

But me, I never did hear *Wodzeewob* talk about them dead comin' back, Mike.

122. *Wodzeewob*, 1870 Ghost Dance Prophet

But he's not a *poweenabe*, good talker, *Wodzeewob*. . . . And same way, too, he's not a singer. 'Cause only Jack Wilson is that [singer]. Same way, too, I don't think *Wodzeewob*'s got *booha* to make it rain [i.e., like Jack Wilson].

But I hear there's another *Wodzeewob* . . . a woman. . . . And they say she used to put up dance a real long time ago—in Schurz. . . . But that's way before Jack Wilson, partner. Yes, sir! Them real early days ago. . . . 'Cause they say someone hit that tub and she faint; sleep like she's dead. . . . 'Cause maybe some Indian from Idaho are comin' down there that time [also]? Got different song, different drum. . . . Scare her with that wild Indian song? And so she faint and come back again? But I don't know her. . . . Only thing is, Jim Wilson, he don't tell me about them kind dance she put up. . . . No, sir! Anyway, the other *Wodzeewob* [Fish Lake Joe], [since] he's a doctor, he help my mom . . . three times!

'Cause that first time, I'm only four. And you see what happen? My mom, she's workin' for Old Man Readin' and Tom Mitchell come to that restaurant. She can give him fifty cent, but Tom, he want five dollar. So, make her to be sick that way [i.e., witchcraft]. So the Old Man, he come down here to this [Mason] valley—to get Fishlake Joe on that cure. . . . What [all] I know about that, anyway. . . .

Second time we get him, you see what happen?

I'm still in Stewart then, and so the Old Man, he's usin' a mustang on our buggy. The bristlin' strap is worn, and so that horse get scared on the downgrade, start to run. Big Mack, he pull back and that strap snap. So my mom, she get scared. Jumps. Get hurt by that way! Not my sister, though. 'Cause Lizzie's O.K. So anyway, Big Mack, he [again] come down here—to get *Wodzeewob*. . . . at that Indian camp [reservation] in Yerington, where he's livin'.

And you see what that *poohaghooma* [shaman] tell 'em? Say they should have paid more close attention to *tabudzeba* [a kind of hawk]! Yes, sir! 'Cause *Wodzeewob*, he say that hawk's tryin' to tell the Old Man to stay home. Yes, sir! 'Cause he know that kind, *Wodzeewob* [i.e., harbingers of misfortune]. . . . What they're doin', anyway. Tells Big Mack that hawk was warnin' him about that accident. . . . 'Cause that kind [of hawk], you know, he cry just like a baby. . . . Came to our house night before [the day of the accident] to tell him that. . . . But you think that Old Man's gonna listen? Hell, no! 'Cause Big Mack, he still wanna go to town! So, should have stayed home! Should have listened to *tabudzeeba*, 'cause otherwise, our horse won't get on the scared side. No, sir! Accident won't happen. . . .

And same way, too, another time we have to get *Wodzeewob* for my mom. . . . 'Cause you see why? Still don't feel good ever since that accident. . . . Them mashed rib, they keep botherin' her all the time. Sick always, my mom. . . . And that time, *Wodzeewob* is back at Schurz. So Big Mack, he go after him there with his wagon.

"*Poogoo tsakarago!*" What he say. "Go hitch them horse!" And so, by God, we do! Then rattle along in two wagon; bring *Wodzeewob* back [to Smith Valley] with us. And he stay one week at our place that time. . . . Jim Wilson's *nuugweegeeyaka* [designated shamanic repeater]—say everythin' back what *Wodzeewob* say [during] that night. And *Wodzeewob*, he has a drum and can dance. Yes, sir! Sing and dance around my mom all night. . . . 'Cause we all gotta be there, you know: family. . . . Same way, too, nobody can go home when he start to doctor. . . . No, sir! Not till after *Wodzeewob* tell us to go, anyway; not till next mornin'. Oh, and you can eat [if] you're hungry—the middle of the night. Get your sleep, though, the next day. 'Cause them *poohaghooma*, they're tough! They can do that [i.e., sing, dance, doctor] all night long! And same way, too, when they sleep, why, you're not supposed to be botherin' 'em. No, sir! 'Cause they say [if] you do, [if] you make noise, why, you might just spoil their dream; so they can get sick and die!

Big Mack, he pay ten dollar to *Wodzeewob* to doctor my mom that time; give Jim Wilson two dollar to be his *nuugweegeeyaka*. Has to sell a horse to pay 'em, though. . . . But *Wodzeewob* don't really doctor my mom that time; he just try to rub. And [since] that don't work, why, next time, he has to doctor by right way [i.e., sucking]. . . . Same way, too, he know who's doin' that [witching] to my mom. Only thing is, *Wodzeewob* won't tell. No, sir! 'Cause you see why? We don't pay enough for that! And says he can't make it [cure Mary Mack] that last time. . . . No, sir! Tell the Old Man he don't have too much power to help her—we should go to that white doctor in town. . . . And so we do, too. He cut her open, then she's better.

Good man, though, *Wodzeewob*: [helps] pull my mom through twice! Dies before his wife, [though]. 'Cause I know last time I seen her was in Schurz [the U.S. Public Health Hospital at the Walker River Reservation]. Come to see me that time I get knifed [sec. 120]. . . . But I never did go to his [*Wodzeewob's*] funeral. 'Cause you see why? Nobody let me know when *Wodzeewob* die. Dies before my mom. . . .

123. Jack Wilson (Wovoka), 1890 Ghost Dance Prophet

Same way, too, I know him, all right! 'Cause Jack Wilson, he's my *hai'ee* 'uncle' [mother's brother or step-father], Big Mack's brother. Well, not really brother. . . . Cousin-brother, by Indian way. . . . 'Cause the Old Man, he's related some way to Jack Wilson. . . . So I just call him [Wilson] *hai'ee*, and he call me back *huzza* [nephew, sister's son]. . . .

Good man, Jack Wilson: always wear buckskin glove, moccasin, and black Stetson hat. And he's from this [Mason] valley, you know. But no more job down here, so Jack, he go up to Smith Valley; work there a good many years. Then after he sell his lumber house to the Old Man, why, Jack can move back down here . . . to Mason [town]. Live right there by the [Walker] river; by his father and mother . . . till he move to that [Yerington Indian] Colony down here when they die . . .[his] wife first.

'Cause I know them [Jack Wilson's parents]. His *na'a*, they call him *Nuumuuraivo* 'Indian-white Man'. 'Cause you see why? Them *taivo*, they stole him! Yes, sir! After that [Pyramid Lake?] War, when them Indian fight them *taivo*, they drive 'em outta here. Make a reservation for them someplace else. . . . And so Jack Wilson's *na'a* is taken away from here by them George Washington soldier. 'Cause too many [Indians] them day! Afraid of 'em, you know. Have to separate 'em. . . . And *Nuumuuraivo*, he's not marry yet, neither. No, sir! Come back to Nevada with his wife; start his family that way. . . . And he's a doctor; pretty powerful, too, by God! But never did hear too much about him, though [i.e., from Jim Wilson, who talks mostly about Jack Wilson]. Wife's name? Never did hear that one, neither, Mike.

Jack Wilson, he's got two brothers: Pat Wilson, he's younger. *Moohoo'oo* man, Pat. . . . Yes, sir! Use that black stuff all the time, and white; then when that [dope] go outta these valley, why, Pat Wilson, he's gonna drink heavy. (Wife's Annie, but she don't use either. They have a bunch of kids. . . . 'Cause Woodrow Wilson, he's one of 'em. . . .) And Jack Wilson's other brother, he's the youngest. Call him *Toyanaga'a*, but I don't know what that mean. Older than me, *Toyanaga'a*, 'cause I see him. Was marry to Nelson Charley's mother [*Apee*]; then he die young. Great big tall guy, *Toyanaga'a* . . . just like Jack Wilson. And he don't use drugs, neither. No, sir! Not savvy yet to *moohoo'oo*—just that half-*Waseeyoo*, Johnny Mack, he's the only one usin' when Jack Wilson's young[est] brother dies. . . .

And Jack's wife's named Mary [Wilson]. . . . They got two daughters, Ida and Lucy. But you see what she [Jack Wilson's wife]'s doin'? Steal that other girl! Yes, sir! *Nomogwet*, Alice Wilson: look just like George Simpson the way she laugh, so everybody say he's her *na'a* [father]. . . . 'Cause three Simpson brothers in all: George, Frank, and Bill. Bill, he's the oldest. And [since] Jack Wilson work for George Simpson in Pine Grove, I guess that fellow sneak on his wife! What them Indian women are doin' a long time ago.... What they're all after, money! But George Simpson, he don't claim her. No, sir! 'Cause he's already marry. So Jack Wilson claim her. Always calls her *"'A-lis,"* though. Won't say *barruu,* daughter, neither. No, sir! 'Cause I never did hear Jack Wilson say, "That's my *baree!"* And Alice Wilson, she marry that government bull I don't like later on ... that Andy Vidovich. Younger than me, Alice Vidovich. And only one them Wilson girl use *moohoo'oo* ... one they call Ida....

124. Jack Wilson's *Booha* ('Power')

Jim Wilson, he say Jack Wilson's a real powerful man! Yes, sir! Say Jack Wilson can light his pipe by [pointing it at] the sun! Don't have to use *koso* [fire, matches], neither. No, sir! Same way, too, he say how Jack Wilson make rain. 'Cause not too much snow that winter, [so] the [Walker] river is dry. Everybody's sufferin' for water.... Cryin' around, you know.... And so Jack Wilson, he put down a big pot ... willow basket, anyway, that can hold water.... And that one fill up quick, all right! Yes, sir! To let everybody to drink outta that.... 'Cause that happen in this [Mason] valley ... where Jack Wilson's always livin', you know: on the Wilson Ranch [Nordyke] ... before Bill Wilson sell....

And same way, too, Jack Wilson don't never mind rain. No, sir! 'Cause he can walk under it, don't get wet! 'Cause they say one time, in Smith Valley, Jack, he work for [Frank] Simpson. Must be irrigatin', 'cause he has a shovel? Dig up small tree, pretty near like cottonwood, pack that on his shoulder. 'Cause his boss, he want him to plant that by a well, you know.... So, anyway, it rain pretty hard. Yes, sir! 'Cause all these other Indian are in the shed. But Jack, he don't mind it. No, sir! Walk with that tree on his shoulder, singin'.... And he don't never get wet, neither! 'Cause Sam Leon, he [also] tell me that story.... And same way, they [also] say that tree's still standin'! So maybe he bring that rain? 'Cause they say Jack Wilson can [also] make it to storm: you know, so our food grow better that way....

And Jim Wilson, he also say he's good singer, Jack. Yes, sir! Used to travel all the time, too.... 'Cause one time I hear Jack Wilson go to Oklahoma—with Tommy Cyphers; second time with Pete Penrose. You know, just to visit around, maybe? 'Cause maybe they might call him over there? You know, to see his *booha*.... Or maybe Jack Wilson just like to go see their country [i.e., curiosity]? Tommy Cyphers, he's from Carson [City]; Jack Wilson's relation, I think. But he don't use dope. . . . Drink quite a bit, though. 'Cause I know him! I go to school with Tommy Cyphers in Stewart. . . . 'Cause Jack Wilson, he's gotta take these young fellow along with him: to help him to talk. But don't take his wife with him. . . .

So he must believe in somethin', ain't it? Jesus, maybe? But Jack Wilson don't. . . . No, sir! Never mention the Lord or Jesus at all. No, sir! Just put up his dance, and doctors later on.

125. Jack Wilson's Dances

'Cause I hear he call for them Big Times in Schurz . . . them kind dance down there. . . . For snow, you know; for them *tuuba* 'pine nut' [to grow]. . . . And tell everybody to get together for that kind. . . . "Get lotta wood, so they can dance all night long." 'Cause he's a singer, Jack Wilson. . . . But not the *poweenabe* [leader]. No, sir! Another fellow do that. . . . Go around, you know; tell everybody how that dance is gonna be . . . what they gonna do. . . . And he's got a long white *moosoowee* [moustache? chin whiskers?] that other fellow: [I] try to catch his name, but can't get it. No, sir! But he's from Schurz, anyway. . . . Want people to get along, Jack Wilson . . . to act good. And I think Big Mack go to that kind? Might [even] be he bring me, too? My early days. . . .

And only two time, I seen what Jack Wilson's doin'. . . . Puttin' up them dance [in] these valley. . . . Yes, sir! 'Cause I'm a little guy, then . . . around about four to five year old. But I remember 'em, all right! First time, that's Pine Nut Dance; second one, Jack's puttin' up a dance for them Bannock—in Wellington, on Fred Fulstone's land. Right across the highway from where Irene Thompson live. . . .

That first dance we call that *tuubanuuga* 'Pine Nut Dance'. 'Cause that's just a Circle Dance, you know. 'Cause like I tell you, Mike, Jack Wilson, he's a *hoovee* [singer]: can sing them kind [pine nut songs] in Wellington. . . . 'Cause there used to be lotta pine nut them early days ago: in Dayton. . . . Virginia City. . . . But you see what happen? Them miner, they just chop 'em down, so *karroo'oo!* Got no more left no more! But Desert Creek, Sweetwater, they've got some left still. And [in] that other direction, too, over toward Hawthorne, Lucky Boy Spring, Mina . . . the other side Tonapah, too. . . . Like I already told you. . . . 'Cause by old-time way, anyway, we have to do that, you know: have that Pine Nut Dance before we pick 'em. . . . Yes, sir! Have to talk [pray] good to that seed, you know, 'cause *tuuba* [pine nuts], that's our [primary] food. So everybody's gotta come to that kind dance. . . . Yes, sir! Come from all over these valley and dance around that fire in that circle. . . . All night long, too! And pretty cold in them mountain, too. that time [fall], I tell you, by God!

So you see what happen? That singer [viz., Jack Wilson], he get his song ready. Everybody's holdin' onto his partner's hand, and all in step, why, they can start up that dance. Get hungry, they can eat *papee* [pine nut soup in] the middle the night. Jackrabbit, too. But you can't [really] tell what that *poinabe* [Good Talker] say. No, sir! 'Cause them old-timers, they're [such] good talker!

And same way, too, when I'm older, I seen that other kind dance Jack Wilson's puttin' up—near where my boss, Macarini's place, is. . . .

'Cause you see what he's doin' that time? Jack, he wanna show off our dance to them Bannock; other Indian from California, too. . . . And them *'aduseeva* [as well]. Call 'em Cheyenne, that kind. 'Cause they wear that kind haircut, you know: sides are bald, center is long and tied. . . . Yes, sir! We can show 'em our dance to them Bannock, they can show theirs. 'Cause they're from Idaho, you know. And I don't know how many days they stay, neither. . . . One week, maybe? Maybe two? And not too big a crowd that dance. . . . No, sir! No gamblin', neither. . . . . 'Cause everybody just dance! 'Cause I know Big Mack and my mom, they go. . . . Not my grandma, though. 'Cause she's real funny woman, my grandma: don't never like to get into no kind fun! No, sir! Don't wanna shake it up a little bit or look at nothin'! 'Cause she just work, that's all! Yes, sir! Hard-workin' *dibeetzotnee* [old woman], my grandma! 'Cause I know I see lotta them [old women] doin' that, too, by God! They can shake [by dancing] the louse off 'em! But not my grandma. . . .

Oh, and maybe we dance three night with them Bannock Indian? Jack Wilson's holdin' in Smith Valley? Dance till them fellow get tired and wanna go home. 'Cause you see what they're doin'?' Them Bannock, they got a drum with bell on it. Wear a loin cloth, and put paint on their face, across their chest. And they got bow and arrow [also], so them *taivo* [visitors?], they have to back up when they dance! Yes, sir! 'Cause otherwise, they might just turn loose their arrow! But they don't. . . . Just makin' believe, you know; makin' believe that's like a war. . . . What they're doin,' anyway. 'Cause somebody beat that tub [drum], so they start hoppin' up and down like they're doin' . . . [whereas] we just slide our feet. . . . Why our women dirty their *soowee* [vagina] that way! 'Cause they make [raise] dust, you know. . . . And nobody try to play handgame with them Bannock Indian, neither. No, sir! We just show 'em how we play football, and that woman's game; they can show us that war dance. . . .

But that's one thing I can't get, though: Jack Wilson's song. No, sir! 'Cause that's a real old-time Indian song, partner. . . .

And so, after Jack Wilson's through singin'—and he can pray real good, too—them Bannock, they wanna shake his hand. And well, so they do that, all right. Only they get pret-ty shake-y, partner! Yes, sir! 'Cause you see why? Jack Wilson's *booha!* His power do that to 'em, you know: shake 'em pretty hard, so they feel scared. . . . And Jack, he just sit there, laugh. 'Cause that's the time he load up his pipe and light by the sun. . . . Yes, sir! Only time I seen Jack Wilson's *booha.* . . .

Anyway, I'm little back, then, so [I] don't really pay too much attention to what Jack Wilson's sayin'. 'Cause otherwise, I might just know somethin', ain't it?

126. Doctored by Jack Wilson

Same way, Jack Wilson, he [also] doctor my mom . . . after that runaway. 'Cause my mom, she's sick pretty near one year afterward. But he can't tell the Old Man who's doin' that [witchcraft], neither. No, sir! 'Cause you see why? Ain't got too much *booha* yet, Jack Wilson; tell Big Mack to get another doctor for that poison [i.e., removal of intruded objects]. . . . Anyway, he [at least], take out some that sickness Tom Mitchell put inside my mom. Some, not all. . . . So that was only a little cure by Jack Wilson.

And same way, too, I'm doctored by him.

'Cause you see what happen? I'm workin' for Macarini, liftin' them [graded] potato sack, and hurt my shoulder. Yes, sir! 'Cause that pain shoot straight across my shoulder! Back, too! And gee, that's a pret-ty tough one, partner! 'Cause I'm already a man that time; marry, too. . . . And so my grandma, she give the Old Man hell:

"Don't you think you better get *poohaghooma* for my *moo'a?*" my grandma tell Old Mack. "Maybe Indian doctor can help my grandson?"

And so that's what we do: Come down from Smith Valley to Jack Wilson's place. . . . 'Cause that time, Jack, he's livin' at the Indian camp in

Yerington, after [post-1917] they line them [houses] up. 'Cause Jack Wilson don't doctor nobody when he's still livin' in Smith Valley. . . . No, sir! And I know we're [riding] on a buggy that time, 'cause I can't ride no horse. No, sir! Hurt too much! And that take one whole day on that trip, partner! Shakin' along, you know; I can hardly draw my breath. . . . And so I'm kind of thinkin' that to myself: [i.e.] "Gee, I work hard all my life, maybe just stretch myself [muscle pull]?" But I'm hurtin' below my kidney, too; close to where my hip is. . . .

And so, Jack, he doctor me, all right—right there in his own house! Work all night long, too, by God! And I know the Old Man, he pay ten dollar for that [cure]. 'Cause some them *poohaghooma*, they charge pretty high . . . even twenty dollar! Not Jack Wilson. Too new that time. . . . Start in too late to bein' a doctor. . . . And he can just wave his [eagle] feather over a person, you know—draw [out] that poison by that way. Yes, sir! Don't have to suck! 'Cause Jack Wilson's *booha* on [in] his arms. . . . But he don't do me no good at all. No, sir! Say he can't help me. . . . So maybe Jack Wilson don't know [i.e., possess *booha*] enough yet?

127. *Hongo,* Virgina City Paiute Rubber

And [since] way later I'm still hurtin' . . . [since I] don't like white operation, *Hongo,* he's gonna try help me.

'Cause he's from Dayton, *Hongo.* Live with his [first] wife in these valleys that time. . . . Close by Old Man Charley all the time. Not a real doctor, though, *Hongo.* . . . No, sir! Not like his mother, anyway. And we call that kind *nodaygit* 'rubbin' doctor', you know. Same way, too, *Pipoosee Nohorr^ha,* he's another one. . . . Call him Barney Miller in English. . . . 'Cause only two Indian doctor doin' that, that time, you know! *Pipoosee Nohorr^ha,* though, he only rub tonsil; *Hongo* is all-over man. Both them use *moohoo'oo,* though. . . . And *Hongo,* he don't sing, neither. No, sir! Rub you at night; charge fifty cent on a rub. . . .

Anyway, that time he doctor me, *Hongo* come right after supper. Give me Indian chalk to chew on—that *ebe,* you know, 'white paint'. Tell me to swallow that. . . . 'Cause that's just like a pill, you know. And so, while I'm doin' that, *Hongo,* he chew tobacco. Use store tobacco, too, not *poowee pahmoo* [Indian tobacco] on that rub. . . . 'Cause you see why? That other kind's [Indian tobacco has] got too many seed, too many little leaf; so he say he can't chew on that too good. . . . Then *Hongo* put that kind [tobacco] on my shoulder, arm, back . . . every goddamn sore place! 'Cause that's his *booha*, you know. So he just know thing by that kind! Then *Hongo* can say [i.e., diagnose] to me:

"Corbett, somebody's tryin' to witch you!"

Yes, sir! 'Cause he can do that [also], you know [i.e., diagnose witchcraft].

"That fellow, he put red paint on his hand," *Hongo* tell me. "Shake your hand first, then he touch your shoulder and head with that. Then he can say to you, 'I don't see you in a good long time, Corbett!' But [even so,] only your shoulder's gonna hurt," he tell me. "Not your head. 'Cause you see why? Can't make it! No, sir! [The witch will] touch your head after he shake your hand, but [since] that don't work, so he's gonna touch your shoulder next. Make you to be sick by that way!"

Only thing is *Hongo* don't tell who's doin' that to me. No, sir! Can't, on account he do ranch work[?]. And [since] we're [also] livin' in Smith Valley that time, in Colony District, and that's potato diggin' time, we don't have a horse or car; so can't meet real easy. No, sir! 'Cause somebody else has to bring *Hongo* to my camp, partner! To rub. 'Cause that's seven miles away! Yes, sir! Have to bring him clear across the valley! 'Cause *Hongo*, he can't foot it. . . .

Ain't got enough time [money?] to tell me who's doin' that to me, . . . but anyway, he can rub where that pain is—across my [left] shoulder, down to right [side] here [kidney]. . . . Chew his tobacco while I take my shirt off, put that where that pain is. And leave that on for a good long time, too, by God! So that's pretty cheap on the rub. . . . Too bad we ain't got enough to pay *Hongo* for that [all-] night rub. . . . Maybe then he can tell who's doin' that to me?

Another time, though, I do . . . have enough money for that. And so *Hongo*, he tell me that. . . . Says,

"You're gonna meet somebody today, Corbett, and he's gonna stop and talk to you. Great big heavyset man; got a *moosoowee* [moustache]. And when you meet him, he's gonna act ashamed, too. Yes, sir! [He's] got a gamblin' house."

And so, by God, *Hongo* was right! 'Cause I do meet Tom Mitchell that time! Came right up to me in the street and try talkin' good. Ask me, "How I'm doin'?" Not ashamed to talk to me, neither. No, sir! Just like *Hongo* say!

"Haven't seen you good long time, Corbett!"

Yes, sir! What that Tom Mitchell say to me. 'Cause you see why? Must be he's got that stuff on his hand? 'Cause Tom Mitchell, he wanna put his hand on my [left] shoulder when he's sayin' that to me: you know, after we shake.... And same way, too, *Hongo,* he tell me,

"*Sa'ab* [witch], Corbett—he's gonna try and trap you. Yes, sir! [He] can put red paint on the door his gamblin' house, so when you go inside there, that's when he can get you—when you brush past [the lintel]!"

And so, by God, that's what that Tom Mitchell's doin', all right! Make me to be sick by that *pizzapee* . . . that red paint them Indian doctor use. . . . Same kind Jack Wilson's sellin', you know.

"*Pizzapee,* that's what's makin' you sick, Corbett"; *Hongo,* he say that to me. "'Cause I know him, all right! What that witch is doin' to you!"

Marry to *Apee* ["Happy" Hooligan] that time, *Hongo.* 'Cause she's also from Virginia City. . . . Same place his first wife is from, and they have one daughter, die young. . . . *Hongo,* he die with earache. . . .

And so you see what I'm thinkin'? Maybe Tom Mitchell do that to me on account I been with too many them young girls [i.e., Mitchell's daughters]!

128. A Different Kind of Cure

But them rubbers, they can't put no kind sickness in you. No, sir! 'Cause they ain't that kind [witch], you know. Still can get mad at you, though. . . . Yes, sir!

But *Hongo,* he ain't the only one [doctor] to tell me not to go into Tom Mitchell's gambling house. . . . No, sir! 'Cause *Wodzeewob* and *Soowee warr^b,* they're also sayin' that same thing. Both! Say to me there's poison inside there. . . .

"[If] you set foot inside, why, you can get sick and die!"

So that's why I know the Old Man and my mom, they won't go Tom Mitchell's gamblin' house. No, sir! Not since what he done to my mom, anyway. Go to Wellington instead to gamble—to Blind Bob's place.

But [since] that pain don't go away, three, four year later, that kind hit me again! Can't sleep, can't breathe too good. . . . So you see what I'm doin' this time? Go to that *tota* [doctor] in Yerington: Dr. Eagleton. And he tap around, all right, but he can't find nothin' wrong with me. Send me to Schurz [U.S. Public Health Hospital, Walker River Reservation]—so they can X-ray me. But they can't find nothin', neither, so, have to send me back to Yerington—to that other *tota*.

Call him Dr. Nye, that one.... Says I got too much meat, veins all grow over that injury, so they can't operate. No, sir!

129. Tom Mitchell!

'Cause he's the one I don't like! No, sir! 'Cause you see why? Tom Mitchell, [if] he don't like a person, why, he's gonna kill him! Regular *sa'ab*, that one ... 'witch'!

Indian name's *Songaibaga'a* 'Hummingbird'.... And he's got two wife, Tom Mitchell.... Sisters, you know; one, he can keep in Smith Valley, the other, she have to stay at the [Yerington Indian] Colony. Doin' that you know, 'cause they don't get along. *Kwoho* ... rival each other. And you see what else he doin'? Tom Mitchell, he run that gamblin' house in Yerington. Then when they line them house up [i.e., formation of the Yerington Indian Colony in 1917], well, so he can move that there.... 'Cause you see what he's [really] doin'? Set a trap by that gamblin' house! So anybody raise heck [i.e., drinking and fighting] inside, why, Tom Mitchell, he can tell 'em:

"Think you're gonna live very long?"

What he says anyway.... And so, by God, they die quick! 'Cause I know him! Yes, sir! 'Cause Tom Mitchell, he pretty near kill my mom! 'Cause you see what happen? She can't breathe good that time.... Was gettin' all choked up, and so the Old Man, he has to ride down here to this [Mason] valley—for *Wodzweewob*. But he says he can't help my mom out.... No, sir! Says Tom Mitchell put that string inside her, and he can't get that out. "Better to take her to that *tota* [white doctor] in Yerington!" Yes, sir! What *Wodzeewob* tell Big Mack. "'Cause he's a pretty powerful man, that one. Maybe he can fix it [cure her]?" And so, by God, we do: hitch up our wagon and take my mom there ... to Dr. Leavitt. And he clean that poison out from her throat, all right. Yes, sir! Make my mom to be a well woman again.... Pretty good doctor, that one, I tell you, Mike! Government doctor, Dr. Leavitt....

And you see why Tom Mitchell's doin' that to my mom? She's workin' in a roomin' house, in Wellington, and Tom Mitchell, he comes inside that restaurant ... time my Mom give him fifty cent for his meal. But he only get mad at her. Says,

"You're a workin' woman, so that's pretty cheap!"

'Cause you see why? His *booha* tell him how much she's got. . . . And you see why he's [really] doin' that? Tom Mitchell, he want us to hire him! You know, to get rid that poison. . . . But we know him! Know what he's doin', anyway. . . . On account what *Wodzeewob* and that other real old-timer tell us about him . . . that *Soowee warr^b.* . . . 'Cause they tell my mom, "Don't give Tom Mitchell nothin'!" And so, ever since that, I know I never like to talk to him. . . . No, sir! His wife, though, I like to talk to. But [I] never like to be close to Tom Mitchell. . . . No, sir! Never [even] to look at him. . . . But gee, I sure like to get close to his daughter[s]. . . .

And same way, another time, too, my wife's niece [Marie Dick] get some kind sickness. . . . Andy Dick's daughter. So they call in Tom Mitchell to doctor her. But he don't help! No, sir! He just play [pretend]! 'Cause that girl's only gettin' sicker and sicker, [meanwhile] Tom Mitchell [just] dance around that stove! 'Cause my wife, you know, she's the one tell me this: [how he] take out his pipe—that *to'eeza,* you know, blue rock pipe them *poohaghooma* always use—and pass it around for everybody to smoke. . . . Then Tom Mitchell can put it away. . . . And that's pretty near like a circle dance what my wife say Tom Mitchell's doin'. . . . Yes, sir! Says he want some woman to dance with him, but my wife says the only one [who] join him are his own daughter: Sadie and Daisy! Yes, sir! 'Cause they're the only one [also] dancin' around that stove! And he's not supposed to be doin' that, neither!

130. *Nuumuu Puharr^* ('Witchcraft')

And same way, too, another time, somebody [else] witch my wife. And so, she hire *Hongo* for that. . . .

'Cause you see what happen? Her belly's all blown up [pregnant]! Yes, sir! And my wife's [a] single woman that time. . . . Divorced, you know, so, her daughter's husband, he has a car—that Logan Williams, from Schurz—has to go to get *Hongo*. And so that rubber, he give my wife *ebbe* [white paint] to swallow: little amount, small pill, you know; then he can rub. 'Cause you see how he's workin' that? every time *Hongo* rub, she's gotta swallow one pill. . . . Then that green stuff come out—come outta my wife's *tsaboo* [rectum]. . . . Then *Hongo* tell who's doin' that to her.

Says,

"When you see George Abe's wife, just look at her eye. See if she'll turn away from you?"

And so, by God, that happen, too! 'Cause that other woman, she don't wanna look at my wife. No, sir! George Abe's wife, that's Sullivan Tom's mother. . . . 'Cause Sullivan, he's a[nother] *nomogwet*. . . . First one [who] hire me to sell *moohoo'oo* in these valleys. . . . *Kawee yarro'a,* that's Sullivan Tom's mother's name. . . . Means 'Talkin' Loud'. 'Cause she's drunk all the time, that old lady. . . . Ride around on their buggy makin' helluva racket! And [if] she don't like you, why, George Abe's wife can get mad—call you a "Cocksucker!" Yes, sir! Cuss you out like that. . . .

From Schurz, *Kawee yarro'a*. But mostly she's livin' in Yerington when she's marry to George Abe. . . . To "Egg" George, what they call him mostly. 'Cause you see why? That fellow's always swallowin' hard boiled egg. . . .

And Sullivan Tom's mother, she call me *meetho'o* 'sister's son'. Still, when I see her, I'm afraid. . . . Always give her two bits. 'Cause she see me and she can say, "Give me two bits!" 'Cause drunk all the time. . . . Yes, sir! So she's just the same as that Tom Mitchell [i.e., witch]. Or that other *sa'ab,* Maggie Milton. . . . One they call *Eehobee* 'Dove'. On account how she laugh. . . . 'Cause they say Maggie Milton kill her own sister—James Keno's wife. But I don't believe that. . . . No, sir! 'Cause my wife, she like Maggie. Good friend together in Sweetwater when they're little. . . . Why I always talk good to Maggie Milton. . . . Anyway, Maggie and Dutch John [Milton, her husband], they're like George Abe and his wife: drunk all the time! Work for Norman Brown, and she call me *wanga'a* [younger cousin-brother]. . . .

Another time, Sullivan Tom's mother is fightin' with George Abe. . . . She take his hankey from his neck and twist it till he nearly die! (Them old-time hanky them *pakyera'a* [cowboys] wear when they ride. 'Cause I know I always wear one. Yes, sir! Make me to show like I'm a cowboy!) So anyway, Adam Dixon, he pull that woman off her husband's throat! So maybe I see George Abe's wife and give her money 'cause I'm afraid she's gonna choke me same way, too?

Another time, I find her in a hole. . . . Have to use my horse to get her out. 'Cause George Abe's asleep under a tree [i.e., drunk]. . . .

But you see how *Kawee yarro'a* can witch my wife? Make her to feel like there's a baby inside her. Yes, sir! 'Cause after *Hongo* rub five times he tell my wife:

"Don't be shamed when you see her, neither. Just walk straight up that woman!"

And so, by God, that's what my wife does. And George Abe's wife acts ashamed, all right! Look away! Ashamed, on account what she's doin'.... Same as she can give a person a peach or plum and they blow up! Yes, sir! 'Cause I hear that happen to this one boy from Yerington. . . . And he almost die, too. But *Hongo* [also] doctor him—tell what *Kawee yarro'a* is doin'.

Same way, you see what George Abe is always tellin' everybody:

"My wife's gonna eat you quick!"

Norr^gwa nuumuuduuka, what we call that kind: 'Indian-eating wife'! 'Cause that's that *nuumuu puharr^*, you know: Indian witchin'. 'Cause George Abe, he know her! Know what his wife's always doin'.... Know she's a witch, you know. Tell everybody that.... 'Cause that kind, they're just no good!

131. Tom Mitchell's Witchin' Way

Same way, too, I know Tom Mitchell [also] try to put somethin' in front my uncle.... 'Cause that's that *Soowee warr^b*, you know; from Schurz. Already told you about him.... Real old-timer, that one. *Poohaghooma*....'Cause you see what he say? Says that feel like steppin' on a nail! Cripple up on his leg, too, by God! And that happen at the [Yerington Indian] Colony ... where *Soowee warr^b* live.... 'Cause you see why he's doin' that, Tom Mitchell? He wanna clean up all them other Indian doctor so he can make more money that way. And *Soowee warr^b*—'cause that mean a mustache on your outfit, partner. And pretty good doctor, too, that one. Yes, sir! [His] son's the one they call *Soobrook* 'Stays Broke on Pussy'. 'Cause you see why? Spend all his money on them Indian girl! So anyway, his father, after Tom Mitchell's doin' that to him, *Soowee warr^b* can throw away that crutch! Yes, sir! Get that poison out by his own *booha!* But still, he walk lame always—on account Tom Mitchell's witchin' way....

Yes, sir! Killin' all them other Indian doctor.... What he's doin', you know, Tom Mitchell: Dick Bennett ... *Wuuyuuduusaqa*—that Little Dick: short fellow that one ... and *Pipoosee Nohorr^ha* [Barney Miller] ... Fish Lake Joe ... *Hongo* ... *Hongo*'s mother ... *Kweenapeeta*.... Jack Wilson, too.... 'Cause Tom Mitchell, he also take away *all* their power! Already told you how *Hongo* die of an earache.... Well, so that's 'cause what Tom Mitchell's doin' to him! Yes, sir! So, pretty bad man, Tom Mitchell.... [For] what he's always doin' around here.... 'Cause gee, there used to be lotta them Indian doctor these valleys. But Tom Mitchell, he clean 'em all up good! So nowaday, *karroo'oo* 'no more'! 'Cause he eat 'em all up, by God! Just like them *Paheezoho* [Giant Cannibal, sec. 153]! 'Cause you see what he's doin', Tom Mitchell: don't never talk mean to a person. No, sir! Talk good all the time. . . . Still, [if] he don't like you, why, he's gonna put some kind sickness in you. Witch you by that way!

132. I Love Tom Mitchell's Daughters

So, like I say, I never even like to look at Tom Mitchell. . . . No, sir! Never get close to him, neither. Don't stop and visit. Or talk to him in the street. [Or] give him money, neither. . . . And Tom Mitchell, he never talk to me, neither. No, sir! 'Cause he's a bad man, I tell you, Mike! [Also] kill Pat Wilson's son, 'cause he haul [transported?] his daughter around. . . . And so these Indian around here [Mason Valley], they complain to Bill and Joe Wilson. But they tell 'em, "[If] anybody's witchin' somebody, don't kill him. We will!" So you see what happen? Them Indian have to back off. . . .

And one time, Tom Mitchell, he [even] go up to my house to bawl out Big Mack and my mom. Says,

"Corbett's been foolin' around with too many girl [i.e., his daughters]. Better to marry 'em!"

'Cause you see what happen? I'm goin' to his gamblin' house, you know—[I] come down here to Yerington lookin' for them young girl . . . them city girl. . . . 'Cause you see who I'm after all the time? Tom Mitchell's daughter[s]! Yes, sir! 'Cause I'm first with Carrie—doin' that [defloration] to her, you know. (She's young, same age like Eddie Mack. . . .) And same way, too, I'm also doin' that with them other Mitchell girl[s]: Minnie, Amy, Daisy. . . . All except for Sadie and Nellie, them two old one. Yes, sir! 'Cause I know I like them young girl best. . . . Wanna make a "friend" with 'em all the time. . . .

And so both them Mitchell girl [Carrie and Minnie], they say to me:

"Come on, Corbett: Let's walk to the brush!"

And they can [also] say to me:

"Don't worry—we won't tell our father!"

And so I do that, too, by God! And sometime, too, I can stay overnight. So, in the mornin', Tom Mitchell's wife, she say to me,

"We got no feed, Corbett!"

Shame me, you know. And so what little change I got in my pocket, why, I gotta do that: go downtown to Yerington, to buy grub for all them Mitchells. 'Cause gee, I know I sure like them two girl. . . . Carrie and Daisy Mitchell, they look alike . . . laugh pretty near same way, too. . . .

And so, Tom Mitchell, he [also] say when he come to visit the Old Man:

"One man's gonna have both them girl for a team on his buggy! 'Cause both are gonna be on one man's horse some day! He can have 'em both for his team!"

So gee, I know I sure feel funny then. . . . But otherwise, like I tell you, Mike, Tom Mitchell talk nice to a fellow: soft, not mean. Work that kind [witchcraft] that way, you know. . . . Witch you in secret way all the time! And so the only way you can find out about 'em, what they're doin', is when another *poohaghooma* tell you that [i.e., diagnoses witchcraft].

So how come the Old Man never mention anything like that to me? No, sir! Never say he's goin' to kill Tom Mitchell on account what he's doin' to my mom. . . .

133. The Death Of Jack Wilson

Witchin' Jack Wilson, too, by God, Tom Mitchell! 'Cause good man, Jack: talk sense all the time. [He] tell the people to get along, make a livin'. . . . [But] never say nothin' about that dope business, neither. No, sir! Never say: "You youngster better quit that." No, sir! 'Cause his own brother's usin' [opium]; daughter, too. And he don't say nothin' about drink, neither. . . . No, sir! Never [even] seen Jack Wilson playing handgame. . . . But he and the Old Man talk all the time. Don't talk about them real early days ago, though. . . . Anyway, good man, Jack Wilson: good head man. Don't drink. Help everybody. . . . And good doctor, too, I tell you, Mike. 'Cause nobody's afraid him. . . .

But that's one thing I [still] don't see [understand] is: how Jack Wilson die? No, sir! 'Cause he's a pretty healthy lookin' guy yet. . . . Die in his house at that [Yerington Indian] Colony, and is buried in Yerington. . . . So you see how I think he die? Tom Mitchell! Yes, sir! Poison him! 'Cause he do that to all them other Indian doctor, you know. . . . Clean 'em up! Why he live to the last end. . . . Have to die last. . . . Yes, sir! Even kill Jack Wilson's brother, and Pat's not a doctor!

'Cause you see what Tom Mitchell can tell him [Jack Wilson]:

"We can put our *booha* together, make more power that way!"

And so Jack, he believe him. Yes, sir! But Tom Mitchell, he just bullshit him! Bullshit Jack Wilson that way. . . . Eat him up!

And there was helluva earthquake when Jack Wilson die. . . . Yes sir! Says [prophesies],

"[If] I go a long way from here, I'm gonna shake this earth!"

And so, after Jack Wilson die, why, this ground sure give us a rock! Look like them tree over there by Central [Smith Valley] are gonna go over, too, by God! So we just have to stay [lay] right there on the ground. 'Cause [if] a fellow stand up, why, maybe he's gonna fall over! Yes, sir! Pret-ty shake-y, that earthquake, I tell you, Mike! So we just have to sit there . . . and stay away from them tree, too. And people are sure scared of that, too. . . . But nobody's prayin'. No, sir! Not least what I seen, anyway. And so after that, they believe him! Yes, sir! Believe what Jack Wilson say is true . . . on account that earthquake when [after] he die. . . .

134. Pneumonia! Exposure!

"Pneumonia!" "Exposure!" "Exposure!" "Pneumonia!" What they're always puttin' [writing] down on that paper [death certificate] when Indian die! Yes, sir! 'Cause lotta them Indian die by that kind. 'Cause them drinkin' guy, you know; they go out at night: catch cold and want more *heebee,* so they get tired, then; tired and lay down some place. Catch cold and just die! But not them *moohoo'oo* men. No, sir! 'Cause [if] they're usin' that kind [opiates], why, they don't go out at night. No, sir! Just stay home all the time. . . .

And same way, too, that *taivo tu'oi* [influenza] . . . that one can [also] kill them Indian. Yes, sir! 'Cause right around that First German War's when that one's bad. . . . 'Cause I know my sister Janie and her husband [Henry Dick], they die of that kind [flu]. And Grover Pitts, too. Gee, lots! 'Cause I know I lost [lots of] good friend on that one, partner! And so them drugstore, they have to sell mask to these *taivo.* And same way, too, I know I [also] get sick with that flu.

Not yet marry that time, neither: I'm workin' at East Walker [River]—at Cheilboy Ranch. And that's fall the year, partner; potato work. I take Steve Johnson's daughter up there with me, and, by God, Edie get sick with that flu! Yes, sir! Hits the bed before me. Then I go down after her. . . . And there's no kind Indian medicine for that one, neither. No, sir! Same way, too, no *poohaghooma* can help. No, sir! Can't fix that kind *nuuma* [sickness] at all, so we just have to stay in that warm bed. . . 'Cause it take around about one whole week before you're better from that kind. . . . And so Edie, she get better before me; then she can go back to work again: get grub from her boss to feed me . . . until I'm better.

And [if] that [flu, i.e., "pneumonia"] don't get 'em, why, they can pass out on the highway: freeze to death out there like that way [i.e., "exposure"] . . . [if] a car don't [just] get 'em!

135. Exposure! Pneumonia!

'Cause I know that's what happen to pretty near all them Mitchells. . . .

'Cause Tom Mitchell's boy, Stewart, he's my good friend. And so, no more *moohoo'oo*, Stewart Mitchell just drink all the time. (Don't have no kind Indian name, neither, Stewart. No, sir! Was single a good many year before he marry Elsie ["Candy"]. Got no kid with her, neither. . . .) And Stewart's always livin' on Fred Fulstone's Ranch, you know: irrigate for him. . . . But he used to be a cowboy, Stewart Mitchell. . . . Yes, sir! Work in Sweetwater with George Keno a long time. . . . After his father take him outta Stewart. . . . Where he get that name, maybe? So you see how Stewart Mitchell die? Him and Elsie, they're both drinkin' pretty heavy—'Cause that's after Stewart's finished usin' that dope: that black stuff. . . . ([He] learn that in Sweetwater. . . . But he don't try sellin' that, neither. No, sir! 'Cause none them Mitchells do. 'Cause you see why? They ain't got enough to buy!) And so, that night, Stewart, he come up to our place. 'Cause we're drinkin' too, you know, and so Stewart Mitchell, he say: "That's my jug!" "*Khai!* Not! That one's ours!" we say right back to him. And lock that door, too. But Stewart Mitchell say, "Then keep your goddamn drink!" Get mad, you know; throw that empty bottle he steal from me on [against] my door. . . . Leave to walk home. And [if] he don't do that, why, I bet you Stewart Mitchell's still livin' today! Yes, sir! 'Cause he's healthy man. . . . Could have just slept [it off] right there on the floor! And so you see what happen? That car don't see him till it's too late. . . . 'Cause, Stewart, he's drunk on that highway—near Central [Smith Valley]. Gets killed that way. . . . Break his neck. . . .

And same way, too, Joe Mitchell. . . . Call him *akw^zo'o*. And he die by that way, too. . . . 'Cause he's the oldest, Joe Mitchell: eat *moohoo'oo* like candy! Was fishing and get sick; die on that typhoid. . . . Sadie—*Saree'ee*, they call her; she use *moohoo'oo* 'morphine', too. But she don't drink too much—she was marry to Hank Brown. . . . And Sadie's older than me. . . . (Younger than Andy Dick, though. . . .) And so, that's how she die, too: get drunk and go out from her house; freeze on that highway! And, by God, Sadie Mitchell [Brown]'s out there three days before somebody find her! The one they call Minnie—she's younger than I am; Minnie Mitchell was marry to Louie Jones, but I bust her cherry—she also die by that same way. . . . "Pneumonia!" "Exposure!" 'Cause she's also passed out drunk on the highway! And real heavy user of that black stuff, Minnie Mitchell [Jones]— that time she's marry to Louie, anyway. Drink afterwards; and heavy. And so, when her husband leave her, Minnie don't wanna live no more. . . . Get drunk and pass out on the highway; die by that same way, too. 'Cause you see what happen? She's comin' home from Fallon all by herself! Amy Mitchell, she's marry to Jess Reymers; but I never did hear how she die, neither. . . . And so her sister, Nellie, she can marry Amy Mitchell's [second] husband . . . that Harry Conway. One we always call "Cigar" Harry: smoke that kind all the time. . . . And he can drink, too, that fellow. 'Cause one day, Harry Conway say, "I don't feel good. [Am] goin' to sleep!" So, that's what he do, by God: go to sleep all day long and die! Anyway, [since] Harry and Nellie—she's way older than me—spend all their money on *moohoo'oo;* and that *heebee,* they can't take care their kids, so Tom Mitchell's wife, she has to. Nellie was [also] marry to Wakeen Brown. But he leave her. Hear of land at Fallon, Wakeen Brown, leave her. . . [Also] die of that flu, Nellie Mitchell!

Yankee—*Haikee doorro* ['Yankee Doodle?'], we call him; but pronounce it by white way . . . Yankee Mitchell, he's oldest. . . . Real short fellow, too, Yankee, like me. Only one them Mitchell boys usin' that white stuff [morphine], too! He need more, so Yankee can just get on his horse and go lookin'. . . . 'Cause you see why? Tom Mitchell won't give him no money to buy! No, sir! And so, that's why Yankee say he don't like his father. . . . Was marry to Addie Mason, Yankee Mitchell; they live in Wabuska. Then Yankee Mitchell marry my wife. 'Cause you see why? She's a real hard worker [i.e., supports him]! And oh, maybe my wife can use some *moohoo'oo* [yen-shee] when she's marry to Yankee Mitchell? Live together at Charley Perry Ranch in East Walker. . . . But she divorce him, all right! On account Yankee's always usin' that *moohoo'oo!* So he never marry again. . . . Yes, sir! Has to work always [then] to buy his own dope. . . . And [so] Yankee, you see what he say always [about his father]? "I don't see how my good friends all dyin' off [i.e., witchcraft suspicion]." Anyway, he die by that same way, too [pneumonia, exposure]. . . . Pretty near my wife's same age, too, Yankee Mitchell. . . . Gus Mitchell, he's younger than me. Call him Lion, so I guess he get that name in Stewart that way? You know, sayin' that all the time, maybe? "I'm a lion!" But [I] never seen Gus usin' that dope, neither. No, sir! Never try to get marry, neither. . . . Never [even] see him goin' around with a girl. . . . No, sir! Just don't like 'em. . . . 'Cause Gus Mitchell, he never touch girl! . . . And they find him near the Armory in Yerington. . . . 'Cause Gus, he has a weak leg, you know. Can't hardly walk: work for Joe Scieroni all the time; in Mason. But that *Aytayay* don't give him wine. No, sir! Just pay him each night. And so, Gus, he has to go buy *heebee*. . . . 'Cause they find him on the ground, frozen like that, you know. 'Cause Gus, he was drinkin' pretty heavy: fall down on a drunk and can't get up no more. . . . And Dave Mitchell's got a weak heart. . . . Younger than me, Dave; just about like Eddie [Mack]. Got no Indian name, though, Dave Mitchell. . . . No, sir! Same way, he's gone through all them *moohoo'oo*. . . . White stuff, too. Then no more dope, so Dave Mitchell, he start drinkin'. Die in Jim Glazier's house [in Smith Valley]. . . . 'Cause they say his sister [Sadie] don't treat him right. . . . Anyway, Dave Mitchell's the one [who] marry his brother's wife, you know: that time Stewart go to prison. 'Cause you see why [Stewart Mitchell was incarcerated]? That fire. . . . 'Cause Stewart Mitchell, he burn down his sister's house when [brother-in-law] Hank Brown die; so they send him to prison. 'Cause you're not supposed to be doin' that no more. *Karroo'oo*. Not after them *taivo* come into these valleys, you know. . . . And same way, too, Dave Mitchell's been to prison: on a jealousy [charge]. For six months. . . . 'Cause Dave Mitchell, he kill this one woman—on account she's goin' around with other men. . . . And walk away from his brother [Stewart Mitchell]'s wife when Stewart gets outta jail. . . .

But nobody know how Doud Mitchell die. . . . No, sir! He was [also] in Stewart, Doud. . . . Father put him in there with Dave [Mitchell]. (Doud's wife, Rosie, she die young—when Johnny Mitchell's still in the basket. 'Cause she's a pretty heavy morphine user, Rosie Mitchell, I tell you, Mike! 'Cause I know her! Use black and white *moohoo'oo* . . . both! Die by that overdose. . . . 'Cause Doud Mitchell, he give his wife a shot of that white stuff, and so her heart can't stand it! First time use, you know. And so Rosie Mitchell, she die.) Then all that dope is gone outta this country, so Doud

Mitchell, he drink heavy. Oh, and he's an Anacin man, too, Doud. Yes, sir! Always gotta take his Anacin when he's sick! So maybe, there's some kind kick in that? Then after his father die [1945], why, Doud Mitchell, he can take over Tom Mitchell's gamblin' house. . . . Daisy Mitchell, she also get drunk and is killed on the highway—over by East Walker Bridge. . . . 'Cause Daisy's marry to Jimmy Summers that time. . . . Head light on their car went, so Daisy's gonna walk to Yerington. Get killed on the highway by that way. . . . And last one them Mitchells is Carrie. . . . Younger than me, Carrie Mitchell . . . like Eddie Mack. But I never fuck Carrie Mitchell, partner. No, sir! Fuck her sister Amy, though. . . . And you see how Carrie die? She's drunk and fall from her bed; hit her head on the stove and die that same way, too. . . .

[So] "Exposure!" "Pneumonia!" "Pneumonia!" "Exposure!" What they're always puttin' [writing] down on them paper [death certificates] when Indian die. . . . 'Cause pretty near all them Mitchells die by that same way! But still, I kind of think somebody's doin' that to 'em! Yes, sir! 'Cause maybe Tom Mitchell's *booha* do that to 'em? Yes, sir! [Maybe] their father don't want 'em to live? . . . 'Cause Yankee Mitchell, he's always sayin' that. Says,

"You see what my father's doin', Corbett. He give me strong stuff, and I can't handle it!"

Says,

"Yes, sir! Always killin' my good friends, [so] I wish he die!"

And same way, Dave Mitchell, too, says that. . . . 'Cause one time, Tom Mitchell's doctorin' Andy Dick's boy, and he point to his own boy. Says to *"Eeshavoo* ['Liar' or Dave Mitchell]":

"He's gonna take my place when I die!"

So maybe that's how come Dave Mitchell die? You know? On his father's *booha*. . . . But [since] he don't know too much about it, so, die on it! 'Cause Dave Mitchell, you know, he want *booha* for battle [war], not doctorin'. And he get that name *Eeshavoo* 'Bullshit Dave', 'cause he think he know everything. . . . Same way, too, Joe Mitchell and Stewart, they don't want their father's *booha;* die, too. . . . So maybe that's how come all them Mitchells die? On account what their own father's doin' to 'em!

136. The Death of Tom Mitchell

And I hear Tom Mitchell's only nine when he first start out to be a *poohaghooma*. . . . 'Cause his mom, you know, she take him everywhere to doctor when he's [that] little. . . . 'Cause I hear, one time, Tom Mitchell, he go to Bishop to doctor somebody. . . . But you see what happen? One old lady, she's watchin' [witching] him! Yes, sir! Chase him all the way back to this valley, and so Tom, he won't go there no more. . . . But you see what he can do? Tom Mitchell can doctor anybody who's eatin' that *hageenop*. . . . that wild parsnip [i.e., attempted suicides]!

'Cause lotta them Indian are doin' that, you know: they get mad, don't wanna live no more; so they can eat *hageenop*. . . . Grows by irrigation ditches, that kind. You eat some, you die fast! 'Cause I know, one time, these two women are after the same man . . . George Decroy. . . . He's livin' with *Apee* then, and she find out George's been goin' around with Steve Johnson's daughter: get mad at other woman, and so *Apee*, she tell her: "I can dig *hageenop*. Let's eat that on a contest! See who win?" But Jennie [Decroy], she spit hers out. And so they have to call in Tom Mitchell to doctor *Apee*. . . . But he make her to be well again, all right. . . . Then, way later, *Apee* get mad again. (Don't know why, but she's livin' in a cabin [Sheriff] George Allen give her that time.) And so *Apee*, she put an apron over her head and set that mattress to fire. . . . *Khaishooname'yoo,* you know: off in the head! And so they have to send *Apee* to Sparks. . . . Same way, too, my wife's sister-in-law [Marie Dick]—she don't wanna live no more. So she eat that *hageenop;* die by that way. Indian name's *Naidebone'e* 'Mean Woman', that one. . . . Get mad on account of a man! And same way, too, Tom Mitchell's own son's doin' that. . . . Yes, sir! 'Cause I know him! 'Cause Yankee Mitchell, he say he don't wanna live no more. Eat that kind, so his father's gotta doctor him. And, by God, Tom Mitchell do, too: make Yankee to spit up all what he's eatin'. . . .

Another time, a bunch these Indians are doin' ditch work in Smith Valley and find *hageenop*—by the side of that irrigation ditch. And so I guess they toss some to Sam Leon. 'Cause you see why? Sam Leon's always sayin' [boasting]:

"I'm a pret-ty tough guy—This [plant] ain't nothin' to me!"

Pozeeda Sam, that's Sam Leon's *na'a* [father]. Real old-timer, that one! Part of Tom Mitchell's [Desert Creek] outfit. . . . So, anyway, Tom Mitchell, he don't wanna help Sam Leon. . . . No, sir! 'Cause you see why? Maybe he don't want nobody else doin' that [i.e., eating parsnip to suicide]? No, sir! But he change his mind after.... Doctor Sam Leon, all right.... And Tom Mitchell use chewin' tobacco on that: spit some in Sam Leon's mouth, make him to spit out that [poison] by that way....

Still, not too many people around here like him.... On account what Tom Mitchell's doin' to everybody! 'Cause I know Big Mack, he don't visit him. No, sir! Won't, [especially] not after all what he's doin' to my mom. Says,

"Tom Mitchell eat [up] his own family!"

So you see who [finally] get Tom Mitchell? Ben Lancaster....

137. Ben Lancaster (Chief Gray Horse), Peyotist

Real old-time lookin' Indian, too, that one.... Call himself Chief Gray Horse. Most powerful one [Indian doctor] that time!

And he's born here, you know, in Wellington. Mother's *Waseeyoo*.... Been workin' in this valley a good many year, too.... And so afterward [after Ben Lancaster's birth], she get with this *Nuumuu*—from Schurz; and they fight.... [He] kill her, so that boy, he go back to Gardnerville.... Yes, sir! Was raised by his own *Waseeyoo* people up there.... Then Ben Lancaster leave this country.... Learn about that *peeyot* business somewhere else ... maybe back in Oklahoma? We can't say that for sure.... But my grandma, she say Ben Lancaster can speak our language pretty good....

'Cause I know I used to see him when I'm around about eighteen to nineteen years.... And Ben Lancaster, he's thirty-five or forty. Was workin' at Ludwig [copper mine, Mason Valley]; live in a boardin' house up there.... Yes, sir! Tall guy, real skinny. But when he come back, Ben Lancaster's fat! And he's got real long hair, too.... Pretty light [-skinned], so maybe he's stolen? Maybe his *hai'ee* [stepfather] kill that woman on account Ben Lancaster's *nomogwet?* Yes, sir! 'Cause maybe she steal him from some *Duts^man* in Gardnerville?

Anyway, Ben Lancaster, he come back here with that *peeyot* business.... Say to everybody:

"I lost lotta my best relation, and Tom Mitchell's the one doin' that!"

Yes, sir! So Ben, he's gonna get him! And so, you see what he do? After he bring that *peeyot* into this country, why, Ben Lancaster can make Tom Mitchell curious. Yes, sir! Make him to come to that *peeyot* meetin' he's holdin' all the time. . . . And so he do, too, by God! Go. So Tom Mitchell, he fall for that trap! [His] life go straight into that *peeyot* drum—where he loses his *booha*. Then Ben Lancaster can put [dispose of] Tom Mitchell's *booha* into that *peeyot* fire. And so when he [Mitchell] go home that night, Tom Mitchell, he get sick. But he can't do nothin' about that sickness, you know. No, sir! 'Cause like I say, Ben Lancaster's most powerful *poohaghooma* [in] these part that time! And so pretty quick, the rest of Tom Mitchell's life goes into that *peeyot* fire. . . . Die!

138. That *Peeyot* Business!

Peeyot—that's the only name that one's got. Named by its *moosoowee* ['mustache' or bristles], you know. And they can also call that *nat^sawabe*, medicine. Same way, I hear this other guy's tryin' to teach these Indian around here about that *peeyot* business—before Ben Lancaster. . . . Name's Runnin' Bear. Or Little Bear? Same way, too, they [also] say White Feather's another *peeyot* man. But nobody like him in Smith Valley. . . .

So anyway, when Ben Lancaster first come back with that *peeyot*, he start it up in Coleville. Yes, sir! Build his roundhouse there. . . . 'Cause them kind [peyotists], you know, they gotta have that kind [open-air] structure to meet in. . . . Yes, sir! Then Ben, when he first start comin' around here, he come to Macarini's place. . . . 'Cause you see why? Wanna buy potato. . . . Put a silver dollar in my boss's hand and talk to Macarini in English. See me there, too; he call me his relation. . . . But really I'm not. Oh, maybe my wife's related to Ben Lancester a little? Anyway, when he shake my hand, Ben Lancaster [also] put a silver dollar in it. Yes, sir! Give that to me, you know; just to be friend. But I can't talk to him by his own language. No, sir! 'Cause you see why? My mom, she won't teach me *Waseeyoo*. . . . And Ben Lancaster, he don't talk to me in *Nuumuu*. . . .

And you see what he's always sayin' about *peeyot?*

"You're sick, why, you can use that medicine. Make you better!"

Yes, sir! 'Cause I know that's what Ben Lancaster's always sayin'. How *peeyot* is like *nat^sawabe*. . . . Medicine for the Indian. . . . Make him to feel better that way. . . . Just like a real old-time Indian medicine that kind! Same way, too, Streeter Dick say you gotta talk [pray] to that kind before you eat it. Or else it won't work. . . .

Only one time, though, my wife go to Ben Lancaster's [peyote] meetin'. 'Cause you see why? Her *moo'a* [daughter's daughter]'s sick all the time. Margaret's daughter ... Paulina [Benjamin]. 'Cause you see what happen? Margaret, she goes wild on the drink, and so her mother, she wanna put that girl in [reform] school. But Willy [Muldoon] won't let us. No, sir! Says to put her in her great-grandfather's [Johnny Jones's] house in Schurz instead. 'Cause that's where my wife's daughter's marry, you know—where Margaret made that girl [i.e., off Logan Williams]. (Named for my boss's wife, Paulina. . . .) Anyway, Paulina, she get headache all the time. She's seven or eight, and don't wanna eat or drink, so her grandma, she take her up to that *peeyot* meetin'. Yes, sir!

But you see what happen? Ben Lancaster, he don't [even] pray for that girl! No, sir! 'Cause only my wife is doin' that. . . . [But] must have helped, though, *peeyot?* On account Paulina's headache, they go away. . . .

Same way, too, one meetin's for my wife's cousin . . . Annie. At her father's [Dick Bennett's] house, that lumber house in Smith Valley, other side Central. . . . 'Cause she's marry to Jack Wilson's brother Pat that time. And sickly all the time. (Heart's no good, same like my wife.) But *peeyot* don't help her, neither. No, sir! So, Annie, she die. . . .

[Yet] another meetin' at my wife's father's house—for Dick Bennett's wife. . . . 'Cause she's [also] sick, you know. And so she take that *peeyot*. . . . But that don't help, so Gerdie, she die. Same way, George Decroy take his boy there. But Ed Decroy don't live very much afterward. No, sir! Got TB and die after that *peeyot* meetin'. . . . And Andy Dick's the same. . . . He and Mamie, they [also] take his boy to *peeyot* meetin', at James Keno's house— in Smith Valley, or right here at Campbell Ranch, after they [federal government] start this reservation [1936]? Can't say which. . . . But you see what he's doin'? Andy, he take him out [in] middle the night, and so, Ben, he get mad: start workin' that [witchcraft] stuff. And Ed Dick don't live very long afterward. . . . Same as Old Man Keno's boy, Jerry, [who] hurt his ankle on a witch and go to that kind meetin'. But *peeyot* don't help Jerry Keno, neither. No, sir! Not like his young[er] brother Wesley, anyway. 'Cause Wesley Keno, he got hurt on a tractor, but go to [the] hospital in Reno. . . . Never took *peeyot* till way later, though. And so he get well, all right. . . . And same way, too, Ben's own cousin-brother . . . [who they] call Muscot. He's a *Waseeyoo*. . . . Ate *peeyot* at a meetin' in Wellington, and got sick and [also] die.

'Cause you see what they're doin?' Act crazy after that [peyote meeting]! Yes, sir! 'Cause I know I seen 'em! I and my wife, both! What they're doin!' Act worse than any drunk. . . . 'Cause we go to my wife's father's house this one time. . . . And that's in the early mornin', partner. . . . Sunday. . . . After that [all] Saturday night meetin'. And so them *peeyot* men, they're all wearin' Navajo blanket around their neck. One of them's Streeter Dick; he's from Coleville, Antelope Valley. . . . 'Cause all them Dicks, they're mixed, you know: *weta* [half] *Nuumuu* and half *Waseeyoo*. . . . Why all them Dicks can talk our language real good! And one boy, Johnson Dick, he's a marijuana man. (Your stuff, Mike, ain't it?) Get that from Reno, I hear. . . . Johnson Dick's marry to Pat Wilson's daughter, Sadie; they stay in Coleville all the time. . . . Yes, sir! And you see what we call them Antelope Valley people? *Ungabeedokado* 'Salt-Eater'. . . .

Anyway, Streeter Dick, he grab hold my wife and says,

"*Hama'a* [younger sister]: you better get them lice out your hair!"

Yes, sir! Tell my wife to shake her hair in that fire! But she don't have lice in her hair! Hell, no! Hair's clean! Same way, too, my wife, she don't see nothin' crawlin' around that moon when she went to that *peeyot* meetin' with her daughter. . . . Actin' crazy outside, them *peeyot* people—dancin', just like they're *pahmoodayp* [smoking opium]!

Then I hear they run Ben Lancaster off Campbell Ranch. Yes, sir! 'Cause you see what happen? Someone call [in] Dr. McGee, and so that *tota* [U.S. Public Hospital contract physician], he send them government bull after him. . . . Run Ben Lancaster outta these part. He can live with his wife in Coleville, then. . . . And so he don't come back no more, neither!

139. Never Mix, Never Worry!

And I only seen that [peyote button] one time. . . . 'Cause Muscot and Willy Dick, they have it in a watch case; show it to me. . . . 'Cause them two, they use *peeyot* in Smith Valley and go crazy: stole a car, went to prison. . . .

But [so] you see what's wrong? Don't use it right around here! No, sir! 'Cause [if] you're sick, well, how come they keep goin' back? Yes, sir! What I wanna know about that *peeyot* business. . . . 'Cause Mike Wallace, he's sick all the time. Cough all the time. So Mike hear about that *peeyot* business and go to Oklahoma. . . . Yes, sir! Hear about that from his partner in Fallon, that

Johnny Wright. Cousin-brother, that one. 'Cause Johnny, he first go to Oklahoma: write his cousin-brother [about] that, and so Mike Wallace, he go, too. (Johnny Wright's son of *Dzog^s* [George] Wright and *Tuugapuuno'o*—from Smith Valley, they go to Fallon when they give land; live there. . . .)

"[Peyote's] for sick people," so Mike Wallace say when he come back here. "Yes, sir! 'Cause that ain't for no healthy people!"

So I kind of figure it must be more like that dope than medicine!

'Cause I hear Ben Lancaster's doin' that, you know: soak that *peeyot* in *toha moohoo'oo* [morphine]—before he give it to 'em to try. Yes, sir! 'Cause my wife, when she go [to a peyote meeting], after she drink that tea, she say *peeyot* taste just like that other kind [dope]! And say that taste dusty . . . got white dirt on it. . . . Same as my wife say them people are throwin' down lotta money into that basket they send around! Yes, sir! Pretty near four bits each, maybe more? 'Cause you see why? It don't mean nothin' to 'em! Same way, too, I hear Ben Lancaster's sellin' that kind. . . . 'Cause not supposed to be doin' that, that way, you know—not if that's Indian medicine, anyway. . . .

Anyway, you see what them kind [peyotists] are [really] doin'? Want you to quit drinkin'! Yes, sir! 'Cause I hear Ben Lancaster's always sayin': "[If] you drink and go to [peyote] meetin', you can go crazy and die!" Yes, sir! 'Cause Streeter Dick, he's the one tell me that. His brother Johnson, too. . . . [Also] tell me not to try that. But not to mix them kind! No, sir! How I'm gonna go outta my head [if] I do. . . .

"Corbett, you don't wanna mix nothin' [e.g., wine, marijuana] with that kind!" What Johnson Dick and Streeter tellin' me. . . . 'Cause you see what I'm doin', partner? I'm finished with *moohoo'oo,* [so] I'm a drinkin' man, that time; still, I try marijuana. 'Cause Johnson Dick, he say a few puff make you to feel good. . . . So I know I don't wanna do that [i.e., "mix" peyote with alcohol or marijuana]. 'Cause Johnson's brother, he drink, so when he start usin' that *peeyot,* why, Streeter Dick have to quit! And Old Man Keno's same way. . . . 'Cause he's been through all them other stuff, Jim Keno: black and white *moohoo'oo* . . . drink. Quit drinkin' when that *peeyot* business come in, that old-timer. . . . 'Cause they say, Ben Lancaster, he know you! *Sooname* [mind or power] tell him what you're doin' [i.e., drinking]. Yes, sir!

So, pretty powerful man, Ben Lancaster. 'Cause that one time he come to Macarini's place to buy potato and shake my hand, why, I know I sure feel funny. . . . But he's not a real Indian doctor. No, sir! Got some kind different song from them *poohaghooma.* . . . Use a rattle. . . . 'Cause all he know about is that *peeyot.* . . .

And nobody know who kill Ben Lancaster, neither. No, sir! Was marry to this one woman from Topaz that time, Mary Summers; then Ben, he marry Louise Byers. . . . So maybe she's the one doin' that to him? Yes, sir! Maybe she kill Ben Lancaster? 'Cause no more Indian doctor left that time. . . .

So anyway, pretty powerful stuff *peeyot:* make you to know somethin' pretty fast. [If] someone steal from your house, well, he tell you who's doin' that, too, and right away!

8

Retirement Years (1954–74)

140. A Falling Out with My Boss

And all them year I'm workin' for Macarini, only twice I quit my boss. . . .
    'Cause that first time, we're drunk in Wellington and miss work the next mornin'; so Macarini, he bawl us out. Yes, sir! Don't say, "Better sleep it off. Work when you feel good." No, sir! 'Cause you see why? My boss don't talk good to a person!
    "Well, [if] you don't like my job, Corbett, [if] I don't give you enough to satisfy, go work someplace else! Get a better boss!"
    What he say. . . . And so, by God, I say right back to him,
    "Well, all right, Amos! I will!"
    So you see what I'm doin'? Come down to Fred Fulstone's place, work there a couple or three week. Then I can do hayin' work for Nuti. . . . But Macarini, he get over that. Come to where I'm workin' and get us back again. . . .
    And you see what happen that second time I get mad at my boss? We're loadin' potato sack on the wagon. . . . Fall the year, partner, and so it's gettin' dark. But you think we're gonna quit? Hell, no!
    "Amos, we better quit!"
    'Cause I know I tell him that. But you think he's gonna listen to me? Hell, no!

"[Just] leave 'em in the goddamn field!" I tell him. "Cover 'em up, they won't freeze!"

And that's I and my wife; and my wife's daughter, Margaret; and Margaret's [new] husband, Willy Quartz. One other Indian from Schurz is workin' with us, too—they call him *Wasa*. . . . Yes, sir! 'Cause we're all workin' for Macarini in Colony District on that potato job that time, and so my boss, he's afraid they [the crop] might just freeze.

"Let Macarini put harness away!" I say. "Let him put them horse in the barn!"

Mad, you know. 'Cause we got a team of four horse, and so, after we're through, I won't unharness 'em, by God! No, sir! Just wanna leave 'em that way. . . . And so Macarini, he get mad at me. . . . So I quit. Quit, and go to work for Hans Crosby that time. . . .

Good man, Hans Crosby: don't work me too hard. 'Cause I know I [only] have to carry them milk can around for him. . . . Yes, sir! Help him out that way. . . . And he give more pay, too, Hans Crosby: five dollar every day. So I know I sure like him! [But] come springtime, though, I'm back on the job for Amos Macarini! 'Cause you see why? He raise my wages! And same way, too, my boss, he give us that cabin to live in. 'Cause these other two Indian had my job when I [we] quit Macarini: Rawhide [Willy John] and Jesse Reymers. . . . Yes, sir! So they [also] get our cabin to live in. . . . But soon as they quit him Macarini come to get us. And I been with him ever since, partner. . . . Till my wife die and I retire.

So, pretty bad, them *Aytayay*, I tell you, Mike: 'cause work the hell outta you!

141. Campbell Ranch Land Assignment?

And so around that time [1935] they first start this reservation [Campbell Ranch, Mason Valley]. . . . Bunch them Big Bug [Bureau of Indian Affair officials], they go up to Wellington. . . . 'Cause you see why? They wanna sign me up for land here. . . . And so that one government man from Schurz, he say to me:

"Got any land some place, Corbett?"

"Well, I got little piece in Schurz," I tell him. 'Cause that time, you know, the Old Man's still livin' yet. . . . And Big Mack, he has a small piece land down there [Walker River Reservation] he's collectin' on. Dennis Bender, he's with 'em—that's Jack Wilson's grandson, you know, Dennis; first chairman these Indian [Yerington Paiute Tribe] got! 'Cause Dennis, he show 'em where Amos Macarini's ranch is . . . where I'm livin' yet. . . . But you see why I don't get one of these [ranch] assignment? 'Cause they don't think I can make it! No, sir! 'Cause that's too much money, partner: [if] a fellow ain't got no horse, no equipment, how he can make it?

Andy Dick, Howard Rogers, Frank Quinn . . . they do [receive original Campbell Ranch land assignments, and miraculously survive on them]. Yes, sir! But lotta them other Indian can't make it. No, sir! Harry Conway, Mack Paddy, Buster Phoenix. . . . *Karroo'oo!* 'Cause Howard [Rogers], he's always usin' [borrowing] his boss's horse . . . that Jim MacKay from Smith Valley. And Howard can make a partner with his *hai'ee* [stepfather], with Andy Dick, my wife's brother. You know, to help each other out on that. . . . Same way, too, Frank Quinn, he's got a little money behind him; so Frank and Hazel can make it at Campbell Ranch. . . .

So maybe [if] I got a few thousand dollar in hand I can do that, too. But I'm a drinkin' man, then. . . . So [I] never did sign up to come down here. No, sir! Only way later do I move to Campbell Ranch, partner. . . .

142. No More Spuds!

No more potato, so my boss, he quit!

'Cause you see why? Potato market's not too good. . . . Nobody's shippin' spud into California no more, so Macarini, he don't plant his thirty-five to forty acre no more. *Karroo'oo!* No more spud! [He] go outta that business, you know. But still, my boss say he want us to stay up there with him.

"Corbett, you been a good friend. [You can] live here all the time!"

Try to treat us good, you see . . . even though he's got too much machinery them day. So, not much work for us to do. . . . Anyway, we do; stay. 'Cause I think I'm livin' in that cabin maybe another three years more after I retire workin' for Macarini [1955-58]? But still, I know I can work around Smith Valley. . . . You know, any kind small job they got. . . .

143. *Ya'eep* ('Death')

My grandma, she's already dead. . . . And so's my mom. Big Mack, he's next. . . . 'Cause them day, you know, somebody die, and so we just call up Stewart. Yes, sir! 'Cause Uncle Sam's the one givin' them box [coffins] to the Indian. . . . And since them old-timers don't make no more [crafts], we don't [even] have to burn anything. No, sir! Just [their] clothes, that's all. Beddin', too. And same way, we have to move our tent. . . . 'Cause like I told you, Mike, they won't let us to burn that no more. No, sir! *Karroo'oo!* And that tent's too expensive to burn. . . . So you see what we're doin'? We keep everythin'. . . especially them [their] pot and pan. . . .

'Cause I know when my mom die—and she die six or seven year before my grandma—three to five year after I get marry—my grandma just sit and cry all the time. Yes, sir! 'Cause that's what all them old-timers are always doin' when somebody die. . . . And bury my mom fancy, too, I and the Old Man: get a box [coffin] from Stewart and haul her up to that cemetery in Smith Valley on horse and wagon; dig that grave and put all my mom's belongin' inside. Say that there [graveside], too, you know: *"Xhai soomayipon,"* 'Don't think about me!' *"Peeza'yoo teepa wetoo meeyakwa."* 'You're gonna go to a good land!' Then cover that up and put rock around that. . . . But when my grandma die, we just bury her back of Andy Shera's place—across from that Simpson Ditch. . . . But not too close to where we're livin' then. No, sir!

And that only cost $7.50 to bury my mom! Old Lady [Annie] Fulstone, she's still livin' yet. She's the one pray for my mom. . . .

Then when the Old Man die [1953], Lena [Rogers] take care his funeral. . . . Yes, sir! 'Cause I'm still livin' in Smith Valley yet, you know; Big Mack, he's down here, at Campbell Ranch. Live with his granddaughter and Howard [Rogers]. . . . 'Cause Old Mack, he [previously] was stayin' with my young sister in Smith Valley. But you see what happen? Lizzie move to Susanville, so he move down here to live. . . . Anyway, they tell me that [Big Mack's death], so I come down here to his funeral: throw dirt on him, too; talk good. . . . Say that to him to forget about me. "Don't come back! 'Cause I don't wanna think about you no more." Yes, sir! 'Cause otherwise, they [ghosts] can come back and bother a person. . . . And we bury Big Mack in Wellington [Smith Valley].

My mom, she's 87 when she die. My grandma's 115. The Old Man, why, I bet you Big Mack's around about 105!

144. Death of a Wife

And my wife's pretty old, too, when she die. Yes, sir! 'Cause, she just go to bed and forget to get up! And so the next mornin', why, my wife's gone!

Die in 1958, you know. [She] was already drawin' a pension. But my wife can still work. . . . Yes, sir! 'Cause she's a hard-workin' woman all her life, I tell you, Mike! Don't hardly miss a day! And you see what's wrong with her? Heart's no good! *Ste'yoo!* Stop every once in a while. . . . And so Dr. Mary [Fulstone], she give my wife some kind medicine for that: she can sniff [?] that [nitroglycerin?] and is good again! Same way, too, my wife get some kind syrup from another *tota* [white doctor]. . . .

She's all right, my wife, when I first marry her; later on, though, that's when her heart [first] stop. And so you see what I'm thinkin'? I kind of think her own father's doin' that [viz., witchcraft] to her. Yes, sir! 'Cause you see why? [To] get rid of her! 'Cause Dick Bennett, he's [also] got that kind [i.e., heart condition]; [also] give that to Ida and Annie, them other girl he's got. 'Cause they all got bad heart; die by that way, too. . . . Annie, she marry Pat Wilson. . . . Mean woman! Always talk about someone that [malicious] way, so I don't like her. . . . No, sir! Never try to make a friend with nobody! And Ida, too, she's also mean: always bawl her father out. . . . So maybe that's why he give 'em that [his] sickness! 'Cause them two don't wanna take care him?

And same way, too, my wife, she always say how she don't like her own father. No, sir! [But she] wasn't raised by *Tseeyanamaqapa* [Dick Bennett], neither. . . . Raised by his other wife, Gerdie; her *beeya* [mother]. . . . 'Cause my wife don't even wanna visit her own father!

'Cause I know that one time my wife hire *Hongo*'s mother to doctor her, she tell her what's wrong. Say,

"Your *na'a* [father] don't want you to live. Put his sickness inside you!"

And same way, too, that *poohaghooma*, she can say to my wife:

"You get heart trouble by your own father! But don't think you're gonna die that quick. 'Cause you're not. . . . You're gonna live a good long time, too!"

Yes, sir! What *Hongo*'s mother tell her . . . after Margaret's hubby [Logan Williams] go for her in his car. . . . And she's a real old lady, then, that Indian doctor. . . . Not a lot of *booha*, so we only pay her ten dollar. . . . Too old to dance, too. And *Hongo*'s mother don't [even] need a repeater. . . .

And so that was true, too, by God! 'Cause like I say, my wife don't die till 1958. And she's around about what? Seventy then? So anyway, after she die—'cause we bury my wife in Yerington—I go to Macarini, and he call that mortician; in Yerington; they take her away. And same way, I call up her daughter at Schurz—to help me to bury her mother. [Then] I know I wanna tear down that cabin. But Macarini, he won't let me. No, sir! So we just burn that mattress and beddin' . . . my wife's clothes, too. And [I] never wanna go back there again.

145. I Move to Mason Valley

And so you see how I quit Macarini that last time? Why I don't wanna stay in his cabin no more? 'Cause by old-time way, you're not supposed to stay in your house when somebody die. No, sir! [And since] can't burn it down no more, so I and Macarini, we argue about that cabin.

"I can move my own house, Amos!"

Yes, sir! What I tell my old boss. . . . Only Macarini, he won't let me do that.

"Well, that's supposed to be my goddamn cabin, ain't it, Amos?" I tell him. But you think he's gonna listen to me? [To] lemme do that? Hell, no!

"Then to hell with you, Amos!" I tell him. "You keep it! I'm movin' to this [Mason] valley."

Cause you see why he's mad at me? [I] start to tear down that [his] cabin! Yes, sir! 'Cause I wanna move that someplace else. And so Macarini, he find out. Bawl me out. . . . Why I move down here . . .

So you see what I do? Move in with Eddie [Mack]—right here, partner: this house! Eddie's wife's dead; [he's] got them two *hooza* [stepsons], so I help him out. Feed 'em, you know; buy grub; cook. . . . And they're not little, then. No, sir! Big enough to work. . . . But they don't try to get a good job yet. . . . 'Cause Eddie, he's my sister Janie's boy, Eddie work up in Bridgeport all summer long: feed cattle, you know. Then he come down here to his assignment every winter. . . .

And so I come down here to Campbell Ranch to live with my nephew—help to take care Eddie's two stepsons. . . . And been here ever since. . . .

146. Attempted Reconciliation with My Boss

Only one time after I move down here my old boss come after me. . . .

Says I should come back to his ranch. . . . Says I can move that cabin if I want to. . . . But I tell him,

"No, Amos! Keep your goddamn cabin! 'Cause I don't wanna stay in it no more!"

No, sir! Don't wanna go back up there, you know. 'Cause [the house] make me to think too much about my wife [if] I do that. . . . Bother me that other [bad] way. . . . Yes, sir!

147. Retirement in Mason Valley

And I'm already gettin' my pension when I first move down here. . . . So, don't supposed to work no more. . . . Forty-seven dollar every month, pension, by God! And I can get $64 on Social Security. . . . So, that give me $111 every month, partner. Pretty near what I'm earnin' [for] one whole year when I first start workin'! And I gotta buy my grocery with that; clothes, too. 'Cause Lena [Rogers], she take me shoppin' to Yerington when Eddie's away. . . . 'Cause like I just told you, Eddie, he work in Bridgeport all summer long: don't come back till winter, so he can take me shoppin' then. . . .

Oh, I can [also] irrigate for Eddie . . . this small ranch assignment he's got here. . . . Not any more, though—too old for that, partner. Yes, sir! 'Cause Howard [Roger], he's [now] doin' that custom work. . . . Howard can cut, bail Eddie's hay, . . . do all that kind work on this assignment after Howard's own crop are in. . . . And same way, too, I know I like to put in garden every summer. . . . Sound pretty near like the Old Man, ain't it? 'Cause Big Mack, he ask them *taivo* he's workin' for for that [privilege]. I grow watermelon, tomato, bean, corn, carrot. . . . Great big *Aytayay* squash in my garden, too! One summer, I [even] put in Heart-of-Gold melon. . . .

So I'm just like a woman [again]! You know, have to keep house, cook for them two boy—send 'em to school in Yerington. . . . But soon as they're big, why, they move outta here. . . . So mostly [now] I'm alone. . . . In the summer, anyway. 'Cause Eddie's with me every winter. . . . And once every while I can go uptown to buy *heebee*. Maybe you wanna take me today, Mike? 'Cause I know I sure like that Tavola Red. Yes, sir! 'Cause that table wine's pretty close tastin' to what them old-time *Aytayay* used to make . . . that homemade wine. . . . Only thing is, I don't like to get drunk uptown. No, sir! Just like to buy my own jug and come back here. 'Cause you see why? Too many fellow botherin' you, then.

"You gonna treat today, Corbett? Buy me a drink, partner! I'm sick!"

Yes, sir! Why I don't like to hang around town. . . . 'Cause too many wino! So I just stay away. . . . 'Cause these Indian, you know, they sure like to go crazy on that drink! You know, tip that bottle all the way, and so, pretty quick, they're outta their mind . . . *Khaishooname'yoo*. Crazy. Staggerin' around drunk like that. . . . Talk real funny, too. Act goofy. . . . Then they can fall down drunk like that and pass out. . . .

'Cause I know, one time, bunch them crazy wino come out here. . . . 'Cause you see what they're thinkin'? Maybe I'm hidin' a jug [of wine]? And so they search all over; but can't find it. 'Cause you see why? I'm hidin' my *heebee* in my mattress!

Another time, I'm robbed!

Ten o'clock at night, I'm drinkin' by myself; so I pass out. But forget to lock my door! And that's first of the month, too, by God; so them wino, they know I'm gettin' my pension check! Both! So, bunch 'em come right in here, and this one fellow—'cause I know him: Joe Moose; long-haired guy—he lift my pocket! 'Cause my money's over here [back pants pocket], you know. And, by God, $380, partner! He steal that from me, so I report him. You know, tell them government bull to put Joe Moose in jail. . . . But [since] nobody don't take me uptown to that trial, I hear he get off. . . .

Another time, Crazy Jackson Sam, he steal a ham from me. I report him, too; and they have to arrest that fellow. . . . My sister [Lizze's] boy. . . .

And same way, too, this other time, bunch 'em crazy wino bring this one woman out here. . . . She's passed out on my bed, and so I'm thinkin',

"Maybe I can have a go at her?"

And so I do, too—get on her, you know, doggie-style. . . . And so, by God, she wake up! Tell me to hurry up! 'Cause she's from Smith Valley, that woman. Can't remember her name, though. . . . Another time, Florence Brown is with 'em.

"Come on sister," I tell her. "Give me some that *soowee*!" 'Cause she's [also] drunk, Florence; but not [yet] passed out. . . . But I get on her, anyway. And so Florence, she just laugh at me. Say,

"We're related, Corbett. How we gonna get marry?"

Anyway, that's one thing about this valley, partner: never did see snow down here! No, sir! 'Cause in Smith Valley, gee, we used to get lotta heavy snow! Snowed in real bad sometime.... Not here, though.... Just cold, that's all, wintertime. 'Cause Mason Valley, why, pretty near look like that [snow alert]. But got no snow.

148. Some (More) Real Old-Timers

Yogho [Cry] Sam, he has two son: *Puweevuuno'o*—'cause maybe he wear same colored sweater all the time? and *Yachapuuno'o*—some kind 'cry', anyway.... Rawhide—that's Willy John—he's brother to Emma Emm, George Emm's *norr^gwa*. Oldest of them three kid, Rawhide.... Trade his name *Wuuxuuri'i* with some Pyramid Lake Indian, and use all kind dope; then Rawhide get drunk and die of pneumonia.... 'Cause I know, one time, he bring this woman to our house; call her *"Siqan"* 'Chicken'. [He] was marry to her a short time.... And she drink too much, so Rawhide, he tell me: "We're cousin-brothers, Corbett. Lay down with my wife!" But I'm too young to know about that that time.... Anyway, Chicken and her sister, they like that dope, too. Stay in Yerington all the time....

Sam Leon, that's *Pozeeda* Sam's boy: he tell how Jack Wilson don't get wet [rained on] that time he's workin' for Simpson and pack that tree [for planting] on his shoulder.... Yes, sir! And that tree's still standin' in Smith Valley, by God! Same as that tree they say Jack Wilson plant at the [Yerington Indian] Colony ... over by that [Assembly of God] Church where he used to live ... before Jack's wife die and he have to move to the other end ... [where he] die in Dennis Bender's house.... 'Cause *Pozeeda* Sam, he's another old-timer ... real old-timer! 'Cause I know him! Always used to see him goin' to Johnny Rogers' ranch [in Smith Valley] ... where my grandma work. And he stay there all day long, too, by God: chop wood, do any kind little job like that they give him.... Don't drink, *Pozeeda* Sam. No, sir! 'Cause I never did see any them real old-timers doin' that: drinkin' or usin' that *moohoo'oo*.... black or white. Just *Hongo* and Barney Miller ... that *Pipoosee Nohorr^ha*.... And same way, too, I used to see *Pozeeda* Sam headed home from work with a bag of grub the end the day.... But he don't say hello to nobody. No, sir! Just put his head down, and walk past I and my brother like that.... So that make me to wonder if he's got a bad mind [i.e., practicing witch]? 'Cause you see what that kind's doin'? They can pass you without liftin' their head, then look back. So we never make fun of them [i.e., *Pozeeda* Sam]. . . . No, sir! And you see how that old-timer's [also] called? *Toona'a yacha* 'Antelope Cry'. 'Cause when *Pozeeda* Sam's [a] young boy, somebody give him them horn from *toona'a* [antelope]. So he can make that sound [antelope cry], you know. Then when he's a man, why, *Pozeeda* Sam have to build a corral way up in the mountain—this side Sulpher Spring, goin' toward Sweetwater. . . . You know, to get [lure] them *toona'a*. Cause he's got *booha* over antelope, you know. Yes, sir! *Pozeeda* Sam's last of them Antelope doctor! Pretty powerful man, too, I tell you, Mike! And gee, there used to be lotta antelope in Smith Valley. . . . Now, *karroo'oo!* No more left!

Maggie West, she's some kind doctor, but I don't know what kind, neither. Used to live in Mason, that old-timer. . . . And Pete Winnemucca, he alway come down here from Pyramid Lake—to peddle *kooyoowee*, that fish they got up there. . . . Same way, too, *Pasheeda*, he's another real old-timer. But I don't know what that name mean. . . . Anyway, gamblin' man, *Pasheeda*. They also call him California Jim. 'Cause you see why? Speak Spanish! Older than Big Mack, *Pasheeda*. . . . Real old-timer. . . . Potato Sam, he's another bad man! *Sa'ab*, that one, you know—witch! 'Cause [if] somebody's doin' somethin' he don't like, why, Potato Sam can get his bow and arrow and throw it! Yes, sir! 'Cause that's what them witch also do to a person, you know. . . . By that *nuumuu pooharr^*. 'Cause I know him! Live with his wife in Smith Valley all the time—Frank Quinn's *goonoo'oo* [paternal grandfather], Potato Sam. . . . And Trottin' Wijo, I saw that fellow doctor Tom Mitchell's mother-in-law. . . . *Pahmoo karree'ee*, that's Tommy Benjamin's father: he's another real old-timer, that one. He's from Schurz, but always livin' at this [Yerington Indian] Colony. . . . And you see what that name mean? *Pahmoo karree'ee?* "Your tobacco tastes good, partner: give me some!" Yes, sir! 'Cause that's what he's always sayin', so they name him by that. . . . [He] was marry to Trottin' Wijo's wife, Annie, after her *gooma* [husband] die. . . . And *Poowee'age'yoo*, that old-timer's name is 'Somethin' Green's Growin'. 'Cause, maybe, that's what that that old-timer always like to eat? And same way, too, *Poowee'age'yoo* is always sayin' how he's a real cowboy. . . . Yes, sir! But nobody don't never see him buckaroo. So maybe he just bullshit everybody? 'Cause you see why? Say, he's [also] a doctor. 'Cause I know one time, *Poowee'age'yoo* try to doctor some woman, but she find out what kind bullshit doctor he is, chase him out! And that's that Annie *Moopa*, Henry McCloud's wife. She's another *nomogwet*. . . . Same way, too,

I hear *Poowee'age'yoo* try to doctor one of Dick Bennett's wife.... 'Cause like I told you, my wife's father's got two wife, you know. Same as Tom Mitchell.... So anyway, she tell him off:

"You carry whiskey. Use that [only] to get a woman!"

But *Poowee'age'yoo*, he answer her right back. Say to her:

"*Nat^sawabe heebeena!*" 'This drink's my medicine!'

Wakeen Brown's father, they call him *Sook wana*. And that's 'cause when he swim in the river, he put his finger inside a girl's *soowee* and say "*Sook wana!*" [i.e., 'Look: One Finger inside Vagina!']. 'Cause he's another one them real old-timers . . . die by that [1917–18] flu! Another they call Poker Bill.... 'Cause you see why? He [also] like them women! Yes, sir! After 'em all the time, by God! So I guess this one time, some crazy women, they're gonna get Poker Bill. Gang [rape] him, you know! And so, by God, they do that, too! Then when they're through, why, they can hold him down and piss on his face! Tom Ricci Sam, he's from Topaz. So they always call him that: *Ungabee* Sam, 'Salt' Sam. 'Cause you see why? That's where them Indian get salt a real long time ago, partner . . . in Topaz. 'Cause them real old-timers, they cook that under the ground; then if you want some, why, you just scrape it in your food. And so we call them kind Indian up there in Antelope Valley, *Ungabeedokado* 'Salt-Eater'. Or we can call 'em Tom Ricci Sam Indian. And like I already [also] told you, they're all *-weta*, up there . . . half: half *Nuumuu*, half *Waseeyoo*.... Anyway, when I see that old man [Tom Ricci Sam], [I] don't [even] call him *wa'eets* [old man]. No, sir! Just call him by that good way, *togho'o* 'grandfather'. 'Cause he's my grandma's age, Tom Ricci Sam. And he's got three wife, so [if] he don't like what one's sayin', why, Tom Ricci Sam can slap all three! Yes, sir! Why they always make a joke by that: call him *Topadzee* Sam, 'Hittin'' Sam! 'Cause he's always hittin' all three....

Waqawee'i—that's your neck or throat; some kind brown markin' there —he's from Fallon. And he live alone in these valleys a long time ago; help them Indian doctor [designated repeater].... Dick Bennett's ... my wife's father ... and they say [he] once got shot during rabbit drive; so you see what them old-timer can do: take off his shirt and shake out them bullet! Yes, sir! 'Cause that other fellow, he wanna shoot Dick Bennett, not them rabbit! But he's not hurt, neither. No, sir! And you see who tell me that? [Another] real old-timer they call Sing . . . *Soowee warr^ba*, my uncle from Schurz. He always call me *nanagwa* 'nephew', that old-timer. 'Cause he's related to my grandma some way.... [The] one they say Tom Mitchell put somethin' in front his leg—get crippled that way at the [Yerington Indian] Colony. ; . . . But like I already tell you, Mike, *Soowee warr^ba*, he's got his own *booha*. So he can throw that crutch away by his own power. Even though he walk lame all the time after. . . . Already [also] told you about Winnemucca *natsee*. . . . And that other Nixon [Pyramid Lake Reservation] Indian [who] visit us all the time . . . *Oho* Joe, 'Bone' Joe, they always call him. One-legged guy, too, *Oho* Joe: has a wooden leg. And so, every time he visit my grandma—'cause he's related to my grandma, *Oho* Joe—why, he's gotta bring *kooyoowee* [Pyramid Lake suckers]! And that fellow never quit singin'! No, sir! Sing all day long! Whistle, too, when he's makin' rawhide rope for me. 'Cause that's all Bone Joe's ever is doin' by God, is to sing, sing, sing. Sing and whistle! So I guess he's a handgame player? Or maybe *Oho* Joe's related to my grandpa, not my grandma? 'Cause my grandma's from Bridgeport, my grandpa, he might be from up north?

Pipoosee Nohorr^ha—that Barney Miller—I already told you how he's named? For some kind bug that live under the ground . . . ? 'Cause you just touch that bug, why, it blow out stink! Like skunk. . . . Pretty near like horsefly in size, that bug. . . . Yes, sir! But can't fly. Just to walk. 'Cause I know him, Barney Miller—good man! Drink that black stuff [yen-shee] and can doctor both way [sucking and rubbing]. And Barney Miller, he can also "fit" [enter trance-states]. Yes, sir! 'Cause you gotta catch that kind [of shaman] once his *booha* knock him out. Catch 'em and put 'em down [carefully]; let 'em sleep that way. . . . 'Cause Tom Mitchell's that way, too. . . . Always doin' that, you know: start to fit, then somebody has to catch him. 'Cause his power just knock him down by that way, Tom Mitchell. . . .

Old Man Charley—that's Nelson Charley's father: Nelson, he's the one put that cross on the hill; over by that cemetery in Yerington—he's another real old-timer. And best doctor, too, that old-timer! Yes, sir! And so, I guess one time, this other old-timer, he find a body in the field: [he] take that head off and put some kind light inside. . . . Pretty near scare everybody half to death! 'Cause I know when my grandma see it, gee, she think them dead people are comin' back. . . . And you see who's doin' that? Name's *Eeza'a kwazee'ee*. . . . some kind Coyote name that old-timer has got. . . .

149. Tales of *Booha*

Same as they say one real old-timer—he was a *poohaghooma*—turn into a rock! Yes, sir! On Jack Wright Hill.... Road outta Wellington to Gardnerville.... 'Cause that rock's there.... And they say [if] you've got any kind sickness, why, just rub it on that *teebee* [rock], then leave money for your pay.... *Tsomeebee* [bird bone beads], them real early days ago.... See, 'cause [if] you're doin' that, well, you'll be all right.... 'Cause [that's] same as when I pick *tsiroopee,* that Mormon tea; for [a] cold. 'Cause they [also] say to throw a nickel down when you're doin' that! Yes, sir! All them medicine you're supposed to pay 'em! Just like we're payin' them *poohaghooma*.... Payin' in the store.... And same way, too, you're not supposed to take any that money you find.... No, sir! But Jim Nuna, I guess he don't believe that—take that rock and that money and them bead that's all up there!

Jim's wife's Annie. No, Daisy! They're from Bridgeport, but mostly live in Sweetwater.... Old Man Nuna's [Jim's father] supposed to be a doctor— 'cause I hear he try to doctor Jerry Keno's leg this one time ... when it went bad. But he can't help him.... No, sir! And same age as my grandma, Old Man Nuna: got two wife from Bridgeport, they all live in Smith Valley. He don't use dope, neither, but Jim Nuna does ... that black stuff.... 'Cause I think he get that habit in Sweetwater? But Jim Nuna's wife don't use at all.... No, sir! Jim Nuna, he die before that white stuff come in.... Real name, Indian name, is *Toghowa* Jim, 'Rattlesnake' Jim. 'Cause he get that kind [rattlesnake skin], you know: hang that on his hat. So maybe he make rattlesnake noise all the time when he's a young guy?

And I'm a pretty good size man when they [Nunas] move into Smith Valley.... Do hayin' work at the Simpson Ranch.... Then I hear Mamie Dick bawl him out this one time. Tells Jim Nuna,

"You better take it back! 'Cause, otherwise, you're gonna get all crippled up! Die by that!"

But you think he's gonna listen to her? Hell, no! 'Cause Jim Nuna, he just laugh! Don't wanna believe Mamie at all.... No, sir! You know, to believe what she's sayin'.... And so that's what happen to him, too, by God: to Jim Nuna and his wife. Both! 'Cause they get crippled up pretty quick after that, both them old-timers; and die ... by that airport in Smith Valley.

And you see what everybody call that rock? *Teebee bahaveena.* Beats me, though, what that means?

Same way, too, there's another *poohaghooma* rock in this [Mason] valley ... on McLeod Hill. Yes, sir! 'Cause everybody's supposed to leave coin up there for a blessing. And you're not supposed to touch that change, neither. ...

150. More Tales of Supernatural Power

One day, Sun went to sleep. And we call that *ya'ayo*, you know: 'Sun's dead'. 'Cause I seen that kind [eclipse]. ... Yes, sir! No more sunlight. ... Start in to be cold, dark outside. ... 'Cause we was workin' in Colony [District, Smith Valley] with some *taivo* that time. ... And so, by God, cold! Colder than hell! And so, you see what Jim Wilson say:

Says, them early days ago, one man, he make that Sun to come back! Yes, sir! 'Cause them old-timers, they're cryin' around. ... Try to make fire but can't. ... Cryin' 'cause they're scared, you know. And can't hide, neither. So they just gotta pray real hard. ... You know, to stop that [eclipse]! But then, pretty quick, this one fellow says, "I think I can turn it over!" And so you see what he's doin'? Call for somebody else's gun. ... Then he can call for his cloud [spirit helper?]. Yes, sir! Shoot that like that [at the Sun], and, by God, pretty quick that cloud start up. ... and that other fellow [Sun], he come back!

So that's a tough power, partner! Pretty powerful man, too, Jim Wilson say. Name's *Natsee Kweeda* 'Shit Boy'. Father of Emory Charley. He's from Sweetwater, *Natsee Kweeda*. ... About like my grandma [in age]. ... And smart man, too. Indian doctor. 'Cause he [also] know how to make rain. ...

'Cause another time, Jim Wilson say there was a big fire in Sweetwater [Valley]. Say my wife's grandmother talks to *Natsee Kweeda:* asks that oldtimer to put that [fire] out. ... And so, by God, that's what he do! But [I] never did find out, though, if he's a *poohaghooma*, Emory Charles's father. ... No, sir! Anyway, he just speak [prays] to that cloud. Say:

"I wish you'd stop that fire!"

Wishes for that [his?] cloud [= source of power], you know. And so, pretty quick, here come that rain!

'Cause I know I seen that place where that fire was. ... 'Cause you see what happen? My wife, she say some *taivo* were cookin' pine nuts. ... They make a fire, and so, pretty quick, there's that other kind [i.e., forest fire]. And so all these Indian are cryin' around. ... You know, "What we gonna do?"

And so my wife's grandmother, she go to Emory Charles's father . . . Tell him,

"Our pine nut trees on fire. You can put it out?"

So, must be he's a pretty powerful man, *Natsee Kweeda?* On account what that old-timer's doin' . . . . Yes, sir! [Even] more powerful than Jack Wilson! Same way, I hear *Natsee Kweeda* try to give his *booha* to his son, only Emory Charles won't take it. No, sir! 'Cause he don't believe in it. So I kind of figure maybe that's why Emory Charles die young?

Earthquake, though, that's a tough one. 'Cause, gee, that ground can sure shake! 'Cause my grandma, she tell me a real long time ago—them real early days ago, partner!—there was [a] tough earthquake. . . . [And] everybody has to hang onto somethin'. 'Cause you see why? [They] think that ground's gonna tip over [i.e., end-time]. . . . Take 'em away! Shakin' so much, my grandma say everybody get scared, you know. Start cryin' around. . . . Think maybe this whole live earth's gonna [finally] turn upside down!

Deepa yutsunga, what we call 'earthquake'.

And I don't think no kind [of] *poohaghooma* has got *booha* to stop that kind. No, sir! Jim Wilson, though, he say my grandfather once walk outta Wellington Mercantile one day and say,

"When I get to the other side that road, building's gonna collapse!"

Mad [angry], must be? And so, pretty quick, all them *taivo* come runnin' outta Old Lady Hoye's store! But it don't collapse. . . . Still, lotta them beam fall—on account what *Poogooga'yoo* is doin'.

And, same way, too, them real old-timers, they [also] got story about Whirlwind. . . .

Call that kind *Pitoomabe,* you know. And they say Whirlwind's a dead Indian. . . . [How if] you don't speak [to the recently deceased], why, that fellow's [Whirlwind = dead is] gonna come back and bother you! Yes, sir! But that's not Wind . . . No, sir! 'Cause anybody can do that [i.e., "Call up the wind"], you know. 'Cause I know my wife's doin' that. . . . 'Cause one time, I bawl her out. She's way up in them mountain gettin' chokecherries, and my wife hear Lightnin'. So she tell him: "Wet my pine trees, 'cause we're poor. We don't have too much that's good to eat nowaday, so go on over that way and make lotta rain!" Yes, sir! What my wife's doin'. . . . Sayin'. 'Cause I know I'm workin' in the field that same time: I and Jerry Keno. We're workin' for this one *taivo,* and so, that lightnin' pretty near hit us! And so afterward, when my wife tell me what she's doin', gee, I sure bawl her out!

"*Keemaho gw^p!*" 'Wind come up!' How they [women] can say that, you know . . . when they want that wind to clean their pine nut [separate seed from chaff] . . .

And you see what else them real old-timers are always sayin'? Not to make fun of Thunder! Don't say, "Come over here and wet me." No, sir! 'Cause you see why? That's a person, Thunder. Turn into that kind. . . . And he can speak our language, too. . . . Why them Indian are afraid of him. . . . So, have to just leave him alone all the time. . . . And same way, too, you're not supposed to point at Thunder. No, sir! Don't talk too loud when you hear that kind, neither! But you see what happen to that fellow? Thunder, he make two baby, and Coyote don't like him. "Take me along," he tell him. But Thunder, he don't wanna. . . . No, sir! So Coyote, he throw them baby to the Sun. . . . Burn up. So Thunder, he won't take him [Coyote] along. . . . No, sir! Just leave him alone, you know; Coyote, he try to hold on but can't. Tell him to come back, but Thunder won't listen!

Nuu naba, that's how we call Thunder in our language, partner. *Tugweezeeba*, how we call that other kind . . . Lightnin'.

151. *Natoon^dweba* ('Animal Teaching Stories')

And there's even [another] *natoon^dweba* [animal teaching story] on them kind [i.e., Thunder], too. . . .

'Cause they say Coyote's daughter, she [also] make two baby, and he don't like 'em. . . . No, sir! So Coyote, he throw 'em both to the Sun. And they [both] burn, all right. . . . 'Cause you see why he's doin' that? Coyote, he don't like who she marry. No, sir! Wanna marry her himself! And so his daughter, she take both them baby inside her house; only Coyote put 'em back outside again. . . . So Thunder, he's the one [who finally] take her away. "Let me go with you!" Yes, sir! What Coyote tell Thunder. . . . But that other fellow, he don't listen to him. No, sir! Try to hold onto Thunder, but he can't. So [Thunder] take his bow and arrow and that girl, and they leave. . . .

'Cause them old people, they say animals made everythin' in this world. Yes, sir! 'Cause they say Wolf, *Eesha*, he's the boss. Coyote—*Eeza'a*—he's his young[er] brother. But he never wanna listen to what his *pavee'ee* [older brother] tell him, Coyote. No, sir! 'Cause I know I used to hear lotta them [animal teaching] story when I'm young. . . . [For example] about them two brother, *Eesha* and *Eeza'a* . . . and *Taboo'oo*, Cottontail Rabbit. . . . And *Ang*, Pine Nut Bird . . . Coyote's *barruu*.

'Cause they say *Moo'esa*, them early days ago, animals can hunt, make a fire, cook pine nut soup. . . . Yes, sir! Everythin' what these Indian do, why, just the same with them! And they can [even] talk our own language, too! Yes, sir! [Even] know lotta them hard word nobody know today. . . . Same like them Indian writin' [petroglyphs], you know. . . . [Which] nobody can understand 'em. . . . 'Cause [they're] just like a Chinese. . . . But them animals them real early days ago, why, they can . . . understand 'em. 'Cause they're real smart.

Wolf, call him *na'a* 'Father'. 'Cause he's the one make them four kid off that Woman . . . after Coyote "fix" her. 'Cause you see what happen? *Moghotnee*, that Woman, they say she and her mother are from Mono Lake. . . . They're livin' on a island. . . . Call it *Pasa chatuu*. And so Coyote, he follow 'em both. But can't catch up. No, sir! So next day, *Eeza'a* go right behind 'em [i.e., almost catches up]. But [then] you see what happen? Must be like a bird, them two women, on account they get away. And so Coyote say he'll dream somethin' [e.g., let the water divide]. And so, by God, he do! And he can go straight through that water to that *pasa chatuu* [island], and so, when he get there, *Eeza'a* see that Old Woman [first]. He wanna jump on her, but she say to wait:

"My daughter's huntin' ducks, *yahee* [son-in-law]. So you can eat lot!"

And so, when that other Woman come back, you see what *Moghotnee* is doin'? Feed them [cooked] duck bone to her *soowee!* Yes, sir! 'Cause you see why? Got teeth inside there, just like a dog! And so, before Coyote go to sleep [cohabits] that night, why, that Woman, she close up all them hole[s] in her house. 'Cause you see why? She wanna cut off Coyote's *peetho'o* [penis]! Yes, sir! Don't want him to escape!

So anyway, he do. . . . And so that Woman, she try to catch him, all right. Throw her club at *Eeza'a*, but he come back with a rock. And when she "bite" [i.e., in intercourse] that rock, why, it break all her [vaginal] teeth. Yes, sir! Then Coyote can file 'em down. . . . Bawl her out good, too, by God! Say to her,

"Ain't supposed to be the way *soowee* work. No, sir! 'Cause [you] ain't supposed to be eatin' all my good friend, *Moghotnee!* No, sir! Not supposed to see that [genital trophies?] on your wall, neither!"

And so next day, that Woman goes huntin', only she can't get no more duck. No, sir! 'Cause you see why? [She previously] was killin' 'em with her *soowee* [vagina]! And so *Eeza'a,* he's gotta get them kind for her now . . . them duck. [So] then she have to go to live with Coyote's brother. . . .

And so Wolf and that Woman, they have four kid: two girl—they're [born] first—and them two boy. Only thing is, they keep fightin' all the time! Yes, sir! Can't get along no-how! 'Cause them two boy, they shoot arrow at each other; [while] them girl, they can hit each other with a basket! And so *Eesha,* he get mad. Say to that Woman:

"[Since] my kids can't get along, I'm gonna separate 'em. Let 'em to be Enemy in this world!"

Then you see what he's doin'? Wolf, he kick 'em both off that island! Yes, sir! Tell that one boy and that one girl, "Live over there!" And tell that other pair [of siblings], "You live over there!"

And so that first pair, they land over here . . . in this country. . . . Who we are, you know, *Nuumuu.* . . . Them other two [pair of siblings], we call 'em, *Sai'ee,* Enemy. . . . And then, *Eesha,* he say to his *norr^gwa* [wife] how he don't wanna live on that island no more:

"I'm gonna leave this place now," Wolf tell her. "Yes, sir! Goin' to that other side. And [if] I make it over there, why, I can shake this world. So don't cry, *Moghotnee,* 'cause when you die, you'll see me again. . . ."

Heaven, that's what them *taivo* call that place. . . . Place Beyond the Cloud. Same as my grandma, she's always sayin' how there's a hole in the sky, and so when you die, you go straight there. Just like an arrow, you know. But them young one [infants], they don't wanna go there too fast, so they can just go along slow. . . . Pickin' flower, you know, all along the way. . . . But them real old-timers, they don't talk about hell. . . . No, sir!

152. The Flood and Other Animal Teachings

And some [also] say this world was [once] all under water. . . . How that Woman wanna kill off them Big Giant [sec. 154]. Yes, sir! And so all them animals, they drown. 'Cause everythin' is under water, then, they say. . . . Everythin' except Mount Grant. 'Cause that's the only one stickin' out, you know, that mountain. . . . Call it *kurr^gwa* 'highest mountain'. And *hootsee* 'Sagehen', he's the only one doesn't die. Save Fire that one. . . . 'Cause Sagehen, he climb Mount Grant and sit up there [covering Fire]. . . . Why they say that fellow's chest is burned black. . . . Tail's always in water, when he's sittin' down. . . .

So, pretty smart Woman, that one: make the water to raise up. Yes, sir! Make this whole land [world] to be covered with *pa'a* [water].... 'Cause she know how to do that. Savvy, you know.... Savvy 'cause she [also] can get away from them Giant.... Yes, sir! Escape to that *pasa gatuuduu* ... that island. 'Cause [if] she's not smart, how she can get away from 'em? 'Cause that Woman, she say she's gonna leave America. Yes, sir! So, take her baby and tell that Old Lady [mother?] who's outside sleepin' what she's gonna do.... Go to Desert Creek; get *yaba* ... them long root, like string, for travelin'. [But] then another one [Giant] come along ... make her baby to cry by pinchin' it. But she know what he's after:

"*Keemaho!* Come over here! Baby's cryin'."

What he's sayin' to her ... to fool her, you know. 'Cause that Giant take that baby from her. Yes, sir! Pick him up like a rabbit, kill him....

And same way, too, them old-timers tell story about Star [i.e., constellations].

'Cause the Milky Way, you know, that one's a rabbit drive. And them three Star in a row [Orion], they say that's *Koip* [Mountain Sheep] ... his family. 'Cause them two in the front, that's the father and son; his wife, she's in back. 'Cause you see what happen? That father, and his son, they don't wanna hunt mountain sheep. No, sir! Too lazy, so his wife, she chase 'em outta bed. Both 'em! But you see how they're foolin' her? They can make believe they're in bed, so when she find out they're not, set fire to it.... And so they try to run away from her.... But she chase 'em, all right!

Same way, *Taboo'oo* 'Cottontail Rabbit', they say he's the one knock Sun outta that Sky! Yes, sir! 'Cause you see why? So he can hunt cottontail rabbit. 'Cause them days, they're [the day] too short; so *Taboo'oo*, he get mad.... Climb this one great big tall mountain east of here, and shoot his arrows at *taba* [Sun]. But everyone burn up quick! Everyone, except that last one [arrow].... 'Cause that's the one *Eeza'a* give him, you know. Made of hard wood.... Same kind wood Coyote use to take [extract] them teeth outta that Woman.... And so that last arrow, it work, all right: Cottontail Rabbit, he knock *taba* down from the sky. Then he have to talk [prays] to that fellow:

"Better travel high[er] across the sky, partner," he say to him. "Give some more light that way; so I can hunt my own kind!"

Yes, sir! Talk good to that fellow.... And *Taboo'oo*, why, he [even] gut *taba*—pull Sun's *boowitwe* [gall bladder] out; buries that, same as any hunter's supposed to be doin'. But when that other fellow [Sun] get high in the sky, he make Fire. Yes, sir! Send *Koso* [Fire] after Cottontail Rabbit ...

chase him, you know. And [since] *Taboo'oo* can't hide under Prickly Pear, that's how come you see them stripe runnin' down his back.... On account what that other fellow [Sun]'s doin' to him! Same as them spot all over, partner—'cause that's that hot dust Sun can spray onto Cottontail Rabbit's back.... You know, for what he done....

Lotta them kind story, you know.... And them old-timers, they [also] say only three can dream. 'Cause Rock, he say,

"I'm gonna be a trap. [So] *Eeza'a* can fall into me, so I can kill him!"

Coyote, though, he dream another way.

"I can smash Rock to pieces!"

Daqa [Arrow], he dream he can go right through deer and kill him.... Only thing is Deer, he don't dream. No, sir! Same as *Kamuu*, Jackrabbit.... 'Cause not smart enough, you know.... Anyway, so that's why them old-time Indian use rock and arrowhead: use Rock to catch Coyote—set that kinda trap on his head—and that Point [projectile] to hunt deer....

And same way, too, I know I hear lotta story about them Bird....

'Cause they say they're all Coyote's daughter, them *hoozeeba* [birds]: *Soogoo* 'Robin', *Ang* 'Pine Nut Bird', *eehobee* 'Dove', *Wuuyu puha'a*—that's 'Red-Spotted Bird'. And Bluebird.... Yes, sir! All them bird! 'Cause he's no good that fellow, *ste'yoo*! Bad man, Coyote. 'Cause *Eeza'a*, all he wanna do is to make *yogho'o* [sexual intercourse] with his own *barruu* [daughter]!

"Go see [if] there's [a] hole in the roof, Daughter!" What Coyote tell that one bird.... 'Cause it's stormy weather, partner, by God, just like today. But there ain't no hole up there! No, sir! 'Cause Coyote, he's a liar! Do that, you know, 'cause he only wanna see his own daughter's *soowee!* Say he like that kind [incest] best! Why he ask that girl to fix that "hole" in roof.... When he's only gonna "fix" her!

And so *Eeza'a* do that, by God! Make his *noho* [testicle] into rabbit; then he say to her:

"*Kamuu* [Jackrabbit] is over there, Daughter. Let's catch it!"

Yes, sir! Tell her to go ahead and catch Jackrabbit! And so [when] he run under the sagebrush, by God, she grab him, too!

"Pull up your dress, Daughter. Make *Kamuu* fatter that way!" Yes, sir! What Coyote tell her ... then he can hit [have intercourse with] her with his own outfit [penis]! And, by God, that break off inside her!

"*Khai yacha!* Don't cry," Coyote tell her. "I got the worst part!"

And so, *Taboo'oo* [Cottontail Rabbit Doctor], he's gotta be the one to fix it.... See, first, Coyote send her to his own brother, but *Eesha,* he can't make it [i.e., extract the penis].... No, sir! So [he] send her to *Kwawa* [Mountain Rat] next. But that other fellow, he can't make it, neither. So *Eeza'a,* he has to send her to *Taboo'oo.* Bad man, Cottontail Rabbit Doctor.... Yes, sir! 'Cause he tell Coyote to go deep[er] into that water.... 'Cause you see why? So he can put his own *peetho'o* [penis] inside that girl! Yes, sir! Pull Coyote's outfit out and stick his own inside her! And tell *Eeza'a* each time to go [a] little deeper into that water ... four times.... Say:

"It's loosenin' up—Maybe we can get 'em [out] next time?"

And [also] tell Coyote to stamp four time before he come inside that house....

"So I can hear you better that way!"

And so, pretty quick [after four turns], Coyote, he drown. River take him away, but *Eeza'a,* he wake up.... 'Cause you see why? Lizard! Yes, sir! That fellow lick his eye!

"How come you don't never wanna let somebody to sleep?" Coyote, he ask him that. So, anyway, he wake up and go into *tseeyabe* [rosebush] ... that house where Cottontail Doctor live.... And you see what Coyote hear? Them kid they two made! Yes, sir! 'Cause they're playin', you know, all them kid Cottontail Rabbit Doctor make after he marry Coyote's daughter.... And so them little Cottontail Rabbit, they call Coyote *togho'o* [maternal grandfather].

"Look good to eat!" Coyote say. And eat 'em all! Only thing is, he leave that small[est] one. And so, when he build that fireplace, Coyote see his own *peetho'o* [buried] underneath it. Try to eat that, too, but he find out that's his own outfit! Yes, sir! So, put his finger in his mouth to puke that one out, and say,

"*Nuuma....* Hurt down here!"

Same way, too, there's another story them old-timers got about Coyote....

'Cause they say, one day, *Eeza'a* is takin' a dump, and he watch that *kweeda* roll down the hill.

"Someone's after us, *Eesha,*" so he tell his older brother. "Yes, sir! Comin' to kill us!" And so *Eesha,* he say:

"Well, then, I can fight 'em, *wanga'a* [younger brother, i.e., alone]. Only thing is, *Eeza'a*, don't look [watch]! Else I might get killed!"

And so, you know Coyote. . . . Don't listen to nobody! Peek and Wolf die. And them *Sai'ee* [Enemies], they can [then] cut off his head. . . . Put that in the middle their dance ground. Yes, sir! Dance around *tsopigee* [head] of Wolf all night long! And so, pretty quick, *Eeza'a*, he find out . . . go there and say how he wanna look at that head—

"[I] wanna see what kind a lookin' man is this one?" What *Eeza'a* tell 'em. . . . And so they do, too. . . . Let him to look. Coyote, then, say,

"*U'wee!*" 'Sleep!'

Yes, sir! Make 'em to go to sleep that way! But Louse, he's away from the bunch. . . . (Call him *Puzeeyaba*). . . . He come back and holler about what Coyote's doin', and so the rest of 'em, why, they wake up. 'Cause you see what Coyote's workin'? He can get all them young girl together away from the bunch, and "work" 'em over! Yes, sir! Then go back to Wolf's *tsopigee;* cover his head with dirt . . . that wet dirt, you know. To soften him up . . . make *Eesha* to wake up better [faster?] that way. . . .

153. Giants and Waterbabies

One Old Lady—she's mother of that Giant Cannibal—and you see what she's doin'? Wanna kill her own son! Yes, sir! So she mix up them *daqa* [projectile points] in a bowl with blood, tell that other Woman: "Bad man's comin. Yes, sir! 'Cause every day he bring another Indian he killed!" And so his own mother do that to him, by God! Feed him [Giant] that in a bowl. . . . And so that glass [obsidian?] start workin' inside him, and pretty quick he can fly straight [up] in the air! So that Old Lady, she call that other one [Woman]:

"Come out! 'Cause we're gonna watch 'em. . . . See how high he's gonna go. 'Cause [if] he's dead," she tell her, "his *kasa* [wings] gonna flop around. And when he's down on the ground, he's gonna be dead!"

And so, Giant Cannibal, he do that all right: hit the ground and start to break his wing. Both! Then they can make a boat outta that kind, them two [women]: you know, to get across to that Island. . . . Fix him, all right! And so that Woman, she tell that other one goodbye. Say to her,

"When I get to that Island, this land's gonna all be under water. . . . [So] I can drown all them other Giant by that same way. . . . Yes, sir! Kill 'em off!"

And so that's how she kill 'em. Before that other one [woman] can marry *Eesha* . . . before she make them four kid; them two boy and girl. . . . 'Cause them Giant, you see, they can eat 'em [Indians] raw! Make a knife outta *daqa* [arrow points]—skin 'em better that way. And Deer, too. . . . What they doin', anyway. Before them *taivo* start comin' to this country. . . .

'Cause they say back of Bridgeport there's a lake, and that's where that one kind Giant live: *Tsana'oho*. (He make a funny noise, that one: "*Wii'moo, Wii'moo* . . ." like that. . . .) And they say a bunch these Indian were gamblin' by that lake this one time: one girl, she's with cherry [menstruating]; so she has to stay outside. 'Cause by old belief, anyway, she can bring bad luck. Yes, sir! And so [when] she hear that noise, she go inside that gamblin' house—try to tell 'em somethin' bad's comin'.

"You're lyin'! You don't hear nothin'!" What they say to her. And keep on gamblin' like that. . . . So she tell 'em that again. Yes, sir! Tell about that whistle *Tsana'oho* keep makin'. . . . But you think they're gonna believe her? Hell, no! So that Giant, he keep comin'. And so that girl, she jump into that cellar—where they keep their food; cover herself with a basket. . . . And so *Tsana'oho*, he keep comin' right along. . . . Yes, sir! Keep on whistlin' like that same way, too. . . . Throw dirt through that door, but still, they don't believe her!

"You're foolin' us!" What they say to her. . . . Think she's tryin' to trick 'em. . . .

"Your eye gonna dry up!" Then *Tsana'oo*, he tell them gambler. . . . And so they do, too, by God! Look at him and die! But he never eat 'em. . . .

And same way, they got another kind Giant, too. And he's [also] that kind [Cannibal]. . . . 'Cause I know I seen that rock belong to *Paheezoho*. . . . What he's always carryin' around on his back, so he can eat these Indian. 'Cause like I already told you, they say that's how come they have that Flood them early days ago. . . . What I hear, anyway. 'Cause too many Giant Cannibal livin' back then, so Flood's gonna kill 'em. . . .

And you see how that Woman can trick *Paheezoho?* He go to that gamblin' house, where them Indian are playin' handgame. . . . And she try to warn 'em, all right! But they won't listen to her! No, sir! And so, *Paheezoho*, he just look [stares] at their eye: put 'em to sleep by that kind [hypnosis?], you know. Then he can grind 'em up on that rock. . . . Eat 'em like paste by that way. And so that Woman, [since] she's got a baby, you see what's she's doin'? Have to dig a hole in the ground and put that big [funneling] basket over their head . . . to hide from *Paheezoho*. 'Cause he's a great big tall man, *Paheezoho*—must be eight feet tall, by God! Great big, long bone. . . . And he's got a real long tail, too. Light come shootin' outta his mouth. . . . Eye like a flame. . . . And same way, too, they say his teeth are like [a] fingernail.

"*Nuunuuha keema . . . Nuunuuha keema.*" 'Wild Animal's comin'! Wild Animal's comin'!' Yes, sir! What he say all the time. . . . You know, sayin' that over and over again to them Indian gambler . . . to trick 'em! But you think they're gonna listen? Hell, no! And so that's how come they die. And same way, too, *Paheezoho*, he say,

"*Boowe pasa!*" 'Eyes gonna turn dry!'

And so they do. . . . Then he can find [out] where that Woman's hidin'. . . . 'Cause she leave that baby alone, you know. Yes, sir! Run away without her own baby! Leave that baby for Giant Cannibal's breakfast! And she's got a great big, long stick, that Woman: use that on the escape . . . like a high jump. . . . Jump clear to Walker Lake [from Desert Creek] . . . where they say she's livin' now. . . . And so, *Paheezoho*, he get mad at her. Put that baby on his belt and pull off his own nose. . . .

But I hear they find one [Giant Cannibal] back of Hudson [Mason Valley]. 'Cause this one prospector, he tell that. . . . Was diggin' in the rocks, you know. . . . And I was thinkin' about goin' there to see them bone, you know. But never did. . . . And you see who [finally] fool *Paheezoho!* Coyote! Yes, sir! Tell that fellow to look down over the side that mountain—at that bunch *koip* [mountain sheep] feedin' there. . . . And so, when he do that, why, that other fellow [Coyote], he push him off! 'Cause some Indian in Smith Valley, they're fishin' in the [Walker] river and climb on that big rock . . . in the river bed, where that *Paheezoho* fall in the water. . . . Yes, sir! And they find that rock that's on his back. . . .

Same way, too, with them Waterbaby. . . . 'Cause they're [also] two kind, you know: that Woman, they call her *Paseeyar^m*, she look like us; the other kind's just like a baby. . . .

Paseeyar^m, she's got long hair. . . . Belong in deep water. And they say her hair's draggin' behind her clean down to the ground, partner! 'Cause some Indian, you know, they [even] seen her; seen her in a [deep] water hole. . . . But nobody don't wanna bother *Paseeyar^m*. No, sir! On account she'll take you in with her! Underwater! 'Cause they say she took this one guy away. . . . Some *taivo* [who] seen her layin' on a rock . . . and same way, too, they can give [offer] you money, them Water Women . . . then take you down in their hole that way [when] you're reachin' for that kind. . . . Anyway, that's not around here . . . [but] in Yosemite. . . . And you don't wanna dream about *Paseeyar^m,* neither. No, sir! 'Cause only one old-timer is doin' that [i.e., Waterbaby as Guardian Spirit]: Winnemucca *natsee.* Yes, sir! Use her hair when he doctor. . . . Rolled up in a little ball. . . .

But that other one, we call her *pa'o aha.*

'Cause that one's real tiny, you see. 'Cause I know, one time, [even] I seen her track . . . over by that Hot Spring in Smith Valley—that lake [Artemisia] up there. And real small tracks, too, by God! Round, you know. Just like a baby startin' to walk. . . . Leading around that shore! And that water's deep, there, I tell you, Mike! Never go dry! Same way, too, I hear there's lotta that kind in Walker Lake. . . . 'Cause one *taivo* I know, he [also] seen a Waterbaby. Yes, sir! Was layin' around on top the rock there, playin'. And she try to give him somethin', too! Her dress, maybe? 'Cause you see what they're [really] doin'? Tryin' to trick you! Yes, sir! 'Cause soon as you reach for that, why, *pa'o aha,* she can pull you into the water!

154. Wolf and Coyote

Yes, sir! 'Cause lotta them kind [animal teaching stories], partner! And them real old-timers. Why, they can take all night long to tell 'em! Say to you:

"Get some wood. . . . Put that on the fire."

Say to you,

"*Natoon^dweba!*" 'We tell story!'

'Cause I know Sweetwater Jim, he's another one always sayin' that. And say how you're only supposed to be tellin' 'em at night, too; not day. And [only] to small kid, not each other. . . . Same way, too, Andy Dick, he also tell 'em. . . . 'Cause he's Sweetwater Jim's grandson, Andy: act like his *nugweegeeyaka* [designated repeater]. . . . You know, one [who's] supposed to be doin' that, tellin' back what he say; and keep on askin' them question to him like that—right along. Like:

"Grandpa, where did Wolf go when he left this world?"

Or

"How come after he leave this world *Eesha* don't wanna stay [down] here with his Indian children no more, *togho'o?*"

You know, like them kind [questions]. . . . Same way Andy's supposed to tell [repeat] back a little at a time after that old man's stopped [narrating]. . . .

But one thing I never seen is no wolf. . . . Seen his young brother lotta time. . . . Yes, sir! But not *Eesha*. And he's real smart, Coyote. . . . He don't want you to see him, he can hide. . . . But they say nobody make *Eesha*. Cause Wolf, he's been here all the time. Yes, sir! No story about where he come from. . . .

Only thing is this wolf we got around here, is a different kind! 'Cause this one, he's *khaishooname'yoo*. Not smart! Don't know nothin'! Kill his own tribe. . . . [But] that other *Eesha*, he's the smart one: leave this country and go to some better place to live! Yes, sir! 'Cause he don't like it around here. . . . Wanna live close to them smart people. . . . And so he go away. . . . Live by them *taivo*, maybe [Europe?]? Or somethin' like that?

And same way, too, them old-timers, you see what [else] they say: [if] you [ever] tell all your story, why, you can make it storm. . . . Only thing is, me, I don't care to learn any when I'm young. No, sir! 'Cause you see why? Too busy on that cowboy business, partner! Yes, sir! 'Cause when I'm young, I tell everybody,

"I'm *pakyera'a!* Real cowboy!"

[So I] don't wanna learn nothin' what them real old-timers are sayin'.

"*Karroo'oo!*" I can say. 'That's nothin' to me!'

155. *Karroo'oo!* No More Nothin'!

[But] today, nobody's tellin' that kind no more . . . them *natoon^dweba* 'animal [teaching] story'. No, sir! And seem like nobody talk our language any more, neither. 'Cause I know I speak Paiute first; learn my English in Stewart. . . . [But] today, it's different. 'Cause I know I try talk to these kid around here in their language, and they can't [even] answer back! No, sir! And some these Indian, why, they only talk to you in your language when they get liquor in 'em. . . . But we oughta hang onto our own language, ain't it? You know, to try to use that all the time? Be better that way, instead of teachin' them little papoosee only on the English side? Yes, sir! To let 'em to learn their "Paiutee" first—save their English word for later. What I'm doin', anyway, when I'm little guy. . . .

And same way, too, they're too doggone lazy, them young fellow! Yes, sir! Don't wanna work! 'Cause I know when I used to be young, I don't wanna loaf around. No, sir! Always workin', by God! Ever since I start workin', anyway. . . . And don't wanna hunt, neither! 'Cause I know, wintertime, I'm always doin' that: huntin' for my grandma rabbit, duck, deer . . . before my eye go bad. . . . 'Cause that's all the meat we got back then, partner! And just so long as that [hunting season]'s still on, what I'm doin' all the time! Then I can help my grandma, my mom, and my wife on the seed [gathering] side. . . . And same way, too, they don't make their basket no more. . . . No more tule house, neither. . . . [We] can't [even] read our own Indian writin' [petroglyphs] no more! Too dumb! So, *karroo'oo* 'nothin'!

Don't even know how we're related today! Hell, no! But them early days ago, by God, the old people, they're always talkin' about that [i.e., kinship]: you know, how this one's your relation and that one's not. . . . Make a fellow to be ashamed when you're doin' that [i.e., sex with too-closely related family members]. . . . But nowaday, *karroo'oo* 'no more'! 'Cause you see why? Nowaday, they just wanna ride around and buy their sister a drink. . . . Make *yogho!* 'Cause I know my grandma, she bawl me out when I wanna go with Hazel Bob [Quinn]. . . .

"That's too close, Corbett! Your cousin-sister!"

'Cause my grandma and Judy [Joaquin], they're sister by long way off . . . not real way, though. . . .

And that's somethin' [else] about these [we] Indian: don't know how to save our money [either]. . . . You know, to buy a ranch . . . not smart like them *taivo* . . . them *Aytayay*. 'Cause they [Italians] know how to do that, by God! 'Cause real cheap! Yes, sir! Always savin' up their money, then one day, they can buy a spread . . . like Macarini's doin' . . . rest of them *Aytayay*. Not these Indian, though! No, sir! Just not smart enough, I figure. . . . 'Cause you see why? Always have to spend their money on *heebee* [drink]! So I kind of think we take after Coyote that way. . . . When we should be more like Wolf. 'Cause he's the smart one, *Eesha*. His young[er] brother, *Eeza'a*, he's dumb!

156. Bad Dreams

And all my life, even though I bury lotta my old people, never did dream about nobody in my family. No, sir! Just put 'em in the ground and talk good to 'em. . . . Tell 'em not to think about me no more. . . . "You got a good place to go to . . . better than this place. So don't come back and bother me no more!" Yes, sir! And throw dirt on top 'em. . . . So they don't bother me. . . . 'Cause seem like all I'm doin' is to bury my people: . . . my brothers . . . my mom, my grandma . . . both my sisters . . . and Big Mack. . . . But none 'em do that to me [i.e., return in haunting dreams]. No, sir! But when I come down here, my wife, she do that to me . . . twice!

'Cause that first time, a woman come into this room and take my blanket; then she's on top me. Yes, sir! 'Cause you know how they can make that racket with them high heel, them woman? And she's cryin' along, too. . . . Well, so, I have to wake up and get outta bed . . . talk good to her . . . tell her not to bother me no more! And gee, I must be screamin' real loud, too, 'cause Eddie, he wake up. Yes, sir! Has to come to this bed I'm sittin' in; shake me real hard. 'Cause you see why? He think I'm on D.T.!

But that woman's not [really] on me. . . . No, sir! Doesn't take my blanket, neither! 'Cause I just dream by that! Dream she grab hold my blanket, and so I wake up that way. . . .

And that other time, she come right through that [front] door! Yes, sir! Jump right between my leg, too! I try and fight her, but can't do nothing at all. *Karroo'oo!* Can't [even] hit her, 'cause you see why? My arm, they're all locked up. So I just wake up. Light my light, and sit [up] on my bed. . . . Tell her to get away from me, 'cause I don't want nobody to bother me that way. And gee, my heart is sure beatin' when I wake up. . . . Scared, you know. . . . Tough feelin' that way. . . .

And I don't see that woman's face, neither. No, sir! 'Cause that's night time, partner . . . too dark. But I feel her hair, though. . . . You know, when she's on top me. . . . And she's got real long hair, too.

That's only a dream, but anyway, you see what I'm thinkin'? I kind of think that's my wife! Yes, sir! What I'm thinkin,' anyway. . . .

"Don't come back and bother me, no more, Celia!"

What I say to her. . . . But I never did try and call her [back]. No, sir! [I] just let her to go. . . .

157. No More, He Comeback(s)

So you see what I'm thinkin' about now all the time? How I work hard all my life! Yes, sir! 'Cause I'm born in Smith Valley; and stay there pretty near all my life . . . till I get to my old age. Marry thirty-six years. . . . And I and my wife, we're workin' twenty-five years for same boss . . . Macarini! Heavy work, too, by God! All I'm ever doin'! 'Cause I don't like no kind easy job, neither. No, sir! And don't never lay off! 'Cause even [if] I'm hung over, why, I'm on the job Monday mornin'! 'Cause some fellows, you know, they can lay off Monday . . . maybe even Tuesday . . . then go back to work again. But not me! Not what I'm doin', anyway! No, sir! We work all the time, except for Sunday. 'Cause that's when you gotta rest.

And so damned stiff-handed now. . . . Can't even lift my shoulder no more! 'Cause I do that potato work all the time. . . . Work like a goddamn mule! Yes, sir! 'Cause them *Aytayay,* they work the hell outta a person!

But you can't get it back again! No, sir! What I'm thinkin', anyway. [How] you can't come back to bein' a lively man again! No, sir! And you see why? Coyote! He's the one doin' that, you know! What I always hear, anyway. . . . What them old-timers are always sayin' . . . them real old-timers. . . .

Say,

"*Moo'esa*" 'early days ago'. . . . And tell how *Eesha* don't wanna see nobody gettin' old. No, sir! 'Cause same way, too, Wolf, he don't wanna see nobody sick, nobody dyin', neither. 'Cause you see why? He's the best, Wolf! *Tonadoo,* we call him—by real old-time way, anyway: 'Chief'. And we can [also] call him *poweenabe* 'Good Talker'! But Coyote, he don't wanna listen to his brother . . . what Wolf sayin':

"All the Animals have to die, *Pava'yoo* 'Big One'. Not fair [for] your [Indian] children to be livin' all the time [forever]!"

Yes, sir! What *Eeza'a* say. . . . Cryin' around all the time, too, you know, that fellow: mad! 'Cause Coyote, he say he [also] wanna see them young girl bleedin' every month.

"Let somebody push down on their belly hard: to make 'em to holler out loud when that papoose come out! Better that way!"

And same way, too, *Eeza'a* want everybody to get sick and old; then die. . . . [He] wanna see old men at home sewin' their *moko,* their buckskin shoe; and makin' their bow and arrow and their *weega* [rabbitskin blanket]. . . . Walkin' down the road with their *goonoo'oo* [digging stick-cane]. . . . Wanna [also] see old lady with their teeth all rotten out . . . so they can't do their willow work no more! Yes, sir! Bad fellow that Coyote. . . . What he doin', anyway. 'Cause he [even] wanna give his Indian children same kind hand [paw] he's got! Only Lizard, he say, "No!"

"How my relation gonna do anythin'?" Lizard say. "*Nuumuu* need a good hand, like mine!"

So he should have listened to his old[er] brother, ain't it? 'Cause when his own [only] son die, Coyote, he start cryin' around. But Wolf, he won't listen to him. No, sir! Won't change thing [back] around, then. Can't....

158. Disillusionment?

Already told what all them old-timers believe.... How when this world's gonna tip, them good people, they're gonna come back again. Yes, sir! [And how] after they die, they can turn into young people again.... But not bad one, though.... No, sir! Only them good one.... Yes, sir! 'Cause they [old-timers] talk crazy that way ... my grandma, Big Mack, my mom.... All believe in that kind.... Then after a while, they quit talkin' about it....

Me? I believe that for a while. Then no more.... 'Cause *karroo'oo!* Don't believe that kind no more.... No, sir! Don't believe what my old people are tellin' me.... 'Cause you see why? *Wodzeewob*, he's been there. Yes, sir! Went to that other place, you know ... heaven. 'Cause you see why? He wanna find out....

So *Wodzeewob*, he say he go through that hole [in the sky]. Only thing is *Eeza'a*, he fool him! Yes, sir! 'Cause Coyote, he also go with him; tell *Wodzweewob* how he's gonna show him them dead people.... Only thing is, when they get to that other side, *Eeza'a*, he disappear! Hide away, you know ... fool him, all right! And so *Wodzeewob*, he just stand up there by himself.

"Where's all the [dead] people?"

What that real old-timer say. 'Cause nobody there, by God! Only a dugout [?], and one great big Owl. Yes, sir! Everythin' else just a shadow... *Haba*, you know. Shade! And so *Moohoo'oo* [Owl], he just blink like that at *Wodzeewob*....

So *Wodzeewob*, he come back and tell everyone that. Say he don't believe in his dream no more ... *Karroo'oo!* Don't believe them dead people are comin' back again to be young.... No, sir! 'Cause I know that's what *Wodzeewob* say all the time ... when I visit him in Mason ... when I come to know somethin'. And same way, too, when he doctor my mom, *Wodzeewob* is sayin' that ... that second time, when I'm old enough to remember....

Say,

"*Karroo'oo!* It's nothin'! Only shadow there!"

So I figure you gotta be an old man. . . . Yes, sir! An old man [who] gotta sit in your house like me, Mike. . . . Yes, sir! 'Cause can't come back to bein' a young man again. . . .

Epilogue

159. Final Visit (1973) with Corbett Mack: A Conversation

"My jug's just about empty, partner!" [Corbett burps]
"Well, I can't buy you any, partner. Don't want Lena gettin' mad at me—"
"O.K., partner! . . ."
"Sorry about that, Corbett! . . ."
[Long silence]
"So, you goin' back to your big town, Mike?"
"My *pava'yoo* city, Corbett! My big city!"
"Oh, your *pava'yoo* city. . . . Maybe I get in there, I might get lost?"
"You bet, Corbett! It's pretty big—bigger than Sacramento!"
"Bigger than Sacramento, huh? Maybe bigger than Los Angeles?"
"I guess it is. . . . Bigger than even that town."
"Uh, huh!"
[Longer silence]
"New York . . . that's pretty close to the ocean, Mike?"
"Right on the ocean, Corbett!"
"Right on the ocean . . ."
"Yeah, and we get some pretty bad storms this season! What they call 'hurricane'."
"What they call 'hurricane', huh? Pretty tough over there when that cold come, huh, Mike? Winter season?"

"You bet, partner! Pretty cold!

[Short silence]

"*Koso* [match], Corbett?"

"Yeah, my fire [cigarette] went out."

[We light up]

"Thanks, Mike!"

"So, I hope I'm gonna come out again next summer, Corbett—"

"Oh, so you're gonna come out next summer, huh, Mike?"

"I hope so, partner! But you're gonna take care of yourself?"

"Well, that is if I'm still alive?"

"Just try and take it easy—and watch out for them wild women!"

"Yeah, them crazy drinkin' women!"

"Yeah!"

"Just wish my arm and knee get all right, though. . . . 'Cause that's what bother me all the time. . . . Make me to feel sick. . . . 'Cause, otherwise, I'm still [a] good man yet!"

"Maybe you ought to go over there and try that new Sweatlodge, Corbett?"

"Maybe I oughtta, huh? 'Cause I hear it help some guys."

"I go! It helps me!"

"Pretty near like that steam bath, ain't it?"

"Uh huh!"

"Well, I drink. So maybe, I better stay away?"

"Don't wanna mix, eh, Corbett? Afraid you might lose your mind?"

"Yes, sir!"

"Well, what about liniment, Corbett? Ben Gay help?"

"Too strong, partner! Gonna make my shirt smell to stink! Then maybe my blanket's gonna smell *ste'yoo*, too. . . . Why I don't like to put that kind on my arm. . . . And too greasy, too. 'Cause I know I used to try that kind a real long time ago—time my knee went outta joint."

"How'd you use that stuff, Corbett?"

"How did I use that stuff? Oh, I just rub it in. Then rub alcohol on top. 'Cause them [white] doctor don't help me at all. No, sir! Just look at that, that's all. Put bandage back . . . don't try to rub me at all. . . . And so, when I go back home, I just take them bandage off."

"And don't let them winos get you drunk, either, Corbett!"

"No, sir! 'Cause I don't wanna do that! Don't want their kind [of] drink, either!"

"How come?"

"Too strong that *taivo* drink! See, 'cause, one time, this one fellow bring me that kind, and I have helluva time with it! Almost a dead man! I just like my Tavola Red."

"Table wine. . . . Does Eddie [Mack] ever buy for you?"

"*Karroo'oo!* No! Have to get it myself!"

"Eddie doesn't want you to drink any more, huh, Corbett? Like his sister Lena?"

"*Khai!* Say, 'Uncle, you been drinkin' so many years, them white people say you get off that altogether, why, you can get sick and die!' So I know I just buy quart of my Tavola Red, partner. Not a gallon, though. Drink a little bit that way, Mike . . . don't guzzle it, neither . . . and don't try to get drunk!"

Appendix A

Local Newspaper Accounts of Opiates in Smith and Mason Valleys, Nevada (1896-1931)

Abbreviations:

    YT   *Yerington Times*
    LCT   *Lyon County Times*
    MVN   *Mason Valley News*

1896

2 May: "Sheriff Littel arrested a Chinaman at Wellington, Smith Valley, this week for running an opium joint for Piutes. The Chinaman is a fiend himself, and about half the Piutes of Smith Valley have formed the opium habit by visiting the joint he conducted." [LCT]

9 May: "Quong Sin, the Chinaman arrested for running an opium joint for Piutes in Smith Valley, was tried before Justice Whitacre in Mason Valley last Saturday, convicted and sentenced to seventy-five days in the county jail. He now languishes." [LCT]

1899

1 Apr: Chinese man arrested for selling opium to Indians. "Efforts are being made to run the opium joints out of the Valley." [LCT]

1907

26 Nov: Chinese man man arrested in Mason found with a can of hop and several packages sewn into his underwear. Estimate worth $165, plus $3000 in cash. Raids made for the next two days in Mason resulting in 9 arrests of Chinese men. "That they were doing a large traffic, principally among the Indians is assured." [MVN]

1908

4 Jan: Jimmie Bobb, Indian from Smith and Mason valleys found high on hop in Yerington. Tells the place of purchase. A raid follows on the Chinese man Ah You's opium joint. "We regret to say this city has a 'hop head' population that would put many larger localities to shame." [YT]

4 Apr: Leo Kingston and Charlie Wye, two Chinese men, and an Indian woman, were found high and arrested in a Yerington laundry west of the city serving as an opium joint. [YT]

23 May: Charley Kee, Chinese man, arrested for selling yen shee to an Indian from his cabin. [YT]

1909

20 Mar: Lee Loy, Chinese man, fined $50 for selling opium to an Indian. [YT]

25 Sep: Bill Muldoon, local Indian charged with stabbing Willie John, at a Chinese opium joint. [YT]

26 Nov: Roundup of 9 Chinese men at Mason by U.S. Deputy Marshall with the help of Constables Ambrose and Dalton, Deputy W.W. Thompson and Constable G. Osborne. Ah Gee was found in his tent near the [Walker] river below the Mason livery feed stable with a can of hop and several packages sewn onto his underwear. Total of 3 lbs worth $55/lb and $300 on his person. Raids in Yerington and around the Valley during the next two days resulted in the arrest of 9 more Chinese men. They had lots of money on their person. [LCT]

27 Nov: Special agents from the Interior Department arrested 5 whites for selling liquor to Indians and Charlie Wye and Gee How for selling yen-shee to the Indians. The Chinesemen were fined $200 each and sentenced to 100 days in jail. "The degrading influence of

APPENDIX A

opium is rapidly reducing the Indian squaws to prostitiution and the bucks to the vile 'employment of procurers.'" [YT]

1913
1 Feb: Dave John, an Indian, broke into Chineseman Louie Bovard's cabin near the slaughterhouse in Yerington, steals a gun, shirt, and the pills used to break the opium habit. [YT]
24 May: The body of a Kong Wau was found. Chineseman was killed from 10 days to 2 weeks ago. Indians are suspected. [MVN]
31 May: Dave Jim and Little Johnny, two Indians, were charged with the smothering death of Yee Young, Mason Chinese man. They had no money for opium and he refused to give them some gratis. [YT]
12 July: The 2 Indians charged with killing of a Chinese man in Mason confessed and each receives a 5 year prison sentence. [YT]

1915
9 Jan: Ah, Sam, Chinese man, was arrested for running an opium den at the Indian camp in Yerington and selling narcotics. [YT]

1916
19 Feb: "Big Charlie," Chinese man, arrested for selling drugs to Indians in Yerington. [MVN]
19 Feb: Charlie Wye, Chinese man, arrested again for selling drugs to Indians at Wabuska. [MVN]

1917
22 Dec: Charlie Foo, Chinese owner of the Grant Saloon and Restaurant in Mason, arrested with $2500 worth of opium and yen-shee on his person. "The place has had a bad name for some time, it being alleged that the Indians secured both whiskey and hop there." [MNV]

1920
11 Aug: Federal officers, George O'Neill and James J. Brown, arrest Sing Lee, Chinese laundry owner in Mason, for having opium on his person. Lee paid a $200 fine immediately and was freed. [YT]
18 Sep: Lee Sing, Chinese restaurant owner arrested in Mason on 11 August had 3 large match boxes of yen-shee and 5 boxes of mor-

phine tablets which he was dispensing. Sing offered federal officers O'Neill and Brown drugs and $30/month if they would permit him to continue. Use of the drug has grown to an amazing degree among the Indians, so that it was found during a recent raid that "at least one member of the tribe in every hut was smoking opium." [MVN]

1921

27 July: Ah Boo, Chinese restaurant man from Wabuska, arrested by Chief of Police Kelley on Monday with 18 packages of yen-shee. He is a known peddler. Pleaded guilty and received a $200 fine. [YT]

1922

29 Mar: Chinese man arrested for 3rd time in Wabuksa for selling opium to Indians. [YT]

1 April: Ah Boo caught with 2 packages of yen-shee during sale to an Indian. He is a repeat offender, always in jail. [MVN]

22 July: Charley Wye, Mason Chinese man, found beaten. $1500 worth of opium and $300 taken from him. [MVN]

18 Oct: Federal Narcotics Officers and a Special Indian Officer arrest Ho Hun, a Smith Valley Chinese man, who worked on the Fulston Ranch in that valley, for possession of yen-shee. [MVN]

1923

6 Jan: Indian Gus Bran, ca. 39, said to be a dope addict was arrested at the Yerington Indian Colony for killing Ah Quong in Carson City. After the killing, he and 3-4 other Indian men and one squaw reportedly went to Wabuska Japanese Ranch where they split up, Bran returning to Yerington, the others to Schurz for a fandango. Bran used a broken spike to beat the old Chinese man to death. He had previously been in prison from 8 November 1918 to 1 January 1920 on a 1-14 year sentence for forging the name "Frank Stickney" on a check. [MVN]

13 Jan: Gus Bran confessed that he attempted to pass a bad check, which the Chinese man refused because of a previous bad check. He then killed him and took his morphine for personal use. [MVN]

APPENDIX A   247

20 Jan: Ho Hun of Smith Valley appeared in court saying he possesses drugs but doesn't sell them. Charley DeBoer, a one-armed white man, was arrested with narcotics on his person. [MVN]

10 Feb: Wong Shew, Chinese laundryman from Mina, was arrested with 21 bindles of yen-shee and the marked money given by an Indian provocateur. [MVN]

23 June: Arrest of Jimmy Burbank for murder:
           "Conditions at the local Indian camp in Yerington are none too good. Drug addicts have been apprehended several times." [MVN]

11 July: Joe Yama was arrested with 60 bindles of yen-shee following a raid on the grocery store at the Yerington Indian Colony that he purchased from Tom the Jap. One Indian, Martin Davis, was also arrested. "Yama stated that he started giving drugs to Indians in order to secure necessary help to harvest his crops, later enlarging the scope of his operations." Yama owns a ranch for the past 2 years and said that the only way Indians would work for him was by providing narcotics. Owned the grocery store for only 2 months and was selling there since. [YT]

14 July: James Brown, Internal Revenue Officer and C. J. Bright, Federal Narcotic Inspector, from San Francisco, Special Indian Officer, George O' Neill, and Yerington Chief of Police, James J. Kelly, combined to raid a grocery store outside the Yerington Indian Colony late Sunday afternoon. They discovered a cache of narcotics: 1 can containing an ounce of yen-shee in his toilet; 1 can containing 29 bindles on the back porch; 5 packages containing 41 bindles in the stove. Joe Yama admitted he'd been selling. Said he'd received the shipment recently and expected another soon. A raid on the huts of the Yerington Indian Colony followed and several pipes were destroyed but no more drugs were discovered. One Indian fled, but shots in the air stopped him. [MVN]

18 July: White person arrested for selling opium to an Indian. [MVN]

18 July: Dewey Clark, Indian of Mason, was sent with marked money to purchase opium. [MVN]

1 Aug: Jake Thompson, white person, arrested for selling yen-shee to an Indian. [YT]

11 Aug: Jim Sing, Chinese cook for the Reading Brothers of Smith Valley, was arrested for selling yen-shee. Had quite a trade, and Indians were waiting for him even as the arrest was being made. [MVN]

20 Oct: Bill Queen [Willy Quinn], Indian, arrested for receiving a package containing opium sent from James Brown of Virginia City. [MVN]

1924

26 Mar: Corbett Williams, Schurz Indian and recent graduate of the Carson Indian School, received 18 months after being caught with yen-shee he had shipped from Sacremento in a crate filled with lettuce. [MVN]

26 Mar: A 3-day festival of booze and dope at the Yerington Indian Colony that began on Sunday and continued through Tuesday resulted in the death of two Indians because of a fight over a woman. An autopsy revealed that alcohol and dope poisoning caused the death. 7 Indians arrested. Gus Lee and Johnny Bob were the deceased. Each was 35. Jailed for 10 days were Henry Bob, George Abe, Johnny Miller, Hank Mitchell, Corbett Mack, Sam Leon, and J. Brown. "It is authoritatively stated that out of the several hundred Indians here, not more than a dozen are free from the dope habit, men, women, and children alike being victims." [YT]

29 Mar: "With the death of these 2 Indians the people beginning to awaken to the fact that conditions are getting pretty rotten at the Indian camp. At present 90% of the Indians in the Valley are hop heads and the time is coming when some dope crazen [sic] Indian is going to run amuck and kill a few citizens. The local bootleggers and hop peddlers' association has decreased in membership during the last few days—several leaving for milder climates and the remaining brothers have crawn in their ears. Now is a good time to call the attention of the government ot the fact that the so-called reservation within the city limits of Yerington is nothing more or less than a clearing house for yen shee peddlers. The place is so damn rotten that it smells to heaven." [MVN]

1927

21 May: Ed Reymers, Andrew Penrose, Henry McCleod, Sam George, Ray Sam, Henry Johnson and Charley Brown were arrested for stealing 25,000 feet of copper from the Truckee River Power Company and several thousand feet from Gelder Mill. Robbery took place over 3 months with the men taking turns thieving the copper. They would chip it from the poles and cut it into small pieces and fill barley

sacks with it. If the wire was insulated they burned off the insulation. Wire sold to the local junk man living near the Yerington Indian Colony, who gave them $40 for it. All admitted to using dope and that dope is now hard to come by. [MVN]

11 June: Two Indians arrested for having opium and other narcotics. $1000 worth of wire has been stolen during the past few months and numerous complaints of petty larceny. [MVN]

18 June: "A dope epidemic among our Indians which resulted in a small crime wave in this part of the country." [MVN]

1928

31 Mar: An Indian dope peddler was arrested with more than 1 ounce of narcotic drugs, which he possessed for the purpose of sale. "Mr. Muldoon, dope peddler, will get a needed vacation." [MVN]

21 July: A raid by Deputy Sheriff McLeod and Bert Miller and the Indian cop, Jack Dalton resulted in the arrest of Billy Schurz, who had opium, morphine, yen-shee, cocaine, and many other derivatives, as well as a home made pipe. [MVN]

18 Aug: Outfit belonging to Billy Schurz called "the most complete dope layout ever seen." It is felt that with this 4th raid by DA Ross that this breaks up the local dope ring. [MVN]

6 Oct: Poisoned alcohol (jackass) kills Harry MacMaster: "One by one Yerington's Indians are succumbing to the ravages of booze and dope. Before long the ranchers will be hard put for hay hands." [MVN]

1929

23 Mar: Secretary of Lyon County Chamber of Commerce, E. W. King, Mrs. Gertrude Webster, and Reverend R. B. Culvertson, were appointed by the BIA to investigate conditions at the Yerington Indian Colony, in Smith Valley, and at the Walker River Reservation: "It is quite probably the question of dope, whiskey and need of better water supply on the reservation will be handled without gloves and that the English language will be put to a severe test to express the view of the committees on these subjects." [MVN]

22 June: Reports of widespread narcotics usage and violations of the Harrison Narcotics Act led to a raid in Yerington which resulted in

arrest of 3 Indian peddlers—James Keno, Billy Muldoon, and Minnie Keno—$1000 worth of morphine and $1084. Were they agents for white peddlers from San Francisco? "The raid constituted the first move in a campaign by which officers hoped to halt the use of narcotics by Indians—a practice that, encouraged by drug peddlers, has spread alarmingly in recent months." [MVN]

16 Nov: "War Against Hop Peddlers Waged by Local Officers:" Tom Benjamin and George Pyle, Indians, were arrested at the Indian camp in Yerington by Sheriff Randall, and others to follow as they return from pine nut camps. Lead came after an Indian (Marston Scott) was arrested for passing bad checks for the sums of $5 and $10, the money used for the purchase of hop. Scott admitted to numerous small crimes in the area and was willing to inform on the other two Indians. "It is safe to say that between $200-$300 is spent by local Indians in the purchase of hop. The average dope fiend using three packs a day."

Benjamin and Pule were hip-pocket peddlers selling 100 packets a week on the average, each packet worth $100, getting $.25 on each dollar, for local dope kings from Carson City or Gardnerville Chinese who imported narcotics from the West Coast or Mexico. [MVN]

1930

11 Jan: Doud Wallace and Dewey Norton, Schurz Indians, were found with dope and needles and sentenced to 5-5& 1/2 years. "A few more stiff sentences like this will make the sale of narcotics very unpopular with the venders. . . . It is about time that our Indian department took some drastic measures to stop the sale of whiskey and narcotics to our Indians if they expect to ever place them on a self-supporting basis and make any kind of citizen of them." [MVN]

1931

1 Aug: Local Indian, formerly of Virginia City and Carson City, caught peddling morphine at the Yerington Indian Colony. [MVN]

1 Aug: Frank Herrera (Mexican) was arrested for selling whiskey to Ray Sam and and Louie Jones (Indian miner in Virginia City mines and

APPENDIX A

           resident of Carson Valley) was arrested for peddling morphine at the Yerington Indian Colony. [MVN]
18 Nov: An Indian was arrested for selling dope. [MVN]
18 Nov: Richard Brown and Louie Jones were paroled from their 1-5 year prison sentences on narcotics violations. [MVN]
28 Nov: Streeter Dick and Andrew Penrose arrested for dope and whiskey. [MVN]
5 Dec: Andrew Penrose convicted of selling narcotics. [MVN]

Appendix B

Report of Narcotic Situation among the Indians of the Walker River Jurisdiction, State of Nevada, 8 June 1931

Some talk about the use of narcotic drugs by the Indians in Nevada, particularly in the Walker River Jurisdiction, dates back at least ten years. The situation previous to 1927 had been investigated and handled mainly by the Indian Service Special Officer. In 1927 a letter was sent to the Indian Officer requesting that he devote his time particularly to the liquor traffic.

In 1929 complaints came to the Federal Narcotic Office that there was considerable narcotic drugs being sold to the Indians in Nevada under the Walker River Jurisdiction, which caused the Narcotic Office to send two officers, Agents Elliot and Robertson, to that district to make an investigation. They arrested at that time James Keno, Minnie Keno, and Bill Muldoon, all Indians. Case No. Nev-39 (James Keno was sentenced to one year and one day in prison and fined $100; Minnie Keno was dismissed; Bill Muldoon was sentenced to three months and fined $50). James Keno has in his possession over $1100 which is proof that he was peddling narcotic drugs. He also had in his possession a quantity of morphine for sale among the Indians. The agents at that time also visited various camps in the territory and found that there were about twenty addicts in the Mason Valley District, about the same number in the Smith Valley District, and about seven or eight in the Walker River Reservation. It was disclosed that no new addicts were made during the past three years. The main source of supply came from Chinese at Carson

City, Nevada, and there were also rumors that Indians went to Sacramento and Bridgeport, California in automobiles and brought drugs back with them.

In February 1930 two Chinese were arrested at Carson City, Nevada, by Agent Robertson, namely, Ah Bong and Lai Num. Case No. Nev-82. Each was sentenced to 18 months and fined $250. Continuing the investigation, in March 1930 Agent Robertson arrested in the Walker River Reservation one Sullivan Tom, who had, undoubtedly, taken over Keno's trade in dispensing narcotics among the Indians. Sullivan Tom stated that he was securing the drugs from a Chinese at Carson City and has purchased for the government agents one ounce of morphine for $165 from Ah Gow, Chinese, who was arrested, Case No, Nev-9\87, and sentenced to one year and one day and fined $100. Sullivan Tom was incarcerated in the Nevada State Hospital for 90 days to effect a cure, and was granted probation for a period of eight months. These arrests were the blow which curtailed the traffic.

In November 1930 there seemed to be some activity in that traffic, centering at Carson City. At this time Agent Robertson and Indian Police Lewis Henniger apprehended Yee Dock at Carson City for selling narcotic drugs to the Indians, Case No. Nev-106, and Yee Dock was sentenced to prison for one year and one day.

During the same period local records show that Special Officer O'Neill, Indian Officer Jack Dalton, the Sheriff's Office, City authorities, and the Federal Narcotic Officers made 31 arrests of Indian addicts and peddlers at Yerington, Nevada. The main arrest was that of William Muldoon (son of the Bill Muldoon arrested in 1929, Case No. Nev-39), who received a sentence of from 10 to 15 years; two others received a sentence of five years each. Twelve of these individuals are still incarcerated.

On May 26, 1931 when the Senate Committee on Indian Affairs held a hearing at Reno, Nevada, one Jack Largen, a Cherokee Indian who lives part of the time at Schurz, made the statement that the narcotic traffic among the Indians was growing fast and many Indians were dying from the effects of drugs, which, according to him, was being distributed by the different farmers who employed the Indians to do ranch work.

On June 1, 1931, Agents DeSpain and Robertson met Miss McGair, Field Representative of the Indian Office, at Schurz, Nevada, at which time Jack Largen was questioned as to the traffic of drugs in the Walker River Jurisdiction. He stated he knew of one Indian who had died from the effect of drugs, and when asked regarding the Indian's age he stated that he was about 105 years old. When questioned as to how he knew the man who had been using drugs and if he had ever seen him use drugs, he stated that another Indian had told him that he was using drugs and that he had never seen him use the same. When questioned regarding actual facts, he stated that of his own knowledge he knew of no addicts but that another Indian had told him about the name. The Indian alleged to have given the information was questioned in the presence of Mr. Largen, the officers, and Miss McGair, and he stated that he had given no information regarding the Indian addicts and that he did not believe that there were many Indian using drugs at this time for the reason that they had no money. During the conversation with the narcotic officers Mr. Largen stated that if he had a United States Marshall's badge he would be able to do something. Seemingly, his object is to secure a position of some kind.

The earning capacity of the average Indians at the present time is $1.50 a day and Superintendent Parrett stated that the average annual income of an adult male Indian was $300 a year. Drugs are worth about $165 an ounce in Nevada, if sold by the ounce, and about $300 an ounce, if sold by the bindle. A bindle [of] morphine is sold for from $2.00 to $4.00 in Nevada, which bindle would last an addict about a day.

Miss McGair, together with Agents Robertson and DeSpain, visited various camps, amounting to twenty-four different homes occupied by Indians and their families. The officers examined the Indians, talked with them, and were unable to find one person who was using narcotics, but did see ten former addicts who would be using drugs if they had the money to buy them and a source of supply. However, the successful arrest of various Chinese curtailed the traffic, and the officers believe that at this time there is no traffic in narcotic drugs in the Walker River Jurisdiction.

According to Sullivan Tom, an Indian, a former addict and peddler, who can be depended upon to know the facts, about 21 years ago there were approximately from 50-60 Indians using the drugs. Owing to the activity of the Indian Special Officer, the local police, and the Federal Narcotics Officers, the traffic has been cut down, no new addicts made, and, according to Agent DeSpain, at the present time there are no addicts. However, at Carson City there are six Indians whom Agent Robertson knows to be users of drugs when it is possible to obtain the same. All the former users of drugs mentioned would, no doubt, use drugs now if they had the money to purchase them and a source of supply.

It is believed that if the Indian Special Officer was instructed by the Indian Office to keep a close watch on conditions with regards to narcotics, the present clean slate would be maintained and also improved, as the only way to prevent the Indians from using drugs is to make it impossible for them to buy it.

Mr. Fred Brooks, who is Night Marshall of the Town of Yerington and, who was born and raised among the Indians, stated that the general conditions, including narcotics, among the Indians was better than it has ever been to his knowledge. He stated that there was absolutely no traffic in narcotics but considerable trouble was had with the "bootleggers" selling to the Indians, and the ranchers dispensing liquor as part payment for work. It is entirely probable that the liquor stupor is being interpreted by the general public, who are not familiar with the action of drugs, as being a drug stupor.

[Signed by Mary Gilbert McGair, Field Representative, Indian Service; V. H. DeSpain, Narcotic Agent; and Daniel K. Robertson, Narcotic Agent.]

SOURCE: ITC Archives

Appendix C

Narcotics in Smith and Mason Valleys, Report of the Grand Jury of the Eighth Judicial District of the State of Nevada, Submitted to James J. Britt, Acting Commissioner of Indian Affairs, by Clark Guild on behalf of the Directors of Lyon County Chamber of Commerce, 18 April 1929

We, the Grand Jury, have further investigated the narcotic situation among the Indians of Mason and Smith Valleys. It is our belief that the officers of Lyon County are making every effort toward the elimination of this traffic among the Indians. We wish to commend their efforts in this behalf.

We are of the opinion, however, that the local officers can not cope with the situation. We believe it impossible for officers, who are known to those engaged in the traffic of selling narcotics, to successfully apprehend those so engaged; that it is of the utmost importance that an under-cover man work in connection with the Office of the sheriff and district attorney. Realizing further that narcotics are almost universally used by the Indians of Lyon, Douglas, Storey, Mineral, Churchill and Washo Counties, we believe that there should be a special officer, with authority to operate in all of the above named counties, it being his duty to pay particular and exclusive attention to this form of law violation.

It is our belief and opinion that the eradiction of the narcotic evil is not a matter of local or state control and should not be left to local and state officers. In most instances those guilty of infractions of the law, and the users of narcotic drugs, are government wards and we deplore the laxity on the part of the government to assist the local officers.

It is to be noted that occasionally George O'Neill is in our community, and is doing all within his power, upon the short time alloted him, to assist local officers and properly perform his duty. However, we firmly believe that O'Neill, or any other government officer engaged in this work, should have the authority to employ under-cover men.

It is to be deplored that when narcotic cases are turned over to the government officers that so small sentences are given and so little regard given to the seriousness of the situation. We regard the fact that the Federal authorities have not more intelligently comprehended the existing situation.

We believe the government should have one man, whose particular duty it would be, to work in the counties above named until the present situation has been corrected.

So serious is the narcotic traffic and so prevalant is the use of narcotic drugs among the Indians of the above named counties, that we recommend, in view of the fact that the government does not seem to be able to cope with the situation:

That the Governor of the State of Nevada, of his initiative or by and with the consent of the several counties named, appoint some person who is qualified to undertake the task of apprehending the sellers of narcotics; that this person be made a member of the State Police, and further that he be allowed when he deems necessary to engage and use under-cover men and decoys of the persons making narcotic purchases.

We believe that the above recommendations, if considered and put into effect, would be of the greatest benefit in eradicating this evil, we further beleive [sic] that in the event that narcotic traffic is ended that violations in the several counties will greatly decrease

*EDITOR'S NOTE: In that same year Charles Burke, commissioner of Indian affairs, wrote James Doran, commissioner of prohibition:"This Service has no funds for the employment of additional officers at present."

SOURCE: ITC Archives

Notes

(Note numbers correspond to section numbers, not page numbers.)

1. *Nomogweta* derives from *Nuumuu* 'Northern Paiute' and *-gwet* 'splitting'. I count nine additional half-breeds who reached maturity between 1892 and 1930: Nellie Emm, Alice Vidovich, George Emm, Jimmy Summers, Nellie Nobe, Mae Jim, Henry Tom, Bill Miller, and Marie Conway. Indeed, four years before Corbett's birth, the local newspaper editorialized about the "stolen" children (*Lyon County Times,* 17 March 1888). More than a decade later, in 1901, The *Lyon County Monitor* was advising that adoption of the Pima system of killing half-breeds "by the local Piute contingent would be likely to result in the extinction of that race in one generation." Walker River Reservation farmer-agent Franklin Campbell wrote the commissioner of Indian affairs on 9 June 1865 that "as yet they have resisted the baneful influence of intoxicating drinks and have preserved with great tenacity the native virtue of their women" (in Canfield 1983:59), and according to Stephen Powers (D. D. Fowler and C. S. Fowler 1970:127), who visited in 1875, "There are no halfbreeds to be seen in Nevada, but on the frontiers of California there are many." The first "stolen" Northern Paiute, then, might have been Maggie or Jennie (Rhodes) James of Pyramid Lake (or Loyalton, California), fathered on 14 April 1878 by an Irishman (Inter-Tribal Council of Nevada 1974).

The life history of Annie Lowry, Lovelock Paiute, wrote Robert Heizer, is the "unadorned and factual recital of a 'half-blood,' the peculiar institution of the advancing western frontier of America" (1966:x).

The Northern Paiute term for stealing, incidentally, is *nat^ruuhanuu*.

2. Corbett was drinking when he told me this and laughed. Ashamed of being a half-breed? Sarah Winnemucca (b. 1844?) said during her 1879 Christmas Eve lecture-appeal for financial aid to establish an Indian school, "Some say I am a half-breed. My father and mother were pure Indians. I would be ashamed to acknowledge there was white blood in me" (Canfield 1983:167). Relevant perhaps also in this regard is the fact that her father, Chief Winnemucca, did not speak to Sarah for two years following her marriage to Lt. Edward Bartlett, a *taivo* (Canfield 1983:79). Nor were any Smith and Mason Valley Paiute shamans the product of miscegenation.

3. Timothy B. Smith, an early settler of the valley named for him, wrote:

> Mr. and Mrs. Hoye came to the valley in 1863 or 1864 and rented a place on the edge of Alkali Flat where they kept a station. They soon left this location for the better one at the head of the river canyon in the lower end of Antelope Valley. . . . Here they were very successful as station and store keepers. All the old-timer travelers on the (La Sue or Rasue or Rissue) road will remember the fine table set by Mrs. Hoye. In the early 80's they moved to the present location (near the Wellington Post Office) and built a fine residence, a large store building, etc. [1911-12:228]

Cora Sayre (b. 1897), daughter of another Smith Valley pioneer and whom I pleasurably interviewed in 1989, recalled for the Oral History Program of the University of Nevada that John Hoye was born in Scotland and died in 1890; his wife, Anne Mary Kingston, was from Ireland. They had no children but raised two nephews, Tom Kingsley and Frank Kingsley, and one niece, Mary Kingsley. Wellington Mercantile, according to Mrs. Sayre, was originally located north of its eventual site, on a well-traveled teamster's road to Virginia City. It relocated south, or near the bridge in Hoye Canyon, before finally moving to Wellington, where the Hoyes took in boarders in their three-story extant house in Smith Valley, one room reserved for the visiting Catholic priest from Carson City. Wellington Mercantile's letterhead in 1882 carried the mailing address "Walker River, Douglas County, Nevada" (Sayre 1977:8-12). The photo of Mrs. Hoye, the nephews and the niece, the Chinese cook, and Jack Wilson (Wovoka) as a teenager, that Cora Sayre gave to the late Mary Ann Cardenal, who with her husband Rene owned Wellington Mercantile in the 1960s, appeared in Hittman (1990, Plate B). Mrs. Cardenal thought only Pioche, Nevada, in 1889 had an older continuously operating store.

The town of Wellington was named for Maj. Daniel Wellington, who in 1863 bought the stage station that Jack Wright and Len Hamilton had owned alongside the bridge they had built over the Walker River. The stage station ran freight between Carson and the mining camp of Aurora. A post office opened on 17 March 1865, the town of Wellington, according to the census, listing 126 inhabitants in 1870 *(Reflections 1988,* annual publication of the *Mason Valley News).*

James J. Corbett knocked John L. Sullivan out on 7 September 1892 in the twenty-first round of their heavyweight championship fight in New Orleans; Corbett apparently conflated this with a subsequent bout between his namesake and Bob Fitzsimmons in nearby Carson City. I note, too, the contemporaneous names Corbett (Williams), Sullivan (Williams), and Fitzsimmons (Williams) on the Walker River Reservation (Walker River Indian Agency, box 315, "Press Copy Books from Farmer Asbury to Superintendent Pugh, RG 75, Federal Archives, San Bruno, Calif.). Long before Corbett Mack's birth, however, *taivo* names were adopted by Northern Paiutes (cf. Magnaghi 1975-76). The tenth federal census (U.S. Bureau of the Census 1880-1920), for example, evidences widespread adoption of first names in Smith and Mason valleys. Surnames, which probably came later, derived from those pioneer families on whose ranches and farms the Paiutes worked and to whom they became paternalistically attached, for example, Bennett, Reymers, McLeod, Bovard, Lancester, Shreck, Webster, West, Smith, and Williams. Jack Wilson, whose name derived from the original *taivo* settler of Missouri Flat, Mason Valley (cf. sec. 123), of course, is the most famous of these. Among the more interesting names, I note in this regard Woodrow Wilson and James Mooney, the latter for the great nineteenth-century Irish-American ethnologist who interviewed the famed 1890 Ghost Dance prophet on the outskirts of Mason Valley on 1 January 1892.

4. "They may name the child for some habit he has acquired, or perhaps for the first word that he spoke clearly," Lovelock Paiute Annie Lowry told Lalla Scott (1966:79). "They like to name their girls for flowers." "Nicknames," no doubt, are prominent in family- or band-level primary group societies (Steward 1938; Stewart 1939; Service 1962), such as Northern Paiutes had. An anecdote about Corbett's family told to me by Russell Dick is revealing in this light. Big Mack and a nephew once cut Sunday Sam's wife's shoes into pieces, and when she challenged them, their reply, "Never mind, Annie!" became her name.

5. See sections 69-71 on Amos Mencarini. In the text, however, I adopt my informant's willful or unintentional practice of referring to his long-time employer as Macarini.

6. The Paiute word *na'a* designates both social father and biological father.

Euroamerican rules for first and last names were not immediately evident to Paiutes. Thus, Andy Dick was the son of Dick Bennett, "Aim" Dick the father of George Aim, which became Emm. Similarly, Chief Winnemucca's son Natchez Winnemucca was the father of Gilbert Natchez, landscape painter and amateur linguist (Inter-Tribal Council of Nevada 1974:42-45).

"Polygamy is practiced, and I have known one case of polyandry," Powers (D. D. Fowler and C. S. Fowler 1970:129) observed in 1875. "A couple of funny old codgers known by the unique names of Ox Tom and Chiquito Winnemuc had a woman in common, and, by general report, they lived together with her in perfect accord" (cf. Steward 1936b, Stewart 1937; Park 1937). Coexistence of polygyny and polyandry, coupled with "sister-exchange," noted in section 7, are no doubt consistent with harsh survival demands and the need for mobility and "flexibility" among this nomadic, foraging Great Basin people (cf. Steward 1938:242-43; D. D. Fowler 1966: 58-62; C. S. Fowler and Liljeblad 1986:446-49).

Informants explained the name *Nop^daka'a* as follows: *no-* 'to carry', *-^daka'a* 'to trot along'. *Tsanorr^*, they said, meant 'to pack anything on your back'. Bert Hooten, Yerington Indian Colony resident, was also called *Tsanorra*. Lena Rogers, one of Corbett's surviving nieces (she took care of Big Mack at the end), verified his other Indian name as *Wasatsabeedoo*. "Kind of a mean guy when we were kids," she told me. "Drinks and hollars to scare a person" (see secs. 10, 79-80). Corbett's other two nieces separately recalled their grandfather's making "the biggest drum there was, out of wagon wheel and cow skin. And Big Mack pounds so loud, my mother gets mad," Bernice Crutcher (b. 1928) told me. Her sister Elsie Sam Ausmus not only reported the additional name *Saya* 'Stork' for Big Mack but also recalled what pleasure he derived singing his own songs:

> Big Mack told Indian stories and made us sit and listen. He was around six [feet] four [inches] with white hair. John Wayne reminds me of him. He used to get mad at us when we were kids because we used to take his picture lots of time. Too bad we lost them! He wore Levi's and work shirts. Had big feet. Wore work boots—wore that same pair nearly all his life. My mother [Lizzie] would yell at him to quit playing his drum and singing: "Sounds like you're going to war!" He also used to make little

drums you could hold in your hand. They had a buckskin cover. He lived with us and took care of us when my Mom goes to work. Corbett used to visit him all the time.

7. I could find no archival evidence of Big Mack's allotment on the Walker River Reservation, yet all three descendants asserted the occasional check for fifty-four cents that he received for heirship-tangled leased land. The only archival reference to Big Mack I found is a letter from Etta J. Shipley, Yerington Indian Colony field matron, to Mr. Horace J. Johnson, superintendent of the Walker River Agency. Dated 2 August 1922, it reads:

> I had a phone call from a Mrs. Day, Smith Valley. She said there was an Indian couple there—the woman has been blind for years and the man is paralyzed. *They are relatives of Big Mack whose wife has been sick for several months*—they [?] Schurz some time ago but are not here under Dr. Leavitt's care. Mrs. Day said this couple was at least 100 years old and [there is] no one to look after them. Pat Wilson's family has been there for some time but they are returning to Mason so there is no one to take care of them. Pat Wilson is a relative also. Please advise me. These Indians are [living] at Simpsons. [Walker River Agency, box 303, Correspondence for 1922 and 1923, RG 75, Federal Archives, San Bruno, Calif.; emphasis added]

Mack Wilson was a son of David (1829-1915) and Abigail Wilson (1836-1910), pioneer settlers of Missouri Flat, Mason Valley.

See section 16 on the settlement of Smith and Mason valleys.

Julian Steward (1938:38-39) wrote the classic description of Great Basin communal rabbit drives, but Powers's earlier account of the role of the rabbit boss on the Walker River Reservation in 1875 is informative:

> Every autumn after the pine-nut harvest is ended [Walker Lake Paiutes] organize a grand drive or hunt in Mason Valley or some other locality where hare abound, in which all able-bodied members of the tribe participate. They advance in line of battle with an interval of some rods between each two, whooping and shouting to flush the hare, which are shot in great numbers. Their flesh is dried for winter use and skins saved for the manufacture of blankets. [D. D. Fowler and C. S. Fowler 1970: 125-26]

A photographed account of a 1907 mudhen drive on the Pyramid Lake Reservation can be found in the papers of Lorenzo Dow Creel, superintendent of the reservation. Creel there also wrote:

> October, 8:00 am/300-400: Boats form a fleet in two rows, one man rowing another shooting. . . . Too fat to fly so die in water or swim

toward shore where Indian women and dogs collect them . . . taken to camps where skinned and dressed immediately. . . . What's not eaten hung to dry. Three or four of these drives in October and November, so they camp at lake. . . . Mud hens arrive in September from the north and leave in November. [Lorenzo Dow Creel Papers, box 8, folder 2, Correspondence, 82-1, 1875-1945, Special Collections, University of Nevada Library, Reno]

Omer Stewart (1939:141-42) defined the *Agaidokado* 'Trout-eaters' of the Walker River Reservation as one of twenty-one Northern Paiute bands. Edward Johnson (1975) wrote a very useful history of the Walker River Reservation.

*Nuumuu pooharr^* (witchcraft) means 'shooting something [evil] into a Northern Paiute'(see sec. 130).

8. Confirmed by all of Corbett's nieces. "Change my name, my real father's name is Tom Wheeler!" Lena Rogers recalled her grandfather telling the "welfare lady." Thomas "Paps" Wheeler was one of several brothers who settled Missouri Flat, Mason Valley. Mormons, they apparently were recalled to Utah. Conceivably, then, Big Mack, after leaving the Walker River Reservation, worked on the Wheeler Ranch before working on the Wilson Ranch in the 1860s.

9. One measure of Corbett Mack's reliability as informant was this discussion of William Douglass.

In the *Lyon County Times* (3 February 1890) we read of a William J. [?] Douglass and Frank McBeth from Smith Valley visiting Greenfield in Mason Valley to see a play. Constables, I was told by Jim O'Banion of Smith Valley, ordinarily assisted the sheriff by serving papers. Phil Earle, curator of the Nevada Historical Society (Reno), located these additional invaluable references to Corbett Mack's putative father: (1) a note card bearing the entry "W. S. Douglass, elected Constable to the Smith Valley township in 1894"; (2) the entry "William S. Douglass" in the 1920 census (U.S. Bureau of the Census 1880-1920), where it is reported that he was born in Canada in 1879 and was living in Carson City, Ormsby County, where he was said to be a "lodger" at the Nevada State Prison; (3) a 7 March 1925 death certificate, which gives Douglass's birth date as 24 January 1855. Cause of death was "gunshot wound in Carson City," his final resting place the Lone Mountain Cemetery in Carson City. Curator Earle then guided me to the *Carson City Appeal*, where the heading of column 7, page 1, for 7 March 1925 reads: "William Douglass Shoots Self to Death." This story accompanies it:

William S. Douglass, Carson resident for many years, committed suicide in his room in a lodging house on South Carson street this afternoon by shooting himself through the head with a rifle. He had been drinking heavily the past few weeks and his resultant physical and mental condition is believed to have prompted him to suicide. That he had considered self-destruction, however, is indicated by a newspaper clipping found in his room telling of a mysterious suicide by cyanide in San Francisco several years ago. Douglass did not arise this morning and Duncan Clark, a friend, called upon him at his room to learn if some aid could be given. Douglass said he was alright and Clark came up town at noon. This afternoon upon returning to Douglass' room Clark found him dead. He had placed a rifle beside him in his bed and evidently placed the end of the barrel in his mouth and pulled the trigger with his left hand. He was a native of Canada, aged about seventy years, a coroner's jury found, and the verdict of the jury was suicide. He leaves no known relatives. Douglass' recent employments had been as caretaker at Eagles' Hall and later as a guard at the prison. No funeral arrangements have been made yet.

Smith and Mason Valley Paiutes are notoriously scrupulous about identifying paternity, yet several gave Charley Hinds or Charley Beamans (both of Smith Valley) as Corbett's genitor. His niece Elsie Sam Ausmus, on the other hand, thought he was fathered by a Simpson. Be that as it may, her sister Bernice Crutcher in 1992 recalled for me that "Uncle Corbett was always talking about his real father, Bill Douglass. 'That's why I'm small and light!' Uncle always said."

10. This nightmare of the dangerous taunting of a wife with a loaded rifle for reason of illegitimacy was replicated within Andy Dick's family. A 6 June 1905 letter from Walker River Reservation farmer-agent Longrove to Superintendent Calvin Asbury similarly speaks of the incarceration of Tom Bob, Indian, as "murderer, wife beater, and general scrapper." He "undertook to do his wife up on the 31st ult.," the letter reads,

> and also went round in the dead of the night looking for his half-breed boy with the intent of killing him, could not find them, so tried to sneak on a policeman and kill him, but the man was not in his wicaup [sic] at the time, so called on me about 11 at night just as I was going to bed and started in abusing me, so took him to the jail where he started into scrap, put the cuffs on him; while resisting the cuffs being put on, had occasion to hit him, but as his mug was too hard, beat him with my gun and brought him into line, and he is lucky I did not shoot him. He is shackled to the wall with a shackle around his ankle, and intend to keep him there

for two months at least. [Walker River Reservation Agency, box 248a, Correspondence, book 2, A-Z, folder entitled "Carson School," Mar.-Dec. 1905, RG 75, Federal Archives, San Bruno, Calif.]

By the same token, Mrs. Edward A. Dyer (b. 1882, Pine Grove), whose husband translated the 1890 Ghost Dance revelation for James Mooney and became Wovoka's business partner in subsequent years, recalled for Peg Wheat in the 1950s that Walker River Reservation Paiute Captain Ben became so angry with one of his two wives for bearing an illegitimate child that both were forced to flee to their Mason Valley ranch one night, fearful for their lives. Their blind (!) husband, or so Mrs. Dyer reports, had threatened to kill them for "running with white men." The women were allowed to sleep on their bedrolls on the kitchen floor, returning in the morning to their husband (Margaret M. Wheat Papers, tape 15, Ed Dyer, 83-24, 1957, Special Collections, University of Nevada Libraries, Reno). On 22 December 1926 the *Yerington Times* reported wife beating and family abuse for illegitimacy as the causes of arrest of the male head of a local Paiute household who had stripped his wife's bed, turned her outdoors, and sold her flock of turkeys. Opiates might have been an additional factor. In addition I observed in the 1960s the hostility directed against a Paiute girl fathered by an American sailor.

Finally, Bernice Crutcher felt that although her grandfather didn't like Bill Douglass, it was her impression that Big Mack and Corbett got along.

11. *Tseehooka*, I am told, might mean 'Stiff Leg', that is, with reference to the thigh or front part of the lower leg. Lena Rogers thought their grandmother was born either in Topaz or in Coleville, California, and said she was called Maddie by whites. Bridgeport Indians were the *Kuutsabeedokado* (also called Kootseebadokado) 'Mono Lake Brine Fly Pupae-Eaters' (C. S. Fowler and Liljeblad 1986:437). Sayre might well have been referring to Corbett's grandmother (and mother) when she recalled "Old Mattie and Big Mary, who were fine [Smith Valley] Indian workers, handling their weekly wash" (1977:42).

Great Basin Indian acculturation was rapid (cf. Lee 1967). As early as 1872 the *Virginia City Territorial Enterprise* (14 June) would observe:

> They [Virginia City Paiute women] were employed as servants washing, house cleaning and the like and are very patient and industrious, and would make excellent servants. With a little training they could be led to take up their residence in any dwelling. [But] They can never be prevailed to stay overnight where they work. Very easy to teach the women. [in Magnaghi 1975-76]

Many years later, Special Indian Agent Lafayette Dorrington would write to Lorenzo Creel (2 January 1917) that Indian women still "received about a dollar a day for washing and the same for ironing. But the women often worked in the potato fields picking up potatoes for which they received $1.00 or $1.50 per day" (Papers of Col. Lafayette A. Dorrington, Special Agent, Bureau of Indian Affairs, 1923, box 14, "Inspection Report of Walker River Agency," RG 75, Federal Archives, San Bruno, Calif.).

"The Paiute women always took their children with them when they went to work," Annie Lowry told Scott in 1936. "It was not unusual to see a Paiute woman with a papoose strapped to her back, bending over the wash tub, scrubbing the clothes. The pay was not so important as giving the family a good feed" (Scott 1966:79).

The Portuguese milker whose worn shoes were given to Corbett's grandmother might have fathered at least one of the children "stolen" by his older sister Janie (cf. sec. 14; Dr. Mary Fulstone's oral history of the Fulstone family [into which she married in Smith Valley], Special Collections, University of Nevada Libraries, Reno).

The theft of Corbett's grandmother's buried earnings prefigured the siege of crime in Smith and Mason valleys during the opiate years (sec. 89).

Buckberries or silver buffaloberries are *Shepherdia argentea* (C. S. Fowler 1989:50). Corbett's comment about hunting ducks is culturally weighted, insofar as the Paiute creation story requires a reversal of gender roles by Coyote before this world can be "made right" (sec. 151).

Sweetwater Valley, California, was called *Atsa-gweeda* or 'Red Canyon'.

12. Lena Rogers thought her grandmother Mary Mack was born either in Smith Valley or in Colevelle (Antelope Valley).

See section 28 on Northern Paiute-Washo relations.

Regarding Northern Paiute prayer, Catherine Fowler in an unpublished paper with Harold Abel transcribes Wuzzie George's (solar) formula for health as follows:

> As you are going along up there
> There into your going down
> You will be with his fever
> It should remain with you as you go there
> You should, where you go down, wash it away in a cool place
> Tomorrow morning you should rise good and healthy on top of it.
>
> [C. S. Fowler and Abel 1992]

Also see Liljeblad (1986) on Northern Paiute prayer.

Sayre recalled that the W. E. Reading Company Store in Smith Valley was originally owned by Zadok Pierce, an early settler. Reading, who was from Bodie, California, purchased Pierce's place, opening a restaurant with upstairs hotel that became "a regular stopping place" for stage passengers (Sayre 1977:9-11). Across the road from the Reading store and under a big tree was Reading's Saloon, Sayre also recalled; Bill Reading was barkeeper. The bar was later moved five miles away and is the Central Bar today. Mary Ann Cardenal, on the other hand, whom I interviewed in 1988, thought the Reading store was purchased from George Wellington. Reading, she told me, closed his stores in Bodie and at Wellington Station, thereafter operating a composite grocery store, restaurant, hotel (with upstairs bedroom), and post office. She also thought Reading spoke Northern Paiute. It should be noted here that my Paiute mother, born in 1917 and raised in Smith Valley, refused my offer of lunch in the restaurant that stands on the site of Reading's General Store today because of her bitter memory of days when her people "could not go in the dining room with their purchased pans of food and tea in pitcher for twenty-five or fifty cents and in general were treated 'like a dog'!"

13. *Poogooga'yoo* 'owner of horses' derives from *poogoo* 'horse' and *-ga'yoo* 'possession'. Eileen Kane (1964:37) learned that Horseman was six feet and six inches tall. She also wrote (1964:48) that he was shot by a Dayton man whose wife he allegedly witched, but that he cured himself by sucking.

Pat Hoye attended Stewart. According to the Carson Indian School Health and Sanitary Records (Walker River Indian Agency, compartment 2167, bound vol. 1, 1897-1910, RG 75, Federal Archives, San Bruno, Calif.), Hoye was sick on 15 December 1909 with pterygium, a chronic condition. According to the *Yerington Times*, he was arrested on 5 February 1910 the sixth time for drinking and was convicted. His age was listed as thirty-two in the 1911 census of the Walker River Reservation (Indian Census Rolls, Walker River [Paiute Indians], 1897-1912, roll 629, microcopy 595, Federal Archives, San Bruno, Calif.). According to Kane (E. Kane 1964:48), Pat Hoye killed his grandfather for witching his (Hoye's) sister. Owl—a harbinger of bad news—supposedly was heard by him in the chimney at the time of Horseman's death. Irene Thompson told me that after Pat Hoye returned from Sacramento, he was nervous all the time: "Can't sit still. Always wears a sheeplined coat, even in the summer." This could relate to his being an opium addict.

If Corbett's grandfather was variantly called Dr. Joe, Sayre might well have been discussing his death with this comment: "Dr. Joe was a medicine man before Jack Wilson, who was the famous 'Wovoka.' Dr. Joe was killed by Potato Pat because Pat's wife was doctored by Dr. Joe before she died" (1977:25). In that case we have newspaper documentation of the incident. On 25 April 1896 the *Lyon County Times* reported that after an Indian woman who had been doctored for several weeks by Dr. Joe finally died of consumption and was buried with her three-month-old infant, her husband shot "Dr. Joe" twice with his own rifle, then mashed his skull with a club, while two other Indians held him. Sheriff Littel reportedly went to arrest him. "The Piutes have carried things with a high hand in that section for some time and it is about time the authorities called a halt," we read. "Or the brutes will be killing white people by-and-by." This tabloid item also noted that Dr. Joe had been shot by a Dayton Paiute named Jim Davis the previous summer!

Killing shamans is explained by Beatrice Whiting (1950) as a technique of social control in small, atomistic societies such as Northern Paiutes had. Powers, for example, early reported: "Yo-wo-wuk-kuh was the name of an old doctor in Mason Valley who was killed in 1872 for this offence. He had lost two patients and was attending a third who lay at the point of death. The relatives were closely and sternly watching him" (D. D. Fowler and C. S. Fowler 1970:137). Eileen Kane (1964:48) was told in 1964 that Dr. Charley, Horseman, Little Dick, and "Dr. Joe" (?) were separately killed for witchcraft. Generations later, on 7 March 1911, Dr. Tom Crow of the Walker River Reservation was "shot by his grandson, Dave Brown, about six years ago, during one of their dances, and thrown into the river. Brown, convicted, received two years" (ITC Archives). Jack Bennett, Corbett's father-in-law's brother, set fire to the house of the Indian agent of the Walker River Reservation (Dr. Hailman), hoping to drive out and shoot him, because Hailman was blamed for the death of Bennett's daughter (ITC Archives). In fact, even as late as the 1960s, a Smith and Mason Valley Paiute attempted to murder an elderly Yerington Indian Colony (female) resident suspected of witchcraft.

Finally, an informant told Willard Z. Park, "This kind of horse is no longer found here" (C. S. Fowler 1989:123).

14. A fire on 15 May 1909 entirely destroyed the Lyon County Courthouse in Dayton, Nevada. The county seat was shifted to Yerington in 1910, where I examined the Lyon County Record of Deaths but was unable to locate death certificates for any of Corbett's siblings.

Toyanabaga'a was a name Lena Rogers thought Janie Mack shared with her (paternal) grandmother. Despite the Paiutes' "fear of the dead," boys, according to Curtis (1926:63) were named for their fathers' fathers, and girls for their fathers' mothers. Northern Paiute also has self-reciprocal kinship terms between alternating generations. The name *Toyanabaga'a* might, according to Ida Mae Valdez, refer to 'hearing something [loud] in the distance', that is, a frightening sound or voice. It is interesting too, in this regard, that she recalled that the Macks not only spoke loudly but had large eyes: *Poowee natsee* 'Eye-Boy' was Corbett's brother's name. He, in any event, also mentioned during one interview that his older sister Janie might have already given birth to Eddie Mack before she met Don Jones. Bernice Crutcher thought her uncle Sullivan Mack died of a burst appendix, possibly following surgery, whereas her mother, Lizzie Sam, died of rheumatoid arthritis and "complications" from "hard work." ("Her fingers were disjointed from washing on washboards.") Corbett's other niece, Elsie Sam Ausmus, listed these Smith Valley *taivo* employers of her mother: Mrs. Monkowski, Edna Day, and Alfa Arentz. Lizzie Mack, both sisters agreed, had no formal education. According to Crutcher, the name Lizzie was given by a Smith Valley school teacher; Ausmus, on the other hand, thought Edna Day had named her. Elizabeth Malina, their half sister, lives in Redding, Oregon. When last heard from, Jackson Sam, their brother, was in Washington State. Neither knew whether he even was still alive.

Compare Lovelock Paiute Annie Lowry's description of her facial tattooing with Corbett's account of his sister's (Scott 1966:19).

15. Lena Rogers suggested that this sibling who died in the cradleboard was a girl.

16. Mason Valley is a twenty-six-mile-long by three-to-four-mile-wide fault in the Sierra Nevadas, bounded by the Singatse Mountains in the west, the Desert Mountains on the north, the Wassuks on the east, and Pine Grove Hills on the south. Smith Valley lies to the immediate south and east. It is nineteen miles long by three to seven miles wide and bounded by the Pine Nut Mountains on the west, the Buckskins on the north, the Desert (Creek) Mountains on the south, and the Singatses on the east. Desert Creek Peak in Smith Valley is the tallest mountain in either valley at 8,969 feet. Artesia Lake, a large alkali body of water, is in the north of Smith Valley, and the West Walker River flows through its northern end, meeting up with the East Walker in Wilson Canyon to form the Walker River, which flows north through Mason Valley before emptying into Walker Lake on the Walker River Reservation, south and east of Mason Valley (Kersten 1961:27-30).

Initial Euroamerican intrusion in Nevada might have begun with the fur trader Jedidiah S. Smith in 1827 (Fletcher 1923-24:24). Joseph R. Walker, Bonneville Company guide, probably saw one or the other of these Great Basin valleys in 1832-33 (Scrugham 1935:55). The Bidwell-Bartelson emigrant party passed through en route to California in 1841, and three years later John Charles Fremont on 20 January 1844 described them on his second expedition (Nevins 1956:344-45), while crossing the East Walker River in Mason Valley "under the guidance of natives near where Walker, Bartelson, and others had crossed before him" (Bancroft 1890:59). On his third expedition Fremont rested at the lake named for Joseph Walker, who was his guide (Nevins 1956:452-54). Both Fremont and his cartographer, Edward Kern, spoke of the "lowly" condition of these Northern Paiutes (Nevins 1956: 454; Kern in Simpson 1876:480). By 1859 Capt. John Simpson (1876:87) indicated the degree of acculturation at Walker Lake, future site of the Walker River Reservation: "Some Pi-Utes from Walker's Lake have come into camp to sell or trade salmon-trout, caught in the lake. The largest talk a little English, and some of them dress like white people."

Timothy Smith recalled the initial appeal of the valley named for him: "The wild grass on Walker River when we reached our destination was a fine sight. In the meadows it was standing practically undisturbed except where the Indians had made trails through it on their way to the river" (1911-12:225). Indeed, it was the very grazing possibilities of "Smith's valley" that would combine with the severe California winter of 1858 to draw him and his brothers R. B. Smith and Cyrus Smith, along with Simon Baldwin, John A. Rogers, Sam Baldwin, Chandler Stratton, and a man named Patterson back into Nevada from Stanislaus County in 1859 or 1860. Meanwhile, N. H. A. (Hoc) Mason in 1859 left San Joaquin Valley for the valley named for him, its fertility similarly recalled from having driven cattle through in 1854 *(Reflections 1988,* annual publication of the *Mason Valley News).* Charles A. McLeod (b. 1878), whose father, Angus, from Arkansas, was a member of the third white family in Mason Valley, related the following about its early settlement in response to an "Early Day Family Questionnaire" prepared by the Nevada Centennial Committee:

> My father, Angus, by bull teams, and 12 other men with around 1200 head of cattle went on to California, and around 1859-60. Father returned to Genoa, Nevada, and worked for Moses Job, there as a clerk

in his store. He came to Mason Valley in 1860. N. H. A (Hock) Mason ... had taken up land in 1859 and built a house thereon.... My father and Mr. Mason had been boyhood friends back in Arkansas. Father returned to Genoa, Nevada Territory, and in 1862 returned to Mason Valley and filed on land east of "McLeod Hill." He also bought land adjoining his and had 1040 acres. His place was the third settlement in Mason Valley, named after Mr. Mason. The Wheelers, father and sons had filed or squatted on land in the south end of the Valley; theirs was the second settlement. Father farmed his land until 1877, when he married Mary Edna Ellis in Virginia City, July 3, 1877. He rented the farm to Charles T. Martin and then moved to Aurora, Esmeralda County, Nevada as he had large interest there.... He and Henry Williams of Sweetwater, Nevada, had the franchise for the toll road, from Wellington to Aurora and every one paid the toll, going over this road. [*Reflections 1988,* annual publication of the *Mason Valley News*]

Mining joined alfalfa and cattle industries as the third leg of what cultural geographer Earl Kersten (1961) calls the "Walker River regional economy." Seven years before the Comstock silver discovery of 1859 there was a gold strike in Mono Lake, fifty miles southeast of Wellington; this led to the establishment of Aurora, a mining town of 3,000, in 1863 (Kersten 1961:90-91). "In the decade of Aurora's greatness, 1860-1869, extensive areas in Mason, Smith, East Walker, Sweetwater and Antelope valleys were settled by men primarily interested in stock raising," wrote Kersten (1961: 90-91). Gold also led to the founding of Bodie, a mining town where Northern Paiutes encountered the Chinese and Chinese opiates (Cain 1956).

Corbett Mack's account of these Northern Paiutes' initial response to white occupation is consistent with the rise of predatory mounted bands throughout the Great Basin (Steward 1938). "The Indians at first kept away from us," wrote Timothy Smith. "But one morning we were greatly surprised when nearly two hundred of them came in from all directions whooping and yelling and driving our cattle on the run ahead of them. Thirty or forty came up to where we were and in no uncertain manner ordered us off their range" (1911-12:225-26). So short-lived were these hostilities, however, that by the end of the first decade of contact, an Indian agent was writing the commissioner of Indian affairs: "The progress made among the Indians herein [Walker River Reservation] enumerated since the year 1860 is very encouraging; then they were sullen, aggressive, and given to nakedness, laziness and stealing" (ARCIA 1869-70:113).

Finally, Blind Bob's name was *Paiseed*. His work-related farm accident blindness, according to Corbett Mack (and others), was interpreted, however, as the result of witchcraft.

17. Eileen Kane (1964) recorded a somewhat different version of what undoubtedly is the 1860 Pyramid Lake War (Hopkins [1882] 1969; Wheeler 1967; Egan 1972). Noting in her field report three rather than four super- human Northern Paiute warriors who combine to defeat the American army— *Tona'ta*, or Winnemucca, Horseman, and Chief Joaquin—she wrote they were "tall men, doctors and cousin-brothers," bulletproof and invincible in battle. Corbett's grandfather created a stream of pure water in the desert mountains and line of fire between himself and confused white soldiers, according to Eileen Kane (1964:34-35). Corbett's account of this battle, in which five American soldiers were wounded and 200-300 Indian horses captured, sounds remarkably like Sarah Winnemucca Hopkins's:

> Sometimes I laugh when I think of this battle. It was very exciting in one way, and the soldiers made a splendid chase, and deserved credit for it; but where was the killing? I sometimes think it was more play than anything else. If a white settler showed himself he was sure to get a hit from an Indian; but I don't believe they ever tried to hit a soldier,—they liked them too well,—and it certainly was remarkable that with all these splendid firearms, and the Gatling gun, and General Howard's working at it, and the air full of bullets, and the ground strewn with cartridges, not an Indian fell that day. [(1844) 1969:177]

Eileen Kane (1964:11), whose comment about Corbett Mack originally influenced my decision to interview him (see the Introduction), quoted him that Winnemucca *natsee* had another name, *Mupi' tawa'ka* 'One with a Hole in His Nose'. *Tona'ta*, she wrote, means 'to punch another'. Sarah Winnemucca Hopkins ([1882] 1969:60-61) noted the role of her cousin in the Pyramid Lake War, and Indian Agent Frederick Dodge wrote that Young Winnemucca, or *Numaga*, led a band of 300 at the shores of Mud Lake in the 1860s (Canfield 1983:17). The war leader, a complex individual, no doubt, who maintained vociferous opposition to the destruction of pine nut trees (Canfield 1983:34), then advocated peace with whites, while demanding recompense for loss of Honey Lake (1983:21-28). "I found him a most intelligent and appreciative man, one who reasons well and talks like a prudent, reflecting leader," James W. Nye, Nevada Territory's first governor, wrote about Young Winnemucca (Canfield 1983:33). What is confusing, however, is Indian Agent Bateman's comment that Young Winnemucca died of lingering consumption on 28 October 1871 (in Canfield 1983:7). Were there two Young Winnemuccas? Chief Winnemucca is reported in the 22 September 1864 edition of the *Gold Hill News* as saying, "Young Winnemucca is not my son!" (Magnaghi 1975-76).

Chief (or San) Joaquin was the name Dodge in 1859-60 gave for the leader of a band of Northern Paiutes at the fork of the Carson River in Carson Valley (Stewart 1939:143). Historian Myron Angel similarly listed Joaquin (or "Yurdy") as leader of a band "on the Big Bend of Carson River and south toward Mason Valley" (Stewart 1939:143). I was unable to find any information about Trotting Wijo, who Corbett thought had died as a result of misuse of his own power.

Northern Paiutes were forcibly relocated to the Malheur Reservation in Oregon following the 1875 Bannock War (Hopkins [1882] 1969:137-202). Similarly, some 900 Owens Valley Paiutes were relocated on the San Sebastian Reservation near Fort Tejon, California, following participation in the Owens Valley War of 11 July 1863 (Lawton et al. 1976:31). According to informants, Jack Wilson's father appears to have been imprisoned as a result of participation in some early resistance struggles (Hittman 1990:29-35).

According to John Wesley Powell (D. D. Fowler and C. S. Fowler 1971: 246, 287), Northern Paiutes believed in individuals who were invulnerable to arrows. Jack Wilson, of course, demonstrated his invulnerability to gunpowder during gatherings that came to be known as the 1890 Ghost Dance (Hittman 1990:82-88).

"Churchill" was Fort Churchill, named for Sylvester Churchill, inspector general of the United States. It was built in 1860 to protect the Pony Express and abandoned on 15 June 1871 (Ruhlen n.d.).

On the designated repeater, see note 29.

Finally, I reiterate that in this interesting hero tale George Washington's troops ultimately are defeated not by gunpowder and the horse but by a precontact cultivated food in Smith Valley (cf. sec. 18)!

18. Powers defined the *Tabooseedokado* as Northern Paiutes residing "On the Carson, up as far as the Washo territory" (D. D. Fowler and C. S. Fowler 1970:123). Omer Stewart wrote that as early as 1850, a "band" of approximately 820 Northern Paiutes called the *Tabooseedako* or 'Grass Bulb-Eaters' occupied

> upper Walker River (country), both the east fork in Mason Valley and the west fork in Smith valley . . . a 2100 square mile territory extending from the *Agaidokado* [Walker River Reservation 'Trout-Eaters'] bound-

ary on Wassuk (Walker) Mountain on the east to the Washo country on top of Pinenut Mountain on the west; and from the edge of the Sierra Nevada and Stillwater mountains—the *Kutsavidokaodo* [Bridgeport Paiute] line—in the south to a short distance beyond the Carson River in the north. [1939:142-43]

Julian Steward, on the other hand, challenged the "band hypothesis." He argued instead for a "family level of sociopolitical integration" in precontact Basin society, that mounted predatory bands arose following contact (1938, 1963). Residence, in either case, was an emic sine qua non for naming and identification of different subgroupings of what more profitably might be seen as a panband or tribal level of sociopolitical integration (cf. Basehart 1967, 1970; Fried 1967). According to Catherine Fowler, the Northern Paiutes "may be regarded as an ethnically, politically, and socially distinct tribe, with a fairly well-defined territory. Within the large group local aggregates of families seasonally exploit the resources of particular regions in the Paviotso habitat" (1989:5).

Stewart's identification of *taboosee* 'grass nuts' with *Brodiaea captiate* Benth has more recently been challenged by Lawton and coworkers (1976). They conclusively show it was based on a misidentification by Steward (1930) and return to its original 1875 identification by Powers as *Cyberus*, "which abounds in low moist places . . . [and] is gathered and dried, then ground on the metate into meal and made into panada. Eaten raw, it tastes a little like cocoanut" (D. D. Fowler and C. S. Fowler 1970:127). Donald and Catherine Fowler add that *taboosee* "was made into a kind of mush or bread" (1970:138). "The common name of 'grass-nuts', 'nut-grass', 'taboose grass' and 'taboose'," write Lawton and coworkers (1976:19-20), is (yellow) *Cyperus esulentus L.*, which sometimes is called chufa, earth almond, or Zulu nuts; it is a small bulb of the lily family and one of two plants cultivated in precontact time in Owens Valley, if not in Smith Valley as well. Mary DeDecker, moreover, showed that "taboose" belongs to a far-ranging (from California to Alaska) weed whose protein content was shown by J. G. Waines to be "almost equivalent to rice as a staple" (Lawton et al. 1976:39). Catherine Fowler's correspondence with Lawton in this regard is important: *taboosee* "is really a 'food-name' rather than a plant name, i.e. the tuber of Cyperus or others" (Lawton et al. 1976:33-36).

Although Lawton and coworkers note that "the Northern Paiute of Mono Lake, about forty miles to the northwest of Owens Valley, did not irrigate" (1976:15), these researchers nonetheless ruled that the absence of continuous distribution of precontact irrigation agriculture did not preclude its existence in Smith Valley. Regarding those two cultigens noted by Corbett Mack, *pozeeda* and *mahaveeta,* Powers noted that Mason Valley Paiutes were called the Pam-mi-toy, "because there was once a lake in this valley yielding tule, where now it is dry; [while] on the north fork of Walker River, [they were called] the Poat-sit-uh-ti-kut-teh [*pozeeda?*] or alfalfa-eaters" (D. D. Fowler and C. S. Fowler 1970:123). Smith Valley Paiutes were called by Powers "Toa-pa-kah" or "Red Bank." "Pam-mi-toy" is unidentified; *Pozeeda,* according to Donald and Catherine Fowler, is *Trifolium,* "wild clover, eaten raw or boiled" (1970:139). *Mahaveeta—nahavita* in Owens Valley—also said to be cultivated in Desert Creek, according to a newspaper correspondent who reported on a trip to Owens Valley in 1861—"grows like an onion, sending up three blades that bear a blue lily-shaped flower . . . [with] a small white root of an oval shape, and the size of a cherry. . . . When roasted, it looks and tastes like the yam" (in Lawton et al. 1976:30). Lawton and coworkers (1976:20) identified this as *Eleocharis,* or spikerush, partially after Steward, who wrote they had a "number of bulbs," and with final corroboration from Catherine Fowler (Lawton et al. 1967:33). In sum, they argue that along with *taboosee, pozeeda* and *mahaveeta* were cultivated in precontact times in two- and three-mile-long communally dug irrigation ditches, not only in Owens Valley, but in Smith Valley as well (Lawton et al. 1976:18).

Corbett Mack also told my predecessor in Yerington that his father as a young man used to plant a crop similar to potatoes in Desert Creek (E. Kane 1964:9), and he told me that Paiutes cultivated sunflower plants in addition. Timothy Smith wrote: "About 1862 Hall and Simpson located on Desert Creek near the place where it bebouches [*sic*] from the mountains. They raised hay and vegetables, using a ditch dug many years before by the Indians and which they now enlarged" (1911-12:227). Compare Angel's report: "When the first white settlers went into the Walker Valley they found the Indians irrigating portions of it to promote the growth of an edible root which formed a great portion of their living" (1881:131).

Smith Valley pioneer rancher Daniel C. Simpson died in 1897. Irene Thompson, "last of the Smith Valley Indians," died in 1992.

Regarding Corbett's mythological derivation of aboriginal farming, Lawton and coworkers write that in Owens Valley, "after water was turned into the ditch, fish were recovered from the dry stream bed" (1976:18). Those rocks flipped by fish were, Corbett told me, the cause of one large Desert Creek boulder's erosion. Andy Dick, another informant, credited *peesee-*

'eeyoo, "a big flatheaded bird," and *tsana anagee,* "some small bird," with having collaborated on petroglyphs found in Desert Creek of Smith Valley (cf. Heizer and Baumhoff 1962).

Whatever the size of the precontact food-named group(s) in Smith and Mason valleys, the tenth (1880) federal census (U.S. Bureau of the Census 1880-1920) listed these valleys' Indian population in June of that year as follows: 39 families or 148 individuals in Mason Valley; 3 families and 18 individuals in Smith Valley; and 17 families, 57 individuals in the mining camp of Pine Grove, twenty or so miles southwest of Yerington.

Yerington was called Greenfield. Its earlier name of Pizen Switch was supposedly derived from poisoned whisky sold at Mason Valley's first saloon, The Switch, though Corbett Mack said it originated from the experience of a Northern Paiute given something poisonous to eat or drink.

Regarding the Yerington Indian Colony, which was purchased in 1917 from Frank Bovard, local rancher and owner of the Rawhide Mine:

> The Piute population of the city is disturbed by a notification that the Piute houses must soon be moved from their present location on the Bovard ground south of Bridge Street. This ground has been leased by the Bovard estate. There is quite a colony of Indians residing there and they are now hunting a suitable location to move to. It is their wish to get a piece of land just north of the city limits, where there are now a number of Piute families living. When it was suggested that they could buy a 20 acre tract for $20 per acre, they demurred on having to pay anything, stating that they owned this whole valley once and that it was hard times not to be able to get a small tract of land now upon which all could live free of charge. [*Yerington Times,* 2 May 1914]

According to the *Mason Valley News:*

> The entire tract is fenced, three wells have been put in, ranging in depth from 23 to 35 feet. A specimen of the water was sent to the State chemist for examination and his analysis proved it splendid for domestic purposes. In addition to these wells another was put down and paid for by an Indian on his own lot.
>
> The Catholics have erected a very attractive building at the entrance to the colony site—a school building and church combined. During the week children too small to be left alone while their mothers are at work are cared for in this building. Sunday church is well attended by the Indian parents and their children. The building has also been placed at their disposal for various entertainments during the year. [5 April 1919]

Owing to its proximity to a house of prostitution and the influenza epidemic of 1919 (Hittman 1984), the day school operated by Father Joseph Cunha of the Roman Catholic Church of Yerington was short-lived.

19. This is not the only instance in which a seemingly traditional folktale undergoes modification as a result of acculturation (cf. secs. 55, 123-24, 133).

20. The discussion by Eugene Hattori of Northern Paiute housing styles following the discovery of silver on the Comstock lode is pertinent:

> One of the earliest modifications on the aboriginal dome was the use of canvas, muslin, carpet, burlap, or sheet metal dome skins. After the fire of 1875 many Indians utilized iron pipe from the burned buildings as a framing material superior to the willow which formerly grew near the city. . . . As early as 1876 the Virginia City Paiutes occupied wooden frame structures resembling those of the Whites. . . . Another house type modeled after the dwellings of the Whites was the pipe framed, sheet metal and wood covered structure occupied by the Paiutes until the 1930s. . . . The roofs were flat and also framed with pipe. These structures were covered with sheet metal or wooden walls attached by the use of wire or nails. Newspaper insulation [was] wired to an inner wall. [1975:20-22]

Similarly, an article in the 14 April 1889 edition of the *Virginia Chronicle*, cited by historian Russell Magnaghi, indicates:

> Here and there the aboriginal conical wigwam asserts itself, but most of the dwellings are gable-roofed cabins built rudely after the white man's fashion. The most impressive structure [built by Captain Bob with county money and occupied by his successor] is an eight by twelve shanty built entirely of good lumber and lightly roofed with shingles. [1975-76]

Most of the other houses were said to be shanties: compounds of boards, gunny sacks and barrel staves,

> homes of semi-darkness, with rabbitskin robes spread on earthen floors, with old stoves in the center, and material objects hanging from the roof and sides: quivers with ancient arrows, ivory headed canes, rubber boots, tattered swallow tailed coats, hairbrushes, prints, and plug hats. "No regard to cleanliness!" [Magnaghi 1975-76]

Annie Lowry (Scott 1966:78) also described the shift from the traditional *kanee* to lumber houses. Not surprisingly, too, recent archaeological research (cf. Arkush 1987) shows how Paiute winter houses in the early historic period followed the aboriginal (winter) tule house design, which was described by

Steward as "conical, 3-4m. high and equal diameter. semi-subterranean and with four main posts around the pit edge and upper ends joined, smaller poles added to the frame with opening at the top for smoke hole . . . covered with pine or juniper needles and bundles of wild rye" (1933:264).

Two of Corbett Mack's nieces, in any event, recalled their uncle's enjoyment in building the traditional domicile for them to play in as children in the 1930s: "It was warm. It had a dirt floor, no window. We'd crawl inside. Our fire was in a willow shade outside, and we'd use blankets or quilts on floor for our mattress" (Bernice Crutcher).

21. Corbett in this section clearly articulates the "flexibility" built into Northern Paiute precontact society, with its extended family or "kin cliques" (D. D. Fowler 1966) and bilateral kinship system, with matrilocal tendencies, at least for first marriages (C. S. Fowler and Liljeblad 1986).

22. The seed of piñon pine was, of course, a staple food (cf. Steward 1938; Lanner 1981). *Kooha* is white stem blazing start, or *Mentzelia albicaulis* (C. S. Fowler 1989:46).

Regarding Corbett Mack's grandmother's frequent assertion:

A joker was a day or two since telling Captain Sam, of the Piute tribe, that pretty soon all the mines would be played out, the white men would all go away, and leave their houses, when the Indians could take possession of them, that he [Sam] might then have the International Hotel all to himself. Sam did not look as if he would give a nickel for the big hotel, did not even care to dwell upon his installation in it as monarch of all he might survey. He looked very serious for a time, then propounded the conundrum: "S'pose white man all go 'way, what Injuns gon' to do?" It would be now nothing less than starvation should the whites all withdraw from the Comstock. . . . Sam took in the situation at once. All the houses in the land would be of no use to the Piutes—grub is all they want and sufficient cast-off clothing to cover up their nakedness. Should the whites now leave it would be necessary for them to take the Piutes along with them in their journeyings in search of a new land of promise. [*Territorial Enterprise*, 23 January 1881, cited by Magnaghi 1975-76]

23. Willard Park (1941:184-87) described the Round Dance, which was the centerpiece of the Pine Nut Festival, as a five-night sacred rite performed by Northern Paiute men and women who gathered from far and wide, painting their faces and dancing till morning around a center pole to the instrumentless singing of ritual officiants. It was held before commencement of the fishing season in May, jackrabbit communal drives in November, and pine nut harvests in the fall.

24. Arie Poldervaart, Wycliffe Bible translator, was kind enough to translate *naaveey^ts* for me: *naavee* 'first kills', *yu* 'into', *tsee*, diminutive form of endearment. Annie Lowry told Lalla Scott that upon her initial menstruation, her mother struck "three black marks across her forehead and rubb[ed] on some extra paint, putting on yellow dots to heighten her cheekbones" (Scott 1966:19). Smith and Mason Valley Paiute women reported that during their first periods, or *namaraghai*, they were not permitted to eat these "firstfruits" brought in by young hunters, lest the latter be misled by trails of blood.

Neighboring Washo Indians had far more elaborate girls' puberty ceremonies (cf. D'Azevedo 1963, Downs 1966).

As a youth Corbett had poor vision, hence he did not hunt very much. One niece speculated, "Someone put seed or dust in them?" that is, witched him.

25. While I was collecting these hunting proscriptions (Hittman 1965), Corbett Mack either claimed he did not know many or did not feel like narrating them.

26. Edward Dyer left this invaluable account of the men's football game described in section 26:

> The Indians used to play a ball game. They had about a half a dozen Indians on each side. They had wickets at each end of the ball park. The ball was make of rags: it was wound around and around with string, and with a covering of buckskin. It was about the size of two or three basketballs . . . the size of a grapefruit. They used to kick this ball around, and sometimes one would try to kick the ball and someone else would try to grab him; to keep him from trying to kick it. . . . And the race toward the goal would start all over again. . . . They were perfectly naked, with the exception of a breechclout or gee-string, and a headband: a narrow headband they had on their forehead to keep their hair in place. And they kick the ball with their bare feet: with the ends of their toes, or anywhere they could. [Margaret Wheat Papers, tape 15 (1), 83-24, 1957, Special Collections, University of Nevada Libraries, Reno]

Watsimuiva was a "football game in which holding, pushing, tripping, wrestling, in fact, almost any tactics, were permitted. The ball was a small one of deerskin, and each of the goals, which were about forty yards apart, was marked by two posts" (Curtis 1926:75).

Lowry described the stick and rag game, which in Lovelock, anyway, was played by men and women. This was "much like hockey," she told her autobiographer,

> but a rag is used instead of a puck. The "rag" is made by braiding cloth, making it hard and about eight inches long with a knot at each end. The stick is a willow, wider at the striking end. The ground is marked off with a goal at each end, and captains choose sides. The object is to get the rag over the opponent's goal. Everyone played. . . . They gambled on the number of strikes to make a goal and on the final result of the games. All the men were on one side and the women on the other. Sometimes they played wild. The women would run for the goal but fall down on the way. The men would try to hit them with rag before they got up. [Scott 1966:89-90]

27. "But we don't talk to white man's medicine," Corbett maintained. Irene Thompson told me, on the other hand, how she always prayed to aspirin before taking them.

Moogoodoohoop, according to Donald and Catherine Fowler, is *dalea,* "stems used in decoction for colds, coughs, rheumatism, etc." (1970:139). More recently, Catherine Fowler (1989:126) described this as mugutuhupi (*Psorothamnus polydenius*), a two- to four-foot-tall brush with greyish-green white leaves growing in sandy soil, which she said was broken and boiled and drunk for flu.

Poowee pahmoo, or green (i.e., growing) tobacco might be *Labelia* (C. S. Fowler 1989:126). In recalling the general store opened and operated in Yerington in 1902 by her husband, Mrs. Ed Dyer told Peg Wheat in 1957:

> Old men came in, they used to smoke cigarettes. Rolled them. . . . But they didn't smoke too much. And the women, and the really young boys, you didn't see them smoking. They didn't chew tobacco, either. But when they had a sore, they used to chew a little and put it on a cut or burn. [Margaret Wheat Papers, tape 15 (1), 83-24, Special Collections, University of Nevada Libraries, Reno]

I speculated (in Hittman 1973a) that tobacco usage was preadaptive for yen-shee addiction. It is also interesting to note how rolling cigarettes becomes a point of identification between Corbett Mack and his stepfather. Ida Mae Valdez told me that her own mother, Mamie Dick, would insert chewed tobacco for earaches.

28. Tom Mitchell told Willard Z. Park (C. S. Fowler 1989:5) that "fights resulted" whenever Paiutes went into Washo country, and Edward Curtis

wrote: "The principal enemy of the Walker River Paviotso [Paiute] was the Washo, whom they regarded as a not particularly worthy foe" (1926:76). One indirect documentary evidence of this hostility is found in the *Gold Hill News*, where on 27 February 1864, we read:

> Indians in considerable numbers, both Pi-Utes and Washoes are beginning to be seen in the streets of this city [Gold Hill and Virginia City]. Formerly the two tribes seldom met without a fight, but contact with the whites appears to have rendered the red men somewhat docile, and now their hatred of each other only finds expression in grunts, shrugs and defiant glances. [cited by Magnaghi 1975-76]

Twenty years later the *Lyon County Times* more directly reported:

> Two Washoe Indians came down to Mason Valley from Antelope Valley last week and had quite a time to get away without losing their horses and lives. It seems that the Piutes in Mason Valley will not allow Washoes among them, and when they got news that two Washoes with horses were at the Switch [Yerington] they made plans to make it exceedingly interesting for the strangers. The Washoes knew the Piutes were after their scalps, and kept hid, until they made [Indian Agent] Sam Wasson acquainted with their situation, and he then piloted them into the foot-hills and advised them to return to their tribe in Antelope as fast as their horses could travel. The day after they departed the chagrin of the Piutes was great, as they had calculated to take the Washoes' horses from them. [25 October 1884]

Also see Sarah Winnemucca Hopkins ([1882] 1969:61).

James Downs (1963a, 1963b, 1966) offered an ecological argument for what was the profoundly different Washo and Northern Paiute initial responses to Euroamerican conquest, that is, Northern Paiutes' adoption of horses and their emergent raiding complex versus the attempted escape by horseless Washoes to the high Sierra environs.

29. In another recounting of this childhood trauma, Corbett claimed to have mashed his left toe after boarding the runway wagon and "dragging" his foot on the brake to stop it.

The "repeater" was an essential part of all cures. Curtis wrote, "There is an old man, hired by the family, to whom the shaman addresses all his remarks, and who repeats them to the others" (1926:83), whereas in Willard Z. Park's field notes we also learn from shaman Joe Green, Pyramid Lake Paiute informant, that

> one special man repeated after him the account of his journey. The visitor would say a few words and then the repeater said those words. He

said only a few words at a time so he would not miss any of the account. When a visitor arrived, if the repeater was not present he had to be sent for, if he were not too far away, before the visitor talked to the assembled people. . . . They always did this. They could not get along without someone's repeating. The repeater is a good man. He talks loudly so all the people sitting around the camps can hear what the visitor has said. . . . This is the same as the interpreter or the repeater for the shaman when he is doctoring. [C. S. Fowler 1989:142]

See also Olofson (1979) and Liljeblad (1986) on the roles of the designated repeater in shamanism and in folktale narration, respectively.

Nordyke is at the mouth of Wilson Canyon in Mason Valley. Named for the individual who installed Marmon machinery at the flour mill on the David and Abigail Wilson ranch, it had a post office from 13 June 1872 to 15 January 1914 *(Reflections 1988,* annual publication of the *Mason Valley News).*

30. Corbett's nephew-in-law, Howard Rogers, a knowledgeable horseman and father of champion rodeo riders, confirmed that he had raised and raced a brown mare in Wellington. Horse racing was, of course, a popular sport before the automobile, as indicated by the *Lyon County Times* on 9 July 1887, which reported one-mile and one-half-mile horse races during Fourth of July celebrations in Yerington. Also included were a 100-yard footrace, sack races, fireworks, a baseball game with Wabuska, a midnight supper-dance, and a "free-for-all race," in which twenty-five Indians participated—and lost. Two years later the same newspaper mentioned Paiutes racing horses against white entries, side bets allowed.

"I had another one after Brown," Corbett Mack also told me, "but he cut himself with a wire. That cut was too deep, don't want him no more; so I turn him loose, so he can go in with someone else." According to Lena Rogers, her uncle "dressed like a cowboy, bought a white horse after selling Brown and rides him in Smith Valley."

31. Edward C. Johnson, a former Walker River Reservation chairman who is writing a long-anticipated history of Stewart Institute, reports that petitions by Nevada politicians, and especially Sen. William Stewart, resulted in the federal appropriation of $25,000 in 1888 for this Indian industrial school. According to Johnson (n.d.), the Virginia and Truckee railroad magnate for whom Greenfield was renamed, H. M. Yerington, a member of the state's Indian School Commission, applied to the U.S. Land Patent Office for 200 acres in Ormsby County on 28 February 1889, purchasing ranches owned by Henry Ross and Charles F. Miller for the boarding school. Stewart Institute—named for Senator Stewart—opened its doors on 17 December 1890. It

was soon renamed the Carson Indian School. In 1894 William D. Gibson, former Pyramid Lake Agency superintendent, became its first superintendent. The name was soon changed back to the Stewart Indian School. With 67 students—Paiutes, Shoshones, and Washoes—on opening, Stewart's enrollment increased to 91 in 1891, 147 in 1899, and 243 in 1900. More than 300 students attended during Corbett Mack's years. Operating on the quarter system, the school year annually began in early September, dismissing students for summer vacation and the odious "outing system" on the first week of June.

A 17 September 1918 letter from its superintendent to Walker River Agency superintendent Robert E. Burris indicates that Native American policemen were hired to bring pupils to the school (Carson Indian Agency, box 248a, Carson School-Walker River Reservation, book 2, A-Z, Mar.-Dec. 1905, RG 75, Federal Archives, San Bruno, Calif.). Irene Thompson confirmed that her grandfather, Tom Mitchell, had a badge to haul kids to Stewart, as does an 11 July 1905 document from Stewart superintendent Calvin Asbury to S. W. Pugh of the Walker River Agency, which alludes to "a letter of Tom Mitchell regarding a student named 'May Johnnie.'" Since Mitchell was said to be in Smith Valley and Pugh could not see him, he was said to be "confused regarding what to do." Another letter dated 18 January 1912 from Asbury to Constable J. A. Carter of Yerington speaks of "sundry Indians up the Walker River . . . who were placed under the supervision of Pugh . . . [and he was] sure he will be glad of any assistance you or Tom Mitchell can give him in suppressing this [drugs or drink] traffic" (Carson Indian Agency, box 248a, Correspondence for Walker River, 1902-5, RG 75, Federal Archives, San Bruno, Calif.).

Howard Rogers recalled the Washo Dick Bender, who gathered up students for Stewart: "He was a big guy, and the night watchman up there. Had a billy club and goes out after runaways." Similarly, Mrs. Ed Dyer recalled how "Schurz Indians were men hired to bring children to the boarding school [and] given Studebaker wagons. They were painted bright green and removed the seat. . . . The man would sit in the front, often with a son, if he had one, women in the back" (Margaret M. Wheat Papers, tape 15, 83-24, Special Collections, University of Nevada Libraries, Reno).

Regarding Buckaroo George Walker's family, Corbett said Elizabeth married a Washo named Willy Moose, who was called "Chip Monkey" in Stewart and who subsequently became a shaman in Gardnerville.

A search of the Carson Indian School records from 1890 to 1921 in San Bruno, California, unfortunately did not result in Corbett Mack's student folder.

32. A post office was opened in Stewart in 1905, the year of Corbett's admission (Johnson n.d.).

33. According to the Indian Census Rolls (roll 629 for Walker River [Paiute Indians], 1897-1912, microcopy 595, Federal Archives, San Bruno, Calif.), more matrons were married than Corbett realized. Names of these women in 1911 and 1912 include Helen C. Sheahau ("literary"), Miss Barnett, Miss Luce, Miss Queen, Miss L. George. In the "Book Agency Issues to Personnel" and "Health and Sanitary Records" (Walker River Indian Agency, compartment 2167, bound vol. 1, 1897-1910, RG 75, Federal Archives, San Bruno, Calif.), we also find a personnel listing for the boarding school in 1903-5, which includes an engineer, a blacksmith, sewing instructors, a disciplinarian, a tailor, a person referred to as a "literary", a matron, a laundry worker, a farmer, a shoe and harness maker, and a baker. A similar list for 1911 and 1912: a baker, a carpenter, a clerk, a domestic science teacher, an engineer, a hospital laundress, a librarian, a shoemaker, and a seamstress.

"Issues Books" from 1908-11 no doubt name Corbett Mack's teachers: Norton, Mrs. Lovelace, Thomas, Stone, Mrs. Fennell, Mr. R. A. McIlvane (who must have taught him geography; cf. sec. 35), Mrs. G. G. McIlvane (who was reported to have received Baldwin's second reader, which Corbett might have used), Sheahan, Richards (who used Black's, Baldwin's, and Taylor's readers in first and second grades), Richards (who received a third grade reader), Mrs. Shanks, Mrs. Carr, Miss Waterman, Miss Burgess, Miss Walker, Miss Mann, Mrs. Burton, and Miss Halfacre.

Since the first issue in 1910 was dated 9 September, we can reasonably assume this was the start of Corbett Mack's last year at Stewart Institute, whose second quarter began on 22 October 1910. The third quarter began on 31 December 1910, which was around the time he was pulled out of school by his stepfather. Misses Petoskey, Ellis, and Howe were said to have joined the staff as matrons at the start of that academic year (Walker River Indian Agency, compartment 2167, bound vol. 1, 1897-1910, RG 75, Federal Archives, San Bruno, Calif.).

On the duties of the matron:

> Appointees under the general direction or supervision, will have charge of the home life of students in the Indian boarding school, including the

performance of one or more of the following tasks: Directing the household departments of the institution; supervising or directing or promoting the social life of students; training or guiding them in correct habits of health; self-discipline, ethics of right living, physical training or recreational work; teaching vocational guidance, housekeeping, care and repair of clothing. [Meriam 1928:361]

34. The aforementioned "Issue Books to Personnel" found in the Federal Archives contains a reference to a "Physiology-Pathfinder."

35. Corbett might have confused some knowledge of Mormonism—the angel Moroni's visit to Joseph Smith's bedside—with this account of Christopher Columbus's discovery of America. On the other hand, dreams and supernatural *booha* or power were vital to Northern Paiute religion (cf. Whiting 1950; Olofson 1979; Miller 1983; Hultkrantz 1986).

Geography, as noted, was a subject of study in the Carson Industrial School's curriculum during Corbett Mack's tenure.

36. Johnson writes that "a work experience program was instituted in 1912" (n.d.), yet Corbett Mack had already left the boarding school by then.

37. Johnson (n.d.) also finds that in Stewart Institute's second decade of existence, from 1900 to 1910, when Corbett Mack attended, "the only major change in school policy was the addition of military discipline—students were required to dress in military uniform and march to meals and classes." Two Northern Paiute runaways (Sam George and Howard Remus) were discussed in a revealing 3 December 1917 letter from the Carson School superintendent to his equivalent at the Walker River Agency: "The Indians around Yerington seem to be about the worst we have to handle, as practically all the runaways we have had this year have been from Yerington and Schurz" (Carson Indian School, box 248a, Correspondence to Walker River Agency, 1902-6, RG 75, Federal Archives, San Bruno, Calif.).

Meals at Stewart prompted its younger graduates whom I knew to jokingly rename it "Bean College."

38. See section 26 on this traditional sport.

39. None of my informants confirmed knowledge of this nickname.

40. Johnson also gives the following comment by the superintendent of this boarding school in its annual report of 1904: "Our weekly socials for the pupils have been very pleasant, and we believe profitable, in amusing the children and cultivating proper conduct in company" (Johnson n.d.).

41. Why students were forced to pay remains unclear.

42. And whether or not Corbett has romanticized his years at the boarding school, Ida Mae Valdez reported that during her years at Stewart (the 1930s), the penalty for speaking Northern Paiute was "packing coal, scrubbing toilets, darning socks on Sunday, and standing with our arms on the wall!" Indeed, her older brother Howard Rogers, who briefly attended earlier (ca. 1915), recalled a certain Mr. McLean, who was "a mean guy. He'd bawl you out if you don't salute him, and beat the hell out of you for speaking your own language!" Similarly, life-long Yerington Indian Colony resident Sophina Smith (b. 1918) told a reporter for *Reflections 1993*, an annual publication of the *Mason Valley News:*

> They said Indians were lousy and dirty, and they shipped us to the Stewart School—a boarding school. If you ran away, you got whupped. They were real strict like the military. The boys wore uniforms and you'd hear the bugle blow to get up. I couldn't get over it. And when you ran away, they tied you with a ball and chain. They had a hot line (for those who broke the rules), and as they ran through, the kids could hit them with anything they had. It was awful. I'd never seen anything like that.

43. George W. Smart (1958) reported that as early as 1874 the Indian agent at the Walker River Reservation preached Methodist-Episcopalianism to Mason Valley Indians and that Robert G. Pike in 1902, with the aid of an interpreter, preached to 120 Indians in Yerington. F. M. Willis, the father-in-law of Carrie Wilson, who belonged to the (Wilson) household in which Jack Wilson learned the fundamentals of Christianity (Hittman 1990), wrote of his own proselytizing (Presbyterianism) efforts in the Walker River area in the late 1870s and early 1880s (Picket Guards, Special Collections, University of Nevada Libraries, Reno).

According to Johnson (n.d.), Christian services at Stewart began in the early 1900s, when Robert G. Pike, a Carson City Methodist, first conducted services there. In time, Reverend Pike established his own church in Schurz. Lillie Corwin of the American Baptist denomination later held services at Stewart, in 1910, a fact that might account for Corbett's apparent confusion regarding the woman preacher he mentions. She was said to have had a permanent residence constructed near the boarding school and marched the students to services at her mission. Christmas presents distributed by Corwin, Johnson (n.d.) also writes, were eagerly anticipated.

Yet, according to Corbett's nieces, he not only regularly recited the Lord's Prayer, but also was frequently seen carrying his New Testament, reading from it, despite chronic eye problems, even when drunk. An anecdote told to me in 1989, and again in 1993, by Alex Miller, longtime Smith Valley resident, is also revealing. One day, this former beekeeper from Poland recalled, Corbett Mack and his wife were staggering home drunk, and he overheard the following exchange:

Corbett: "I believe in Jesus."
Celia: "Jesus is bullshit!"

"All churches are alike," Corbett himself once told me. His—pragmatic—view of faith seems wholly consistent with the Northern Paiute approach to religion (cf. Stewart 1941).

And finally, Johnson (n.d.) also writes that Stewart children were allowed to ice skate on Sundays on nearby ponds in 1904.

44. In contrast to the figure of 100,000 men, a mere 8,848 Chinese women emigrated to the United States between 1850 and 1882, the period of unrestricted immigration. In 1890 only 3,868 Chinese women were reported in the federal census, which also reported 102,620 Chinese men (Lyman 1970). Those women who came, if they had not been "kidnapped, sold into indentured servitude by their parents, captured by pirates or raiding bands, or lured abroad by a meretricious promise of proxy marriage," upon arrival in America were ordinarily placed "under contract [of prostitution] to individual Chinese, or more often to others in the Chinese quarter," as controlled by San Francisco-based secret societies (Lyman 1970:18, 19). Henry Tsai (1986: 40–42) writes that the majority of these "daughters of joy" were not from mainland China but from Hong Kong.

The list of fourth graders forwarded by Frank A. Thackery, supervisor-in-charge, to Walker River Reservation superintendent Pugh on 11 June 1912 include Corbett Mack's classmate-friends: David Bobb, Steve McCloud, Doudy Mitchell, Gus Mitchell, Sullivan Tom, Willie West, Sadie Dyer, Amy Mitchell, May Steve, May Jim, Minnie Dock, Rosa Dock, Lizzie Calvin, James X. Willie, Bert Summerfield, and Charles Abraham (Carson Indian School Correspondence, box 248a, RG 75, Federal Archives, San Bruno, Calif.). Six of the nine boys in that list became opiate addicts.

45. During another interview, Corbett alternatively recalled that the superintendent (Asbury?) gave him permission to leave because there were "too many students" in Stewart. When queried why he did not then return next fall, he mentioned his mother's accident in a runaway buggy (sec. 122), lamenting (again!) that he might otherwise have graduated from eighth grade and come to "know something."

Sayre recalled Blind Bob as a Paiute who "could wander about the valley with his cane. He sat at Readings and listened to white people talk. He was a very wise, old Indian" (Sayre 1977:25). This Northern Paiute's granddaughter, Sophina Smith, also recently commented that he "could feel anybody coming a long ways. He'd say, 'Who are you?' when someone arrived" (*Reflections 1993*, annual publication of the *Mason Valley News*).

46. Johnson (n.d.) found that band instruments originally were furnished in 1896. Edwin Schanandore, an Oneida, was hired the following year as band instructor-disciplinarian. He began the Stewart marching band, which not only performed at the Carson City Memorial Day Parade, but also regularly gave concerts on the steps of the state capitol.

47. Jimmy Burbank, age 28, was arrested on 1 August 1923 and sentenced in the Eighth Judicial District to one to fourteen years for attempted rape. From his "Narrative of Circumstances," we read that Burbank

> went to the Wilson Ranch, near Nordyke, in Lyon County, Nevada, on the 18th of June 1923 . . . [and] had one [bottle] with him when he reached the ranch. . . . [He] in the company of another Indian, had found a couple of bottles of whiskey near the town of Mason; they . . . drank one of the bottles . . . rode around the ranch first, and then . . . [Burbank] asked Mrs. Geena Lommori where the boss was; was told that he was in town . . . [It was lunchtime, Burbank asked for something to eat and was given eggs and bread, after which he] rode toward the hay corral, and the horse evidently galloping too fast, the meal was spilled. So, Burbank returned to the house and made insulting remarks to the lady, which were heard by the witness, Jeannette Menesini, a little thirteen year old girl . . . [Alarmed, Mrs. Lommori phoned three times for help] while the Defendant was in the house, which he had entered unceremoniously, when he started toward her . . . she ran out in the yard and upon the public highway . . . [Burbank then allegedly followed and] attacked her, threw her down, and as the evidence shows, but for the timely arrival of the neighbors his desire might have been accomplished. [cf. Nevada State Prison Records and District Attorney Narratives, State Archives, Carson City, Nev.]

Burbank's prison record indicates that he "bore a very good reputation previous to the commission of this crime," as well as medical pleas (claims of cataracts and imminent blindness) for parole during his four-year prison sentence. Also included was a 17 March 1927 note to the Board of Pardons from Corbett Mack's former employer, Charles Hinds, who agreed to pay for surgery: "Jim has worked for me quite a number of time before he got into trouble, and I always found him a trust and faithful worker." Then, following his release, Jimmy Burbank was reported on 2 June 1927 to be working for W. L. Blackwell in Smith Valley, on the Belmonte Ranch in Smith Valley on 21 June 1927, and on Ambrose Rosachi's ranch in East Walker River (30 August 1927) (Nevada State Prison Records and District Attorney Narratives, State Archives, Carson City, Nev.). According to the Lyon County Record of Deaths (Lyon County Courthouse, Yerington), Burbank, about thirty-five, died in an automobile accident on 11 October 1931.

48. Corbett's decision to begin wage labor, which he represents as pride in the face of parental pressure, reflects Northern Paiute adaptation to Euroamerican occupation. Timothy Smith, for example, after describing initial hostilities by *Tabooseedokado*, commented:

> Yet a few years later I do not see how we would have managed without their assistance in the harvesting of our large crops of hay as well as in some other lines of work. What they did was generally pretty well done. As hay stackers and in the use of the horse fork they excelled. [1911-12:226]

Indeed, example after example from the Annual Reports to the Commissioner of Indian Affairs from the 1860s indicate the same. For example, "Many of them [Paiutes] are employed as laborers on the farms of white men in all seasons, but they are especially serviceable during the time of harvest and haymaking" (ARCIA 1865-66:115). Not surprisingly, then, one component of the 1 January 1889 Great Revelation of Wovoka, a.k.a. Jack Wilson, was the prophet's revealed Protestant work ethic, "They must work!" (Mooney 1896:776).

49. An excellent summary of technological advances in Smith (and Mason) Valley agriculture by Sayre is relevant. She describes old-fashioned dump rakes, hayforks, and hay wagons giving rise to the wooden-toothed rake pulled by a horse, which flopped over the hay and made it into bunches, as followed by the side-delivery rake, which along with the mowing machine left "nice rows of alfalfa; and on to derricks, cables, compressors" (1977:19). "The pay was not so important as giving the family a good feed," Annie Lowry emphasized for Lalla Scott (1966:79).

Significantly enough, Corbett's word for irrigator is close to the term used by Owens Valley Paiutes—*tuvaiju'u* (Lawton et al. 1976:18). If, indeed, there was precontact farming in Desert Creek, this might well be seen as a preadaptive reason for the Northern Paiutes' apparent willingness to engage in farm and ranch wage work.

Writing about the Smith Valley Artesia Lake land boom of 1910, Kersten (1961:132-35) reported that Frank W. Simpson subdivided his large ranch into eighty-acre parcels for sale to homesteaders and dug eleven wells.

50. They obviously were cutting wood without permit on U.S. National Forest land. "Nowaday, it's hard cuttin' pine nut wood," Corbett elsewhere told me. "'Cause you see why? Them *taivo*, they claim everythin'! But them days, they don't really bother you too much." Pine nuts, the seed of *Pinus monophylla*, were, of course, long the staple of these Great Basin Indians, hence "The Theft of the Pine Nuts" (sec. 55) is a constant in all of their folktale collections (cf. Lowie 1924:217-21; Kelly 1932:395-403; Powers, cited in D. D. Fowler and C. S. Fowler 1970:135). Wholesale destruction of piñon pines occurred during the great nineteenth-century silver and gold booms in Nevada; that was the tree used for charcoal for mining, among other purposes (cf. Lanner 1981). As for faunacide, the *Lyon County Times* on 1 April 1893 reported Smith and Mason Valley Paiutes catching gophers for "$1.00 per hundred and feasting on them, while ranchers purchased strychnine for their complete termination." On 22 April 1893 the same newspaper wrote that "thousands upon thousands" of gophers were poisoned. On 18 August 1894: "Rabbits are dying off so fast that the odor of the decaying carcasses is a nuisance on the ranchers." And on 1 June 1895, thousands of unwanted carp were said to be trapped in ditches and to have perished *(Lyon County Times)*.

51. Sayre (1977:13) recalled that Hinds Hot Springs originally was owned by a Mr. Schneider and John Fairchild. They sold to J. C. Hinds, who, in turn, sold to John O'Banion and a Mr. Snell. There was a rooming house attached, and the swimming pool at the hot springs was believed to cure rheumatism. After a fire destroyed Hinds Hot Springs, O'Banion rebuilt it, Sayre recalled. But another fire permanently closed Hinds Hot Springs. Howard Rogers thought the Gallaghers of Smith Valley were also former owners. This health resort, where Corbett Mack's younger sister Lizzie washed dishes, was recalled by this Paiute as a "two story house with bar, dining hall, dance hall, rooms to rent, and place to change your clothes in. They had bathing suit and towels for rent before they [whites] go into that steamed pool." According to Howard Rogers, Mike Sava, who also owned the hot springs, leased it to Harry Powell, perhaps its penultimate owner. Sava, he said, was a "mean guy. Buys jackass and sells it. Don't speak English too good." Elsie Sam Ausmus recalled that Charley Hinds used to frequently visit Big Mack, and that he spoke some Paiute.

52. Corbett, mockingly, contrasted the paltriness of this annual salary with what he could earn selling opiates on a Saturday night alone (sec. 98).

53. "I never knew an Indian to ever go in any mine," Ed Dyer told Wheat. "They seemed to be afraid. Why, if they had to go in a mine, they had all kinds of jobs . . . Pine Grove. . . . Never did anything underground" (Margaret M. Wheat Papers, tape 2, 83-24, Special Collections, University of Nevada Libraries, Reno). Yet Henry Clay, who possibly introduced opium among Smith and Mason Valley Paiutes (sec. 84), was said to have worked in the Bodie mines.

On Northern Paiute shamanism, compare Park (1934), Stewart (1941), Olofson (1979), and Miller (1983).

Kersten (1961:124) wrote that cattle dominated the Walker River regional economy until the early 1900s, when sheep (in Smith Valley) achieved enough prominence during the 1930-39 decade to rival beef. "Aw" or Art Jones, according to Howard Rogers, owned a small ranch in Smith Valley, while his brother-in-law leased from Frank Simpson. Joe Yeager, he recalled, was another Simpson lessee. According to the Lyon County tax lists, J. D. Yeager was assessed $26,187 on properties in 1924 and an additional $8,400 for his band of 1,400 sheep (Lyon County Library, vertical files, Yerington, Nev.).

Yet sheep shearing was a regular enough Northern Paiute occupation. Frank Quinn, former Yerington Paiute tribal chairman and an original Campbell rancher, for example, once told me that he sheared sheep for a living, whereas Henry Fredericks, informant, recalled that Andy Bill was engaged in the same on his *taivo* father's Sweetwater Ranch. According to one document found in the Federal Archives, the Washo Eddie Rube was called

> captain of the sheep-shearing gang, composed of a number of Indians, two white men . . . [who] sheared some 3,000 sheep [in Smith Valley] out of a herd of 5,000 . . . [until] probably urged on by the white men, they struck for a raise from $.08 a head to $.09. Had they held out for $.09 in the beginning they probably would have gotten it readily enough, but under the circumstances, the manager refused. This happened in the afternoon. In the evening Eddie Rube, who had in the meanwhile been imbibing, returned to the store and became abusive and it is alleged threatened to kill Mr. Cunningham. [Bishop Agency, box 251, Bishop, California, 1925-26, RG 75, Federal Archives, San Bruno, Calif.]

Corbett's lingering query "Where them Basqo come from?" reiterates the importance given to subsistence and place of residence in Paiute definitions of identity.

54. On 12 August 1919 the *Mason Valley News* would report that Charles E. Day of Wellington owned the purest-bred sheep in the county, 100 French Rambouileet from Utah and Idaho.

55. Sarah Winnemuuca's brother Natchez harvested sixty acres of wheat, thirty bushels to the acre, in Lovelock, Nevada, and some of the profits were used to pay fellow Paiutes for assisting him during planting and harvesting on land connected with her short-lived Peabody Indian School (Canfield 1983: 216). Indeed, Smith and Mason Valley Paiutes frequently mentioned ownership of these valleys prior to white settlement, as well as of acreage acquired from former employers. Howard Rogers, for example, told me that Dan Simpson gave his grandfather (Blind Bob) a piece of land in Smith Valley (without water rights) that family members helped clear: "They piled brush and burned it, but when he [Simpson] died, they just gave it up." The 1890 Ghost Dance prophet became embroiled in a dispute in 1916 regarding a piece of land on the Wilson Ranch in Mason Valley that Wovoka claimed had been given to him (Hittman 1990:149-51). The most intriguing stories, however, concern a treaty that burned, according to one version, or was buried, according to others. "Blind Bob told stories about a terrible earthquake, and he said the land at Desert Creek was his land, but the BLM took it," Mary Stevens, wife of a former Yerington Paiute Tribal chairman, related in *Reflections 1993,* an annual publication of the *Mason Valley News.*

> The young people listened and believed. They were [also] told that the leader of their tribe was buried with a treaty that gave all the lands in Smith Valley and Desert Creek to them. Our family has tried to find that grave and retrieve the treaty, but we haven't been able to find it.

George and Annie (Fredericks) Fulstone relocated from Carson to Smith Valley in 1902, purchasing Johnny Rogers's ranch in Wellington. Their children were Ed, Fred, Juanita, Frank, Dick, Margeurita, and Harry (b. 1887, Genoa, Nevada), who also was nicknamed Hike *(Mason Valley News,* 4 April 1958). These Fulstones, along with Louis Scieroni, a West Coast real estate and candy manufacturer, in 1919 purchased the recently completed (Scieroni) canal for $250,000, allowing an additional 5,000 acres to come under cultivation in an area in Smith Valley named the Grant District.

The dispute between Corbett's stepfather and the white rancher who employed him might also have concerned fence posts cut by Big Mack that were claimed by George Fulstone.

56. According to the thirteenth (1910) federal census (U.S. Bureau of the Census 1880-1920), Bridgeport Joe (b. California, age 60?) was listed in Smith Valley as a "boarder." In Sam Newland's autobiography, Steward wrote that this Owens Valley Paiute's sweathouse was large enough to accommodate "old men and the young unmarried men" (1934:434). On the other hand, "Sweathouse" was not listed in Stewart's 1941 culture traits for Smith and Mason Valley Paiutes. Corbett Mack's allusion in this section to Ivan Hanson concerns the diffusion of Arapaho Raymond Harrison's religion to Campbell Ranch in 1972 (Hittman n.d.b). Indeed, following the Death Valley Shoshone shaman's unfortunate death in 1975, family members similarly were afraid to tear Ivan's structure down, and it remained until it crumbled from natural causes.

57. "Even when I have a sex dream, I talk to the night, because if I should pay no attention to them, they would continue and lead to fits," Jack Stewart, Owens Valley Paiute, similarly told Steward (1934:432). Coyote's philanderings were told with obvious delight (sec. 151).

58. The town of Mason grew to 275 people and 100 homes in 1912 during the copper strike in the Singatse Mountains and rivaled Yerington (population 700) for Lyon County capital. Wabuska, a railroad stop today consisting only of a grocery store, also formerly thrived, boasting two hotels and a two-room schoolhouse in 1918. Yerington itself grew steadily from 682 in 1910 to 1,169 in 1920, then declined to 1,005 in 1930 as the fortunes of copper waned (Kersten 1961:150-59). Sweetwater, California, according to the *Lyon County Times* (18 March 1882), was a vital mining community in 1882, consisting of the Summers, Homestake, Silverado, Patterson, Teddy Brodan, Messmore, and Williams mines.

Land was provided for the Yerington Indians to build houses in Mason Valley:

> There was purchased for the Indians in Mason Valley a ten acre tract about one-quarter of a mile from Yerington [for $1,025.64 from Frank Bovard]. This tract was sub-divided into lots large enough for each Indian family to erect a house and have sufficient grounds for a small truck garden. 34 houses were built by the Indians, all neat frame houses, some few painted and papered, and most of them screened. A wide street down the center with shade trees planted on each side and a flag-pole at

the entrance makes a huge improvement over their previously scattered group of tents in which they took no pride. [ITC Archives]

Many Yerington Indian Colony residents belonged to the Walker River Reservation, having migrated to Mason Valley for seasonal farm and ranch work. In his December 1920 "Report on Living Conditions," Special Inspector Dorrington wrote Commissioner of Indian Affairs Cato Sells about the

> lack of industrial opportunity, destruction of incentive to make progress, exposure to vices exterior to Indian life, engendering immorality through the crowded conditions prevailing in a [Yerington] camp of primitive character; . . . the arrangement invite[s] epidemic and is likely to engender contagions, and generally . . . the colony is calculated to prevent progress, to insure retrogression, to wreck the physical and damn the spiritual man. [ITC Archives]

Dorrington, who "utterly condemned" the place, counted 135 residents on 14 June 1920, a population he said swelled in winter to 300, and which was dependent on two wells. The land was said to be entirely intractable, any goal for Paiutes to raise gardens doomed to failure. Weekly reports by the Yerington Indian Colony field matron Etta J. Shipley lend support to the view taken by Joseph Jorgensen (1971) of western reservations as "satellite communities" created to satisfy the labor demands of those who were either wealthy or becoming wealthy. In the week ending 27 May 1922, for example, we read that Shipley visited five Paiute families living and working on the Fallon Ranch, two at the Salles Ranch, and one on the Rosachi Ranch. On 3 June 1922, Field Matron Shipley would also report having visited eleven additional families working at ranches in Wellington, Smith Valley, and another ten at the Colony District (Walker River Agency, box 303, Correspondence for 1922 and 1923, RG 75, Federal Archives, San Bruno, Calif.).

According to the "Health and Sanitary Records, 1897-1910" (vol. 1) of the Walker River Indian Agency (compartment 2167, RG 75, Federal Archives, San Bruno, Calif.), Edith Johnson attended Stewart Institute in 1901-2. She was hospitalized for hemorrhaging from the lungs in June of 1904.

Finally, it should be noted here that Owens Valley Paiute Jake Stewart similarly boasted of sexual exploits:

> I also was interested in women. My soul confessed it. It once said to me in a dream: One thing I cannot get away from is love for women. I can get along without other things, but I cannot get along without women. I

shall never be able to outlive this. I found that this was true and spent much time in the company of women. [Steward 1934:427]

59. The *Yerington Times* would report on 3 March 1926 that Nellie Natchez, a student home on vacation from Stewart, mysteriously disappeared while in the custody of Judy Dyer (Miller), her inebriated aunt. Judy Dyer, along with sisters Sadie and Agnes Dyer, were half-breeds. Their father was Bob Dyer, Indian trader on the Walker River Reservation, who spoke Paiute as well or better than his brother Ed Dyer, James Mooney's interpreter and eventual amanuensis of the 1890 Ghost Dance prophet. These Dyer girls' (full-blooded) half-brother was named for a Yerington merchant. Arrested on 13 January 1923 for the murder of Ah Quong in Carson City—after serving a prison sentence (8 November 1918-1 January 1920) for forgery, Gus Brann, according to his state prison records (Nevada State Prison Records and District Attorney Narratives, State Archives, Carson City, Nev.), reportedly killed the elderly Chinese man for refusing to sell opiates. In a 24 January 1923 letter about him from Yerington Indian Colony field matron Etta J. Shipley to Horace J. Johnson, superintentent of the Walker River Reservation Agency, we also read that "at one time he [Brann] aided [Treasury Agent] Mr. O'Neil [informant] and the Indians threatened him so he left here and has not been in Yerington for many months" (Walker River Reservation Agency, box 303, Correspondence for 1922 and 1923, RG 75, Federal Archives. San Bruno, Calif.). Brann commmitted suicide in his house at the Yerington Indian Colony.

60. Such ribaldry continues today, as indicated by the name I was given, *Atsa Moosoowee* 'Red Beard', which immediately degenerated (by women!) into *Soowee* 'Vagina'.

61. Edward Treadwell (1931) wrote about the vast Miller-Lux cattle empire, which included a large portion of Mason Valley, employed many *taivo* cowboys, and today is a part of Campbell Ranch.

62. Because Corbett more frequently referred to Celia Mack as "my wife," and because of the Northern Paiute prohibition against naming the dead—and for stylistic reasons as well—in all but one instance, I respectfully delete her name from the text. Celia Mack—"Seal," *Seeya*—was the daughter of shaman Dick Bennett and a Sweetwater Paiute woman named Gerdie or *Seeyeqarone'e* 'Pine Cone Blossom'. Her father's second wife, Maggie Bennett (b. 1831, d. 20 Feb. 1938[?]), was Henry Dick's mother. Part of my Paiute family disliked Celia. They also resented the fact that Andy Dick, her brother, buried her next to him. No doubt drinking was one cause of friction.

But Corbett's niece Bernice Crutcher had only nice things to say about her, for example, "Auntie liked prairie dogs, and we'd hunt them together."

At the end of his life history, Corbett Mack relates an attempted sexual tryst with Florence Brown (sec. 156).

63. As stated, Paiute women frequently were named for flowers or flora.

64. The classic treatise on magic was written by Evans-Pritchard (1937).

65. Corbett, in fact, frequently emphasized how well he got along with his wife, that is, contrasting himself with other marrieds who drank. I found no evidence to contradict this assertion.

66. This hypersensitivity is revealing in light of the macho image created by Corbett Mack throughout his life history.

67. Albin Cofone (1982:116) wrote that Swiss-Italians and Italians from northern Italy were originally attracted to Nevada by wage labor from mining booms in Eureka and on the Comstock lode. "The majority came from Genoa, but the neighboring provinces of Tuscany, Lucca and Umbria also contributed. Many also came from Ticino, the ethnic Italian canton of Switzerland." "They saw themselves as hardworking and industrious," Cofone stated, and "had not developed the same mistrust of the world" as southern Italians, but were "more willing to go it alone" (Cofone 1982:120, 122). According to census figures, 655,888 Italians emigrated to America between 1890 and 1900, a figure swelling between 1900 and 1910 to 2,104,309 (Wittke 1958). In Nevada in 1910 they were but 2 percent of the population, and 3 percent of foreign-born immigrants (Wittke 1958:116). In Smith and Mason valleys, the tenth federal census of June of 1880 (U.S. Bureau of the Census 1880-1920) reported 151 Italians in Smith Valley and 557 in Mason Valley, which combined with 176 in Pine Grove for a total of 884 Italians. (Recall that there were 66 Smith Valley Indians, by contrast, 149 Mason Valley Indians, and an additional 37 in Pine Grove, for an overall count of 252). Lyon County's Italian population was 2,268 in 1900 and 4,078 in 1920 (U.S. Bureau of the Census 1880-1920). The census also reported 103 foreign-born whites owning farms in Lyon County to 190 native born. In addition, 46 tenants (21 of them foreign born) owned 297 farms, or 15.5 percent of all. These were mostly of Italian descent, as indicated by Otto Schultz, a former Lyon County agricultural extension agent, who told Earl Kersten (personal correspondence) that in 1928, 75 percent of Mason Valley's families were Italian. Louie Gardella, another former Lyon County extension agent, and of Italian extraction himself, related that in 1934 "there were more Italians in Mason Valley than there were in Smith Valley

probably. . . . And they were more livestock-minded in Smith Valley . . . [with] holdings in Antelope Valley and in Bridgeport . . . [and] summer range for their livestock" (1975:172).

Hard work, frugality, and a pattern of corporate mine ownership in Nevada, which contrasted with individual placer mining in California, were, according to Cofone (1982:123), the factors responsible for successful Italian-introduced row crop cultivation—potatoes, garlics, and onions—and that led to this alteration in the regional economy, formerly based on mining, hay, and livestock (cattle and sheep). But potatoes were especially important in Smith and Mason valleys. According to the *Mason Valley News* (30 May 1958), they were first planted in nearby Dayton in 1899, reaching these valleys in 1904, when Fred Panelli and Fred Lommori (b. 1878) leased the Higgens Ranch in Mason Valley in 1904. A 25 April 1896 item in the *Lyon County Times,* however, noted Italians already leasing the Gold Hill Ranch near Wabuska. By 1905, in any event, the *Lyon County Times* (11 March) would report Charles Snyder's ranch leased to "4 Wops" for $1,200 per annum. Another early Italian was Fortunata Nuti, who leased farms in Mason Valley in about 1908.

According to the *Lyon County Monitor* (17 August 1901), Missouri Flat (at the southern end of Mason Valley) right away began producing between 400 and 500 tons of potatoes; this short-lived newspaper called the potato business a "new industry in that section." Indeed, as early as 1899, 2,235 acres were already under potato cultivation in Nevada, yielding 361,188 bushels for sale, whereas state figures for 1909 reveal 4,864 acres yielding 766,826 bushels. The state figures decline thereafter, for example, 3,692 acres yielding 541,599 bushels in 1929. More important, Lyon County ranked first in the state in potato production. In 1899 503 acres were reported under cultivation, yielding 117,332 bushels for sale. In 1910 219 acres yielded 244,108 bushels of potatoes, as compared with 766,826 bushels sold for the entire state (U.S. Bureau of the Census 1880-1920, 1920, vol. 6, pt. 3)!

Eileen Kane (1964) also found that Smith and Mason Valley Paiutes interestingly excluded Italians from the racial taxon *taivo* or white.

68. Note that on 21 July 1894 the *Lyon County Times* reported a general strike of harvest hands in both valleys for $1.50 per day. Paiutes were said to have participated. Regrettably, I have no information further.

69. Following his 1863 honorable discharge from the Union Army, David Wilson (1829-1915), along with his two brothers and his wife Abigail Jane Butler Wilson (1836-1910), homesteaded Missouri Flat at the southern end of Mason Valley. Their Bible teachings influenced Jack Wilson (Wovoka), 1890 Ghost Dance prophet (Hittman 1990).

I interviewed Amos (Armedo) Mencarini on 17 October 1982 in his Smith Valley house. Mencarini said he was born in a small town near Crusta Lucca, in central Italy. At seventeen and a half he came to America under another Italian's (Arthur Poli's) sponsorship. After working two years for his benefactor, Mencarini said he worked three years for David Wilson. Having earned twenty dollars per month in 1912, most of which he recalled that he saved, Mencarini said his savings enabled him to lease 160 acres from the Wilsons in 1915, mostly brush. In 1923, he said, he leased his first piece of land in Smith Valley (Colony District). Recalling the Great Depression with appreciation, Mencarini said that as a consequence of it he was able to purchase for $200 per acre land that in 1982 cost $1,200 per acre, as ranches were selling for $3,500 that in 1982 cost $100,000! Characterizing himself as one of the biggest potato growers in either valley—the second leading grower in Smith Valley—Amos Mencarini stated that he owned five large ranches and shipped forty-five carloads of potatoes to California, twenty tons to a carload, during his prime (ca. the 1930s).

Less inclined was he, however—no, even suspicious—to discuss his lifelong Northern Paiute employees Corbett Mack and "Seal." "I did nothing I'm ashamed of!" Mencarini too quickly blurted out as soon as I turned the conversation to my subject. He said he did not remember when Corbett first came to work for him, though he did recall that they met while he leased Wilson's Nordyke Ranch. Corbett worked for him for thirty to forty years, Mencarini stated, for which service he built him (them) a small one-room house and provided a stove. "Corbett does anything!" Mencarini characterized the hired hand. "Seal," he continued, "washed dishes, graded winter potatoes, and sewed potato sacks. She speaks better English than me!" He laughed when reflecting. "I pay Corbett $30/month and Seal $20." Before I could broach the subject of opiates—or payment in homemade wine—Amos Mencarini recalled Corbett and Celia Mack's treks to the Smith Valley Bar, sometimes in the middle of the week. "But they hardly missed a day's work," he commented. The interview was then abruptly ended by him, the elderly Mencarini saying he had a cold and needed rest. In parting, he related how his brother had died in 1968 and his wife on 29 January 1981.

"Poor Corbett," informants so frequently related. "He worked for wine!" Because they were wont to claim that Mencarini—and by implication other Italians—became wealthy as a result of Corbett and Celia Mack's ruthless exploitation for wine, I looked up assets in the Lyon County tax lists. In the 1920s, or right before Corbett became employed by them, the Mencarinis were assessed at $2,820: five work horses, one saddle horse, a barn, one milk cow, forty hogs, twenty pigs, a Ford T, machines, and so forth. By contrast, Fred Fulstone, a wealthy rancher, and Mary Fulstone, his wife, a physician, were assessed at $60,672. In 1941, however, the Mencarinis were assessed at $6,848, $7,030, and $2,926 for various properties. Amos's brother Ettore was assessed at $4,400. And in 1965-66, or right after Corbett Mack retired, the Mencarini brothers were assessed at $9,816 in real estate, $3,130 for improvements, and $9,700 personal, totaling $22,646, plus additional amounts of $9,380 and $12,280 on other properties with a different partner (Shehady) (Lyon County Library, vertical files, Yerington, Nev.).

Bernice Crutcher and Elsie Sam Ausmus each told me that the Mencarinis annually provided flowers for Celia Mack's Smith Valley grave.

70. Corbett's account is unclear, if not confusing, but Irene Thompson did state that Northern Paiute women nicknamed Ettore Mencarini *gween'a* 'horny'.

71. According to the *Lyon County Times* (31 May 1890), Smith Valley farmers signed an agreement among themselves to pay $1.25 per day for common labor and $1.50 per day for hay stacking, binding only if Mason Valley ranchers concurred. Newly arrived Italians on the Carson River were in that same year already earning $35 per ton of potatoes. Implications of this change in the regional economy for opiate addiction is spelled out below.

72. "The Indians are about thru working in the potatoes," the Yerington Indian Colony field matron Etta J. Shipley wrote in a weekly report to the superintendent of the Walker River Agency for the week ending 29 April 1922. A further indication of the impact of row crop culture can be gleaned from her report for the week ending 14 October 1922: "No families at the Colony, except where there is sickness—All are working in the potatoes," and for the week ending 13 January 1922: "The Indian women are at work sacking potatoes" (Walker River Agency, box 303, Correspondence for 1922 and 1923, RG 75, Federal Archives, San Bruno, Calif.).

Columbina Venturri Beullentini, longtime Dayton native (b. 1904), fondly recalled butchering pigs and making blood sausage *(Reflections 1991,* annual publication of the *Mason Valley News).* See note 70 on the number of hogs owned by the Mencarinis. Spam, incidentally, was Corbett Mack's favorite lunch. His niece Bernice Crutcher also related how much Corbett hated the way the Mencarinis boiled the head while cooking chicken.

Carson City. And though Washoes were characterized as more frequently addicted to the "flowing bowl," "something new to the Piutes" was reported on 17 February 1881: Captain Sam, the so-called Paiute Apostle of Temperance, was caught taking a drink of whiskey "for his stomach sake" (*Territorial Enterprise*, 25 Mar. 1887).

"Too mean and too rough," Yerington Paiute Elder Ed Williams complained of Paiute cowboys or *pakyer'a* to Karl Fredericks, my reporter for *Numu Ya Dua*, the Culture History-Language Newspaper Project of the Yerington Indian Tribe (Hittman 1979-82). "Too noisy when they get drunk. Whites, same way. That time, some of those cowboys come in from the mountains; maybe raise the ceiling in the saloons. But the Indian can't go inside the saloon, so he does the same outside." Indeed, the *Lyon County Times* on 13 November 1887 would mention cowboys riding into the saloon at Pizen Switch and shooting up the lamps—a frontier behavioral pattern that diffused to or was emulated by Smith and Mason Valley Paiutes, among them Corbett Mack's social father, Big Mack.

80. Bernice Crutcher recalled her uncle Corbett rebuking his wife once for speaking Italian while drinking wine: "Talk Indian!" When Celia Mack repeated herself, he snapped, "Shut up!"

Alcohol, like opiates, shredded the very fiber of Smith and Mason Valley Paiute life after the 1890 Ghost Dance movement. Walker River Agency superintendent Ray R. Parrett, for example, would on 1 November 1928 write the commissioner of Indian affairs:

> I desire to renew my request that all assistance possible be given in bringing about some action to check the distribution of liquor among the Indians of the Yerington Colony. The situation is a very serious one. The Indians from the reservation go to the town on Saturday nights, also through the week at different times in search of work and fall prey to the bootlegger. There are a number of foreigners in and about the town of Yerington, who continue to sell liquor to the Indians. Occasionally an offender is apprehended and fined or sentenced to imprisonment for a term, but the activities continue, and at the present time, the situation is indeed very bad, with the Indians getting drunk and fighting and beating their wives, and a consequent demoralization of all married life in many instances. The local citizens of the town should take a stand to rid the community of these menacing foreign elements, who have no care whatever of the welfare or survival of the Indian, but on the other hand, they apparently give the matter far too little attention. With conditions as they are, there is a depressed outlook for the good of the Indians. . . .

Two Indians have died in recent months from an overdose of bootleg liquor. [ITC Archives]

In another letter from that year, Clara A. Rees, Yerington Indian Colony field matron, wrote Walker River Reservation Superintendent Parrett (15 August 1928) about off-reservation trouble as a result of drinking: how a Saturday night fight among several Indian girls and boys over two gallon jugs of whiskey and wine occurred

> about six miles out of town on the road to Schurz. They laid out all night intoxicated. . . . It seems that something should be done to stop this sale of liquor to Indians. It is getting worse all the time, and the young girls are all going to the bad. Liquor can be obtained from all of these Italian ranches. We simply must have an officer in the field who will go after these people. [no. 42213, ITC Archives]

And Field Matron Rees would write Superintendent Parrett of the Walker River Agency four years later (23 April 1932):

> Jimmie Bob came to me yesterday morning asking for Mr. O'Neill, and reported conditions which are existing at several of the Italian ranches. As Mr. O'Neill was not here, he went to the Chief of Police, Frank Brooks. I do not know whether he interested himself in same or not, but it seems as if something should be done to stop this furnishing liquor to the Indians. [Walker River Agency, box 313, Correspondence of the Superintendent, folder 3, RG 75, Federal Archives, San Bruno, Calif.]

Under the headline, "How a Smith Valley Rancher Saved His Watermelons," we read in the *Lyon County Times* on 7 October 1893 that a Paiute caught stealing a watermelon was revenged by this rancher's solution of "belly racket" shot into his best melons. Indians were also poisoned during Prohibition for cooperating with federal prohibition officers. Hank Bender, for example, plaintiff versus J. S. and Mrs. A. Grulli in federal court in Carson City, died. According to Special Officer O'Neill:

> Nov. 24, I attended the Federal court at Carson city as witness in the joint case of the United States versus A. Grulli and Mrs. A. Grulli charged with selling liquor to Hank Bender an Indian on July 29th, and 30th 1923, to which charge A. Grulli entered a plea of guilty and served a term of sixty days and paid a fine of $100.00. Mrs. Grulli decided to plea 'non guilty' and the jury rendered a verdict accordingly, in as much as her husband had paid the penalty for the offense and his wife was released from the charge. The case was weakened further by our inability to produce the Indian witness, Hank Bender, who died between the time of the offence . . . and the date of the trial of Mrs. Grulli. [Nevada Indian

Agency, box 116, Law Enforcement Agency, George O'Neill, Special Officer, Suppression of Liquor Traffic, RG 75, Federal Archives, San Bruno, Calif.]

One year later, a letter from O'Neill to the commissioner of Indian affairs on 8 December 1924 similarly would note: "Several Indians who have worked as possemen during the last year or two have died suddenly and many Indians in Mason and Smith Valley are of the opinion that the Italian ranchers against whom the Indians testified were responsible for the death" (Nevada Indian Agency, box 116, Law Enforcement Agency, George O'Neill, Special Officer, Suppression of Liquor Traffic, RG 75, Federal Archives, San Bruno, Calif.).

"They were funny when they used to drink," Dr. Mary Fulstone, the caring country physician and wife of a wealthy Smith Valley rancher who regularly employed Paiutes, trenchantly would recall.

> They'd fight amongst themselves, but you know, they never fought with the white people. And lots of people used to think—I was always picking up the Indians and giving them a ride from here to Yerington or someplace else, whether they were drunk or not. And I say—well, I had no fear of drunk Indians, because they never attack the white people or fought with them. They fought with their closest friends, you know. [1980:41-42]

"Hobos and tramps" in Smith and Mason valleys, finally, are mentioned in the *Lyon County Times* as early as 17 June 1893.

81. Frederic Snyder, the Carson School superintendent, wrote H. J. Johnson, superintendent of the Walker River Reservation, on 26 September 1922 that Margaret Jones and Logan Williams had not yet returned to the boarding school from summer vacation (Walker River Agency, box 303, Correspondence for 1922 and 1923, RG 75, Federal Archives, San Bruno, Calif.).

82. Corbett was drinking when I posed this question. He always self-referentially contrasted "real [i.e., irresponsible] winos" with "those who keep steady job and don't miss Monday work," that is, himself.

83. "When you consider the terrible havoc that opium and liquor have played with these people, especially the younger ones, the last few years, I think they have done fairly well," Walker River Reservation Agency superintendent Pugh wrote on 1 March 1910.

> Their advanced knowledge of civilization makes it the more easy for them [cities surrounding Stewart] to take advantage of the evils attending

it, and there is plenty of opportunity at Carson City, Reno, and other nearby towns for them to secure opium and liquor, which has been the ruin of some of the best of them. . . . Out of about 9 of the male graduates from the Carson School who have returned here, 5 of them are disappointments. Chronic gamblers, lazy, they drink when off the reservation, and some of them use opium, which they know better how to get, and conceal the source. [Walker River Indian Agency, box 316, FY 1909-1916, Official and Unofficial Correspondence, RG 75, Federal Archives, San Bruno, Calif.]

A year later we read: "Two days ago [1 August 1911] I was at Yerington, which is in Mason Valley, where most of our Indians find work during this season, and was informed that several of the Carson School pupils, of both sexes, had been industriously looking for 'Booze &C' this past week" (Walker River Indian Agency, box 316, FY 1909-1916, Official and Unofficial Correspondence, RG 75, Federal Archives, San Bruno, Calif.).

Superintendent James Jenkins of the Walker River Agency contrasted reservation life for the commissioner of Indian affairs on 25 March 1924 with "the lure of the 'villages,'" that is, the Yerington Indian Colony, which "attracted many of the young people . . . scores of them [who] became dope addicts" (ITC Archives). "Many of these young people were returned students who had come back from the Government's advanced schools with the brightest of futures, but they were unable to withstand such disheartening environments," we read in another federal document the same year (ITC Archives). Jenkins's successor, Ray R. Parrett, in requesting a replacement for the transferred treasury agent, George O'Neill, on 17 August 1928 condemned the "foreign element" in Yerington, before going on to state, "The conditions which exist with respect to the young people and returned students is deplorable" (ITC Archives).

Another early source that should have alerted us to the problem of opiates in Smith and Mason valleys ought to be mentioned: the dissertation "Missions to Nevada: A History of Indian Missions," in which its author, George William Smart, quotes an unnamed missionary at Stewart Institute who in 1928 observed:

Opium, yen-shee, cocaine and morphine [were found] on the street in Reno. . . . Some Negroes and Indians and Chinese also [use]. . . . At Yerington . . . Indians sitting around with shirts off shooting dope into each other. Some of them have abscesses on arms, legs, bodies, from unclean methods of injecting. . . . Young educated Indians sell it to other

Indians. . . . Proprietors taken to jail, paid $1500 fine and went back to selling it again. [Smart 1958:38-39]

Finally, Margaret "Peg" Wheat (1908-1988), lifelong student of Nevada Paiutes, astutely queried on a slip of paper about the "Extent of opium trade?" (Margaret M. Wheat Papers, box 4, 83-24, Special Collections, University of Nevada Libraries, Reno).

84. H. H. Kane (1882:1) reported the first white male addict in America in 1868, a Californian named Clendenyu. Diffusion of this innovation (cf. Coleman, Katz, and Menzel 1957) was so rapid that "in a few months" opiates reached Virginia City and the related mining camps of Gold Hill, Dayton, and Silver City (Courtwright 1982:71). This resulted in the appearance of smoking dens in small and large towns such as Truckee, Carson, and Reno. William L. Kennedy of Nevada in 1871 became the second (white male) opiate addict (H. H. Kane 1882:4).

The earliest evidence of Paiute addiction I found was 1885. Under the headline "Slaves of the Pipe," a reporter for the *Lyon County Times* on 25 April wrote: "The red man is rapidly becoming civilized; and he is as readily falling into the bad habits practiced by some of the whites." The reporter had discovered an "old Piute buck" in a Virginia City opium den with an elaborate Chinese layout. Fearful of arrest, the Indian initially "pretended not to understand, but upon closer questioning he replied that it was 'heap good' and that he 'catch up maybe six, maybe seven year.'" This Paiute, who was from Wadsworth (the Pyramid Lake Reservation?), said he had been in jail once with withdrawal symptoms, but he liked opium so much that he "wanted to know what the object would be in stopping. . . . [We told] him that we needed some wood chopped at this office and that if he would come around in the morning he could have the job," the reporter continued, "[so] the next morning he succeeded in working up a cord of wood before noon for which he was paid a big dollar. Upon which a broad grin spread over his face and he said he guessed he'd go down and 'hittum pipe again.'" Ella M. Cain (1956:150-56) also presented evidence that Northern Paiutes used opiates somewhat prior to Henry Clay's putative introduction of them to Smith Valley Paiutes. Relating the pathetic tale of sixteen-year-old Maggie, befriended by Tong Sing Wo, a wealthy Chinese man, she stated that the girl committed suicide on *hageenopa* (wild parsnip) when her patron abandoned her (cf. note 136).

On 7 May 1896 the *Yerington Times* would report a Chinese man receiving a seventy-five-dollar fine or 150 days in jail for the sale of opium to

Smith Valley Indians. Two days later the *Lyon County Times* (9 May 1896) reported this incident as follows:

> Sheriff Littel arrested a Chinaman [Ouong Sin] at Wellington, Smith Valley, this week for running an opium joint for Piutes. The Chinaman is a fiend himself, and about half the Piutes of Smith Valley have formed the opium habit by visiting the joint he conducted.

In fact, though, there is indication that opiates reached Walker River area Paiutes one year earlier. On 25 or 28 March 1895, L. A. Ellis, farmer-agent of the Walker River Reservation, warned District Attorney Charles A. Jones of Reno, "It is undoubtedly true that Chinamen are engaged in selling both whiskey and opium to Indians just south of here at several places and it is demoralizing them very much" (Walker River Reservation, box 314, Press Copy Book for 1895-98, RG 75, Federal Archives, San Bruno, Calif.). The *Lyon County Monitor* (1 April 1899) reported the arrest of Ah Sam for opium sales in Yerington four years later: "Efforts are being made to run the opium joint owners out of the valley," leaving it unspecified whether or not Paiutes were involved.

A 19 July 1905 letter spoke of the transportation of "booze and opium bought in Carson" to the Walker River Reservation (Carson Indian School, box 248a, Carson School Correspondence for the Walker River Reservation, 1902-5, book 2, A-Z, Mar.-Dec. 1905, RG 75, Federal Archives, San Bruno, Calif.). Then on 12 January 1907, a letter to Superintendent Asbury from the Walker River Reservation farmer-agent, Lovegrove, stated: "Levi Smith—a young halfbreed, belonging here, who stays at Hawthorne, & who is a confirmed opium and booze fighter[?], is also reported running around Hawthorne . . . as loco" (Carson Indian School, box 248b, Correspondence, folder 4, 1907, RG 75, Federal Archives, San Bruno, Calif.). Walker River Agency superintendent Pugh on 27 January 1909 wrote the commissioner of Indian affairs: "The Opium traffic here has been more harmful to the Indians than the liquor traffic but there seems to be no U.S. Law covering such cases, we are doing what we can in such cases and are making some progress." Two days later, the superintendent of the Walker River Indian School wrote Chief Special U.S. Officer William E. Johnson in Salt Lake City requesting cooperation from the commissioner of Indian affairs "pertaining to the sale of liquor and opium to Indians of this Reservation." Similarly, Superintendent Pugh on 6 March 1909 would write the commissioner of Indian affairs: "Because of my eleven years intimate acquaintance with these Pah-Utes, and the prestige I think I have over them, I count on being able to correct these evils [i.e., opium, liquor, gambling] (Walker River Indian Agency Correspondence, box 316, FY 1909-16, Official and Unofficial Correspondence, RG 75, Federal Archives, San Bruno, Calif.).

Henry Clay, age 25, is listed in the 1910 federal census (U.S. Bureau of the Census 1880-1920) as living in Smith Valley and married to Annie, age 28. Interestingly, his Paiute name derives from the food identifying Paiute residents of Smith and Mason valleys, *Tabooseedokado*.

85. "It's a poor town now-a-days that has not a Chinese laundry, and nearly every one of these has its lay-out," a white male opium addict in 1883 remarked (in Courtwright 1982:73). Corbett also mentioned "this one *taivo* guy, and his wife in Mason, they also smokin' that [raw] *'oopeey^n* that time."

86. Loren B. Chan (1982:267) wrote that the Chinese population in Nevada rose dramatically from 23 in 1860 to 5,416 in 1880. In an unpublished manuscript, "The Chinese Experience in Nevada: Success despite Discrimination", Sue Fawn Chung (n.d.) reported that in 1890 there were 2,749 Chinese males to 84 females in Nevada; 1,283 males to 69 females in 1900; 876 males and 51 females in 1910; 630 males and 59 females in 1920; and 440 males and 73 females in 1930.

According to Magnaghi (1981:156-57), the Virginia City mining depression and Pioche 1870 boom were what attracted the Chinese; following Pioche's depression, they moved on to Bodie and Tuscarora. Tuscaroa, in fact, had the state's largest Chinese population outside the Comstock lode in the 1870s:280, a figure that rose to 500 in 1889, before dropping to 250 in 1890 and even more dramatically afterward (L. B. Chan 1982:279). Story County itself (Reno) had 642 Chinese in 1890, down by half from its prime. By 1900 this county's Chinese population had fallen to 62. Dayton in Lyon County had between 150 and 200 Chinese in 1885 (*Lyon County Times*, 13 February 1885).

"The smoking of opium, a habit-forming narcotic had developed among the Chinese in the seventeenth century," Magnaghi wrote:

> Foreign traders [the English] introduced vast quantities in the 1830s and 1840s. By 1838 nine out of ten Chinese in Kwantung Province were addicts. The importation of opium into the United States was legal in the nineteenth century, and in 1870, 2,413,073 pounds of opium worth $13,824,535 were legally imported into the United States. The Chinese who arrived on the Comstock carried on this tradition of opium smoking. Opium dens were a feature of Chinatown and the smell of opium wafted throughout the quarter. The Chinese were firmly entrenched as operators

of the dens and their clients were both Chinese and whites. The exteriors of the dens were similar to surrounding structures, but the interiors consisted of a labyrinth of tiny rooms and numerous doors to be used as exits in case of a police raid. The dens were scattered throughout Chinatown and beyond, although a large number of them were concentrated on B Street. Opium smoking became extremely popular among whites by the mid-1870s. Both males and females as young as twelve years of age, young adults and older people made the trip to the dens.... In some cases they added special rooms for women. By 1875 some fifty young men were identified as addicts and after the great [Virginia City] fire of that year, opium dens were some of the first structures to be constructed in Chintatown. [1981:139]

David Courtwright also wrote:

The [Chinese] immigrants who landed in California came from a society in which opium smoking was commonplace, the opium den an institution. Moreover, the overwhelming majority . . . came from the area around Canton, a region that had long been associated with the opium traffic, serving as the sole (though illegal) point of entry for the drug prior to 1842. [1982:67]

According to this student of drugs, the prototypical Chinese laborer-opiate addict was "A young man of peasant stock. He had come to America as an indentured laborer, hoping to earn enough money to support his family, repay his creditors, save more money, and eventually return to his village." And whereas the average opium smoker in China was between 20 and 55, the age in America was between 18 and 30 (Courtwright 1982:63).

In Lyon County, Loren B. Chan would write, Chinese laborers—woodchoppers, fruit and vegetable peddlers, and placer miners who worked for gold in areas on the Comstock lode abandoned by whites—built the Carson and Colorado Railroad. "A small number . . . were cooks on some of the many farms and ranches in the Smith and Mason valleys in the southern portion of the county" (1982:291-93, 293). In fact, according to the tenth federal census (U.S. Bureau of the Census 1880-1920), there were in 1880 five Chinese in Mason Valley, sixty in Smith Valley, four in nearby Sweetwater Valley, and ten in the mining community of Pine Grove.

Loren B. Chan also showed that close socioeconomic ties between Virginia City and San Francisco's Chinese communities were mediated by the Six Companies, that is, the transportation of foodstuffs and herbal medicine, and in particular, the Triad Society, which began as an anti-Manchu political group in 1674 and subsequently "engaged in gambling, narcotics, prostitution, extortion, murder-for hire, and other criminal activity" (1982: 300, 272 n. 17). This, no doubt, was the way opiates reached Smith and Mason valleys. Another way was suggested by a 19 May 1919 headline in the *Nevada State Journal:* "Clever Celestial Used Spuds as $1,000 Dope Camouflage." The article related that C. W. Charlie from San Francisco was in Reno City jail after police found 6 bins of opium and 202 bottles of "snow" hidden in a paper sack of potatoes in his rooming house—opium lacking the federal stamp required by the 1914 Harrison Act (p. 6).

"Cannot something be done to put a stop to Chinamen selling opium to Indians at Hawthorne and Dayton?" Walker River Reservation Farmer-Agent Longacre wrote Superintendent Asbury as early as 8 May 1905.

> Cannot the Gen [?] Govt be induced to put a special restriction in some way or form on the Chinamen? Prohibit Indians from entering the Chinese dens—or kill them off in some genteel manner? This most damnable business is rising to serious proportions among the young Indians and I don't know any way to stop it. This was the reason I asked you some time ago if it was not possible to get me appointed Dept. U.S. Marshal so I could legally make the Chinese glad to leave Indians alone with their dope. [ITC Archives]

At the end of this destructive cycle, Superintendent Parrett of the Walker River Reservation, in discussing narcotics before the Senate Committee on Indian Affairs, wrote that Walker River area Paiutes "go considerable distances [to purchase opiates]. I understand they go to Carson City, to Reno here, and it is brought in. I have understood it has been brought in all the way from San Francisco and Oakland and handled through a long drawn-out line apparently" (U.S. Senate Committee on Indian Affairs, *Survey of Conditions of the Indians in the U.S.: Hearing before the Committee on Indian Affairs,* part 21, 71st Cong., 3d sess., 26 May 1931, 11529-31). In chronological order, here is a sampling of previously unpublished data to supplement newspaper and informant accounts that document Chinese involvement in the Walker River area Indian opium trade:

- George O'Neill wrote on 10 August 1918:

> Lieutenant Myers, Intelligence Office, United States Army, stationed here just advised me that Minnie Gould Robinson of Mason, Nevada, can give you very valuable information concerning the activities of a certain "Big fat chinaman" who is supposed to be selling "hop" to Indians there. She has made mention of Mr. Henry Allen (mule skinner) whom she says has knowledge of the same. [ITC Archives]

- In a 4 December 1919 letter from Walker River Reservation superintendent Jenkins to the commissioner of Indian affairs, we learn:

  [Loose women and gambling are] the besetting sin[s] of the Indians of this [Walker River] reservation, as well as of practically all Piutes and Utes. . . . Women appear to be have become more completely demoralized as a result than the men. . . . The "dope" habit is also a menace to the progress of these people. Opium, or yen shee, is sold by Chinamen to Indians in a dozen or more towns and apparently local authorities take little or no interest in the matter, notwithstanding it is as demoralizing to the communities as to the Indians. . . . We should stop the introduction of this drug, put the Chinese who are in the business out of the country and cure the many Indians who have become afflicted with the "dope" habit. [ITC Archives]

- A "traffic that is more demoralizing than liquor and is steadily increasing among the people," Jenkins wrote again on 20 December 1919. "The drug can be obtained in a dozen or more towns, generally in Chinese laundries or restaurants" (ITC Archives).

- In 1920 Jenkins complained about "Chinaman Charles," who was caught with $4,000 of opium, yet received only a $150 fine and a thirty-day jail sentence (ITC Archives).

- "This Chinaman has been a constant source of trouble over a long period of time and the Office was very anxious to secure a conviction in his case," E. B. Merritt, assistant commissioner of Indian affairs, wrote the Walker River Reservation superintendent on 9 January 1922, regarding the disappearance of Ah Boo: "The records show that this dope peddler has been arrested on several occasions, being notorious for the sale of yenshee" (Reno Agency, box 116, Liquor Matters 1916, 1917, 1918, and 1922-23, 1924-25, RG 75, Federal Archives, San Bruno, Calif.).

- According to a letter of 6 November 1922 from the superintendent of the Walker River Agency to Mrs. P. J. Bryson of Los Angeles:

  They dispose of everything of value they have in order to pay the Chinese for this poison at a high rate, and it would appear that nothing much is done to free the country or the locality by Missionary work or other-wise of such undermining and destroying influence, and the Agent of the Government finds it difficult, almost impossible to secure convictions of dispensers of such poison in the courts." [Walker River Agency, box 303, Correspondence, 1922 and 1923, RG 75, Federal Archives, San Bruno, Calif.]

- "I have given David Bob and Corbett Williams every opportunity to make good in the promise both made to turn up the Chinaman who shipped the dope to Schurz on December 13, 1923," Treasury Agent O'Neill wrote Walker River Reservation superintendent Jenkins (Walker River Agency, box 303, Correspondence, 1922 and 1923, RG 75, Federal Archives, San Bruno, Calif.).
- O'Neill noted on 9 June 1924:

  During the afternoon [of 26 January 1924] accompanied by Indian policeman Sam John I assisted Narcotic Inspector James Tuite in procuring evidence against a narcotic drug vender named Lee Loy Pak, also helped search the premises occupied by the Chinaman at 206 Front Street [Reno] where marked money and a small quantity of yenshee were found. [Reno Indian Agency, box 116, Law Enforcement Program Correspondence from Indian Prisoners to Police Report, RG 75, Federal Archives, San Bruno, Calif.]

- On 8 December 1924 O'Neill wrote the commissioner of Indian affairs that he was leaving Mina to catch the train for Carson City, to answer a subpoena at federal court as a witness in *United States v. Lee Sue Tom*. Tom was charged with "opium, cocaine and morphine to be shipped through the mail from San Francisco to Reno, Nevada" (Reno Indian Agency, box 116, Law Enforcement Agency, George O'Neill, Special Officer, RG 75, Federal Archives, San Bruno, Calif.).
- Lede Loy Pac, according to George O'Neill's notes from 6 July 1925, was charged in Reno on 28 January 1925 with violation of the Harrison Narcotics Act, indicted, and fined $250 on 11 March 1925. He was sentenced to three and one-half years at McNeil's Island. The case against Lem Mou or Sam Low, charged with "furnishing" Indians at Carson City on 6 April 1925, however, was said to be pending (Reno Indian Agency, box 116, Law Enforcement Agency, George O'Neill, Special Officer, RG 75, Federal Archives, San Bruno, Calif.).
- A 13 April 1929 letter from E. W. King, Lyon County Chamber of Commerce director and chairman of its grand jury report on narcotics (cf. Appendix B), mentioned a Chinese seller of narcotics on the Pyramid Lake Reservation who was married to a Paiute woman (ITC Archives).
- Finally, as late as 16 February 1934, "Tom Fong [was arrested] for selling Yen Shee at Carson City, Nevada. Sheriff informed agent that Tom Fong was sending some narcotics to Reno. It was the source of supply around Carson" (ITC Archives).

Dr. Mary Fulstone recalled these tragic years of Paiute addiction to Chinese opium as follows:

> There was a time when there was a narcotics ring that sent out narcotics here to the Indians. They just got in a terrible state. It was early in my practice here, and we discovered that the Indians here were all taking something, but of course we didn't know what it was. At that time we had a Chinese cook here, who was a very fine cook, and we were very fond of him but we finally discovered, when they were working out this problem, that he had something to do with the drug that was coming in here. So, anyway, the agents came in here and got him. He was taken. [1980:40]

Ed Dyer told Peg Wheat: "About that time [1902] they got to buyin' what they call 'Chinaman cart'[?]. And they bought a lot of them. . . . Then I found out that there was some kind of opium in it. It made them woozy, so I closed down on that" (Margaret M. Wheat Papers, tape 15, 83-24, Special Collections, University of Nevada Libraries, Reno). The Yerington Indian Colony's contract physician, Dr. John T. Rees, testified on 4 November 1931 before the Senate Committee on Indian Affairs that "A Chinaman in Sacramento, in Reno, and Carson City is selling my Indians narcotics. He is sentenced to one year and a little fine. My Indians are sentenced to five or six years in the penitentiary. That is a comparison in reference to the sentences" (U.S. Senate Committee on Indian Affairs, *Survey of Conditions of the Indians in the U.S.: Hearing before the Committee on Indian Affairs*, part 21, 71st Cong., 3d sess., 4 November 1931, 11551-54).

And from members of Karl Fredericks's family we learn:

> • I also remember Woe Fong, the Chinese cook. He was full of fun that one. Old Woe would attend the Paiute fandango [on the Fredericks Ranch] in the Fall and mix right in with the other Paiutes. Both Woe and Kee [gardeners] sold that Chinese opium to the Paiutes that worked on the ranch. I [also] used to watch Old Natze[?] take that: he would put the black stuff in the palm of his hand and eat it. The opium was sold in small bottles. I guess it made the Paiutes high when they used it. . . . I never did see anyone use Morphine. [Tommy Fredericks, b. 1912]

> • I remember when the Paiutes took to using that Chinese opium—*moohoo'oo* as the Paiutes call it. Most of the Paiutes that lived on the Fredericks Ranch used it. They would buy it from gardener Kee. I don't where Kee could have gotten his supply from to sell, maybe Bodie? The men who worked on the Fredericks Ranch said that they smoke [yen-

shee] because it made them strong. . . . My uncle also used that opium when he got the chance. [Helen Allen, b. 1889]

• Grandmother [Ida Pagomi] said that she even used yenshee when she was young. She bought it from one of the Chinese who worked on the Fredericks Ranch. Ida could have purchased the opium from the Chinese gardener Kee. [Josie Tom, b. 1926]

Regarding Corbett's comment about domestic attempts to grow opium, H. Wayne Morgan (1981:2) wrote about poppy cultivation in the Sun Belt, in many southern states, and in Pennsylvania, Vermont, Massachusetts, New Hampshire, and Connecticut as well.

Vernon Shears was the son of Ah Sam. Billy "Bacon" Tom, who was arrested for selling opiates, belonged to a large family of descendants of "Chinaman Tom" at the Nine Mile Ranch in East Walker River. Also, Leo Kingston, according to the *Mason Valley News* (29 August 1969), was said to be the son of "Old Hully, Dayton peddler." Nevertheless, evidence exists of initial tension between Paiutes and Chinese: "Indians despised the Chinese for their aggressive work ethic, their tendency to use even the scraps of the environment such as the roots of pine nut trees, and their proclivity to take Indian jobs," wrote Magnaghi. "As whites initially moved into the area, Paiute males found employment as wood choppers, and females as servants and launderers. The Chinese cut into this activity by selling precut wood and returning finished laundry" (1981:155-56). A frequently recounted incident of Paiute-Chinese hostility occurred on 13 June 1891, when Poker Tom from Schurz went to Bridgeport to gamble with Ah Tia and won $200, then was found dead in the river six weeks later with his legs and head cut off, his trunk (salted to prevent smelling) sawed open from neck to stomach. After the perpetrator had been caught by Sheriff Cody of Bodie, Paiutes stationed twenty men outside the jail. Following his release, Ah Tia was systematically tortured to death.

Loren B. Chan objects to the word *Chinaman*, "the way most whites referred to the Chinese during the late nineteenth century and a good part of the twentieth century. Use of the term is now considered in poor taste, and offensive to Chinese ancestry. The proper term is 'Chinese'" (1982:291 n. 89). My usage is not intended to offend. It is both historical and regional, and of course it was part of Corbett Mack's vernacular.

87. "How, where, and precisely when the boiling, evaporating, and straining processes for refining opium were developed is not known," wrote

Courtwright. "Once it is properly 'cooked' and distended, the opium is transferred to the pipe's bowl, where it is rolled into a small 'pill'" (1982:65, 72). Lester Hilp, a Reno pharmacy owner who later worked in Yerington, told the Oral History Program of the University of Nevada:

> I recall that we used to sell opium. It was legal for a doctor to write for opium, and some of these early addicts liked to prepare their own opium, and smoke it like the Chinese did. Some of them made it into pills and chewed it, just like you do snuff. They would heat it, and prepare their opium—made little balls out of it, about the size of these penny gumballs. Then they'd chew that for the morphine that was in it. [Hilp 1978:33-34]

Yen-shee, wrote H. H. Kane, "was the scraping in the ash left after smoking gum opium: in Chinese *yen tshi*" (1882:35-36). In a 3 August 1928 letter to M. C. Guthrie, chief medical director, Washington, D.C., Dr. Rees, Contract Physican to Smith and Mason Valley Paiutes, stated: "Yen shee is the bi-product produced by smoking Opium, or the residue which forms in the bottom of the Opium pipe, which gives nearly the same action as Opium, but is not as injurious or as powerful in action as Opium or Morphine" (ITC Archives). And Courtwright wrote:

> Opium prepared for smoking contains up to 9 percent morphine[;] when it was smoked only a fraction of the morphine is sublimated up the pipe. Most of it remains in the ash, called yen shee, which since less of the morphine was consumed, dependency took longer, a full 15 days of regular smoking, by one account. [1982:69]

Moohoo'oo 'Owl', Corbett Mack related, had trouble pronouncing his words, hence the old people did not always understand him. All the same, when he heard an owl in 1953, the very next day Corbett learned that Henry Greely's son was killed. For the role of *Tabudzeeba* 'Chickenhawk', another harbinger of misfortune, in his mother's accident, see section 122.

Compare Courtwright's comment that opium smoking is a "social enterprise, carried on in a communal place" (1982:64).

88. "They have a crude method of using the drug," the *Reno Evening Gazette*, under the headline "Capture Chinese Opium Dispenser Lee Sing, Restaurant Owner in Mason," reported on 18 September 1920. "A small glass vial with a hole drilled in the side, and a hollow stick in the neck of the body of the bottle permits them to draw the deadly fumes through the body of the bottle." Irene Thompson recalled family members using a three-corner file to work a hole in Sloan's Liniment bottles into which they fit rose twigs as stems. Bailing wire, she also recalled, was used to cook the narcotic over homemade lamps, which in the case of raw opium they worked with their thumbs until cooked.

89. "In order to become physically dependent, one must consume the drug continuously over a period of time, perhaps 10 to 14 days," wrote Courtwright (1982:47-48). What H. H. Kane said about Chinese addicts in the nineteenth century was certainly true for Smith and Mason Valley Paiutes:

> What is desired is a condition of dreamy wakefulness . . . at peace with himself and all mankind, a pleasant, listless calm and contentment, with light and easily interrupted dreams. At one and the same time it puts out of sight the real and unpleasant crudities of daily life, and magnifies and elevates into view a pleasant bubble[; a] whole play of colors and misty outlines are born of the pipe alone. [H. H. Kane 1882:61]

H. H. Kane, in also emphasizing the social aspects of opium smoking, commented that he had "never seen a smoker who found pleasure in using the drug at home and alone, no matter how complete his outfit, or how excellent his opium" (1882:70).

Regarding these arrests of Chinese, George O'Neill on 20 June 1912 wrote:

> The case of Leon, the Chinaman, before Com. Fairbanks, [which] seems to have been a decided farce, will of course encourage the traffic more than ever. I can't see that the evidence could have been better. Mencacci and John Dock were there, but from what Mencacci says it was plain that they did not want to convict him. The Chinaman admitted everything, it seems, and said he had been selling it right along, but that it was medicine for the cure of the opium habit, and that the Com. decided that there could be little opium in it and that it did not amount to much anyway, so he was released. I am sorry you were not there. [Walker River Indian Agency, box 316, FY 1909-16, Official and Unofficial Correspondence, RG 75, Federal Archives, San Bruno, Calif.]

On that same date the secretary of the state board of physicians wrote from Carson City, Nevada:

> Is it not possible to prosecute certain Chinaman under the state law, for selling to the Indians of the Reservation, forms of opium, or pills containing opium, ostensibly for the cure of the opium habit, without license? If so, I will undertake to secure evidence looking to a prosecution. [Walker River Indian Agency, box 316, FY 1909-16, Official and Unofficial Correspondence, RG 75, Federal Archives, San Bruno, Calif.]

One year earlier, in fact, pressure mounted for the arrest of these Chinese opium sellers: "I have been intending for some time to ask you to send a man to me and let me post him regarding offenders who are selling liquor and opium to Indians in the vicinity of Yerington, Hawthorne and Wabuska," Treasury Agent O'Neill wrote. And in a letter to Harold F. Coggeshall, chief special officer, U.S. Indian Service, in Denver, Colorado, he stated on 11 November 1911: "Conditions are very bad. You can't depend on the local county officers. You have a representative, Mr. Henry, located here but they all know him and he can do little. Should be someone else. If your man will come right to me I will do what I can to help him" (Walker River Indian Agency, box 316, FY 1909-16, Official and Unofficial Correspondence, RG 75, Federal Archives, San Bruno, Calif.).

Indeed, a 21 March 1910 letter from Walker River Reservation superintendent Pugh to the commissioner of Indian affairs, that is, months after Corbett's removal from the Indian Boarding School in Carson City, revealed:

> When you consider the terrible havoc that opium and liquor have played with these people, especially the younger ones, the last few years, I think they have done fairly well. . . . Their advanced knowledge of civilization makes it the more easy for them to take advantage of the evils attending it, and there is plenty of opportunity at Carson City, Reno, and other nearby towns for them to secure opium and liquor, which has been the ruin of some of the best of them. . . . Out of about 9 of the male graduates from the Carson School who have returned here, 5 of them are disappointments. Chronic gamblers, lazy, drink when off the reservation, and some of them use opium, which they know better how to get, and conceal the source. [Walker River Indian Agency, box 316, FY 1909-16, Official and Unofficial Correspondence, RG 75, Federal Archives, San Bruno, Calif.]

The overall impact of opiates on Smith and Mason Valley Paiutes was such that the word *catastrophic* would not be an exaggeration. In a 27 January 1912 letter to Yerington Indian Colony gambling casino owner and shaman Tom Mitchell (cf. secs. 129, 131, 136), we read, for example:

> Supt. Asbury sent me the letter written by your friend Jack Carter, and I have been too busy to answer it before. I heard about the death of that man Johnson, but in such cases you Indians could get at the truth of such matters better than we can if you would. Some of your people know all about this and can find it out if they try hard enough, and then we can do something. I know how bad the opium and whisky business is in Mason Valley and about Sweetwater and Wabuska, and the Government has

spent lots and lots of money every year trying to stop this business, but the worst part of the matter is that your poeple [sic] won't listen to me and your other friends that are working so hard all the time to try to protect you. Your people, and especially the young people, are getting worse all the time about looking for such stuff, and just as long as they look for it they can find men who will sell it to them. The death of your [?] Johnson and also that . . . young squaw near Sweetwater was no doubt caused by either whisky or opium. And such matters are happening right along, and yet the young men and women keep on looking for whisky and opium. It is simply killing your people off just as fast as it can. I and your other friend know what is best for your poeple [sic] and are doing all we can to save you, but unless you listen to us and work with us you can not expect us to do much. I can tell you the only way that your people can get on their feet and save themselves and that is to make homes for themselves where they will have plenty to eat and work and stop looking for "boose" and opium. But just as long as they continue to spend their money gambling every time they get a few dollars, they can never get started to make a home. So you are doing wrong in allowing so much gambling there. There is a way that I can stop this opium and whisky business but it would be pretty rough and I don't like to have to do it. If you think you can help me with your people I will be glad to have a talk with you. . . . They know there is no good in it and that it is very bad for them, and that they are simply sending their money to white poeple [sic] or Chinamen for stuff that is killing them, so why don't they cut it out. [Walker River Indian Agency, box 316, FY 1909-16, Official and Unofficial Correspondence, Federal Archives, San Bruno, Calif.]

And again, the chamber of commerce of the town of Mason would alert Superintendent Hailman of the Walker River Reservation in 1924: "The Paiutes of this community are in a notoriously deplorable condition, caused by the uses of alcohol in different forms, and opiates in some matter obtained by them; it being common to witness intoxicated men, women, and children" (Reno Indian Agency, Indian Welfare, ITC Archives, Mason, Nev.). "A number of the Indians from the surrounding neighborhood are now working in the vicinity of Yerington and their money is being freely spent for liquor and narcotics," Superintendent Parrett of the Walker River Agency wrote the commissioner of Indian affairs on 23 July 1929. "The women give as much trouble as the men. . . . [The distribution of yen-shee] seems to be more active now than under general conditions" (ITC Archives). And while Rosie Brown's account of her father, Jim Davis, a.k.a. Jim George, is probably in the extreme, it nonetheless provides some idea of the catastrophic impact opiates had on Smith and Mason Valley Paiute lives:

> I was the one that stayed there to feed them [siblings]. I used to go out and work all the time. And that's all he does [opiates]. Oh, he goes out and works, alright—but don't buy nothing! Everything goes for that dope! Once in a great while he buys food, but that's all. . . . That makes it pretty hard when you got a big family, you know.
>
> He sleeps home—after he gets his dope, he's home, alright; if not, then he bothers me for money. And he'd get rough with me if I don't give him money. Bawls me out. . . . He used to be mean with everybody for money if he can't get enough money for his dope. Gets mean with his sister, his brother, me . . . so, to save my own hide, well, I'd dish out $.50. I don't gonna give him more.
>
> One time I thought we was all gonna eat good. He sells two pheasants to me and I fix 'em up. I cooked them, alright, but in the night, here my birds are gone! He stole 'em! The Old Man took 'em himself, then he sells 'em to somebody else! He got my money, alright. . . . Or, if I'd buy something from somebody else, then he'd be there. Night time, you know, when I'd go to sleep, [he'd] steal what I got. Really awful.

Also, the Lyon County Sheriff Department blotter reveals, as Corbett stated, that plenty of crimes were commited not only against local Chinese (theft and violence), but against white Smith and Mason Valley ranchers and farmers as well. The most serious incident occurred in 1927, when the Yerington Indian Colony Paiutes Ed Reymers, Andrew Penrose, Henry McCloud, Sam George, Ray Sam, Henry Johnson, and Charley Brown furtively worked for three months to chip a mile of copper from the high-power electric transmission line running from the Walker River Copper Company property to the main line of the Truckee River Power Company, filling barley sacks that they sold to junk men living nearby: "These Indians . . . made repeated trips to the line, each time stripping the same length of copper cable," according to the district attorney's narrative statement (Nevada State Prison Records and District Attorney Narratives, State Archives, Carson City, Nev.).

> In all, some fifteen hundred dollars worth of copper wire and copper cable was taken, which copper wire and cable was the property of the Truckee River Power Company and the Walker River Copper Company. These forays on the power line were made during the months of February and March of the year 1927 . . . [by] self-confessed victim[s] of yen shee. . . . The trips were made apparently when the Indians were in

need of money to purchase the needed yen shee. [*Mason Valley News*, 21 May 1927; cf. Appendix A]

And finally, though few Paiute addicts worked as steadily as Corbett (and Celia) Mack, generalizations about the inability of opiate addicts to work, such as the one made by Lindesmith (1947:36), can be challenged by these data.

90. See the "Report of Narcotic Situation among the Indians of the Walker River Jurisdiction . . ." (Appendix B) for drug prices and the average income of the Indians in this area in 1931.

"At its peak in 1880, the Chinese population numbered around 800 in Carson City, and the state capital's Chinatown stretched for five blocks. It was the largest Chinese quarter of any town or city in Nevada," wrote Loren B. Chan. "As late as 1910 and 1920, Carson City still had a Chinatown, but it was only a shadow of its former self" (L. B. Chan 1982:271, 273). Even so, Carson City's Chinatown had twelve opium dens. In the town of Mina, where Gee Jon, a member of Hop Sing Tong, in 1921 murdered seventy-four-year-old laundryman Tom Quong Kwee, nominal member of the Bing Kung Tong (reputedly the final instance of tong warfare in Nevada), Chinese entered as railroad workers when the Carson and Colorado was built through Esmeralda County in the 1880s. "At Mina, a stop on the railroad, a small Chinese community existed during the period from about 1905 down to the 1920s" (L. B. Chan 1982:294). O'Neill wrote to Anna B. Matheson, clerk for the U.S. Indian Service, on 13 December 1919:

> Conditions at Mina, Nevada have been reported to me as being very bad, but it is almost impossible to obtain evidence against a Chinaman who makes delivery of a small package of yenshee to an Indian in a darkened rambling shack with locked doors misleading in all directions without resorting to the use of a decoy. . . . It is also reported that Indians are obtaining yen shee at Carson City and Gardnerville, Nevada, and I am of the opinion that all of these towns can be covered in the time indicated. [ITC Archives]

Nonetheless, this special agent persevered, as indicated by his 21 January 1920 letter:

> On December 29th, accompanied by deputy C. R. Edison I visited the town of Mina, Nevada and on the following morning succeeded in obtaining evidence against two Chinamen named Charlie Lee Tung and Ham Nun Tung, the latter named clestial [*sic*] furnishing bond in the sum of one thousand dollars for his appearance at the next term of the Federal Court at Carson City, Nevada. [ITC Archives]

Free transportation on the Carson and Colorado derived from a 21 November 1892 agreement with the Walker River Reservation, allowing its Paiute inhabitants, along with fish, game, and other products, to travel at no cost to and from all points on tracks operated by this line, provided only reservation right-of-way remained (Johnson 1975). Although this allowed cheap labor supplies among California hop growers (cf. Jorgensen 1971), enterprising Paiutes took advantage of the agreement as opiate dealers. "For some reason, the Indians have been getting passes to Mina more than usual and I am suspicious that there is a reason"; G. A. Trotter, superintendent of the Walker River Reservation, would write George O'Neill on 20 November 1924 (Nevada Indian Agency, box 116, Law Enforcement Agency, George O'Neill, Special Officer, RG 75, Federal Archives, San Bruno, Calif.). And when Yerington's field matron, Etta J. Shipley, wrote Trotter's predecessor, Horace Johnson, on 15 August 1922 about Mason Valley Indians requesting such passes, she was told on 21 August 1922, "No Indians except those on the Walker River reservation roll are entitled to passes" (Walker River Agency, box 303, Correspondence for 1922 and 1923, RG 75, Federal Archives, San Bruno, Calif.). Not surprisingly, Paiute opiate addicts and sellers were eventually blacklisted, for example, Adam Dixon in 1918 and Henry Greely, who on 26 September 1922 was said to want "a pass from Mound House [to] return in 6 days" (Walker River Agency, box 302, Official and Unofficial Correspondence, RG 75, Federal Archives, San Bruno, Calif.). Indeed, as early as 23 December 1911 a letter to the Walker River Reservation superintendent (Asbury) recognizes this point:

> But the manipulation of the pass business has been the most effective. Now I will give you a few individual cases:-This Johnny Hall is among the worst. He is constantly under the influence of either liquor or opium and has made considerable trouble at Yerington for other Indians by furnishing booze to their wives &c. He knows better than to ask me for a pass. [Walker River Indian Agency, box 316, FY 1909-16, Official and Unofficial Correspondence, RG 75, Federal Archives, San Bruno, Calif.]

In another letter, this one from Pugh on 30 March 1912, we learn: "You will readily see what an effective means I can make of the regulation of the pass privilige [sic] to curb drunkenness, opium fiends, gad-abouts, and inveterate gambling" (Walker River Indian Agency, box 316, FY 1909-16, Official and Unofficial Correspondence, RG 75, Federal Archives, San Bruno, Calif.).

Crimes against local Chinese include the 24 May 1913 murder of Kong Wan, the 31 May 1913 killing of Yee Young in Mason, the beating of Charley Wye of Mason on 22 July 1922, and the killing of Ah Kong of Carson City on 6 January 1923 (cf. Appendix A). A case involving the aforementioned Jim Davis, imprisoned on five separate occasions (5-8 years for manslaughter on 9 July 1913, 2-5 years for burglary on 30 August 1920, 2-5 years for burglary on 28 April 1924, 1-5 years for burglary in 1927, and 1-5 years on 3 February 1931 for burglary), is instructive: "[These] Indians [Davis and Little Johnny Walters] killed a Chinaman who had been selling Yen shee at Mason, this County," or so we read in a parole letter from Davis's prison file in 1916, and "The evidence tends to show that Johnny choked the dead man to death while Jim remained outside the door of the cabin where the Chinaman carried on business." Then on 31 January 1931 Davis "was apprehended in the act of taking a sack of flour out of the Warehouse owned by Fabri and Company, Yerington, Nevada. Defendant undoubtedly a narcotic addict and [was] stealing flour to purchase morphine" (Nevada State Prison Records and District Attorney Narratives, State Archives, Carson City, Nev.).

The following anecdote by Howard Rogers might well represent how opiates permeated the fabric of Smith and Mason Valley Paiute life during these years:

> I was taken to Stewart by my uncle [Henry Dick] and Andy [Dick, stepfather]. We left by wagon to Minden and took the motor car. But I ran away after two days. Hit the rails. . . . My partner was Lee Pete, from Sweetwater. He got caught in the tracks and almost lost his leg. We went to Minden because my stepdad and uncle were a bunch of hopheads—went to where they put up their horses in the livery stable and took 'em and went home. Left Andy and Henry there stranded! They were sure mad at us!

91. "October 25th, I operated at Mina and spent the day observing a Mexican named Nicolas Palmo, and a Japanese known as Jap Joe, both being suspected of furnishing Indians with intoxicating liquor and yenshee," George O'Neill wrote Superintendent James E. Jenkins of the Walker River Reservation on 27 October 1924. "The Japanese is employed as section foreman for the Southern Pacific R.R., at a point 9 miles south of Mina, and is said to make weekly visits to Mina either on Saturday or Sunday for the purpose of peddling to the Indians" (Reno Indian Agency, box 116, Law Enforcement Program, Correspondence from Indian Prisoners to Police Report, RG 75,

Federal Archives, San Bruno, Calif.). In an earlier letter O'Neill wrote: "I would like your advice on the following matter: Two Japanese and a Chinaman are living with Paiute women at Wabuska. I recently saw one of the Japs and informed him that it would be necessary for him to marry the woman legally if he wished to live with her, and likewise the other Jap. He expressed his willingness to do so and I thought the other would be" (Walker River Indian Agency, box 316, FY 1909-16, Official and Unofficial Correspondence, RG 75, Federal Archives, San Bruno, Calif.).

Joe Yama, according to the *Mason Valley News* (14 July 1923), was arrested in 1923, after four law officers visited his grocery store adjoining the Yerington Indian Colony. They reportedly found an ounce of yen-shee in a can in the toilet, one can containing twenty-nine bindles on the back porch, and forty-one additional bindles hidden in the store. After the raid Yerington Indian Colony homes were "inspected," and several opium pipes, no drugs, were found. The *Yerington Times* (11 July 1923) added that Yama admitted to selling opium to Indians who worked at his ranch in Wabuska. He said that he had purchased the store "two months ago," when he began selling drugs: "Yama stated that he started giving drugs to Indians in order to secure necessary help to harvest his crops, later enlarging the scope of his operations." Etta J. Shipley, Yerington's field matron, commented about this individual: "The Jap [Joe Yama] is doing a wholesale business with dope and if an officer would get in there during the night they would find Indians there. The Indians are surely not to blame for their crimes and I would like to see every Chinaman deported" (Walker River Agency, box 303, Correspondence for 1922 and 1923, RG 75, Federal Archives, San Bruno, Calif.). Moreover, Special Officer O'Neill on 24 November 1924 wrote about an Indian who bought whiskey from "Jap Joe [Yama?]" with marked money for four dollars (Nevada Indian Agency, box 116, Law Enforcement Agency, George O'Neill, Special Officer, Suppression of Liquor Traffic, RG 75, Federal Archives, San Bruno, Calif.).

In the 1910 federal census (U.S. Bureau of the Census 1880-1920) seventeen Japanese were listed as "hired men" in the Wabuska Precinct of Lyon County. The 1920 census data for Nevada (U.S. Bureau of the Census 1880-1920) list the following Japanese in Smith and Mason valleys: Ben Fukushima (37), prospector; M. Watanabe (29), waiter; Sam Kikumote (?), prospector.

D. O. Komoto in the 1920 Lyon County tax lists was assessed at $2,065, and Joe N. Yokoyama at $2,029. In 1921 Y. Kimura was assessed at $2,386,

Tom Kuranishi at $1,275, Jake Sikora at $1,744, and Joe Yama at $2,624. Yama and Kimura in 1923 were assessed together at $1,600, Yamacuchi and Yama at $1,090 and $450, respectively. And in 1926 Joe Yokoyama, the only Japanese listed, was assessed at $2,120 (Lyon County Library, vertical files, Yerington, Nev.).

I count only one Paiute offspring sired by a Japanese in my genealogies.

Hattie Bennett, according to a 26 March 1917 letter from the Walker River Reservation superintendent to James B. Royce, superintendent of the Carson School, was said to be "suffering from the effects of an abortion caused by herself and a Jap last December" (Walker River Agency, box 302, Official and Unofficial Correspondence, Health, Hospitals, Sanitoriums, etc., 1917, RG 75, Federal Archives, San Bruno, Calif.). Treated by Dr. Knox, the local contract physician, she was described by this source as mad and committed to Sparks Asylum.

92. According to the Lyon County Sheriff Department Arrest Book (Lyon County Courthouse, Yerington, Nev.), the following local Chinese were arrested between 1912 and 1928 for sale of opiates to Paiutes: Leon Kingston, Charley Wye, Ah Tim, Ah Bo, Charles Lee Tong, Sing Lee, Ho On, Ben Hon, Wong Jake, Wong Shew, Jim Sing, and Mrs. and Mrs. Lew Soon. Superintendent Jenkins of the Walker River Agency discussed this situation in a 6 April 1920 letter to the commissioner of Indian affairs:

> Some months ago I advised the Office of the arrest and conviction of a Chinaman, one Ah Bo, for selling "yen shee," an opium derivative to Indians near Yerington. . . . Last week I was called to Carson as a special witness in the Charlie Wye case, having assisted Special Officer O'Neill in searching the Chinese quarters at Mason last September 21st. . . . Wye was found guilty and sentenced to serve 13 months in the penitentiary and to pay a fine of $300. There were six other cases of the same character, all found guilty and assessed fines of about $125 and costs. In the case against Wye, five or six Indians, who belong to our Yerington Colony, testified that they could buy yen shee without difficulty, that they bought it many times of [sic] Charlie Wye, etc., etc. . . . But it seems that the protection of these dirty Chinamen is more to be desired than the protection of our Indians from this demoralizing traffic. [ITC Archives]

I record three Paiute-Chinese domestic unions in my genealogies.

As early as February of 1877 the Nevada legislature passed acts to regulate the sale or disposal of opium and to prohibit places of resort for smoking opium and the possession of opium pipes (Nevada Statutes, 1877, chap. 27, secs. 1-4). These resulted in thirteen Chinese being sent to Nevada State Prison between 1877 and 1904 ("Biannual Report of the Warden of the State Prison, 1901-1902," *Appendix to Journals of Senate and Assembly, 1903*, Legislature of the State of Nevada, 21st sess., Carson City, Nev.). Two of the famous early cases involved Ching Gang, a Chinese doctor, who was arrested by an undercover agent in January of 1881 while pretending to be ill, and Ah Chew, also convicted for the unlawful sale of opium in that same year. Both Magnaghi (1981:141) and Elmer Ruscoe (n.d.) evaluated state laws against opium and the arrests of Chinese.

"Low has done his share of poisoning and his death will give little in regret," a 20 April 1928 article in the *Carson City Appeal* stated. "The dope-stricken Indians are about as usual as the hound dogs that follow their camps."

Gus Brann or Bran, a Paiute, after he was released from prison for the murder of Ah Quong on 1 June 1930, committed suicide in his cabin at the Yerington Indian Colony by cutting his jugular vein and gashing both arms. Brann's blood-spattered message on the wall was for Dennis Bender, grandson of Jack Wilson and the Yerington Paiute Tribe's first chairman, to "make arrangements for disposal of my furniture!" "Hemorrhage due to self-inflicted wounds with pocket knife," the newspaper wrote about the Lyon County coroner's report (*Mason Valley News*, 3 March 1939).

93. Mr. and Mrs. Ralph Hall, who purchased Austin's grocery store in 1928-29, told me that one Mason Valley Italian would routinely smuggle morphine in a truckload of watermelons. A 12 February 1916 letter about Hawthorne from C. H. Asbury to Jesse Flanders of Reno mentioned not only liquor illegally brought in by the mail and by freight truck from Schurz, but also "a butcher running on that [train] line who peddles dope all along the line and had some customers among the Indians."

Ray Sam and Willy Wallace were arrested for narcotics in 1929.

94. See section 9 about William S. Douglass.

95. Superintendent Parrett of the Walker River Reservation discussed the "dope traffic" in a 7 February 1921 letter to the Honorable John H. Miller, State Senate, Carson City: "The drug most commonly sold these Indians is known as 'yen shee' and is said to be largely introduced by Chinamen, although some Indians are known to be engaged in passing the stuff around," (ITC Archives). Lamenting difficulties in arresting opiate sellers, Superintendent James Jenkins of this reservation in a 4 January 1934 letter to John Collier, commissioner of Indian affairs, noted that "direct sales were handled by Chinese and mixed-blood Indians" (ITC Archives). Dr. Rees wrote: "Some of the Indians here who peddle the drug, make regular trips out of the State by automobile, buy a quantity of same, bring it in and peddle it out to those who use it. It is used to such an extent that as fast as one peddler is caught, another takes his place" (3 August 1928 letter to M. C. Guthrie, ITC Archives). And similarly, Congressman Arentz stated:

> It would be well to understand that on a number of occasions I have called attention to the fact that Coleville, Calif. is a center for distribution of dope in the Smith Valley. People have seen it often. In previous years there was a car that would stop in different sections of the valley and the Indian would come from the different directions to meet it. It would not stop in the same place, but there is only one place it can come from, and that is Coleville, into Smith Valley. . . . That car goes over one pass and it is always the same car and unquestionably can be caught if they [agents] will merely send a stranger in there. It is the most terrible thing that can be dispensed to people. It not only makes them slaves to the drug but kills them eventually. It is worse than death. [U.S. Senate Committee on Indian Affairs, *Survey of Conditions of the Indians in the U.S.: Hearing before the Committee on Indian Affairs,* part 21, 71st Cong., 3d sess., 26 May 1931, 11532]

The following information on Indian drug sellers was culled from the Federal Archives, San Bruno, California (Nevada Indian Agency, Law Enforcement Agency, box 116, George O'Neill, Special Officer, Suppression of Liquor Traffic, RG 75):

1. George Orange, "[who is] employed at the Fulstone ranch, was engaged in selling Yenshee to other Indians," wrote Special Inspector O'Neill on 20 October 1924, in reporting his investigation of "blind pigs" (soft-drink parlors in Mason), as well as the Mason Hotel and Tavern and Martin's Pool Hall in Wellington, Smith Valley, where bootlegging and opiate sales were suspected. On 15 December 1924, O'Neill noted that he left Schurz for Wellington at 8:00 A.M., in his unsuccessful attempt to "locate George Orange, an Indian who is strongly suspected of peddling yenshee." On 7 July 1925, however, O'Neill reported the arrest of George Orange for violation of the Harrison Narcotics Act. Orange pleaded not guilty on 6 April 1925 but was convicted by jury in federal court in Carson City on 5 June 1925; he was fined $100 and sent to Leavenworth for one year and one day.

2. Sullivan Tom. A letter from G. A. Trotter, superintendent of the Walker River Indian Agency, to Special Inspector O'Neill in 1924 noted Yerington field matron Clara Rees's suspicion that "Sullivan Tom was selling

dope at the Yerington Colony . . . [and] Dave Bobb is now away for a load of the stuff . . . [probably] in California for the dope." O'Neill reported on 2 August 1924 that during one surveillance he was unable to catch "an Indian named Sullivan Tom . . . [rumored to be] engaged in selling dope to other Indians in the Walker River Reservation." "I overtook a suspected peddler of Yenshee, named Sullivan Tom and though I searched his person and his car thoroughly I failed to find anything by way of dope or liquor," he also wrote on 20 October 1924. "The Indian had in possession a large amount of money, but was unable to state just how he earned it and since [he] has performed little or no work for more than one year I believe it is safe to say that he did not acquire the money legally." And on 24 November 1924 O'Neill, operating out of Reno, wrote: "November 18th I left Schurz at 9:30 A.M. for Carson City and spent several hours investigating conditions at Wellington where it is reported an Indian named, Sullivan Tom, is in the habit of transporting and peddling Yenshee to other Indians."

3. Charley Brown. "Indians here are using more than usual lately and [Indian informant Shaw] thinks that if the tents over around the gambling hall were raided or if someone would drop in at a tent used by Henry Benjamin, Jim McMasters and a couple of Indians by the name of Brown that a supply could be found" (Reno Indian Agency, Law Enforcement Agency, box 116, George O'Neill, Special Officer, Suppression of Liquor Traffic, RG 75, Federal Archives, San Bruno, Calif.).

Turning now to the importance of the automobile in Paiute opiate sales and addiction: "The conditions which exist with respect to the young people and returned students is deplorable. By means of the automobile these young people can reach practically any location." So we read in a 17 August 1928 letter from Walker River Agency superintendent Parrett (ITC Archives). Note 99 contains a list of opiate sellers who owned automobiles.

Few arrests of Indians for opiate addiction were made prior to passage of the Harrison Narcotics Act of 1914, which was primarily a revenue tax, according to Courtwright, "not a prohibition statute per se . . . [it] merely required physicians, pharmacists, and certain other persons who dealt in narcotics to register with the U.S. Department of the Treasury, pay a nominal tax, and keep records of the narcotic drugs they dispensed" (1982:1). Paiute arrests would also have been limited prior to 1914 because Indians were not permitted to patronize opium dens (cf. Courtwright 1982:78-82). The first national anti-opium law was passed on 9 February 1909, banning "all importations of the drug . . . [with] fines ($50 to $5,000) and imprisonment (up to 2 years), and [which] stipulated that mere possession of smoking opium was sufficient to warrant conviction 'unless the defendant shall explain the possession to the satisfaction of the jury'" (Courtwright 1982:83). This law obviously little impeded Smith and Mason Valley Paiutes from obtaining opiates. The Harrison Narcotics Act was slow-working, insofar as only 175 enforcement agents were assigned to the newly organized Narcotics Division within the Treasury Department in 1920. Additional national legislation included the Narcotic Drugs Import and Export Act of 1922, which permitted the federal government to monitor movements of legitimate narcotics and check on the illicit traffic, and a 1924 act by which Congress forbade the importation of opium for manufacture of heroin (Morgan 1981:118-19).

Bureacracy also impeded law enforcement. "It occurs to me that the Office is in error in this respect," wrote George O'Neill, for example, arguing that officers in his employ be permitted to pursue "dope to the Indians" cases:

> Your attention is called to the Indian Appropriation Act approved May 24, 1922, Pub. No. 224, page 10, in which it specifically states under the heading "Suppressing Liquor Traffic:" "For the suppression of the traffic in intoxicating liquors *and deleterious drugs among Indians*, $30,000." [Reno Agency, box 311, Liquor Matters 1916, 1917, 1918 and 1922-23, 1924-25, RG 75, Federal Archives, San Bruno, Calif.]

Finally, Irene Thompson told me she accompanied her uncle Jimmy Summers to Placerville once to purchase opiates that were hidden in his daughter's cradleboard during the return trip home.

96. Corbett also stated: "Sullivan Tom, he want me to sell for him. 'Cause you see why? Grover's doin' [so] well. But I won't do that. No, sir! 'Cause I say to him, 'Not enough profit, Sullivan!'" Elsewhere he remarked: "'Cause the rest them sellers, they see how much I'm makin'. And fast, too! So, they start up."

97. "To-day am sending you Willie Muldoon, aged 9 years. You will find him a very bright boy," Walker River Reservation superintendent Pugh wrote Carson Indian superintendent Asbury on 19 November 1910 (Walker River Indian Agency, box 315, Press Copy Books from Farmer Pugh to Asbury, RG 75, Federal Archives, San Bruno, Calif.). Muldoon suffered from bronchitis (9 November 1909, 11 January, 17 January, 22 January, 29 January, and 15 February 1910). This boarding school student also had battles with eczema pustular on 19 December, 21 December, and 29 December 1909 and 1 January 1910, as well as an abrasion of the ankle a few days later (Walker River Indian Agency, compartment 2167, Health and Sanitary Records, bound vol. 1, 1897-1910, RG 75, Federal Archives, San Bruno, Calif.). Carson Indian School superintendent Jesse Mortsolf, in yet another medical report of Willy Muldoon's boyhood, wrote Walker River Reservation superintendent Pugh on 13 March 1913:

> The doctor thinks now that the limb can be saved, although it will probably be an inch shorter than the other. The bone was broken in such a way that there is not enough periosteum at the end to allow it to unite, and the probability is that the end will have to be sawed off. His brother is here, and Willie is very cheerful. [ITC Archives]

Mortsolf, on 16 March 1913, would also write that the rumor of Willy Muldoon's death was so convincing, he gave Muldoon's train pass away to Corbett Williams, said to be a brother (Walker River Indian Agency, box 316, FY 1909-16, Official and Unofficial Correspondence, RG 75, Federal Archives, San Bruno, Calif.).

Irene Thompson thought Willy Muldoon was the oldest of four siblings, only two of whom were full-bloods, and that their parents were from Hawthorne, Nevada. Willy's brother Ed Muldoon received a ranch assignment on Campbell Ranch in 1937; his sister Myra Muldoon joined the WAC during World War II; she married a doctor and left the area; his brother Jimmy Muldoon moved to Oregon, while Willy himself "lived in a nice house in Carson City after he got out of prison. He worked as a mechanic in the garage he owns thanks to his Washo wife Ida's money," according to Thompson. She also suspected that Willy Muldoon's father was Japanese.

Regarding the grocery store near the Yerington Indian Colony that was owned by Muldoon, an article in *Reflections 1990*, an annual publication of the *Mason Valley News*, entitled "'Modern' Era for Mason & Smith Valley Indians Actually Began in 1930s," reported: "There was also a store located on the corner of the property, originally owned by Bovard but with several others operating it in early years; some owners allegedly using it as a front to sell drugs to the Indians."

Finally, when Stewart Institute's superintendent was interrogated by Nevada's congressman Samuel Arentz on 26 May 1931 about opiate addiction at the Yerington Indian Colony—"How prevalent is the use of narcotics here?"—he responded: "Among our Indians we do not find it so bad, but among the Yerington Indians it is pretty bad. . . . It is not very bad here [Reno]" (U.S. Senate Committee on Indian Affairs, *Survey of Conditions of the Indians in the U.S.: Hearing before the Committee on Indian Affairs*, part 21, 71st Cong., 3d sess., 26 May 1931, 11495).

98. The mining town of Ludwig, which had 750 residents and 65 buildings at its peak, was named after the German immigrant John D. Ludwig, who discovered its copper vein in the Singatse Mountains in September of 1911. High-grade ore almost impossible to drill was shipped to the local smelter at Thompson. The Ludwig quarry also produced 96-98 percent pure gypsum *(Reflections 1990*, annual publication of the *Mason Valley News)*. Thirty claims were made during this copper boom, which ended in 1923 when prices fell. The agricultural community of Artemisia in Smith Valley, originating in 1907, shipped food to Ludwig and surrounding mining towns (Kersten 1961:100, 142-57).

99. Walter Cox, former owner of the *Mason Valley News*, recalled in 1988 for its annual publication *Reflections* that the best time for a trip from Reno to Yerington in the early "horseless carriage" was five hours and twenty-eight minutes. The Lyon County tax list allows us to determine how many Paiute opiate sellers owned automobiles: James Keno (1920 Ford), Jerry Keno (1917 Ford), Mike Rube (1924 Chevy), and James Summers (1927 Chevy) (Lyon County Library, vertical files, Yerington, Nev.).

100. Andy Dick, according to his son Russell, served nine months in federal prison in Reno in 1923 for turning a one-dollar bill into a ten-dollar bill with pen and india ink—to purchase opiates. Treasury agents, of course, would rely on the likes of suffering Paiutes such as Ray Sam and Henry McCloud as part of a "elaborate network of stool pigeons and spies," nor were they "above using entrapment and legal harassment, or threatening to file indictments, or offering to drop shaky charges to keep suspected doctors and users in line" (Morgan 1981:121).

"Referring to letter to you by Supt. Trotter, of Schurz, dated 20th instant," Reno Indian Agency superintendent James E. Jenkins wrote George O'Neill on 9 June 1924 about "conditions around Mina, Schurz, Yerington, Wellington and intermediate points in Mason and Smith Valleys." He advised, "You are therefore directed to proceed to that territory as soon as possible, confer with Supt. Trotter and take ample time to cover all details of the situation" (Reno Indian Agency, box 116, Law Enforcement Program Correspondence from Indian Prisoners to Police Report, RG 75, Federal Archives, San Bruno, Calif.). O'Neill was given a Durham Chevrolet after pursuing Reno bootleggers for many years in an old Ford.

Regarding Andrew Vidovich, whom Corbett obviously disliked, I interviewed him in 1968 about his father-in-law, Jack Wilson, 1890 Ghost Dance prophet, regrettably not about opiates (Hittman 1990). On 13 December 1934 a letter of support from Superintendent Parrett stated that Vidovich was formerly employed by Public Works on Walker River Reservation and Fallon Indian Reservation roads before being shifted to narcotics:

> In maintaining such conditions where, Mr. Vidovich has apprehended bootleggers and violators of law in the surrounding towns of Fallon, Yerington, Wellington, Hawthorne, and Mina, in addition to general patrol of the reservations and Indian colonies located both at Yerington and Fallon . . . [ITC Archives]

Parrett thus praised his importance, urging that he be paid from the Emergency Conservation Fund in order to continue law enforcement work in narcotics. Fellow narcotics investigator Mueller, on the other hand, wrote on 7 March 1935 that James Vidovich of Carson City was the superior officer (ITC Archives). In the testimony before the Senate Committee on Indian Affairs, the charge against George O'Neill, for example, was that he was "too independent" and had developed the attitude after so many years of: "I am sleeping, let them drink" (U.S. Senate Committee on Indian Affairs, *Survey of Conditions of the Indians in the U.S.: Hearing before the Committee on Indian Affairs*, part 21, 71st Cong., 3d sess., 26 May 1931, 11558).

101. On the prison interview form of Henry Quinn, he lists "Big Mack of Wellington, Nevada" as his nearest adult relative. Billy Miller, charged at age 26 with "assault with intent" after accidentally shooting his sister-in-law during a quarrel with his wife, was referred to in this same source as follows: "The sheriff found Miller at the Yerington Indian Camp, in the place of business of one Willie Muldoon, an Indian, who runs a grocery store in the camp" (Nevada State Prison Records and District Attorney Narratives, State Archives, Carson City, Nev.).

"Muldoon is the reputed brains of the dope runners who are supplying the Piutes with yen shee in this region," we also read in the Nevada State Prison records. Arrested on 25 February 1928 with the charge of "possession of narcotic drugs, in a quantity over one ounce, for the purpose of sales," Muldoon was said to have been "for several years one of the largest sellers of narcotic drugs in this community. I think him one of the most vicious men sentenced in this Court in the past two years," the district attorney inserted in his prison file. Remarkably, Willy Muldoon pled not guilty (Nevada State Prison Records and District Attorney Narratives, State Archives, Carson City, Nev.).

A letter from Stewart Institute superintendent Frederic Snyder in 1932 in behalf of Willy Muldoon's early prison release stated: "I recommend leniency in his case and I trust the Board will grant him a parole in view of his good behavior in the institution." O'Neill, incidentally, had been after Willy Muldoon since 1925. For example, he wrote the commissioner of Indian affairs on 7 July 1925: "July 2nd I left Reno at 9:15 A.M. for Carson City, Nevada arriving an hour and a half later to investigate a report that an Indian named Willie Muldoon was making trips by automobile from Yerington to Carson City for the purpose of transporting both intoxicating liquor and yenshee." Muldoon, however, was not in town, so the following day O'Neill continued to operate at Chinatown, "where there are several Chinamen who are strongly suspected of selling yenshee to Indians." After this O'Neill wrote how he made other abortive efforts "to learn the whereabouts of Muldoon, the suspected half breed peddler" (Reno Indian Agency, box 116, Law Enforcement Agency, George O'Neill, Special Officer, RG 75, Federal Archives, San Bruno, Calif.).

102. Regrettably, in the oral history of Clark Guild, the state supreme court judge who tried most Paiutes for opiates, there is nothing about narcotics. All the same, Judge Guild was praised in an editorial in the 3 April 1928 edition of the *Reno Evening Gazette* for his involvement in "narcotic control," which the editor called the "curse of the Indian race in this state."

103. Dr. John T. Rees testified as Yerington Indian Colony contract physician before Senator Lynn J. Frazier as follows:

> In the year 1924 I took the position as physician for the Walker River Indian Agency. I found at that time that I entered Yerington that the narcotic principally used was yen-shee, and that was used by the Indians hypodermically. Therefore there was blood poisoning and several deaths from the use of this yen-shee. [U.S. Senate Committee on Indian Affairs, *Survey of Conditions of the Indians in the U.S.: Hearing before the Committee on Indian Affairs,* part 21, 71st Cong., 3d sess., 26 May 1931, 11552]

And in the aforementioned 3 August 1928 letter to M. C. Guthrie, chief medical director, Washington, D.C., Rees observed: "These Indians make a tea out of it, and [use it] by the improvised method of a hypodermic needle on the end of medicine dropper . . . [and they] inject the solution into their arms or legs" (ITC Archives).

Regarding Emory Dick, Yerington Indian Colony field matron Etta J. Shipley reported for the week ending 7 October 1922 that she was forced to move his sick child "uptown," inasmuch as there was no suitable place at the Indian camp, and that Emory Dick had another residence, on an East Walker

River ranch (Walker River Agency, box 303b, Correspondence for 1922 and 1923, RG 75, Federal Archives, San Bruno, Calif.).

104. A letter to C. H. Asbury mentions Albert [Elbert] Coffin's being refunded three dollars on 4 February 1916 for the poll tax collected from Indians working as section men on the railroad company (ITC Archives). George O'Neill apparently also gave notice of this individual: "I operated at Carson City during the afternoon [of 19 November 1924] and was engaged for some time in making efforts to obtain evidence against an Indian named Albert Coffin, who is strongly suspected of conducting an opium den in his home near China town" (Nevada Indian Agency, box 116, Law Enforcement Agency, George O'Neill, Special Officer, Suppression of Liquor Traffic, RG 75, Federal Archives, San Bruno, Calif.).

Could Corbett in section 103 mean that Emory Dick was the first Northern Paiute to teach *him* to shoot yen-shee? In any event, the hypodermic needle, first brought to America in 1856, was developed so as to avoid "the unpleasant gastric side effects of opiates administered orally. . . . [It] produced stronger feelings of relief and euphoria . . . [more] quickly" (Courtwright 1982:47). Indeed, Morgan (1981:22) characterized it as "the greatest boon among the new therapeutic agents." He wrote that in less than a generation it took the world's medical profession by such storm "that by the 1880s, when drug addiction was a national concern, one editor would warn that every doctor 'carries his hypodermic syringe, ready, like a pocket pistol, to repel the attacks of disease'" (Morgan 1981:25). Courtwright likened it to a "magic wand"(1982:47).

Among Smith or Mason Valley Paiutes, there is no evidence for the "bad to worse" scale drawn by H. H. Kane (1882:139), a status ranking of addicts from those who used morphine by hypodermic injection to those who took it orally or anally, to those who smoked opium. Similarly, the nineteenth-century attitude among opium smokers who felt superior to morphine addicts (Morgan 1981:37) does not apply to Smith and Mason Valley Paiutes; Morgan's generalization that nineteenth-century opium users felt superior to alcohol users, however, seems to hold.

Morgan (1981:26), finally, wrote that mainlining did not become popular until well into the twentieth century, a habit of drug abuse about which Courtwright reminds us: "Sepsis of every imaginable variety, hepatitis, endocarditis, embolisms, tetanus, overdose, and early death, were the consequences of the needle, and no small part of the damage done" (1982:112).

105. H. H. Kane commented, "The injector of morphia or the taker of opium inserts his dose or swallows his bolus and there the matter ends, but the opium smoker spends hours in the tedious cooking and preparing of the *tsanlu* for the bowl" (1882:132).

106. During another interview Corbett said Jerry Keno might have been the first Paiute to inject morphine. He also thought Keno's father James (cf. sec. 101) was "First one showin' everyone around here how to use that kind! Yes, sir! First one to bring that white stuff into these valley!"

Dr. Rees, in any event, wrote in 1928:

> It has only been within the last two years that they have begun the use of Morphine. From what we can understand this is procured from Chinamen. It is mixed with some other ingredient. The younger generation are following in their footsteps. We now have about 14 Indians in the State Prison serving terms who have used Morphine and Yen-she. They have been there one year, and we have reason to believe that [they] are cured of this habit, but when they are released it will be a hard matter for them to resist the temptation again. [ITC Archives]

John Ross, Yerington's district attorney, also wrote on 7 August 1928 that morphine had recently become "more popular with Indians of this community than yen shee." Ross, incidentally, estimated that "90% of all the Indians in Lyon County are drug addicts," a figure he estimated as 1,200-1,400, worrying that "in a matter of a few years . . . this habit will entirely dominate the Indian population of this county" (ITC Archives).

"'Yen shee' seems to be more active now than under general conditions," Superintendent Parrett on 23 July 1929 characterized the liquor and narcotic situation at the Yerington Indian Colony, relating how Indian men who worked in the vicinity spent their money "freely" [*sic!*] for both; how the women gave as much trouble as the men; and how in general they "seem to obtain liquor with very little difficulty" (ITC Archives). "They also smoke it," Dr. Rees wrote in the 3 August 1928 report quoted above: "At least 75% of these Indians are using both Yen-she and Morphine" (ITC Archives).

A 16 February 1934 letter from Agent Edmunds to Indian Commissioner Collier suggests that whites might have been the primary sellers of morphine:

> At Mina, Nevada, agent finds that Dollie O'Niel sells some narcotics among the whites. At Fallon, Nevada, agent finds that Eva Coffee and Blackie Denver deal in narcotics among the whites. At Austin, Nevada, Dr. Dillenger sells among the whites and at Battle Mountain, Guy Mitchell is more or less in the wholesale business and takes care of the east part of the state and hauls some to Butte, Montana. Dollie O'Niel,

Eva Coffee, Blackie Denver and Guy Mitchell are more or less in together dealing in Narcotics. Agent was informed that most of the narcotics were coming from Las Vegas. [ITC Archives]

In any event, morphine, whose addiction was called the "Army [i.e., Civil War] disease," was opium's principal alkaloid, isolated in 1817 (Courtwright 1982:54, 45). Named after Morpheus, the Greek god of sleep, the advantages of this narcotic were immediately apparent to addicts: reduction of nausea, fewer headaches, no stomach irritation (Morgan 1981:12). H. H. Kane, on the other hand, wrote earlier that "while the sleep following the smoking [of opium] was calm and perfectly free from dreams, that following the taking of morphia was filled with horrible phantasmagoria." Since morphine "was one of the first substances injected beneath the skin . . . [it] became popular after it was packaged in bottles and then ampules for hypodermic use" (1882:51, 12).

Regarding morphine, Lester Hilp recalled:

When they would need morphine, for twenty-five cents they could buy two cubes of morphine. A cube of morphine was about a half a dram. Just about thirty grains. That thirty grains would last them a day or two, unless they were pretty hard on it. We used to sell it, in the early times when I first went to work in the drugstore in 1909. [1968:31]

"I think at the time we used to pay about thirty-five, forty cents an ounce for it," the Reno and Yerington pharmacist further recalled (Hilp 1968:33).

107. Here, too, Corbett was confused, crediting both Jimmy Summers and Jerry Keno with selling morphine first. Special Agent O'Neill, in any event, wrote about the latter on 8 December 1924:

I left Carson City at 10:15 A.M., arriving at Wellington Nevada at 1:15 P.M. en route to Yerington. Some time was spent at Wellington endeavoring to obtain evidence against a suspected dope peddler named Jerry Keno, but I was unable to secure the services of a posseman and failed to note any violations of the law. [Reno Indian Agency, box 116, Law Enforcement Agency, George O'Neill, Special Officer, RG 75, Federal Archives, San Bruno, Calif.]

Billy Schurz

was sentenced on 15 August 1928 to not less than five years in the Nevada State Prison by Judge Hawkins of Winnemucca on Wednesday. . . . [Born in 1871, Schurz was] arrested some time ago when officers raided his cabin and seized the most complete dope layout ever seen in the county. The cabin was equipped with everything from an opium pipe to cocaine. [ITC Archives]

We also read in an oft-cited 3 August 1928 letter from Dr. Rees that "an Indian, Billy Schurz, was caught peddling who had the most complete outfit of Opium pipes, Hypo-dermic needles, medicine droppers and Morphine and Yen-she which was ever found in anyone's possession" (ITC Archives).

George Sam, age fifty, was sentenced on 20 October 1928 for five to six years and paroled on 27 May 1932. From the narrative statement by District Attorney Ross:

> The defendant, so far as can be ascertained, was engaged in his first venture of selling narcotics. He had purchased ten bindles from a squaw for one dollar a bindle, and when arrested was busily working at disposing of the said ten bindles, at the original price of one dollar per bindle. So far as figures are to be relied on his business appeared to be non-profit sharing. However, since defendant insisted that it was his first venture in selling, one can presume that experience was sought rather than material gain. [Nevada State Prison Records, State Archives, Carson City, Nev.]

108. In reply to Senator Frazier's question about narcotics in Nevada, Hank Pete, Washo, testified in 1931 that "one Washoe [was] in the penitentiary for a narcotic peddler . . . [and there] were some narcotic users among the Washoe Indians, but they all died off" (U.S. Senate Committee on Indian Affairs, *Survey of Conditions of the Indians in the U.S.: Hearing before the Committee on Indian Affairs*, part 21, 71st Cong., 3d sess., 4 November 1931, 15162–63).

Andy Dick, as stated, was arrested for forgery in 1923.

109. According to Lindesmith, "Apparently drug addicts in all countries show a strong tendency to relapse" (1947:50).

Doud Wallace was also sentenced on 10 October 1930 from five to five and one-half years for "making sales of morphine in the Indian camp, adjacent to the City of Yerington" (Nevada State Prison Records and District Attorney Narratives, State Archives, Carson City, Nevada).

110. Morgan described the symptoms of withdrawal:

> The first stages of withdrawal from opiates produced symptoms that were both physically painful and emotionally exhausting. The patient experienced copious discharges from the mucous membranes, vomiting, and diarrhea. This reduced him to an infantile condition, which heightened his sense of degradation and helplessness. There was sharp pain in the muscles, often seeming to make the bones ache, spasms, and a

general sense of aching throughout the body. The skin usually became hypersensitive. The prick of a needle might feel like impalement, or crucifixion. . . . The craving for relief with morphine became intense. . . . The process seemed endless, which caused a general feeling of despair and misery. [1981:69]

One nineteenth-century addict stated in 1883: "I believe hell is composed of opium eaters, and the punishment consists of withdrawing from the drug, as that is the greatest torture I can imagine" (Morgan 1981:69-70)!

Dr. Mary Fulstone recalled that "the Public Health Service, the Indian Division, sent up medicine to help the Indians during their withdrawal time." But the Paiutes "were awfully cute," she added:

They needed a lot of sedation and a lot of help, but they hated to admit that it was for themselves. So maybe an Indian lady would come up and [say], "Oh, my husband is terrible today. I just have to get some medicine for him," you know. So I'd give her the medicine to kind of calm him down a little bit, but it was for herself that she wanted it. And then maybe an Indian man would come and say, "Oh, my wife's very bad today. I had to get something for her." [Fulstone 1980:41]

Also in a poignant letter, Ray Parrett, Walker River Reservation superintendent, on 5 December 1923 wrote of a Bishop, California, Paiute woman who came into his office with a plea for money to buy "medicine from a local Chinese. She was in a very nervous condition, her body trembled and twitched, and the color in her face was of a pale, sallow nature. . . . It was morphine that she wanted," the woman finally broke down and confessed, then revealed that she'd been stealing money from her husband for several months for tablets to break the habit (cf. sec. 111). A sting operation reportedly followed, as Narcotic Agents used Paiute informants with marked money to catch the Chinaman Law Tung, who was released because the tablets he sold contained insufficient amounts of opium (ITC Archives).

In 1917, the proposed scheme to use the infirmatory-tuberculosis sanitorium at Stewart to "carry on treatment for the drug addicts on the Walker River Reservation" was dashed upon the discovery that it "is filled beyond its capacity and we are turning patients away. We would not be able, at any rate, to handle these drug addicts unless we had a man assistant to watch them, because, as the Office knows, at times they become violent and require men to handle them," Dr. Phillons on 22 October 1917 wrote (Carson Indian Agency, box 302, superintendent of Carson School to commissioner of Indian affairs, Official and Unofficial Correspondence: Health, Hospitals, Sanitoriums, etc., 1917, RG 75, Federal Archives, San Bruno, Calif.). When Senator Frazier, the chair of the Senate committee investigating conditions among Indians in the early 1930s, asked the Walker River Reservation superintendent whether "any of these Indians [are] dying from the use of narcotics," Parrett answered, "There have been some during the past year" (U.S. Senate Committee on Indian Affairs, *Survey of Conditions of the Indians in the U.S.: Hearing before the Committee on Indian Affairs*, part 21, 71st Cong., 3d sess., 26 May 1931, 11529-31).

Finally, I was told that Dr. Mary Fulstone allegedly administered morphine shots to Yankee Mitchell, addict, in the employ of her husband (cf. secs. 134-35).

111. "The Chinese make two kinds of pills (both of which contain opium) that are used by some smokers to assist them in breaking the habit," H. H. Kane (1882:105) wrote. H. A. Larson, chief special officer in Denver, Colorado, discussed on 29 November 1912 the "pills" confiscated by George O'Neill:

> I am not certain whether the pills he left with me were taken from the Indian at that time or taken from the premises of the Chinaman, Kingston, which I think would make a difference. If you do not have the pills please have McNeil write me regarding the matter. This was a strong case and it is too bad to lose it. [Walker River Indian Agency, box 316, FY 1909-16, Official and Unofficial Correspondence, RG 75, Federal Archives, San Bruno, Calif.]

In a letter from Superintendent Parrett to the commissioner of Indian affairs dated 5 December 1923, there is mention of an Indian woman who requested morphine in a drug store, then instead purchased a "small tube marked X containing round tablets. . . . Testimony has since been obtained to the effect that several local Indians are procuring and using the same drugs furnished by local Chinese . . . which as yet [haven't] been determined to have opiate or morphine" (ITC Archives).

112. "Patent medicines . . . were secret formulas marketed, usually with the most extravagant claims, by entrepreneurs seeking to capitalize on real or imagined ills," observed Courtwright. Thus, the typical American druggist in the 1890s could say: "If it were not for this stuff [morphine] and my sodawater I might as well shut up shop" (Courtwright 1982:56). This situation, however, began to change in 1895-1910, as doctors subscribing to the germ theory ceased "shooting first and asking questions later," as Courtwright put it. Warnings had begun to appear in medical journals, and states and municipalities passed laws limiting the sale of narcotics (Courtwright 1982:52, 53). Passage of the 1906 Pure Food and Drug Act ended the sale of patent medicines containing narcotics (Courtwright 1982:58). Hilp, discussing patent medicines, recalled that "anything that was asked for over the counter, [formerly] used to be advertised." He said that he carried more than 200-300 of them on the shelves—"one whole side of the store, nearly every one of them containing a narcotic": Lydia Pinkam's Compound, Sloan's Liniment, Doan's Kidney Pills, DeWitt's Kidney Pills, Nature's Remedy Tablets, Carter's Liver Pills, and Caldwell's Syrup of Pepsin, to name a few (1968:19, 20). Hilp also recalled:

> These are still on the market but their formula has changed . . . [because of] federal restrictions and regulations and limits on dosage and change in advertisements. But we had a great many of them that were made with morphine and opium, and cocaine, and they were wonderful medicines, they just produced wonderful results. [1968:20-21]

And again: "But the trouble [was] . . . they didn't know that they were becoming addicts," he commented. And, in particular, "the Indians really went for Chamberlain's Colic Cure [prior to 1906], because it had quite a bit of morphine in it." Hilp further recalled that while he was working in Yerington, "on Saturdays and Sundays they [Walker River Reservation Paiutes] used to climb in their horse and buggy and their buckboard and their flat wagons, and stock up for the weekend or the week coming. One of the things that they always wanted was Chamberlain's Colic Cure . . . [which] we used to buy . . . for the drugstore by the gross. . . . I started to make a collection of Indian baskets, and I used to trade Chamberlain's Colic Cure for Indian baskets [when Indians could not pay]. . . . I had about three hundred Indian baskets. . . . I would trade a fifty-cent bottle of Chamberlain's Colic Cure or a seventy-five cent bottle of Chamberlain's Cure, for baskets which were priceless" (Hilp 1968:21, 22).

Laudanum, a popular patent medicine, was opium mixed with water. Paregoric was used as a cure against dysentery and was available in cordials, syrups, and such popular elixirs as Black Drop and Mrs. Winslow's Soothing Syrup (Morgan 1981:3). Hilp mentioned another over-the-counter patent medicine, so-called embrocations, which

> were either external or internal. They worked either way. I remember the dosage on them was rather small, because they had quite a bit of morphine in them. But externally you could rub them on as much as you

> The most of these Indians find plenty of employment in the surrounding communities during the summer and fall but few of them are benefitted thereby as by the time the work ends they have little or nothing left, having spent it in gambling and drunkenness and for opium. Most of their employers are Italians and Japanise [sic]. The Italians practically all keep wine and it seems to be the practice of many of them to pay them largely in wine, or at least secure them easily and cheap by furnishing them wine, and yet we have been unable to catch them. Then during Sundays they all flock to towns and are debauched with booze of all kinds and at exorbitant prices. So while their labor furnishes them temporary relief it is more than counteracted by the . . . debauchery it makes possible. If Mr. Dagnett can enter into contracts on behalf of Indians I do not see why I could not do the same and require payment through this office, thereby securing to them some benefit for their labor. [Walker River Indian Agency, box 316, FY 1909-16, Official and Unofficial Correspondence, RG 75, Federal Archives, San Bruno, Calif.]

Similarly, Nurse Clara Rees, the wife of Dr. J. T. Rees, contract physician, and Yerington Indian Colony's field matron, wrote Superintendent Ray R. Parrett of the Walker River Reservation on 15 August 1928:

> It seems that something should be done to stop the sale of liquor to Indians. It is getting worse all the time, and the young girls are all going to the bad. Liquor can be obtained from all of these Italian ranches. We simply must have an officer in the field who will go after these people. [ITC Archives]

"There are a number of foreigners in and about the town of Yerington, who continue to sell liquor to the Indian," Parrett, in turn, would write the commissioner of Indian affairs on 1 November of that same year.

> Indians go from the reservation to the town on Saturday night and fall prey to bootlegger. . . . [Despite arrests] the situation is indeed very bad, with the Indians getting drunk and fighting and beating their wives, and a consequent demoralization of all married life in many instances. . . . The local citizens of the town should take a stand to rid the community of this menacing foreign element, who have no care whatever of the welfare or survival of the Indian. [ITC Archives]

76. Louis Isola, who also emigrated from Lucca (in 1920) and was owner of Yerington's Peoples' Packing Company, the largest of its kind in the state, told the Oral History Program of Nevada: "All the Italians made their wine, and quite a few of them made whiskey, and a few of 'em, they were bootleggers. . . . I never made any whiskey, but we could buy the bootlegger

Quoting from a 1922 flyer that circulated within the Interior Department, these duties were defined for the field matron:

> To give instruction with respect to ventilation, proper heating, and sanitary care, of the place of abode, be it a home, or a tent, or a teepee; and to show the necessity for more room when such places are too small; pointing out the dangers and evils of overcrowding. In suitable cases the question of interior decorations and other matters that would add to home attractions should be given attention. [Meriam 1928:592-93]

Urging "helpfulness that finds expression in a fervent desire to better the condition of a worthy race that is struggling upward to a realm of higher life," the pamphlet demanded respect for "the sacredness of womanhood," Indian women being characterized as "burden bearers" (Meriam 1928:592).

73. "At Mason we obtained evidence against a countryman of mine named Dugan for possession of intoxicating liquor and furnishing some to squaw with whom he was living." So George O'Neill, the treasury agent assigned to Yerington, wrote the superintendent of the Reno Indian Agency on 22 January 1924 (Reno Agency, box 116, Liquor Matters, 1916, 1917, 1918, 1922-23, and 1924-25, RG 75, Federal Archives, San Bruno, Calif.). This is the same Annie Dugan mentioned by Corbett.

74. Recalling her uncle's cabin on the Mencarini Ranch in Smith Valley as a tiny, kerosene-lit wood structure with one window and a wood floor, Bernice Crutcher stated that clothing had to be hung inside. Corbett and Celia Mack were also forced to cook outdoors, where they kept dishes and food, she said, even in winter. "Uncle was a good cook. He made a good stew, and baked bread in the Dutch oven I now have."

75. On 17 July 1924 G. A. Trotter, superintendent of the Walker River Indian Agency, wrote the following to George O'Neill: "Mrs. Shipley reports that the liquor situation among the Indians at Yerington is appalling . . . The ranchers are even paying the Indian laborers with intoxicant and that there is a joint near the colony where they can get liquor at any time; that there are two parties . . . who have been coming to the colony about the midnight hour and disposing of their booze" (Nevada Indian Agency, box 116, Law Enforcement Agency—George O'Neill, Special Officer, Suppression of Liquor Traffic, RG 75, Federal Archives, San Bruno, Calif.). Dr. Mary Fulstone, lifelong Smith and Mason Valley physician, recalled for the Oral History Program of Nevada that "during the Prohibition here . . . [Paiutes]'d work for this certain party and he'd just pay them off in wine that he made" (Fulstone 1980:42). And that these were Italians is made clear by the following:

want and they'd really relieve pain, because they rubbed that morphine into the skin and got results. [1968:30]

Indeed, Henry A. Larson, the chief special officer whose headquarters were in Denver, Colorado, on 3 September 1913 wrote C. Asbury, special Indian agent in Reno, about the "sale of patent medicines containing alcohol by a certain druggist at Yerington" (Reno Indian Agency, box 116, Law Enforcement Program Correspondence from Indian Prisoners to Police Report, RG 75, Federal Archives, San Bruno, Calif.).

"Over one Memorial Day weekend, we had a rash of them [addicts] in here, to buy anything that had codeine or morphine," Hilp wrote about the days when patent medicines helped suffering Smith and Mason Valley Paiute addicts. "[They wanted] certain cough syrups and things that have a small amount of codeine and a small amount of morphine or something in it. . . . 'Do you have any turps?' . . . They called a mixture of terpenhydrate and codeine, 'turps'" (1968:35–36).

In a 27 March 1924 letter, Walker River Reservation superintendent Jenkins spoke of efforts being made to halt the sale of denatured alcohol (ITC Archives). Meredith Crooks, Indian posse man under George O'Neill, no doubt also discussing the suffering that accompanied the suppression of morphine, told Senator Wheeler in 1931 that Nevada Indians were then purchasing canned heat from the dime stores: "Mexicans and whites sell canned heat, rubbing alcohol and denatured alcohol to Indians" (U.S. Senate Committee on Indian Affairs, *Survey of Conditions of the Indians in the U.S.: Hearing before the Committee on Indian Affairs*, part 21, 71st Cong., 3d sess., 26 May 1931, 11497). "There has been an epidemic of rubbing alcohol unconsciousness at the Indian camp lately and Chief of Police Fred Brooks hailed Queeno Laner, Chief dispenser before Commissioner Vic Bernard this week," we also read in the *Mason Valley News*. "The local officers are determined to dry up the liquor traffic to Indians and to date have the problem under control" (14 October 1932).

113. "The position of contract physician was created to avoid this emergency expense," Superintendent Parrett on 26 December 1916 wrote, discussing Dr. Knox, a Yerington physician who secured this position by making the lowest bid to the Indian Bureau. Knox, however, had "some difficulty in getting some of the Indians to go to . . . [him] (ITC Archives). "Efforts [are being made] to abate the opium using habit among the Indians in the Mason Valley," this letter also noted. Granville Leavitt, World War I veteran, replaced Knox. The Yerington Indian Colony field matron Idella

Hahn had this to say about these two doctors in a 8 February 1917 letter to Special Indian Agent Dorrington. Dr. Knox, she wrote,

> has accused me from the first of working for Dr. Leavitt and fielding the Indians in his favor, which is not true. I have always urged them to go to Knox, but many of them will go to Leavitt and pay rather than go to Knox and get free treatment. One man said to me a short time ago, "What you mean always come ask me how I am tell me go Dr. Knox, your doctor no good. I go him and he no do anything for me. When I get money I go Dr. Leavitt. He alright." Another man said to me a short time ago, "Dr. Knox no good, one day he say something, next day he say something else. He tell too many lies. He crooked." [ITC Archives]

Mary Fulstone inherited Leavitt's practice in Smith Valley, after the contract physician "drowned in a tule pool in the northern end of Smith Valley while hunting birds with big gum boots" (Fulstone 1980:39). Leavitt also worked on the Walker River Reservation, as its farmer-agent, Arthur Ellison, wrote on 26 December 1901 that the government doctor would regularly visit Wednesdays through Fridays at 2:00 P.M., though staying overnight in the summer because "two thirds of the Indians work in Mason Vallie and his services are rendered there as Yerington is in the center of Mason Vallie and they go to his office or send for him" (Carson School, box 248a, Correspondence, book 2, A-Z, Mar.-Dec. 1905, RG 75, Federal Archives, San Bruno, Calif.).

Regarding John T. Rees, who replaced Leavitt in Mason Valley from 1926-32, Superintendent Parrett wrote the commissioner of Indian affairs on 5 August 1928 that Dr. Rees had submitted a sample of the drug used by Indians (ITC Archives). Some of Rees's testimony before the Senate committee investigating conditions among Indians in 1931-32 has been cited above. From his previously quoted 3 August 1928 letter to M. C. Guthrie, chief medical director, Washington, D.C.:

> Words cannot express the terrible and pitiful condition which exists here among these Indians, both men and women. Our offenders are doing everything in their power to stop this drug traffic. We had a Special Officer, George O'Neill, in the field here for some time who was doing good work, but for some reason he was transferred and now we have no one whom we can rely on, as he was more familiar with the situation than any other person. We have had a number of deaths resulting from the use of these Drugs, and there are a number more who are past doing anything for the younger generation are following in their footsteps. We now have about 14 Indians in the State Prison serving terms who used

Morphine and Yen-she. They have been there one year, and we have reason to believe they are cured of the habit, but when they are released it will be a hard matter for them to resist the temptation again. [ITC Archives]

George McGee was the last contract physician to the Yerington Indian Colony (and Smith and Mason Valley Paiutes in general). I wrote him in 1971 regarding the allegation that his predecessors were like those notorious scrip doctors "who simply wrote narcotic prescriptions for a fee, or who maintained a clientele of addicts" (Morgan 1981:105). His reply is as follows: "I can remember only a few times when it was necessary to give morphine to an Indian. The contract physicians I knew prescribed it infrequently" (personal correspondence, 23 Oct. 1971).

Exactly why Corbett waited in the back alley or did not shoot up immediately and rather risked waiting until he returned to Smith Valley, which by car took another hour, remains unclear.

114. In his 4 November 1931 testimony before that joint House-Senate subcommittee, Dr. Rees (p. 11551-54) stated:

At Yerington, Nev., in that colony, as they have said, the conditions is [sic] bad on account of the fact that there are no narcotic officers in that field to stop it and the narcotics come in from six or seven different points. Several deaths [were prompted by it]; more prior to this time than at the present time, owing to yen-shee being used instead of the pure narcotic. They use the yen-shee.

Rees's additional statement—"They use another preparation called peyote hypodermically"—reflects distortions surrounding the hallucinogen (cf. Stewart 1987).

Imprisoned on 3 August 1931 for one to five years, Louie Jones was "reputed to be a seller of narcotics." According to his prison file Jones was

under observation relative to said activities. On July 29th a purchase was made from him by another Indian who immediately informed the officers and delivered over to them the purchase. The Money the buyer paid for the narcotics was found on the person of the Defendant at the time of his arrest. The Defendant stated that he had previously been a resident of Carson City and upon being questioned as to his previous records stated that he had served a sentence on a liquor [charge]. [Nevada State Prison Records and District Attorney Narratives, State Archives, Carson City, Nev.]

Irene Thompson told me local Italians frequently shipped pine nuts to Italy, and we might wonder whether Amos Mencarini sent pine nuts gathered by Corbett and Celia Mack, accepting them in payment for hauling the two of them to and from the mountains.

115. Corbett's impression of the distribution of opiates among Indians in surrounding communities appears to be confirmed by historical documentation. The Lyon County grand jury report of 18 November 1929 (Appendix C), for example, stated that narcotics were evident in the following counties: Lyon, Douglas, Storey, Mineral, Churchill, and Washo. On 4 January 1934 Superintendent Jenkins, in praising the successful campaign against narcotics (and liquor) wrote Indian Commisioner Collier as follows:

> [Yen-shee was found] . . . particularly in the Indian communities (or "villages") at Reno, Yerington, Fallon, Winnemucca, Elko, Ely, etc., and around various camps wherever employed. . . . [Years of neglect made] mental and physical wrecks among those Indians, every one of which was an added burden to the Government. [ITC Archives]

Jack Largen, a self-promoting Cherokee from Sequoyah, Oklahoma, and a Yerington resident, told Sen. Lynn J. Frazier, chair of the Senate committee investigating conditions among Indians:

> They are badly ridden by the dope traffic. . . . It is going on unrestrained. . . . I can bring in people to make the statement and prove to you, gentlemen, that in the town of Yerington the dope peddler sits right in front of his gate and peddles dope to the Indians. . . . You can not stop a red Indian from taking a drink of fire water whenever he gets a chance. He gets drunk and he sobers up: but the dope traffic destroys the Indians. . . . Furthermore, these young Indians who graduate from school come right down to the town of Yerington with their diplomas in their hands, red Indians who can not have the Jim Crow law put to them in any place in the United States, walk into a restaurant there and get kicked out into the back to eat in a big pen, but the scum of Europe, and . . . the low class of the United States [can eat]. They are Jim Crowed in the town of Yerington. That is very humiliating to the Indians. We do not like it because we are a proud people. There is the position, gentlemen, which is brought on by the dope traffic. [U.S. Senate Committee on Indian Affairs, *Survey of Conditions of the Indians in the U.S.: Hearing before the Committee on Indian Affairs,* part 21, 71st Cong., 3d sess., 26 May 1931, 11525-26]

When Senator Frazier interviewed the Walker River Reservation superintendent—"What is the dope situation up here on this reservation of yours?"—Parrett replied: "Well, it is very bad around the town of Yerington. The colony of Indians at Yerington and Walker River are related, and they go back and forth. It is a condition that is very bad. The white people in the vicinity of Yerington are a class that do not give us much help" (pp. 11529-31). Indeed, Congressman Arentz (p. 11532) acknowledged that dope peddling had been going on in Nevada "for 25 years."

We also found that E. S. McNeil, special U.S. officer in Reno, wrote on 4 April 1912:

> Glad to hear you are coming. Wabuska is worst place. Opium is sold by the chinaman there running a laundry. He has sold an enormous amount of it. Is very bold about it apparently. I believe it will be better for you to come here first if you can and maybe we can formulate a plan together. . . . Both opium and liquor traffic are also very bad at Mina and Hawthorne. Then comes Yerington, Mason, and Sweetwater. At all these places the opium traffic is worse than the whiskey—especially the first three places mentioned and Sweetwater. [Walker River Agency, box 316, FY 1909-16, Official and Unofficial Correspondence, RG 75, Federal Archives, San Bruno, Calif.]

A letter from E. B. Meritt, assistant Indian affairs commissioner in 1917 to J. B. Royce, superintendent of the Carson Indian School, stated:

Special Physician Phillips advises the Office that there are now on the Walker River reservation a number of drug addicts. He has been endeavoring to treat a number of these cases who desire to be cured, but they have had scarceful a fair chance there owing to numbers of their friends who furnish them with the drug. [Walker River Agency, box 302, More Official and Unofficial Correspondence, RG 75, Federal Archives, San Bruno, Calif.]

A 27 January 1912 letter to F. L. Yparraguerre, deputy sheriff of Sweetwater, Nevada, an early mining and ranching settlement southwest of Smith Valley in California, whose name derives from its sweet-tasting water, that is, lack of hydrominerals *(Reflections 1988,* annual publication of the *Mason Valley News),* emphasized the "demoralizing influences among Indians [there]. . . as far as the opium traffic is concerned" (Walker River Agency, box 316, FY 1909-16, Official and Unofficial Correspondence, RG 75, Federal Archives, San Bruno, Calif.).

On 21 January 1920, O'Neill again wrote Miss Matheson that after obtaining evidence against Charlie Lee Tung and Ham Nun Tung in Mina, he'd heard rumors that a "Chinaman [in Minden] was [also] engaged in selling yenshee to Indians." But though he and his posse man "searched both places [Gardnerville restaurants in January, they] . . . succeeded in obtaining evidence [only] against Charlie Gib for having ten packages of yenshee in his possession." "At Gardnerville, Douglas County, Nevada," we also read of

> one [Walker River Paiute named] Charley Brown, who is employed in the post office and whose uncle is postmaster at Gardnerville, [who] appears to be cooperating with law violators. It is openly charged by Rev. J. Winfield Scott, in charge of the Indian school four miles from Gardnerville, that Brown is in sympathy with Chinese who have been convicted of selling "dope" to Indians, going on the bond of one or more of them and threatening Indians who have been subpoenaed as witnesses in the court not to testify against such Chinese. Further, that Morris Harris, a merchant of Gardnerville, states that the said Charley Brown kept one of the Chinese drug vendor's supply of yenshee concealed in his (Brown's) cellar, dealing it out as was required by the dope-sellers. [Reno Indian Agency, letter from Superintendent Jenkins to the Chief Post Office Inspector S.F., 31 January 1923, Liquor Matters 1916, 1917, 1918 and 1922-1923, 1924-1925, RG 75, Federal Archives, San Bruno, Calif.]

Since there was nothing suspicious in Tonapah, O'Neill on 7 October 1924 was directed by Superintendent Jenkins of the Reno Indian Agency to proceed from

> Reno to Derby; then to Wadsworth, Fernley, Wabuska, Yerington, Mason, Wellington, Schurz, Hawthorne, Millett and other camps or settlements in that vicinity; returning to Tonapah, thence to Goldfield, Ash Meadows, Pahrump, and such camps and settlement along that route that may appear to justify investigation of violations of liquor and narcotic laws among Indians. [Nevada Indian Agency, box 116, Law Enforcement Agency, George O'Neill, Special Officer, RG 75, Federal Archives, San Bruno, Calif.]

Six months earlier, Jenkins on 24 May 1923 had stated, "Many Indians outside the reservation come to Reno to see the sights, but most proceed at once to get in touch with bootleggers or dope peddlers." Chief Special Officer Louis C. Mueller, however, would complain one decade later (1 May 1933) of lack of cooperation with the federal narcotics officer, Andrew Roberts, in Reno: "The narcotic situation at Reno is bad. . . . Narcotic resorts [are in] operation within one and one half blocks of the city hall and police station." On 17 January 1934 Special Officer Edmunds wrote Mueller in Denver, Colorado, "There is very little used among the Indians in this vicinity [Reno, Carson City, Gardnerville and Yerington]," whereas on 2 May 1934, L. E. Moulton wrote Mueller that "the narcotic situation at Reno [along with alcohol was growing] . . . continually worse." No evidence of continuing Indian addiction, however, is given (ITC Archives).

"With reference to locating the source of supply of narcotics at Reno, Carson City, Gardnerville and Yerington," Edmunds related further in the previously cited 16 February 1934 letter,

> I beg to advise that I made investigation at Gardnerville and Yerington but have been unable to locate same among the Indians or whites. Talked to Superintendent Parrott [sic] at Schurz, Nevada and he advised me that there has been no narcotics in or around that vicinity for over two years or more. [ITC Archives; see note 106 for the remainder of this letter, which shows white involvement in morphine sales in Mina]

The *Lovelock Review-Miner* on 7 June 1929 noted that the "uses of booze and narcotics by the Indians on the Fallon reservation is increasing at an alarming rate." And, finally, a letter from Superintendent Parrett on 23 July 1929 mentioned only "the liquor situation in Bishop and Owens Valley . . . [whose] considerable amount of bootlegging . . . [is] a curse to the community" (ITC Archives).

Clearly, more historical and ethnohistorical research is required to determine the full extent of Native American opiate addiction throughout Nevada and adjoining portions of California, if not elsewhere.

116. Corbett Mack's suspiciousness of Sullivan Tom and Willy Muldoon parallels his fear of Tom Mitchell, who gets blamed for much family and personal misfortune. Witchcraft—"the second spear," as the Azande taught Evans-Pritchard (1937)—was indeed a Northern Paiute cultural belief (Whiting 1950).

117. A letter from Superintendent Jenkins on 7 April 1920 estimated that "probably 50 to 75 per cent of this [narcotics] traffic is among the Indians of Nevada and eastern California . . . as a portion of yen shee the size of a pea brings approximately $10" (ITC Archives). On 11 February 1921 he expressed opposition to J. E. Miller, Senate Chamber, Carson City, regarding a bill to eliminate the dope traffic, the "yen shee traffic—which is largely carried on by Chinamen with Indians—having become so wide-spread that practically one-half of the 5,900 Indians in the State are addicts" (ITC Archives). My own figures are presented in the Introduction, along with an interpretation of Smith and Mason Valley Paiute opiate addiction (Hittman 1973a). The William Burroughs thesis, praised by Courtwright (1982:6), that drug addiction is caused merely by exposure, in other words, sounds trite if not self-serving, in light of the Smith and Mason Valley Paiute historical situation. What becomes translucent, I believe, is the complex way in which domination and opiates and labor and opportunity interfaced. Writing about the Late Ch'ing Dynasty, Jonathan Spence showed how "escape to the pipe" was undertaken not only by bored court eunuchs, members of the imperial clan, wealthy merchants, and the like, but also by Chinese laborers and peasants seeking alleviation from the drudgery of their lives (in Courtwright 1982:66). The comment of a former slave to her daughter about marijuana also makes this point: "T'ain't no fun, chile. But it's a pow'ful lot o' easement. Smoke away trouble, darter. Blow ole trouble an' worry 'way in smoke" (Genovese 1972:644). And finally, I note that black stevedores in New Orleans began taking cocaine "to perform more easily the extraordinarily severe work of loading and unloading steamboats" (Courtwright 1982:97).

118. "The addicts have gone to drinking," Bureau of Indian Affairs commissioner John Collier was informed on 16 February 1934 (Reno Indian Agency, box 116, Law Enforcement Program Correspondence from Indian Prisoners to Police Report, RG 75, Federal Archives, San Bruno, Calif.). Here, then, we see reversal of a Prohibition pattern common in the American South, namely, "poor drunkards seek a substitute for the alcohol from which they have been forcibly separated, and they think they find it in the extract of the poppy" (Morgan 1981:34). Indeed, both of Corbett's nieces thought alcohol was worse than opium, at least insofar as addicts would stay up all night washing dishes. "Drink," on the other hand, they separately maintained, "makes them go out of their mind!"

The idea that "mixing" stimulants would prove fatal recurs in section 139.

119. SS was still alive at the time of this writing, and I respectfully protect her identity.

120. On 26 March 1924 the *Yerington Times* reported Corbett Mack's arrest along with the arrest of six other Indians, Henry Bob, George Abe,

John Miller, Hank Mitchell, Sam Leon, and John Brown. They were sentenced to ten days in the local jail following "three continuous days [of] orgy of booze and dope" and a fight reportedly precipitated by jealousy over a woman; the fight led to the deaths of Gus Lee and John Bob, whose bodies were said to evidence "narcotics and alcoholic poisoning of all the organs." "With the death of these 2 Indians the people are beginning to awaken to the fact that conditions are getting pretty rotten at the Indian camp [Yerington]," the *Mason Valley News* on 29 March 1924 commented. It continued:

> At present 90% of the Indians in the valley are hop heads and the time is coming when some dope-crazed Indian is going to run amuck and kill a few citizens. . . . Now is a good time to call the attention of the government to the fact that the so-called reservation within the city limits of Yerington is nothing more or less than a clearing house for yen shee peddlers. The place is so damn rotten that it smells to heaven.

Corbett's other arrest might well have been the subject of this reminiscence by Dr. Mary Fulstone:

> One night I was called up on a ranch here, because a couple of Indians were having a fight. It was a ranch where I think the people were paid a good deal in wine or something like that. . . . These two fellows had had an awful fight and I know they'd gotten all their wine right from this ranch. I wanted to take care of them right there and wanted to go into this house, you know, where they had been working—the people they were working for. I remember they were so reluctant to let me take these two Indians into their kitchen to wash them and clean them up, and I was kind of put out about it. But anyway, they were quite drunk and we called the sheriff. After I got them cleaned up and fixed so that we could send them to Schurz—we phoned to Schurz and the sheriff came and put 'em in the back seat—he said to the two fellows, "Now, you fellows sit right there and don't you fight." The fellow said, "We no fight; he my best friend." (Laughing) He'd already cut him up. And this one fellow did die eventually, because he was cut so bad and had such hemorrhaging. But I'll always remember that. [1980:65-66]

Recalling what might have been this knife fight, Bernice Crutcher said: "The other fellow cut a piece of meat out of my uncle's arm. They were drinking." She said he visited Corbett in the former U.S. Public Hospital on the Walker River Reservation, Schurz, Nevada.

121. Bone Jim, according to Andy Dick, assisted Jack Wilson, but as a singer during 1890 Ghost Dance ceremonies at the Walker River Reservation (sec. 125). On the 1870 Ghost Dance, see Kroeber (1904), Spier (1927, 1935), Gayton (1930), Nash (1937), Du Bois (1939), and Hittman (1973b).

Hazel Quinn (b. 1897) confirmed this cure of her sister, Mamie, by the 1870 Ghost Dance prophet *Wodzeewob*. I date the incident about 1895. Annie Lowery (Scott 1966:92–94) narrated a similar cure of her son Willy by the Lovelock Paiute shaman, Coffee Charley. "Return of the dead" is a subject Corbett Mack returns to in the concluding sections of his life history.

122. In contrast to Cora Du Bois (1939), who believed he died about 1872, I argued that *Wodzeewob* lived until the first decade of the twentieth century (Hittman 1973b). Who the "other *Wodzeewob*" is remains unclear. Be that as it may, in support of Corbett Mack's assertion that *Wodzeewob* was also known as Fish Lake Joe, and that he might have gotten his name from ritual infraction, causing premature graying, might be added: first, the Indian Census Rolls for the Walker River Reservation, 1897–1912 (roll 629, microcopy 595, Federal Archives, San Bruno, Calif.), list Joe Fishlake on 30 June 1897 as married to "Annie." His Paiute name is given as "Wa-ge-wa"; they are said to have had a son named William [Frank?]. Second, the *Virginia City Territorial Enterprise* reported on 11 February 1872 that Paiutes absent from Virginia City were still awaiting the next prophecy of the "Boy Prophet." Two weeks later, on 25 February 1872, this newspaper stated that the "Boy Prophet" was prophesying how next spring mountains would be leveled, as past and present would come together in a new world order. "Will whites also be resurrected?" the reporter queried. "The Prophet preaches often and sometimes through the night" (in Magnaghi 1975–76).

Fish Lake Joe was said to have visited the Walker River Reservation hospital infirmary for treatment for rheumatism in 1898 or 1899, and "Mrs. Fishlake Joe" was treated for syphilis in about 1897 (Walker River Agency, compartment 2167, Health and Sanitary Records, bound vol. 1, 1897–1910, RG 75, Federal Archives, San Bruno, Calif.). A letter from Walker River Reservation superintendent Pugh to Carson School superintendent Asbury on 7 May 1909 noted that "Joe Fishlake" signed line ten of the allotment for goods (Walker River Indian Agency, box 315, Press Copy Books from Farmer Agent to Asbury, RG 75, Federal Archives, San Bruno, Calif.). In 1917 Agreement 15 mentions unspecified articles totaling $32.55 purchased by Fish Lake Joe, for which he had reimbursed $5.00 (Walker River Agency, box 298, Official and Unofficial Correspondence: 1915-1923—Semiannual Report—Sales of Property and Other Transactions Arising under Reimbursement Regulations 5-337, from 1 January 1917 to 1 June 1917, RG 75, Federal Archives, San Bruno, Calif.). And in the Walker River Reservation census for 1902 (microcopy 595, 1897-1912, Federal Archives, San Bruno, Calif.), the age of Fish Lake Joe is given as fifty-one. He is listed each year through 1910, or approximately when Corbett Mack thought he died.

Regarding the 1870 Ghost Dance prophet's half-breed son, Walker River Reservation farmer-agent Longacre wrote Superintendent Asbury of the Carson Industrial School on 30 August 1905: "Willy Frank has been sick, and is now sick with malarial fever and a weak heart. Dr. is not sure yet whether it is organic or not. Dr. says boy is not fit to go to School at present. Will advise you later as to his condition" (Walker River Agency, box 248a, Carson School, book 2, A-Z, Mar.-Dec. 1905, RG 75, Federal Archives, San Bruno, Calif.).

On Northern Paiute curing see Park (1934) and Harold Olofson (1979).

123. See Hittman (1990:27-46) for a sketch of Jack Wilson's family. His brother Pat Wilson, according to the Lyon County Record of Deaths (Yerington, Nevada), died of "intestinal obstruction" on 18 August 1932. Also, contrary to what I wrote (Hittman 1990), Jack Wilson's youngest brother was married. Alice Wilson, the 1890 Ghost Dance prophet's "stolen" daughter, was called *pozi' nee'ee* 'Patchquilt'. Interestingly enough, her birth also resulted in marital tension (cf. Hittman 1990:42-45). Because Jack Wilson's wife Mary worked for the Simpson family in Smith Valley and her daughter was said to resemble George Simpson, informants posited his paternity. Eileen Kane (1964) reported this earlier, but not until I reread her outstanding National Science Foundation field report while preparing my study of the 1890 Ghost Dance did I realize this.

124. Cf. Hittman (1990:75-88) on Wovoka's miracles.

125. Corbett appeared to laugh nervously when I called it a ghost dance. Ed Dyer, relating a visit by Idaho Bannock to Smith and Mason valleys during the heyday of Jack Wilson's 1890 Ghost Dance religion, humorously wrote:

> Here's something very few white men know: The Bannock Indians, up in Idaho, speak the same language as the Paiute. . . . It varies a little, there's a few words in there. For instance, they call a dog *saduu;* the Paiute calls it *wuuzeeboo.* . . . The Paiutes call the Bannock *Kuuutsuuuduuka,*

Buffalo-eaters. [Margaret M. Wheat Papers, tape 17, 83-24, Special Collections, University of Nevada Libraries, Reno]

126. See Hittman (1990:143-49) regarding Jack Wilson's activities as shaman following the 1890 Ghost Dance (also see Hittman 1992).

127. "One time we went to Nixon and he [her husband] was treated by a new kind of Indian doctor," Annie Lowry told Scott. "The man was a faddist and popular for only a short time. He rubbed Pascal and gave him some herb pills which he concocted himself" (1966:104).

Magnaghi (1975-76, 1981), as stated, culled intriguing data about both Paiutes and Chinese in the Virginia City area from early newspapers. A 24 June 1879 entry from the *Virginia City Territorial Enterprise*, for example, spoke of fire signals on high places in Como that the Indians nightly sent to their brethren in Mason Valley—reportedly an economically motivated event, insofar as the Chamber of Commerce was then paying Paiutes one dollar each to appear in Fourth of July parades. A month later we read in an entry about Smith and Mason Valley Paiutes:

> Capt Sam wants more than a dollar a head or he won't turn out [re: Fourth of July pageantry in Virginia City]. For two dollars he will bring in 50 mounted Paiutes and show the war charge, fighting harnesses and decorated horses. He wants $15 for his services and $2 to each private.
> [*Virginia City Territorial Enterprise*, 2 July 1879]

Regarding these Paiutes, by 1917 Lorenzo D. Creel, in a piece entitled "Destitute Paiutes of Virginia City," stated there were only 65 left: 28 men, 25 women, 9 children, and 3 infants: five families living in nine lodges between Gold Hill and Virginia and Ninth Streets (Reno Indian Agency, Social Services, RG 75, Federal Archives, San Bruno, Calif.). A year later, on 9 November 1918, Lafayette A. Dorrington reported that the worldwide epidemic had resulted in the deaths of five of them and that "the majority of the Indians present [were] affected to a greater or less degree." In one house, Special Inspector Dorrington noted, "the stench which greeted us when we entered [the windows and doors were nailed shut] was most horrible and could be endured but a short time" (General Report on Investigation of Influenza among Indians at Virginia City, Nevada, RG 75, Federal Archives, San Bruno, Calif.).

128. Yet Corbett another day recalled being X-rayed and given medicine to drink three times daily by an unnamed white physician (Nye?), who told him surgery was not necessary. And he said the medicine helped.

129. There are other mentions of Tom Mitchell. In an 11 July 1905 letter from Walker River Reservation superintendent Pugh to Mitchell, who was then living in Smith Valley, Mitchell was said to have a brother named George Young and an (unamed) sister (Carson School, box 248b, Correspondence, file 4, 1902-6, book of 1 May 1905-5 Dec. 1906, RG 75, Federal Archives, San Bruno, Calif.). "Tom Mitchell has no land here," Superintendent Pugh on 4 March 1910 also wrote the head of the Carson Indian School (Asbury).

> I wish he had. It was him here a few days ago and wanted to have a talk with him about living on the allotment belonging to the father of the two young girls in your school. I think they are his nieces, and it may be it can be arranged for him to work the ground for them. However, this will not interfere with him getting land elsewhere. Tell him to come and see me when he returns. [Walker River Indian Agency, box 315, Press Copy Books from Farmer to Asbury from Pugh, RG 75, Federal Archives, San Bruno, Calif.]

"Tom Mitchell, a Paiute from Yerington used to come to the Fredericks Ranch, and the Paiutes there would get scared of him," Karl Fredericks was told by his grandfather Henry's sister in 1983. "For nothing! For nothing!" Helen Allen stated. "The Paiutes would give him gifts because they were scared!" (Fredericks n.d.).

Gambling, which ironically was to become a staple industry of Nevada (cf. Ostrander 1966; Thompson 1986), joined Northern Paiute shamanism as anathema to Indian agents (cf. Forbes 1967:168-76). "Your Office is no doubt familiar with the fact that gambling is the besetting sin of the Indians of this reservation, as well as of practically all Piutes and Utes," Walker River Reservation superintendent Jenkins wrote the commissioner of Indian affairs on 4 December 1919.

> These Indians, however, possibly for the reason that they have more money appear to have gone gambling mad in recent years and a large majority of them spend half their time, night and day, playing cards for money and other things of value. It is not unusual, I am told, for an Indian to win or lose from $100 to $200 at a sitting. Both men and women play, and the women appear to have become more completely demoralized as a result than the men. [ITC Archives]

All the same, Tom Mitchell struggled to operate a gambling house—both before the Yerington Indian Colony was founded in 1917, and on its premises afterward. These letters, one to him and one about him, are instructive:

On 3 May 1911 Superintendent Pugh, writing to "Tom Mitchell, Indian, Yerington, Nevada," stated:

> I talked with the Mayor of Y. and am satisfied you are mistaken in thinking that the white people are gambling there. The Mayor does not intend to permit any such thing and of course you must stop also. As I explained to you yesterday, your gambling is breaking the laws of the state and I am giving special attention to you because your allowing the Indians to come there and gamble causes my Indians to leave their work here to go up there and gamble, and if they earn money in Mason Valley they lost it gambling there instead of trying to develop their ranches. You stated your willingness to stop the 1st of July, but neither I nor any one else have the right to authorize you to continue till that time. If you want to be safe, the only thing for you to do is to stop it at once and tell all the other Indians to gamble no more. When you gamble anywhere off the reservation you are breaking the laws of the state and I can not authorize you to gamble off this reservation. You can stop it, and save trouble for yourself and the other Indians. [Walker River Indian Agency, box 316, FY 1909-16, Official and Unofficial Correspondence, RG 75, Federal Archives, San Bruno, Calif.]

On 1 May 1911 the Walker River Reservation superintendent wrote Dr. Joseph A. Murphy, medical supervisor, Denver, Colorado:

> State law last Fall prohibits gambling . . . [and having heard that Walker River Reservation Paiutes were secreting to Mason Valley, Pugh and Reverend Johnson disguised as Indians on 29 April and] found most of my Indians in the middle of a big game, in the house belonging to the recognized leader, Big Tom Mitchell, of the Paiute Indians, resident in those parts. Just what I wanted. You can imagine their surprise and discomfiture when our identity was made known, but our backs were against the only door to the house so no one got out till we were through with them. Big Tom has been conducting this gambling place for some time. He at first claimed immunity from my interference because he and many of the others were not enrolled here. . . . [Pugh then offered a deal: if Mitchell would only quit enticing "his Indians" into "bad habits," there would be no proceedings against him]. Their gambling house was within the city limits of Yerington, the county seat of Lyon Co. so I went to the Mayor, who promises to do all he can to help in the matter, but I don't think he will. . . . P.S. [After Mitchell had agreed to quit] One of my policeman just returning from Yerington, brings word from T. M. that he is not under my jurisdiction and will continue to gamble. So I guess it means a scrap. [Walker River Indian Agency, box 316, FY 1909-16,

Official and Unofficial Correspondence, RG 75, Federal Archives, San Bruno, Calif.]

Irene Thompson told me how in winter her grandfather used his Yerington Indian Colony home as a gambling house, erecting an outdoor shelter or shade *(haba)* for this in summer. Gambling, she recalled, could take place every day, including Sundays; drinking was not allowed. Tom Mitchell, she recalled, owned several decks of cards and gambling sticks. He acted as arbiter, "correcting" any arguments:

> Women played *tuuheemakwuu,* 5 Card. Each woman takes 5 cards, one turn, high card wins; bets are usually for $.10, $.20, and $.50. My grandfather takes the first bet on each game. And sometimes he makes one daughter give them gamblers food. Or, they can go to that Jap restaurant in Yerington to eat for $.50 to $.75—where they're fed in back like dogs!

130. Etta J. Shipley, Yerington Indian Colony field matron, wrote in her report for the week ending 20 May 1922:

> Indians reported (Sunday) that George Abe and wife were drunk and fighting with the Indians, I called the police and had him go down Sunday night. George is a very good worker, but spends all his earnings every Saturday and terrorizes the Indians. George belongs at Schurz and if possible he should be kept away from the Colony. His wife and he fight also and she was badly bruised this week. [Walker River Agency, box 303, Correspondence for 1922 and 1923, RG 75, Federal Archives, San Bruno, Calif.]

Arie Poldervaart told me in 1988 that *sa'ab* or *tsa-ab* probably derived from *tsa* 'killed one' and *ab* 'ghost'. In her classic study of Paiute witchcraft, Whiting (1950) defined the practice as a technique of social control in band-type societies. Corbett already alluded to the witching of his father's sister by Jack Wilson's father (sec. 7) and the killing of his own grandfather by Pat Hoye for a similar reason (sec. 13). Data of this sort can amply be provided. Topsy Quartz from Bishop, for example, the wife of Abe George, Walker River Reservation policeman, judge, and "Chief of the Walker River Indians," was charged with witchcraft (Walker River Agency, box 302, Official and Unofficial Correspondence, Health. Hospitals, Sanitoriums, etc, 1917, RG 75, Federal Archives, San Bruno, Calif.); Dave Brown killed "Dr. Tom Crow," his grandfather, a crime for which he spent two years in jail (Walker River Agency, box 316, FY 1909-16, Official and Unofficial Correspondence, RG 75, Federal Archives, San Bruno, Calif.); and Jack Bennett,

Corbett's wife's uncle, reportedly set fire to the Walker River Reservation Indian agent-physician's house on 28 January 1914 to drive out Dr. Hailman following the death of his daughter, in order to shoot him as a witch (ITC Archives). More recently, in the late 1960s, Maggie Milton, elderly Yerington Indian Colony resident, was attacked in her own home with an axe by an unidentified male charging the former peyotist with witchcraft; she hit her head on the stove and subsequently died. Indeed, Eileen Kane wrote that "Maggie Milton, sister of Jim Keno, present-day resident of the Colony, still has witching powers, and is the successor of the past peyotists in the sense that she is a constant user herself, although it plays no part in her cures" (1964:36).

131. Park (1938b:18) reported Tom Mitchell was "acknowledged as the most powerful shaman in recent years." He listed Eagle, Weasel, a small unidentified mountain bird, and an unidentified fourth spirit as sources of Mitchell's *booha*. In Eileen Kane's discussion (1964:36) of these Smith and Mason Valley Indian doctors' sources of power, Tom Mitchell was said to have obtained *booha* from deer hooves, as well as from eagle feathers. She also listed these other shamans and their sources of power: Winnemucca, waterbabies; Horseman (?); Chief Joaquin (?); Jack Wilson, eagle feathers; Dick Bennett, waterbabies; Little Dick (?); Doctor Joe (?); Doctor Charley (?); Tom Mitchell, eagle, weasel, mountain bird, and ?; Ben Lancaster (?); Jim Keno (?); Lillian McCloud (?); Barney Miller, waterbabies; Jack Dalton, waterbabies; Rosie Quartz (?); and Maggie Milton, peyote.

Russell Dick told me in 1993, "Tom Mitchell has a rock which he can turn into a bear. He just gets his gun and shoots [at] it! And it's still there—at Desert Creek. Call it 'Rock Bear'. 'Cause one doctor told me that's his *booha*."

Bernice Crutcher, interestingly, further related that her grandfather even blamed his lack of success in hunting on Tom Mitchell, saying the feared shaman sent Bumblebee around Big Mack's hat to distract him whenever he went out. She also said the same occurred whenever he ate, interpreting this to mean Tom Mitchell expected to be given food.

132. Much of this section is deliberately repeated from section 59 (cf. the Introduction for discussion of repetition in Northern Paiute).

133. According to the Lyon County Coroner's Death Certificate (no. 32-000996, Lyon County Courthouse, Yerington, Nev.), Jack Wilson died at 1:00 A.M. on 29 September 1932 in his house on the Yerington Indian Colony of nephritis. Enlarged prostate and cystitis were also given as contributing whiskey for about four dollars a gallon then . . . several places we could buy whiskey" (Isola 1980). Sayre (1977:35), similarly, remembered the existence of stills in Red Canyon and Hudson. And in a 15 December 1924 letter from George O'Neill, treasury agent, to the commissioner of Indian affairs, we read of his discovery of a still on the Mason Valley Wilson Ranch

> in a dugout . . . and the following contraband articles were seized and destroyed: One 40-gallon copper still, two pressure burners, one tank, one 15-gallon oil drum, one 25-gallon cooling barrel, one 40-gallon cooling barrel, eight 50-gallon fermenters, one wash tub, one three-burner oil stove, 300 gallons of corn sugar mash, 25 pounds cracked corn, three funnels, one five-gallon keg and 10 gallons coal oil. . . . No one was found in possession of the still, and no arrest was made. [Nevada Indian Agency, box 116, Law Enforcement Agency, George O'Neill, Special Officer, Suppression of Liquor Traffic, RG 75, Federal Archives, San Bruno, Calif.]

77. On 14 July 1920 the *Yerington Times* would report the arrest of Mike Sava for selling jackass brandy at the Smith Valley Hot Springs. Sava, age thirty-five, listed in the 1920 federal census (U.S. Bureau of the Census 1880–1920) as a bartender-owner of a saloon in the Morning Star Precinct of Smith Valley, was said to be married to Marie Sava, age thirty-eight.

George O'Neill stated in a letter on 19 August 1924 to J. E. Jenkins, superintendent of the Reno agency: "If I had to wait until there was nothing doing in the liquor suppression work in Nevada I fear I would never be able to get any time off as liquor conditions in that section have changed but little in the last twenty-five years." After investigating "an Italian named Lemori, a reputed bootlegger," O'Neill noted on 20 October 1924 the "Charley Day ranch which is leased by several Italians who are suspected of selling wine to Indians." O'Neill also wrote the commissioner of Indian affairs on 30 November 1924 about an "Italian rancher named Jake Sikora who operates a ranch near the Yerington Indian village." He had no luck catching him, but on November 28

> I obtained a search warrant for the premesis [sic] of the Martin Ranch operated by Jake Sikora, and spent the forenoon searching for intoxicating liquor and found two half pint bottles containing degrees of alcoholic liquor both bottles being very simelar [sic] to the one taken from George Charley on the night of November 25, 1924. During the afternoon I filed a charge of selling liquor to an Indian aganst [sic] Jake Sikora. [Nevada Indian Agency, box 116, Law Enforcement Agency,

George O'Neill, Special Officer, Suppression of Liquor Traffic, RG 75, Federal Archives, San Bruno, Calif.]

Charles De Boer, a repeated offender, was arrested by O'Neill on 30 July 1924 in Mason for selling intoxicating liquor to Yerington Paiute Andrew Penrose (Nevada Indian Agency, box 116, Law Enforcement Agency, George O'Neill, Special Officer, Suppression of Liquor Traffic, RG 75, Federal Archives, San Bruno, Calif.).

To'eeshaboowee 'chokecherry' is *Prunus demissa* (C. S. Fowler 1989: 49).

Finally, Karl Fredericks in this regard kindly lent me his "Notes toward a History of the Frederick Ranch of Sweetwater, California" (Fredericks n.d.). His father's sister (Edith Keely, b. 1894) told him: "Auntie [Sanchey Fredericks] would sell shots of watered down whiskey to the Paiutes that worked on the Fredericks Ranch. It would cost the Paiutes twenty-five cents a shot. Paddy Conway, owner of the Conway Ranch, would also sell whiskey to his Paiute workers."

78. A 4 June 1916 letter from the Lyon County clerk, John Pohland, to C. H. Asbury of the Reno Indian Agency reported Mike Rube's brother Eddie being "very fond of liquor and [he] often goes on a 'jamboree' and is then inclined to be unreasonable and assertive and a troublemaker" (Bishop Agency, box 251b, Bishop: 1925-1926, folder 267, RG 75, Federal Archives, San Bruno, Calif.).

79. The earliest reference to Indian drinking in the *Lyon County Times* was 22 July 1893. Following the arrest of the second bootlegger in a month, the newspaper's editor remarked: "It behooves the people of the valley to be pretty strict with the Paiutes, as at this season they are quite numerous there, outnumbering the whites two to one, and there is no telling what they might do should a number of them get on a big drunk." On 29 April of that same year, after the appearance of a number of drunk Indians in town on the Christian Sabbath, this same newspaper would report: "The Indians in this valley (Mason) seem to be able to get whiskey whenever they want it—and that is all the time." Within the state, however, earlier evidence of Northern Paiute drinking can be cited. Magnaghi (1975-76), for example, found a 25 March 1877 article in the *Virginia City Territorial Enterprise* mentioning how the presence of numerous drunken Indians in Virginia City inspired local police to send an Indian with a marked coin to a gin mill and dandy shop operated by a Kennedy who sold them whiskey in a pop bottle. Complaints about drunken Indians in 1881 were said to be mounting both in Virginia and causes of death. He is buried on the Walker River Reservation (Hittman 1990:166-76). Like the Northern Paiute demiurge, Wolf or *Eesha*, the 1890 Ghost Dance prophet prophesied he would shake this earth upon reaching heaven. Indeed, Wolf was one of Wovoka's sources of *booha* (Park 1938b: 18; Hittman 1990:143-49).

134. Whiting (1950) also listed their medical causes of sickness, despite arguing that Northern Paiutes did not believe in "natural death."

135. "It has been reported to us several times the last few days that the Indians are being furnished liquor in Wellington and Smith Valley," Clara Rees, field matron for the Yerington Indian Colony, wrote the Walker River Reservation superintendent on 23 April 1932:

> ... that instead of money, they are being paid in liquor for their work. Thursday April 21st, the Indian Police and myself called at the Nooner cabin over there, and found Herman Nooner, a young boy completely down and out with liquor. His father, Jimmie Nooner [Nuna] also was in a similar condition, although not quite as bad. He had set fire to his wife's clothing and destroyed all of them, and was crying from the effects of the liquor. Last night April 22nd a call from W[ellington] came for the Doctor, saying that Herman Nooner was sick with Pneumonia which was caused by exposure to the cold from being drunk and laying out on the ground. [Walker River Agency, box 313, Correspondence of Walker River Superintendent, folder 3, RG 75, Federal Archives, San Bruno, Calif.]

According to Lyon County death certificates (Lyon County Courthouse, Yerington, Nev.), Nellie Conway died of cholecystitis and septicemia in childbirth on 1 December 1926; Daisy Mitchell Summers was struck by a car and killed in 1937; Stewart Mitchell was struck by a car on 23 January 1955 and killed; Carrie Mitchell Hooten died of "natural exposure" and alcohol on 29 February 1955; Dave Mitchell died of "natural causes" on 24 December 1955; and Sadie Jones died in Wellington of alcoholism and exposure on 5 December 1956.

Regarding this house-burning incident involving Stewart Mitchell, Dr. Mary Fulstone recalled

> poor Stewart Mitchell [who burned his sister's place] because they had this superstition. And so one day when he got good and drunk, he burned it [she laughs] ... was put in prison.... [Then after she and her husband wrote letters to have him paroled] he was afterwards killed. He got drunk one night and walked right in front of a car. [1980:67]

"Too many ghosts [i.e., deaths] in the house," Russell Dick whimsically commented to me about this incident in 1993. "So, Stewart douses it with gasoline. I guess he was going to educate the people!"

According to Irene Thompson, her grandfather Tom Mitchell had also attempted to bequeath his *booha* to each of his daughters, and they all separately refused it.

Jimmy Burbank was struck by an automobile in Mason sometime between Christmas and New Year's. Billy Miller, who was also drinking, died outdoors of exposure and pneumonia.

136. Sayre recalled Tom Mitchell as someone who "proved to be a good, popular medicine man. He had herbs for remedies and some people thought the remedies were good in the influenza epidemic." She also remembered his wives' names as Little Jennie and Blind Kate (1977:43).

Hageenop, or wild parsnip, is *Aulospermun longipes*, more popularly known as water hemlock. "Eating of wild parsnip to commit suicide was not an uncommon method among the Indians," wrote Ed Dyer (1990). "I personally witnessed the demise of one deluded victim [during an 1890 Ghost Dance performance] and can attest that it was a long drawn out and agonizing death." In the *Yerington Rustler* we read on 30 September 1899: "A [Paiute] mahala [Indian woman] took parsnip and died yesterday." On 17 March 1906 the *Lyon County Times* reported that a middle-aged Paiute named Emma committed suicide by eating *hageenop* because her husband left her for a younger woman—after administering a beating and stealing twenty dollars. Donald and Catherine Fowler identify *hageenop* as genus *Angelica*, "a root which is grated and made into a decoction [for] rheumatism or sore throat" (1970:139).

Tom Mitchell died in his home at the Yerington Indian Colony on 18 August 1945. The age of death listed on his death certificate was ninety-seven. Apparently he was unconscious when taken to Ben Lancaster's peyote meeting.

Eileen Kane (1964) was also told that both Mitchell and Jack Wilson had lost their lives as a result of peyote.

Corbett's fear of this shaman notwithstanding, my dear, late, lamented friend Irene Thompson of Smith Valley not only loved her grandfather, but also discounted any suggestion that he might have practiced witchcraft. Among the many things she said about him: "Tom Mitchell is greater and a more powerful man than Jack Wilson!" My Indian mother, Ida Mae Valdez, similarly recounted her mother's (Mamie Dick's) feeling that Tom Mitchell was the "best doctor," even though her father, Andy Dick, agreed with Corbett that he was a witch. These additional letters about this remarkable figure are intended to balance Corbett's one-sided portrait of Tom Mitchell.

J. A. Carter of Yerington on 17 January 1912 wrote Walker River Reservation supertintendent C. H. Asbury as follows:

> I am requested by Tom Mitchell, Indian, to drop you a few lines in regard to things happening here. There was an Indian found in the brush who had died there. His name was Billy Johnson. The white man that reported to the officers saw him there for 2 or 3 days before he reported it. The indians took the body and buried it on the 13th inst. He also asked me to see if you could do anything with the opium sellers as there is a Chinaman that runs a wash house at Wabuska that sells by wholesale to the indians and there is one at Mason that sells to the indians but as i understand them sells are 95 percent opium. Tom brought up from Wabuska 3 squaws and one man and gave them a hearing at the indian camp. The young men and women are getting so they don't want to work and Tom gets after them and talks to them and they go way for a while but come back to camp. Tom says if there was a raid made on these places by [?] officers that it would do good for the county officers don't seem to take a hand in it. There are 2 or 3 ranchers where they sell opium but not so much. Tom Mitchell wants you to write a letter that will give the Boss [?] a little understanding of what the opium habit is and what it will do to them if they keep on using it.

This second letter, signed by Adam Dixon and "Tom Mitchell, Captain at Yerington," speaks in 1916 of an informal committee of Paiutes that requested "to have some action by the Govt. and the Indians Bureau to set aside the pinenuts on the vacant [Forest Service] lands of the United States, for the use of the Indians, who have no land off the Reservation," that is, because they "would be quite a revenue for Indians."

"While we appreciate the fact that such an arrangement would be of material benefit to the Indians," Commissioner of Indian Affairs E. B. Merritt would write back that same year,

> we do not know of any plan which could be adopted that would restrict the gathering of the nuts so that they would be available exclusively for the use of the Indians, unless you can make some arrangement with representatives in charge of the forest reserve in your locality under which you can gather the nuts in consideration for services rendered by you.

And in a follow-up letter on 16 December 1926 requesting clarification on the ranger's point, Commissioner Merritt wrote:

"Does he [Tom Mitchell] want the Piutes to help or not? He says that he will make his plans . . . to guard against very serious or permanent damage. But he does not say whether he wants and [sic] co-operation of the Paiutes or anything about the pinenuts."

Finally, in an 8 June 1929 letter from John T. Reid of Lovelock, Nevada, to "Mr. Tom Mitchell, Jack Wilson and Pete Penrose," the subject is narcotics:

The whiskey, the morphine and the opium, to which you refer are, as you say, very bad drugs for the Indians to take, and they should not use any of them. Some white people who lack good judgement, sence [sic] and wisdom use it and always to their sorrow. Anyone with a bit of common sense will leave it alone and you should tell all your people about this being so.

I am indebted to Ernie Conway of the Yerington Indian Colony for allowing me to reprint these letters about his grandfather.

137. In the first of his two published autobiographies, Albert Hensley also complained about peyote not being used for its "original" purpose (Radin [1923] 1970:353). Eileen Kane (1964:36) reported that Ben Lancaster, a.k.a. Grey Horse, was also called White Feather. See note 138 about the famed Washo peyotist (cf. Stewart 1944, 1987; Siskin 1983; Hittman n.d.a).

138. "Famous Indian moves to Smith Valley," the *Mason Valley News* reported on 4 June 1937. "Ben Lancaster, noted Indian medicine man, is staying at James Keno's place. Services are held on Sundays." Yet, three years later the newly formed Yerington Paiute Tribal Council by a five-to-one vote passed a resolution in their 28 February 1940 meeting banning peyote. Reasons given were: (1) Lancaster's practice of medicine without a license, (2) unsanitary conditions, (3) "demoralization of the mind," and (4) because peyote allegedly "gives false information in the line of religious training." Wesley Keno, peyotist, was the lone dissenter. George McGee, U.S. Government contract physician—with help of the Lyon County sheriff—was a factor in the eviction of Lancaster (cf. Stewart 1987:275-85). In any event, Eileen Kane (1964) reported that in December of 1936 Ben Lancaster held a peyote meeting in the Mason Valley ranch house lent or rented to James Keno by his Italian employer and that nearly all sick Indians in the valley attended, including Keno's own son. Ed Reymers and Ed Decroy, she wrote, attended a two-night cure at the Yerington Indian Colony in January of 1937. Each had advanced tuberculosis. The former died at home on 24 January, the latter on 8 February, at the Walker River Reservation. I was told that Ed Dick, whose premature death also militated against Ben Lancaster's chance for success in these valleys, had been working in the Smith Valley potato fields when he precipitously "swelled up"; red dots appeared all over his shoulder. His mother refused to permit Dr. Mary Fulstone to examine him because of fear of surgery, so the Paiute was taken to Lancaster's peyote meeting. He died one month later (Hittman n.d.a).

139. Ben Lancaster died in 1953, and his wife Louise remained active in the peyote religion in Coleville (cf. Stewart 1987:285). Charges that Lancaster was "not usin' peyote right," that is, selling peyote, no doubt, had something to do with Smith and Mason Valley Paiutes' prior experience with opiates (Hittman n.d.a). When Ivan Hanson introduced his short-lived sweathouse religion on Campbell Ranch in 1972, not only were there similar suspicions of marijuana and orgiastic sexual behavior, but also charges of exorbitant amounts of money being given to this shaman.

"And, so, after that *peeyot* went outta here," Corbett also told me, "Old Man Keno, he start in to drink. Yes, sir! Drink, drink, drink! 'Cause you see why? X-ray show pus [?], so that doctor, he tell him to quit peyote. And so he start drinkin' again"—A comment that seems perfectly consistent with Corbett Mack's fear of mixing substances (Hittman n.d.b).

140. Alex Miller no doubt alluded to one of these incidents when he repeated in 1993 what he had originally told me in 1991:

"Once Corbett got mad at Mencarini and took a job with his neighbor. Well, so, Mencarini went over there looking for him. . . . Corbett was eating his breakfast, and Mencarini told his new boss: 'You got my man! I want my man back!' 'Well, so, you can have him back,' the other one said. 'He just came this morning!'"

Jess Reymers (b. 1893 in Mason Valley) died en route to the U.S. Public Health Hospital on the Walker River Reservation as a result of an automobile accident in Wilson Canyon on 1 April 1958. His parents were Bill and Susie Reymers (Remus) of Schurz, Nevada.

141. Campbell Ranch originally was a 1,108.11-acre, $25,000 purchase of land by the federal government under the Indian Reorganization Act. Formerly part of the vast Miller-Lux empire, which included 20,000 acres in Mason Valley (Treadwell 1931), Campbell Ranch was owned in 1937 by the Farmers Bank of Carson Valley, which apparently foreclosed in 1931 on the Italian potato farmer Ambrose Rosachi. After Smith and Mason valley Paiutes voted to incorporate as the Yerington Paiute Tribe in 1934 and adopted a constitution and bylaws, members were eligible for 20-acre land assignments on Campbell Ranch. Corbett Mack's name does appear on a revised list of prospective ranchers (cf. Hittman 1984:43), which also included Henry Fredericks, Charley Brown, Mack Paddy, Henry Tom, Andy Dick, Frank Quinn, Harry Conway, Howard Rogers, Archie Penrose, Richard Conway, Richard Brown, and Brady Emm—six of them being former opiate addicts, four having been sent to prison for selling. Those who survived shared resources with kinsmen, and the perseverence and hard work of Andy and Mamie Dick, Frank and Hazel Quinn, and Howard and Lena Rogers is a remarkable human story (Hittman 1973c).

142. Kersten (1961:205), for example, wrote how the hay baler in these years reduced the labor force of Smith Valley's Plymouth Ranch from twenty-five men to five.

143. According to the *Lyon County Book of Deaths*, Mary Mack died in January of 1923 (Lyon County Courthouse, Yerington, Nev.). Cause of death was given as "parenchymatous nephritis." Lena Rogers, culturally disinclined to discuss death or deaths, nonetheless mentioned that Corbett's grandmother died in 1926. Also, Big Mack Wheeler's death date is given as 2 August 1953. Age was said to be 110; cause of death "natural-senility."

"Indians are invading some of the Church property and it seems they have no respect for anybody," Reverend Joseph Cunha of the Roman Catholic Church in Yerington wrote on 10 June 1922 with alarm. "The case is that they are burying their dead all over the Catholic cemetery. I offered them a little place for them, but they don't take it. Something has to be done" (Walker River Agency, box 303, Correspondence 1922 and 1923, RG 75, Federal Archives, San Bruno, Calif.). Research needs to be done on this interesting sociological correspondence between the nomadic Paiutes' custom of burying their dead in unmarked, unvisited graves in the mountains, and the current practice, which involves annual visits to decorated grave sites on Memorial Day by these sedentary-living people.

144. According to her death certificate (Lyon County Courthouse, Yerington, Nev.), Celia Mack died of natural causes on 2 February 1958; approximate age given was 68. Elsie Sam Ausmus told me that Celia had walked from her house on Mencarini's Ranch to the general store in Central for a bottle of wine that day. Upon returning home, she complained of fatigue and lay down to rest, without ever wakening.

145. Sherman and Claude Sanders are the (living) stepsons of Eddie Mack. In 1954 the Yerington Paiute Tribal Council assigned Eddie Mack the (vacated) ranch assignment of Buster and Ada Phoenix. According to the Lyon County tax list for 1958, he and his wife, Helen, from Bridgeport, were assessed at $19,746: 4 cuttings on 30 acres, furniture, 2 saddle horses, 4 bulls, 1 milch cow, 150 stock cattle, 4 hogs, 25 pigs, a 1949 Buick sedan, a 1957 Chevy pickup, a 1948 Willy's jeep, a 1956 International pickup, a 1953 Dodge truck, and a 1940 Hyde Trit; they were assessed at $3,710, $7,350, and $8,110 on various other properties as well (Lyon County Library, vertical files, Yerington, Nev.). Eddie Mack was legally blind when he died on Campbell Ranch in the middle 1980s.

146. See Whiting (1950) on "ghost sickness" as the perceived cause of death among elderly Paiutes.

147. I did not know Eddie Mack very well; he was friendly, though suspicious, especially when he came upon me interviewing his uncle in his house. Superintendent James E. Jenkins of the Walker River Agency wrote Eddie Mack on 9 June 1924 as follows:

> My Friend: Complaints have been made that you are causing trouble by your presence at the Dresslerville Indian Colony near Gardnerville; that you have no visible means of support and that you are suspected of peddling intoxicants among the Indians of that vicinity. It is therefore ordered for the best interests of that community that you keep away from the Dresslerville Colony and refrain from interfering in any way with those Indians. Any violation of this order will be sufficient cause for your arrest. [Reno Indian Agency, box 116, Law Enforcement Program Correspondence from Indian Prisoners to Police Report, RG 75, Federal Archives. San Bruno, Calif.]

In 1971 I transported a gift home from Corbett's impressive garden—an oversized squash.

148. Timothy Smith left this account both of antelope found in the valley named for him and of their fate following contact:

> A band of antelope grazed in the valley . . . and in the mountains there were deer and some mountain sheep. For the killing of such game the Indians would dig pits beside the trails leading to the river. In these pits they would crouch and cover themselves with brush or grass and shoot the animal with an arrow as it passed. Such methods, however, were so uncertain that there was little danger of thinning out the game. . . . [But] with the assistance of these rifles they were able to kill off the game more rapidly, and the result was that in a few years none of the antelope

were left, while the deer were considerably reduced in numbers. [1911-12:226]

Both Steward (1938:34-36) and Stewart (1941:366-67) reconstructed the antelope hunt on the basis of informants' memories, whereas Lorenzo Creel, as already indicated, documented one at Pyramid Lake.

149. McCloud Hill, along with Mason Butte or Rattlesnake Hill, is a granodiorite outlier rising above the alluvium-covered sagebrush-grass zone that is Mason Valley (Kersten 1961:28).

150. This information on Thunder and Lightning was elicited in the midst of a summer thunderstorm, as Corbett and I sat cowering beneath a cottonwood tree outside his nephew's house at Campbell Ranch.

151. According to Wycliffe Bible translator Arie Poldevaart, *moo-*, in the word *moo'esa*, means 'first' or 'out in front', much as one is tempted to assert the role of maternal grandmother *(moo'a)* in Corbett Mack's life. Sven Liljeblad told Eileen Kane (1964:9) that the *Sai'ee* were Columbia River Indians. In another version of the Northern Paiute creation story, however, Corbett Mack stated that whereas the first set of mixed siblings who went to Schurz were Northern Paiutes, the others went to Fallon and became the modern-day Shoshones. Cf. Lowie (1924), Kelly (1932), Steward (1936a), and D. D. Fowler and C. S. Fowler (1971) for versions of the creation story.

"There is a legend among the Paiutes that one time the earth shook so nobody could stand up," Annie Lowry told Lalla Scott. "The Indians all were thrown to the ground for half an hour. They had to hold on to sagebrush to keep from being tumbled in all directions. The earth shook violently as it never had before and never has since" (1966:137 n. 61). The similarity of Jack Wilson's final prophecy to what *Eesha* or Wolf, Northern Paiute demiurge, said upon leaving this world has already been noted (note 133). Another way in which myth melds or merges with history will be seen in section 158.

152. When I asked Corbett Mack, "Who made the birds?" he thought and he thought before finally replying, "Maybe Coyote make 'em!"

153. Eileen Kane (1964) also learned that the Northern Paiute shamans Winnemucca *natsee*, Dick Bennett, and Jack Dalton obtained *booha* from Waterbaby. The Pyramid Lake Paiute Dewey Sampson told a University of Nevada, Reno, undergraduate this about waterbabies: "Don't make fun of them. . . . Fishing in Pyramid Lake and one guy can't get any. Says, 'I wish I could catch a water baby.' He does. Scared and runs off" (1980). One of my informants reported that Corbett Mack had told him about the "lady in the pond" he met while herding sheep in the mountains: "That was over toward Sweetwater. . . . Corbett said he kicked the ground and the mermaid came out. She had a pearl necklace. Scared him, too. So Corbett told her to go back to the water. And that's not made up, neither! This was real! And he wasn't drinkin', neither." Bernice Crutcher confirmed. Her uncle, she said, "went to that pond in Sweetwater to see that lady. Stomped his feet. 'I want to see you,' Uncle said. Well, so, real waves came up, and she appeared. No fins, though. And she was a real lady . . . naked, too. Was wearing a pearl necklace. . . . Had black hair. 'Go back,' my uncle told her. 'I've seen all I need to see!'" Crutcher further recalled Big Mack having seen one. "Another old-timer was using them for medicine," she said. "So Mack, he joined him. And they saw their footprint, all right. And places where they sat on the ground. So they called one out of the water. But when Big Mack tries to pick her up, she's too heavy, so he just lets her go. Doesn't get any power that way, neither. [But] Other Indian doctors can hold onto them."

Eileen Kane (1964) in her field report also reported the Paiute Giant Cannibals Tsana-oho and Pai-zoho. Bernice Crutcher remembered being frightened as a child by Big Mack's stories about an Old Lady who would come into camp posing as their grandmother—"Because he don't want us playing around at night!" She was told a similar story by her grandfather about Giant Cannibals living in the Hot Springs area in Smith Valley. Her uncle Corbett, she added, never narrated such stories. Russell Dick, in any event, described *Paheezoho* as "man-eating. . . . He goes after anything with blood in it. And he's on two legs, just like a man!" Russell said that his father, Andy Dick, had told him *Paheezoho* "packs a rock with a hole in it, and pounds you and makes you to mush. He can look at you and put you to sleep." Interestingly, both Sarah Winnemucca Hopkins ([1882] 1969:11-12) and Annie Lowry (Scott 1966:7) replace Giant Cannibal in this tale of a Paiute child buried in the sand by its mother to prevent it from being devoured with invading whites. Hopkins even referred to *taivos* as "cannibal owls!"

154. Though suspicious of the contribution "Indian autobiographies" might make toward our understanding of Native American culture, Boas at the end of his life wrote that the study of folktales was "indispensable for a clear understanding of the relations of the individual to the culture in which he lives" (Boas 1943:335).

155. Marplot Coyote also characterologically says, "That's nothing to me!" (cf. Lowie 1924; Kelly 1932; Steward 1936a).

156. During one visit, Corbett, who was drinking, confided this recurring dream about his deceased wife, which he said caused insecurity:

"I always dream she don't like me, partner. See me, you know, and go the other way."

"I wonder why you have that kinda dream, Corbett?" posturing, I psychoanalytically asked.

"Well, it's natural, you see," Corbett Mack wisely, transculturally (cf. Redfield 1953:130-33) replied. "'Cause you see why, Mike? You gotta have your dream! Yes, sir! To sometimes, not always, though, see [dream of] your own [dead] wife!"

157. Andy Dick, my oldest Smith and Mason Valley Paiute informant, and Corbett's brother-in-law and drinking companion in retirement, independently related something similar. In his late eighties, when I went to say goodbye to him at the end of the summer of 1969, Andy encouragingly invited my return to the reservation, when he expected his crippled legs to get better (i.e., "He come back!"), whereupon we could drive together up in the mountains in my Volkswagen for buried gold treasure, which I was assured by him that his (broken!) geiger counter would direct us to! Any old man's yearnings for rejuvenated youth? As the final sections of Corbett Mack's life history suggest, this can be seen as consistent with Northern Paiute traditional beliefs.

158. "They believe that the happy world of the hereafter lies in the south," wrote Stephen Powers in 1877. "According to their philosophy, the good experience a resurrection, but the bad 'stay dead'" (D. D. Fowler and C. S. Fowler 1970:132). Du Bois, in her masterful study of the 1870 Ghost Dance, after mentioning its prophet's "abandoning his pretensions," wrote: "Although Wodziwob later denied it, his followers believed that he had dreamed of the return of the Indian dead and that dancing would aid their reappearance" (1939:4). Also compare Forbes (1967:7) in this regard. Was "disillusionment" part of the traditional culture? If not, Wodziwob's reaction (cf. Mary Lutyens 1975 on Khrisnamurti) might be likened to the reactions of others whose "gods have failed" (cf. Crossman 1949; Festinger, Riecken, and Schacter 1956). Annie Lowry, in any event, told Scott (1966:105) that Lovelock Paiutes believed in heaven, a place where "we will meet our loved ones in the next world and we will know them and they will know us . . . all the Indians gonna come back [she laughs]: that's what they believe." "When are the dead coming back, Corbett?" I once asked. "Oh, some day, Mike," he vaguely answered. "'Cause nobody know when. Only Jack Wilson, he know that. Only, he don't preach that kind, neither." Another time, when I pushed him to define good and evil, that is, Who is resurrected when this world tips? Corbett Mack inexplicably snapped: "All them Indian!" And still another time, while pursuing the same line of investigation, he proved a skeptic: "People die, so how they gonna come back?" Corbett quoted something his father-in-law, the shaman Dick Bennett, allegedly had said: "'Cause they got body, and so they rot. So how they gonna come back to turn to young again?" Then, in a voice derivative of what might have been the 1870 Ghost Dance prophet's bitterness, or the traditional culture, or both, Corbett Mack added:

> And you see why? 'Cause some Indian doctor [e.g., *Wodzeewob*], they just don't believe it. No, sir! Say that's not true. . . . [They] Say you're dead, you're dead. How they [the Dead] just go away. And stay away. 'Cause you see why? They say they been there! Yes, sir! Been where them dead people are. . . . Say only shadow there.

His own bitterness? A reworking of tradition? The result of acculturation? Or was Corbett Mack more of a tribal philosopher than my concern with opiates allowed me to give him credit for? I leave this to the more critical reader.

159. For James Mooney's comment on this repetitive pattern of speech in Northern Paiute conversation, see the Introduction.

Bibliography

Aberle, David F.
    1966   The Peyote Religion among the Navaho. Chicago: Aldine Publishing Co.

Angel, Myron, ed.
    1881   History of Nevada: With Illustrations and Biographical Sketches of Its Prominent Men and Pioneers. Oakland: Thompson and West.

Annual Reports of the Commissioner of Indian Affairs (ARCIA)
    1869-70   Washington, D.C.

Arkush, Brooke S.
    1987   Historic Northern Paiute Winter Houses in Mono Basin, California. Journal of California and Great Basin Anthropology 9(2):174-87.

Bancroft, Hubert Howe
    1890   The Works of Hubert H. Bancroft: History of Nevada, Colorado, and Wyoming (1540-1888). San Francisco: History Co.

Basehart, Harry W.
    1967   The Resource Holding Corporation among the Mescalero Apache. Southwestern Journal of Anthropology 23:277-91.
    1970   Mescalero Apache Band Organization and Leadership. Southwestern Journal of Anthropology 26:87-106.

Becker, Howard S.
    1964   Perspectives on Deviance: The Other Side. New York: Free Press.

Beeching, Jack
    1975   The Chinese Opium Wars. New York: Harcourt Brace Jovanovich.

Bidwell, John, Hubert H. Bancroft, and James Longmire
    n.d.   First Three Wagon Trains to California, 1841, to Oregon, 1842, to Washington, 1853. Portland: Binford and Mortes.

Boas, Franz
    1943   Recent Anthropology. Science 98:311-14; 334-37.

Brumble, H. David III
    1988   American Indian Autobiography. Berkeley: University of California Press.

Burroughs, William
    1969   Junky. New York: Penguin Books.
Cain, Ella M.
    1956   The Story of Bodie. San Francisco: Fearman Publishers.
Canfield, Gae Whitney
    1983   Sarah Winnemucca of the Northern Paiutes. Norman: University of Oklahoma Press.
Carter, Gregg Lee
    1975   Social Demography of the Chinese in Nevada: 1870-1880. Nevada Historical Society Quarterly 17(2):73-90.
Casagrande, Joseph B., ed.
    1960   In the Company of Man: Twenty Portraits of Anthropological Informants. New York: Harper and Row.
Chan, Loren B.
    1982   The Chinese in Nevada: An Historical Survey, 1856. Nevada Historical Society Quarterly 25(3):266-314.
Chan, Sucheng
    1986   This Bitter-Sweet Soil: The Chinese in California Agriculture, 1860-1910. Berkeley: University of California Press.
Chung, Sue Fawn
    n.d.   The Chinese Experience in Nevada: Success despite Discrimination. In A Guide to the Elmer R. Rusco Papers on Ethnicity and Race. Special Collections, 88-28. University of Nevada Libraries, Reno.
Clifford, James, and George Marcus
    1986   Writing Culture: The Poetics and Politics of Ethnography. Berkeley: University of California Press.
Cofone, Albin J.
    1982   Themes in the Italian Settlement of Nevada. Nevada Historical Society Quarterly 25(2):116-30.
Coleman, James, Elihu Katz, and Herbert Menzel
    1957   The Diffusion of an Innovation among Physicians. Sociometry 20: 253-70.
Courtwright, David T.
    1982   Dark Paradise: Opiate Addiction in America before 1940. Cambridge: Harvard University Press.
Crossman, Richard, ed.
    1949   The God That Failed, edited by Richard Crossman. New York: Harper and Row.
Curtis, Edward S.
    1926   The North American Indian, vol. 15. Norwood, Mass.: Plimpton Press.
Dangberg, Grace
    1984   An Interview with Grace Dangberg (26 June 1984). Oral History Program. Reno: University of Nevada.

d'Azevedo, Warren L., ed.
  1963   The Washo Indians of California and Nevada. University of Utah Anthropological Papers 67. Salt Lake City.
DeMallie, Raymond J., ed.
  1984   The Sixth Grandfather: Black Elk's Teachings Given to John G. Neihardt. Lincoln: University of Nebraska Press.
De Quincey, Thomas
  [1821] Confessions of an English Opium Eater. Reprint. New York: Penguin Books, 1971.
De Ruff, Arlene
  1946   General Summary of the Chinese Immigration Problem and Bibliography of the Chinese Immigration Problem, 1880-1890. Special Collections. University of Nevada Libraries, Reno, 10 May.
Downs, James F.
  1963a   Differential Response to White Contact: Paiute and Washo. *In* The Washo Indians of California and Nevada, edited by W. L. d'Azevedo, 115-37. University of Utah Anthropological Papers 67. Salt Lake City.
  1963b   Washo Response to Animal Husbandry. *In* The Washo Indians of California and Nevada, edited by W. L. d'Azevedo, 138-52. University of Utah Anthropological Papers 67. Salt Lake City.
  1966   The Two Worlds of the Washo: An Indian Tribe of California and Nevada. New York: Holt, Rinehart, and Winston.
Dressler, Fred
  1984   An Interview with Fred Dressler (10 April 1984). Oral History Program. Reno: University of Nevada.
Du Bois, Cora A.
  1939   The 1870 Ghost Dance. University of California Anthropological Records 3(1). Berkeley.
Dyer, Edward A.
  1990   Wizardry. Special Collections, University of Nevada, Reno. Reprinted *in* Wovoka and the Ghost Dance: A Sourcebook, by Michael Hittman. Carson City, Nev.: Grace Dangberg Foundation.
Egan, Ferol
  1972   Sand in a Whirlwind: The Paiute Indian War of 1860. New York: Doubleday.
Evans-Pritchard, E. E.
  1937   Witchcraft, Oracles and Magic among the Azande. London: Oxford University Press.
Festinger, Leon, Henry W. Riecken, and Stanley Schacter
  1956   When Prophecy Fails. New York: Harper and Row.
Fletcher, Frederick N.
  1923-24 Earliest Crossing of the Deserts of Utah and Nevada to Southern California: Route of Jedidiah S. Smith in 1826. California Historical Society Quarterly 2:228-37.

Forbes, Jack D.
  1967   Nevada Indians Speak. Reno: University of Nevada Press.
Ford, Velma
  1976   History of Lyon County. *In* Nevada—The Silver State, 135-40. Carson City: Western States Historical Publishers.
Fowler, Catherine S.
  1978   Sarah Winnemucca, Northern Paiute, 1844-1891. *In* American Indian Intellectuals, edited by Margot Liberty, 33-44. Proceedings of the American Ethnological Society, 1976. St. Paul, Minn.: West Publishing Co.
  1986   Subsistence. *In* Great Basin, edited by Warren L. d'Azevedo. Handbook of North American Indians, vol. 11, 64-97. Washington, D.C.: Smithsonian Institution.
  1989   Willard Z. Park's "Ethnographic Notes on the Northern Paiute of Western Nevada." University of Utah Anthropological Papers 114. Vol 1. Salt Lake City.
Fowler, Catherine S., and Harold Abel
  1992   Northern Paiute Prayer: Some Features of the Genre. Paper presented at the 91st Meetings of the American Anthropological Association, San Francisco.
Fowler, Catherine S., and Joy Leland
  1967   Some Northern Paiute Native Categories. Ethnology 6:381- 405.
Fowler, Catherine S., and Sven Liljeblad
  1986   Northern Paiute. *In* Great Basin, edited by Warren L. d'Azevedo. Handbook of North American Indians, vol. 11, 435-65. Washington, D. C.: Smithsonian Institution.
Fowler, Don D.
  1966   Great Basin Social Organization. *In* The Current Status of Anthropological Research in the Great Basin: 1964, edited by Warren L. d'Azevedo, Wilbur A. Davis, Don D. Fowler, and Wayne Suttles, 57- 74. Publications of the Desert Research Institute, no. 1. Reno, Nevada.
Fowler, Don D., and Catherine S. Fowler
  1970   Stephen Powers' "The Life and Culture of the Washo and Paiutes." Ethnohistory 17:117-49.
  1971   Anthropology of the Numa: John Wesley Powell's Manuscripts on the Numic Peoples of Western North America, 1868-1880. Smithsonian Contributions to Anthropology, no. 14. Washington, D.C.
Fredericks, Karl
  n.d.   Notes toward a History of the Frederick Family of Sweetwater, California. Manuscript in Hittman's possession.
Fried, Morton H.
  1967   The Evolution of Political Society: An Essay in Political Anthropology. New York: Random House.

Fulstone, Mary
  1980   Recollections of a Country Doctor in Smith, Nevada. Oral History Program. Reno: University of Nevada.
Gardella, Louie A.
  1975   Just Passing Through: My Work in Nevada Agriculture, Agricultural Extension, and Western Water Resources. Oral History Program. Reno: University of Nevada.
Gayton, Anna H.
  1930   The Ghost Dance of 1870 in South-Central California. University of California Publications in American Archaeology and Ethnology 28(3). Berkeley.
Genovese, Eugene D.
  1972   Roll, Jordan, Roll: The World the Slaves Made. New York: Vintage Books.
Glass, Alton E.
  1966   The Life of Alton E. Glass. Oral History Program. Reno: University of Nevada.
Gottschalk, Louis, Clyde Kluckhohn, and Robert Angell
  1945   The Use of Personal Documents in History, Anthroplogy and Sociology. Social Science Research Bulletin 54:77-173.
Green, Donald E.
  1993   The Contextual Nature of American Indian Criminality. American Indian Culture and Research Journal 17(2):99-120.
Guild, Clark J.
  1971   Memories of Careers with Nevada Bench and Bar, Lyon County Office, and the Nevada State Museum. Oral History Program. Reno: University of Nevada.
Hattori, Eugene Mitsuru
  1975   Northern Paiutes on the Comstock: Archeology and Ethnohistory of an American Indian Population in Virginia City, Nevada. In Nevada State Museum Occasional Papers 2, edited by Donald Tuohy and Doris Rendall, 1-82. Carson City.
Heizer, Robert F.
  1966   Preface to Karnee: A Paiute Narrative. Reno: University of Nevada Press.
Heizer, Robert F., and Martin A. Baumhoff
  1962   Prehistoric Rock Art of Nevada and Eastern California. Berkeley: University of California Press.
Hilp, Lester J.
  1968   Reminiscences of a White Pine County Native, Reno Pharmacy Owner, and Civic Leader. Oral History Program. Reno: University of Nevada.
Hittman, Michael
  1965   Field Report. Tri-Institute Field Training Project in Anthropology. Special Collections. University of Nevada Libraries, Reno.

1973a   Ghost Dance, Disillusionment and Opiate Addiction: An Ethnohistory of Smith and Mason Valley Paiutes. Ph.D. diss., University of New Mexico.

1973b   The 1870 Ghost Dance at the Walker River Reservation: A Reconstruction. Ethnohistory 20:247-78.

1973c   Factionalism in a Northern Paiute Tribe as a Consequence of the Indian Reorganization Act. *In* Native American Politics: Power Relationships in the Western Great Basin Today, edited by Ruth Houghton, 17-32. Bureau of Government Research. University of Nevada, Reno.

1984   A Numu History: The Yerington Paiute Tribe. Yerington: Yerington Paiute Tribe.

1990   Wovoka and the Ghost Dance: A Sourcebook. Carson City, Nev.: Grace Dangberg Foundation.

1992   The 1890 Ghost Dance in Nevada. American Indian Journal of Culture and Research 16(4):123-66.

n.d.a   Opiates: Why Smith and Mason Valley Paiutes Rejected Ben Lancester's Peyote Cult in 1936? Manuscript in Hittman's possession.

n.d.b   Sweating It Out . . . in Yerington. Manuscript in Hittman's possession.

Hittman, Michael, ed.

1979-82   Numu Ya Dua [tribal newspaper of the Yerington Paiute Tribe]. Yerington, Nevada.

Hopkins, Sarah Winnemucca

1882   Life among the Piutes: Their Wrongs and Rights. Reprint. Bishop, Nev.: Sierra Media, 1969.

Horowitz, Irving, ed.

1967   The Rise and Fall of Project Camelot: Studies in the Relationship between Social Science and Practical Politics. Cambridge: MIT Press.

Hultkrantz, Åke

1986   Mythology and Religious Concepts. *In* Great Basin, edited by Warren L. d'Azevedo. Handbook of North American Indians, vol. 11, 630-40. Washington, D.C.: Smithsonian Institution.

Ingalls, George W.

1913   Indians of Nevada, 1825-1913. *In* History of Nevada. Vol. 1, edited by Samuel P. Davis, 20-132. Reno: Elms Publishing Co.

Inter-Tribal Council of Nevada

1974   Life Stories of our Native People. Salt Lake City: University of Utah Printing Service.

n.d.   Inventory and Description Records of the Inter-Tribal Council of Nevada, 1964-1986. Reno: Reno-Sparks Indian Colony.

Isola, Louis J.

1980   Immigrant: I Made Good in the United States. Oral History Program. Reno: University of Nevada.

Johnson, Edward C.

1975   Walker River Paiutes: A Tribal History. Schurz, Nev.: Walker River Tribe.

n.d. Stewart Indian School. Manuscript in Johnson's possession.
Jorgensen, Joseph C.
1971 Indians and the Metropolis. *In* The American Indian in Urban Society, edited by J. O. Waddell and O. M. Watson, 66-113. Boston: Little, Brown.
Jourard, Sidney M.
1964 The Transparent Self: Self-Disclosure and Well-Being. New York: Van Nostrand Reinhold.
Kane, Eileen
1964 Field Report. Special Collections. University of Nevada Libraries, Reno.
Kane, Harry Hubbell
1882 Opium Addiction in America and China: A Study of Its Prevalence, and Effect, Immediate and Remote, on the Individual and the Nation. New York: D. P. Putnam's Son.
Kehoe, Alice B.
1989 The Ghost Dance: Ethnohistory and Revitalization. New York: Holt, Rinehart and Winston.
Kelly, Isabel T.
1932 Ethnography of the Surprise Valley Paiute. University of California Publications in American Archaeology and Ethnology 31. Berkeley.
1938 Northern Paiute Tales. Journal of American Folklore 51:368-438.
Kersten, Earl W., Jr.
1961 Settlements and Economic Life in the Walker River Country of Nevada and California. Ph.D. diss., University of Nebraska.
1964 The Early Settlement of Aurora, Nevada, and Nearby Mining Camps. Annals of the Association of American Geographers 54:490-507.
Kluckhohn, Clyde
1945 The Personal Document in Anthropological Science. *In* The Uses of Personal Documents in History, Anthropology, and Sociology, 77-173. Social Science Research Bulletin 53.
Kroeber, Alfred A.
1904 A Ghost Dance in California. Journal of American Folk-Lore 17:32-35.
1952a The Superorganic. *In* The Nature of Culture, edited by Alfred A. Kroeber, 22-51. Chicago: University of Chicago Press.
1952b The Use of Autobiographical Evidence, 1945. *In* The Nature of Culture, edited by Alfred A. Kroeber, 320-22. Chicago: University of Chicago Press.
Krupat, Arnold
1982 Ethnocriticism: Ethnography, History, Literature. Berkeley: University of California Press.
1985 For Those Who Come After: A Study of Native American Autobiography. Berkeley: University of California Press.

1989 The Voice in the Margin: Native American Literature and the Canon, Berkeley: University of California Press.

Langness, L. L.
1965 The Life History in Anthropological Science. New York: Holt, Rinehart, and Winston.

Lanner, Ronald M.
1981 The Pinion Pine: A Natural and Cultural History. Reno: University of Nevada Press.

Larson, Burnell
n.d. Our Desert Friends. State of Nevada, Department of Education. Vertical Files, Lyon County Public Library. Yerington, Nevada.

Larson, Vic
n.d. Notes on Antelope Valley. Manuscript in possession of Earl W. Kersten, Jr.

Lawton, Harry W., Philip J. Wilke, Mary DeDecker, and William M. Mason
1976 Agriculture among the Paiute of Owens Valley. Journal of California Anthropology 3(1):13-49.

Lee, Shirley W.
1967 A Survey of Acculturation in the Inter-Montane Area of the United States. Occasional Papers of the Museum of Idaho State University, no. 19. Pocatello.

Liljeblad, Sven
1986 Oral Tradition: Content and Style of Verbal Arts. *In* Great Basin, edited by Warren L. d'Azevedo. Handbook of North American Indians, vol. 11, 641-59. Washington, D.C.: Smithsonian Institution.

Lindsmith, Alfred R.
1947 Opiate Addiction. Evanston: Principia Press.

Lowie, Robert H.
1924 Notes on Shoshonean Ethnography. American Museum of Natural History Anthropological Papers 20(3). New York.

Lutyens, Mary
1975 Krishnamurti: The Years of Awakening. New York: Avon Books.

Lyman, Stanford M.
1970 The Asian in the West. Edited by Don D. Fowler. Social Science and Humanities Publication no. 4. Desert Research Institute. University of Nevada, Reno.

Magnaghi, Russell M.
1975-76 Index to: "Chinese and Indians on the Comstock, 1975-1976." Bancroft Library. University of California, Berkeley.
1981 Virginia City's Chinese Community. Nevada Historical Society Quarterly 24(2) (Summer):130-57.

Mandelbaum, David G.
1973 The Study of Life History: Gandhi. Current Anthropology 14:177-96.

Maule, William M.
  1938   A Contribution to the Geographic and Economic History of the Carson, Walker, and Mono Basins in Nevada and California. U. S. Forest Service. Berkeley, California.
Maurer, David W., and Victor H. Vogel
  1967   Narcotics and Narcotic Addiction. Springfield, Ill.: Charles C. Thomas.
Meriam, Lewis
  1928   The Problem of Indian Administration. The Institute for Government Research. Baltimore: Johns Hopkins University Press.
Merton, Robert K.
  1957   Social Structure and Anomie: Continuities in the Theory of Social Structure and Anomie. In Social Theory and Social Structure, edited by Robert K. Merton, 131-94. New York: Free Press.
Miller, Jay
  1983   Basin Religion and Theology: A Comparative Study of Power (Puha). Journal of California and Great Basin Anthropology 5:66-86.
Mooney, James
  1896   The Ghost-Dance Religion and the Sioux Outbreak of 1890. Smithsonian Institution, Bureau of American Ethnology, Fourteenth Annual Report, part 2. Washington, D.C.
Morgan, H. Wayne
  1981   Drugs in America: A Social History (1860-1980). Syracuse, N.Y.: Syracuse University Press.
Nash, Dennison, and Ronald Wintrob
  1972   The Emergence of Self-Consciousness in Ethnography. Current Anthropology 13(5):527-42.
Nash, Philleo
  1937   The Place of Religious Revivalism in the Formation of the Intercultural Community on Klamath Reservation. In Social Anthropology of North American Indian Tribes, edited by Fred Eggan, 377-442. Chicago: University of Chicago Press.
Neihardt, John G.
  1932   Black Elk Speaks: Being the Life Story of a Holy Man of the Ogalala Sioux. New York: William Morrow.
Nevins, Allan
  1956   Narratives of Exploration and Adventure, by John Charles Fremont. New York: Longmans, Green.
Olofson, Harold
  1979   Northern Paiute Shamanism Revisited. Anthropos 79:11-24.
Ostrander, Gilman M.
  1966   Nevada: The Great Rotten Borough, 1859-1964. New York: Alfred A. Knopf.
Park, Willard Z.
  1934   Paviotso Shamanism. American Anthropologist 36:98-113.
  1937   Paviotso Polyandry. American Anthropologist 39:366-88.

1938a The Organization and Habitat of Paviotso Bands. American Anthropologist 40:622-38.
1938b Shamanism in Western North America: A Study in Cultural Relationships. Evanston, Ill.: Northwestern University.
1941 Cultural Succession in the Great Basin. *In* Language, Culture and Personality, edited by L. A. Spier, A. I. Hallowell, and S. Newman, 180-203. Menasha: Sapir Memorial Publication Fund.

Petersen, William
1969 Population. New York: Macmillan.

Poldervaart, Arie
1987a Paiute-English/English-Paiute Dictionary. Yerington, Nev.: Yerington Paiute Tribe.
1987b Yerington Paiute Grammar. Edited by Tupou L. Pulu. Anchorage: Bilingual Education Services.

Radin, Paul
1920 The Autobiography of a Winnebago Indian. Reprint. New York: Dover Publications, 1963.
1923 The Winnebago Tribe. Reprint. Lincoln: University of Nebraska Press, 1970.

Redfield, Robert
1953 The Primitive World and Its Transformations, Ithaca: Cornell University Press.

Reed, Flo, ed.
n.d. Use of Native Plants by Nevada Indians. State of Nevada, Department of Education. Vertical Files, Lyon County Public Library. Yerington, Nevada.

Riddell, Francis A.
1960 Honey Lake Ethnography. Nevada State Museum Anthropological Paper 4. Carson City.

Ruhlen, George
n.d. Military History. Special Collections. University of Nevada Libraries, Reno.

Ruiz, Allura Mason
1964 The Basques: Sheepmen of the West. Master's thesis, University of Nevada.

Ruscoe, Elmer
n.d. A Guide to the Elmer R. Rusco Papers on Ethnicity and Race. Special Collections, 88-28. University of Nevada Libraries, Reno.

Ryder, Norman B.
1965 The Cohort as a Concept in the Study of Social Change. American Sociological Review 30:843-61.

Sampson, Dewey
1980 A Pa Oha Warning. Audio tape recorded by Peggy Lear Bowen, 28 June. Special Collections. University of Nevada Libraries, Reno.

Sayre, Cora Gage
  1977   Memories of Smith Valley. Oral History Program. Reno: University of Nevada.
Scott, Lalla
  1966   Karnee. Reno: University of Nevada Press.
Scrugham, James G. Nevada
  1935   A Narrative of the Conquest of a Frontier Land. Vol. 1. Chicago: American Historical Society.
Service, Elman
  1962   Primitive Social Organization: An Evolutionary Perspective. New York: Random House.
Shepperson, Wilbur S.
  1970   Restless Strangers: Nevada Immigrants and Their Interpreters. Reno: University of Nevada Press.
Short, Shelton Hardaway
  1965   A History of the Nevada Livestock Industry Prior to 1900. Master's thesis, University of Nevada.
Simmons, Leo W.
  1942   Sun Chief: The Autobiography of a Hopi Indian. Reprint. New Haven: Yale University Press, 1971.
Simpson, Captain J. H.
  1876   Report of Explorations across the Great Basin of the Territory for a Direct Wagon-Route from Camp Floyd to Genoa, in Carson Valley, in 1859. Engineer Department, U.S. Army. Washington, D.C.
Siskin, Edgar E.
  1983   Washo Shamans and Peyotists: Religious Conflict in an American Indian Tribe. Salt Lake City: University of Utah Press.
Smart, George W.
  1958   Missions to Nevada: A History of Nevada Indian Missions. Diss., Central Baptist Theological Seminary.
Smith, Timothy B.
  1911-12 Recollections of the Early History of Smith Valley. Nevada Historical Society, Third Biennial Report. Reno.
Smith, William F., Jr.
  1975   American Indian Autobiographies. American Indian Quarterly 2(2): 237-45.
Spier, Leslie
  1927   The Ghost Dance of 1870 among the Klamath of Oregon. University of Washington Publications in Anthropology 2. Seattle.
  1935   The Prophet Dance of the Northwest and Its Derivatives: The Source of the Ghost Dance. General Series in Anthropology 1. Menasha, Wisconsin.
Steward, Julian H.
  1930   Irrigation without Agriculture. Papers of the Michigan Academy of Science, Arts, and Letters 12:149-56.

1933 Ethnography of the Owens Valley Paiute. University of California Publications in American Archaeology and Ethnology 33(3). Berkeley.
1934 Two Paiute Autobiographies. University of California Publications in American Archaeology and Ethnology 33(5). Berkeley.
1936a Myths of the Owens Valley Paiute. University of California Publications in American Archaeology and Ethnology 34(5). Berkeley.
1936b Shoshoni Polyandry. American Anthropologist 38:561-64.
1938 Basin-Plateau Aboriginal Sociopolitical Groups. Smithsonian Institution, Bureau of American Ethnology Bulletin 120. Washington, D.C.
1963 Theory of Cultural Change. Urbana: University of Illinois Press.

Stewart, Omer C.
1937 Northern Paiute Polyandry. American Anthropologist 39:368-69.
1939 The Northern Paiute Bands. University of California Anthropological Records 2. Berkeley.
1941 Culture Element Distributions 14: Northern Paiute. University of California Anthropological Records 4(3). Berkeley.
1944 Washo-Northern Paiute Peyotism: A Study in Acculturation. University of California Publications in American Archaeology and Ethnology 40(3). Berkeley.
1956 Three Gods for Joe. Tomorrow: Quarterly Review of Psychical Research 5(3):71-76.
1964 Questions regarding American Indian Criminality. Human Organization 23:61-66.
1987 Peyote Religion: A History. Norman: University of Oklahoma Press.

Swann, Brian, ed.
1983 Smoothing the Ground: Essays on Native American Oral Literature. Berkeley: University of California Press.

Tedlock, Dennis
1983 On the Translation of Style in Oral Narrative. *In* Smoothing the Ground: Essays on Native American Oral Literature, edited by Brian Swann, 57-77. Berkeley: University of California Press.

Thompson, David
1986 Nevada: A History of Changes. Carson City: Grace Dangberg Foundation.

Treadwell, Edward F.
1931 The Cattle King. New York: Macmillan.

Tsai, Shih-Shan Henry
1986 The Chinese Experience in America. Bloomington: Indiana University Press.

Underhill, Ruth M.
1936 Papago Woman. Reprint. New York: Holt, Rinehart, and Winston, 1979.

U.S. Bureau of the Census
1880-1920 Federal Censuses of the United States. Microfilm. Washington, D.C.: National Archives and Records Administration.

Wall, C. Leon
    1952   A History of Indian Education in Nevada from 1861-1951. Master's thesis, University of Nevada.

Wheeler, Sessions S.
    1967   The Desert Lake: The Story of Nevada's Pyramid Lake. Caldwell: Caxton Printers.

Wheelis, Allen
    1966   The Illusionless Man: Some Fantasies and Meditations on Disillusioment. New York: Harper and Row.

Whiting, Beatrice B.
    1950   Paiute Sorcery. Viking Fund Publications in Anthropology 15. New York.

Willis, F. W.
    1913   Picket Guards: Recollections of a Methodist Circuit Rider, Nevada, 1862-1885. Special Collections, 83-10. University of Nevada Libraries, Reno.

Wittke, Carl
    1958   We Who Built America. Ann Arbor: Press of Western Reserve University.

Corbett Mack
The Life of a Northern Paiute

AS TOLD BY
Michael Hittman

University of Nevada Press
Reno // Las Vegas

University of Nevada Press, Reno, Nevada 89557 USA
www.unpress.nevada.edu
Copyright © 1996 by University of Nebraska Press
New preface copyright © 2013 by University of Nevada Press
All rights reserved
Manufactured in the United States of America

Library of Congress Cataloging-in-Publication Data
Hittman, Michael.
Corbett Mack : the life of a Northern Paiute / as told by Michael Hittman. — First edition.
　　pages cm.
Includes bibliographical references and index.
ISBN 978-0-87417-915-6 (pbk. : alk. paper) — ISBN 978-0-87417-916-3 (ebook)
1. Mack, Corbett, 1892–1974.　2. Northern Paiute Indians—Biography.　3. Northern Paiute Indians—History.　4. Northern Paiute Indians—Social life and customs.　5. Smith Creek Valley (Nev.)—Social life and customs.　6. Mason Valley (Nev.)—Social life and customs.　I. Title.
E99.P2.M335 2013
305.897'4577—dc23
[B]　　　　　　　　　　　　　2013016218

The paper used in this book meets the requirements of American National Standard for Information Sciences—Permanence of Paper for Printed Library Materials, ANSI/NISO Z39.48-1992 (R2002). Binding materials were selected for strength and durability.

University of Nevada Press Paperback Edition, 2013

This book has been reproduced as a digital reprint.

For my wife, Meryl whose courage through life-threatening illness inspires this book, and my daughters Julie, who learned to walk on Campbell Ranch to Grandma Ida's "Hey-na Hey-na" song, and Eliza, whose love of animals was nurtured there.

Contents

List of Illustrations   xiii
Acknowledgments   xiv
Note on Orthography   xvi

Introduction   1

1. Birth and Family (1892)
    1. A Stolen Child   23
    2. Sticks and Stones . . .   24
    3. A Name and a Birthdate   24
    4. My *Nuumuu* Name   25
    5. Another Name for Me   25
    6. Big Mack's Name(s)   25
    7. Big Mack   26
    8. Big Mack's Final Name Change   29
    9. My Real Father   29
    10. Big Mack's Rage   30
    11. My Grandma, *Tseehooka*   30
    12. My Mom   33
    13. *Poogooga 'yoo* ('Horseman')   35
    14. Three Brothers and Two Sisters   37
    15. Sibling Solidarity   40

2. Boyhood (1892–1905)
    16. Them *Taivo*, They Come to Smith (and Mason) Valley!   43
    17. World's War!   44
    18. *Tabooseedokado*: Smith (and Mason) Valley *Nuumuu*   47
    19. One Real Old-Timer   49
    20. Growing Up in Smith Valley: Our House   50
    21. The Outfit   52
    22. Some Traditional (Plant) Foods   52
    23. *Tuubanuugwa* ('Pine Nut Dance')   54

24.	*Naavey^ts* ('Firstfruits'): Male Puberty Rite	55
25.	Hunting Proscriptions	56
26.	Games and So Forth	56
27.	*Pahmoo* ('Indian Tobacco')	58
28.	My *Waseeyoo* ('Washo') Indian Relations	60
29.	I Lose My Little Toe	60
30.	My Horse Brown	61

3. Boarding School (1905–10)

31.	Stewart Institute	65
32.	Why I Change My Name?	67
33.	Readin' and Writin' and 'Rithmetic	67
34.	Books and Grades	68
35.	Christopher Columbus	68
36.	Civilization	69
37.	Meals and Order	70
38.	End of the Day	71
39.	My Stewart Nickname	73
40.	Stewart Girls	73
41.	Parties in Stewart	74
42.	The Disciplinarian: Punishment and Jail	74
43.	That Jesus Business . . .	75
44.	Saturdays in Carson City	77
45.	Why I Leave Stewart?	78
46.	*Nuumuu skooruunobee* ('Indian School House'): Stewart Reprise	80

4. Work and Girls (1912–23)

47.	Back Home Again in Smith Valley	81
48.	First Job	82
49.	Ranch Work	83
50.	Some Other Early Jobs	84
51.	Yet Another Early Job	85
52.	Workin' for the Man	86
53.	Jobs I Don't Like	87
54.	One Boss I Especially Like	90
55.	Ownin' Land	90
56.	My Grandma Remarries	93
57.	Coyote Dreamin'	94
58.	Girlfriend(s)	94
59.	Them City Girl(s)!	98
60.	*Waseeyoo* Girls	99

61.	Ranch Work in Mason Valley	100
62.	My Wife	101
63.	Celia Mack's Real Name	104
64.	*Pashˆp!* ('Childless!')	104
65.	Marital Bliss	106
66.	Reflections on Bachelorhood	107

5. Italians, Potatoes, Homemade Wine (1923–58)

67.	Them *Aytayay* ('Italians')!	109
68.	*Aytayay* Stinginess	111
69.	My Boss, Amos Macarini [Mencarini]	112
70.	The Boss's Wife	113
71.	Working for Amos Mencarini	113
72.	Life on the (Potato) Plantation	114
73.	One *Nuumuu* Death, One Bunkhouse	116
74.	Our Own House to Live in	117
75.	The Real Deal	118
76.	Homemade *Aytayay* Wine	119
77.	Bootleggin'	121
78.	Indian Bootleggers	122
79.	How I Learn to Drink?	123
80.	Hard Drinkin'	124
81.	One Time, Though . . .	127
82.	Why Indians Drink?	128

6. Chinese Opium (1896–1931)

83.	*'Oopeeyˆn* ('Opium')	129
84.	Beginning of Opiate Addiction in Smith (and Mason) Valley	130
85.	Alternative Origin	131
86.	The Chinese Connection	132
87.	*Moohoo'oo* ('Yen-Shee')	134
88.	Your Own Outfit	135
89.	The Life of the *Nuumuu* Addict	136
90.	Buyin' *Moohoo'oo*	138
91.	Other "Celestial" Connections	140
92.	No More Chinaman!	141
93.	An Unlikely Connection!	142
94.	A Meeting with My Real Father	143
95.	The Indian Connection	144
96.	I Sell	147
97.	Willy Muldoon's Base of Operations	148
98.	Sellin' for Willy Muldoon	150

99.	Driving Mishap	152
100.	I Am Nearly Arrested	153
101.	Willy, He Get Caught!	155
102.	George Emm, Last of the Yen-Shee Sellers	156
103.	Shootin' *Moohoo'oo*	156
104.	Shootin' *Moohoo'oo*: Alternative Version	157
105.	Sanalow	158
106.	*Toha Moohoo'oo* ('Morphine')	158
107.	Sellin' Morphine	159
108.	*Waseeyoo* Morphine Sellers	161
109.	Mike Rube, Last of the Indian Sellers?	162
110.	Withdrawal Symptoms	164
111.	What to Take for Withdrawal Symptoms?	164
112.	Over-the-Counter Remedies	166
113.	Contract Physician	166
114.	Once More, Once	167
115.	Geography of Addiction	169
116.	My Gripe	170
117.	Opiates: Reprise	170

7. Some Real Old-Timers (1896–1940)

118.	Never Mix, Never Worry!	173
119.	Another Time . . .	174
120.	I Am Arrested!	175
121.	One Real Old-Timer's Belief	175
122.	*Wodzeewob*, 1870 Ghost Dance Prophet	177
123.	Jack Wilson (Wovoka), 1890 Ghost Dance Prophet	179
124.	Jack Wilson's *Booha* ('Power')	181
125.	Jack Wilson's Dances	182
126.	Doctored by Jack Wilson	184
127.	*Hongo*, Virginia City Paiute Rubber	185
128.	A Different Kind of Cure	187
129.	Tom Mitchell!	188
130.	*Nuumuu Puharrˆ* ("Witchcraft")	189
131.	Tom Mitchell's Witchin' Way	191
132.	I Love Tom Mitchell's Daughters	192
133.	The Death of Jack Wilson	193
134.	Pneumonia! Exposure!	194
135.	Exposure! Pneumonia!	195
136.	The Death of Tom Mitchell	199
137.	Ben Lancaster (Chief Gray Horse), Peyotist	200

138.	That *Peeyot* Business !	201
139.	Never Mix, Never Worry!	203

8. Retirement Years (1954–74)
140.	A Falling Out with My Boss	207
141.	Campbell Ranch Land Assignment?	208
142.	No More Spuds!	209
143.	*Ya'eep* ('Death')	210
144.	Death of a Wife	211
145.	I Move to Mason Valley	212
146.	Attempted Reconciliation with My Boss	213
147.	Retirement in Mason Valley	213
148.	Some (More) Real Old-Timers	215
149.	Tales of *Booha*	219
150.	More Tales of Supernatural Power	220
151.	*Natoonˆdweba* ('Animal Teaching Stories')	222
152.	The Flood and Other Animal Teachings	224
153.	Giants and Waterbabies	228
154.	Wolf and Coyote	231
155.	*Karroo'oo*! No More Nothin'!	232
156.	Bad Dreams	233
157.	No More, He Comeback(s)	234
158.	Disillusionment?	236

Epilogue
159.	Final Visit (1973) with Corbett Mack: A Conversation	239

Appendix A:
  Local Newspaper Accounts of Opiates in Smith and
  Mason Valleys, Nevada (1896–1931)   243
Appendix B:
  Report of Narcotic Situation among the Indians of the
  Walker River Jurisdiction (1931)   253
Appendix C:
  Narcotics in Smith and Mason Valleys (1929)   257
Notes   259
Bibliography   371
Index   385

Index

Acculturation, 31, 43-44, 49, 266-67, 271, 278, 282, 290
Afterlife, 236, 368-69
Agaidokado 'Trout-Eaters', 9, 24, 264, 274
Agriculture, 48, 92, 110, 272, 275-76, 290, 298
Alcohol, use of, 123-28, 173-75, 256, 304-7, 350-51; and attempted rape, 82, 289; causes insanity, 37; and illness and injury, 194-98, 359-60; and opiates, 19, 130, 171, 173, 350; prohibited to Indians, 99
Animal husbandry, 43, 87-88, 272, 292-93, 296
Animal teaching stories, 16, 222-32, 235-36. *See also* Folktales
Antelope, 365-66
Antelope doctors, 216
Arapaho religion, 294
Artemisia, Nev., 333
Artesia Lake, 270, 291
Aurora, Nev., 272
Autobiographies, 1, 2, 8, 19-20
Autobiography and ethnography, 8-9
Aytayay. See Italians

Bannock Indians, 182-84, 353
Bannock War, 1875, 274

Basques, 88
Bears, 89
Boarding schools, 11. *See also* Schools
Bodie, Nev., 272
Booha. See Power
Bootlegging, 119-23, 174, 256, 302-4, 349
Bridgeport, Nev., 169
Bridgeport Indians, 266
Brumble, H. David, III, 1
Buckskin, Nev., 51
Buckskin Mountains, 270
Burial, 38-39

Campbell Ranch, 2, 208-9, 363-64
Carson City, Nev., 169, 323
Carson City Indian Colony, 77
Carson Indian School, 65, 284. *See also* Stewart Institute
Cattle industry, 43, 272, 292, 296
Caves, 88-89, 292
Cheyenne Indians, 183
Chief Gray Horse (Ben Lancaster), 15
Childbirth, 104
Chinese, 13, 132, 288; introduced opiates, 13; origin of opium smoking among, 311-12; Paiute hostility toward, 317;

Chinese (*continued*)
  population, 312, 323;
  prostitution among, 78, 288. *See also* Opiates, sale, by Chinese
Churchill War, 35. *See also* Pyramid Lake War of 1860
Cocaine, 149, 350. *See also* Opiates
Coleville, Cal., 169, 329
Columbia River Indians, 366
Columbus, Christopher, 68, 286
Conquest, reactions to, 282
Contact with whites, 9, 43-44, 271, 272, 290
Contraception, 105
Conversational style, Paiute, 17, 239-41
Copper mining, 51, 294, 333
Cottontail Rabbit, 225-27
Coyote, 89, 222-24, 225-28, 230, 232, 233, 235-36, 367; causes sex dreams, 94; and origin of pine nuts, 85, 90-91; and reversal of gender roles, 267
Cures, 176-77, 184-85, 352-54

Dances, 182-83
Dancing, 54, 74, 182-83, 189, 279-80
Dead, the, 6, 35, 39, 296; burial of, 38-39; raising to life, 176-77, 352
Death, 16, 210, 212, 364
Desert Creek Peak, 270
Desert Mountains, 270
Designated repeater, 16, 60-61, 179, 231, 282-83
Doctors, 216. *See also* Indian doctors; Shamanism; Shamans
Drug use. *See* Alcohol; Alcohol, use of; Bootlegging; Chinese; Cocaine; Marijuana; Opiates; Peyote
Dwellings, 50-51, 85, 117-18, 278-79, 294-95

East Walker River, 270
Eesha. *See* Wolf
Eeza'a. *See* Coyote
End of the world, 175-76
Ethnography, 2, 8-9
Extended family, 12

Face painting, 4, 38, 88
Fallon, Nev., 169
Fish, 48
Fish Lake Joe. *See* Wodziwob
Folktales, 278, 283, 367; constellations, 225; Cottontail Rabbit, 225-27; Coyote, 89, 222-28, 230, 232, 233, 235-36, 367; end of world, 175-76; events of nature, 49, 220-22; Giants, 228-31, 367; Old Woman, 223-25, 228-30; Owl, 236; Sun, 222, 225-26; theme of pine nut theft, 291; Waterbabies, 228-31, 366-67; Wolf, 89, 222-24, 231-32, 233, 235-36
Foodlore, 2-3
Foods, 47-48, 53-54, 275-76, 279
Fort Churchill, 45, 274
Fremont, John Charles, 271

Gambling, 34, 188, 355-57
Games, 57, 71-72, 280-81
Gardnerville, Nev., 169
Ghost Dance, 1870, 6, 352. *See also* Wodziwob
Ghost Dance, 1890, 9, 352. *See also* Wovoka
Ghost sickness, 213, 365
Giants, 228-31, 367
Gold mining, 272
Grass Nut Eaters (*Tabooseedokado*), 2, 47-49, 274-75. *See also* Yerington Paiute Tribe
Great Basin Indians, 266-67
Guns, 45-46
Gypsum mining, 333

*H*ageenopa. *See* Wild parsnip
Half-breeds *(nomogweta)*, 10, 23, 24, 259, 260, 353; taunting of mother of, 30, 39-40, 265-66
Harrison, Raymond, 294
Harrison Narcotics Act of 1914, 166, 313, 329, 330-31
Hawthorne, Nev., 347
Heebee. See Wine, homemade
Hopkins, Sarah Winnemucca, 21, 273, 367. *See also* Sarah Winnemucca
Horses, 35, 62, 81, 283
Houses. *See* Dwellings
Hunting, 27-28, 55-57, 263-64

*I*llness and injury: and alcohol use, 194-98, 359-60; dancing to cure, 189; and peyote, 202, 362-63; prayer for curing, 32, 34-35, 276-78; and shamanism, 199-200; venereal disease, 45-46, 97; and witchcraft, 184-92, 357-58
Illness and injury, treatments for, 32, 38, 58, 89; hot springs, 58; *moogoodoohoop*, 58, 281; rubbing, 185-86; tobacco, 58, 61, 281
Indian Affairs, Senate Committee on, 254
Indian autobiography. *See* Autobiographies
Indian doctors *(poohaghooma)*, 216, 219, 220; and caves, 88-89; curing of venereal disease, 45-46; put facial mark on patients, 88; use rubbing as cure, 185-86, 354. *See also* Shamanism; Shamans
Indian names, 24, 25, 26, 28, 261, 262, 296
Indian Reorganization Act, 363
Indian reservations, 2, 6, 9, 77, 271, 295

Informant pay, 4
Inter-Tribal Council of Nevada, 2
Invincibility, 45-46, 273-74
Italians *(Aytayay)*, 12-13, 102, 109-28, 297-307

*J*apanese, 140-41, 325-27

*K*ane, Eileen, 3
Kinship systems, 52, 270, 279
Krupat, Arnold, 1
Kuutsabeedakado Mono Lake 'Brine Fly Pupae-Eaters', 9, 266

*L*ancaster, Ben (Chief Gray Horse), 15
Life history. *See* Autobiography
Life Stories of Our Native People, 2
Lovelock, Nev., 281, 293
Lovelock Paiutes, 259, 368
Lowry, Annie, 2, 10, 259
Ludwig, Nev., 51, 333

*M*agic, 297. *See also* Witchcraft
Marijuana, 7, 350. *See also* Opiates
Marriage, 26-27, 52, 103, 104, 262, 279
Mason, N. H. A. (Hoc), 9, 271
Mason, Nev., 51, 294, 347
Mason Valley, 9, 270, 271
Mina, Nev., 140, 323, 347-48
Mining, 51, 88, 272, 292, 294, 333
Missouri Flat, 49
Mitchell, Tom, 15, 61, 188, 199-200, 355-58, 360; suspected of witchcraft, 98, 178, 186-88, 191-92, 349
Mono Lake, Nev., 272
Moohoo'oo. See Opiates, yen-shee
Morphine. *See under* Opiates
Mythology, 48, 56, 276-77. *See also* Folktales

*N*ames, customs concerning, 24, 25, 26, 28, 261, 262, 296

Nature, events of, 220-22
Nixon, Nev., 45
Nomogweta. See Half-breeds
Nordyke, Nev., 283
Northern Paiute language, 232, 287
Northern Paiutes, 2, 6, 16-17, 88, 90, 264, 293; relations with Washo Indians, 33, 60, 281-82
Nuumuu 'Northern Paiute', 47-49, 259. *See also* Northern Paiutes
Nuumuu pooharru: See Witchcraft
Nuumuuraivo (Wovoka's father), 26-27, 180

Old Woman, 223-25, 228-30
'Oopeey^n 'raw opium', 131. *See also* Opiates
Opiates, 6, 14, 18, 129-72, 243-58, 307-50; and alcohol use, 19, 130, 171, 173, 350; availability, 307-9; cost, compared to wages, 255; counties involved, 346; extent of use, 5, 169, 255, 337, 350; methods of using, 135, 156-58, 317-19, 335-37; mixing substances, 7, 173, 204; morphine *(toha moohoo'oo)*, 6, 158-64, 168, 336-39; in over-the-counter medications, 166, 341-43; and peyote, 204; and prostitution, 244-45; provided as wages, 142; reasons for use, 6, 14, 18, 129-30, 350; regulation of sale and use, 13, 166, 257-58, 313, 330-31, 333-34, 342, 350; sale, by Chinese, 132-33, 138-47, 253-54, 255, 311-17, 323, 325, 328-29; sale, by Indians, 15, 144-52, 153-56, 159-63, 249-51, 253-54, 324, 329-31, 339; sale, by Japanese, 140-41, 325-27; sale, by whites, 321, 337-38; sanalow, 135, 141-42, 151, 158; withdrawal, 164-67,
339-41; yen-shee *(moohoo'oo)*, 6, 15, 131, 134-35, 318, 328. *See also* Chinese
Owens Valley War of 1863, 274
Owls, 134, 236, 268, 318

Paiute-Chinese hostility, 317
Peabody Indian School, 293
Peer pressure, 14
Peyote, 15, 200-205, 345, 362-63
Pine Grove (mining camp), 277
Pine Grove Hills, 270
Pine Nut Bird, 91
Pine Nut Dance, 182-83
Pine Nut Festival, 279
Pine Nut Mountains, 270
Pine nuts, 52-53, 85, 167-68, 291
Piñon pine, 291
Polyandry, 262
Polygamy, 26, 262
Polygyny, 26, 262
Poohaghooma. See Indian doctors; Shamanism; Shamans
Population: of Chinese, 312, 323; of Italians, 297; of Northern Paiutes, 6, 277; of Yerington, Nev., 294
Potato industry, 110-11, 114-15, 209, 298-300
Power *(booha)*, 286; bequeathing of, 360; of the blind, 79; and caves, 88-89; and Christopher Columbus, 68, 286; and fertility, 105; and opiate selling, 15; and peyote, 201; and Pyramid Lake War of 1860, 45-46; sources of, 358; and tobacco, 186; in war, 45-46; of Wovoka, 181-82, 184
Pragmatics, Paiute, 17, 239-41
Prayer, 54, 58, 76, 94, 267, 281
Prohibition, 102, 173-74
Prostitution, 78, 288
Protestant work ethic, 290
Puberty rites, 55, 280
Pyramid Lake Indians, 169

INDEX

Pyramid Lake Trout-Eaters, 45
Pyramid Lake War of 1860, 9, 35, 44-47, 273-74

Rabbit drives, 28, 263
Radin, Paul, 8
Rattlesnakes, 89
Red Ant, 105-6
Relocation of Northern Paiutes, 45, 274
Reno, Nev., 169, 349
Repeaters, designated, 16, 60-61, 179, 231, 282-83
Reproduction, 104, 105
Reservations, Indian, 2, 6, 9, 77, 271, 295

Salvage ethnography, 2
Sanalow, 135, 141-42, 151, 158. *See also* Opiates
Schools, 65-80, 111, 277-78, 283-89, 332
Schurz, Nev., 49
Senate Committee on Indian Affairs, 13, 254
Shamanism, 24, 38, 89, 269, 283, 292, 352. *See also* Designated repeaters; Indian doctors; Shamans *(poohaghooma)*
Shamans, 199-201, 218, 219, 358, 360, 362-63. *See also* Indian doctors; Shamanism
Sheep industry, 87-88, 292-93
Shoshone Indians, 93-94, 153-54, 168, 284, 294, 366
Sierra Nevada Mountains, 270
Silver mining, 272
Singatse Mountains, 270, 294, 333
Sister exchange, 26-27
Smart, George William, 308
Smith, Timothy, 9
Smith Valley, 9, 43, 260, 270, 271
Sterility, 105
Stewart, Jake, 2

Stewart Institute, 65-80, 111, 283-89, 332
Sun, 32, 34-35, 222, 225-26
Sweathouse, 93-94, 294
Sweetwater, Cal., 294
Sweetwater, Nev., 169, 347

Tabooseedokado 'Grass Nut Eaters', 2, 45, 47-49, 274-75. *See also* Yerington Paiute Tribe
Taboosee 'grass nuts', 47, 275-76
Taivo. See Whites
Tattooing, 38, 270
Thunder, 222
Tobacco, 58-60, 185-86, 281
Toha moohoo'oo. See Opiates, morphine
Trapping, 85
Trees, 84-85, 291
Tri-Institute Field Training Project in Anthropology, 2
Trout-Eaters *(Agaidokado)*, 9, 274

Venereal diseases, 45-46, 97

Wabuska, Nev., 138-39, 294, 347
Wages, 255
Walker Lake, 271
Walker River, 270-71
Walker River Reservation, 9, 271
Wars, 9, 35, 44-47, 273-74
Waseeyoo. See Washo Indians
Washington, George, 45-46
Washo Indians *(Waseeyoo)*, 200-201, 280, 284, 305; and opiates, 131-32, 145, 158, 161-64, 169, 339; relations with Northern Paiutes, 33, 60, 281-82
Wassuk Mountains, 270
Waterbabies, 228-31, 366-67
Water hemlock, 199-200, 309, 360
Wellington, Nev., 47
West Walker River, 270

Wheat, 9
Whites *(taivo)*: dependence on, 279; guns of, 45-46; sale of opiates by, 321, 327-38. *See also* Contact with whites
Wild parsnips *(hageenopa)* or water hemlock, 199-200, 309, 360
Wilson, David and Abigail, 9, 298-99
Wilson, Jack. *See* Wovoka
Wilson Canyon, 270
Wine, homemade *(heebee)*, 12-13, 118-19, 299-302. *See also* Alcohol, use of
Winnemucca, Sarah, 2, 11, 260. *See also* Sarah Winnemucca Hopkins
Witchcraft *(nuumuu pooharru)*, 15, 35-36, 189-92, 264, 268, 349, 357-58; and blindness, 273; and bow and arrow, 216; and death, 35-36, 211, 269; diagnosing, 186; and Tom Mitchell, 38, 178, 186-87, 188, 191-92, 349; and toe injury, 61; and Wodziwob, 179; and Wovoka's father, 26-27
Wodziwob, 15, 49, 176; and afterlife, 369; also called Fish Lake Joe, 49, 176, 352-53; cures by, 176-79; date of death in question, 352; disillusionment of, 16-17; and folktales, 236
Wolf, 89, 222-24, 231-32, 233, 235-36; and origin of pine nuts, 91; a source of Wovoka's power, 359
Women, employment of, 31, 266-67
Wovoka, 15, 260, 261, 293, 353, 354; and afterlife, 368-69; bicultural adaptation of, 10; dances of, 182-84; death of, 193-94, 358; family of, 11, 26-27, 179-81, 193, 353; influences on, 9, 298-99; power of, 181, 184-85, 215, 359; prophecies of, 6, 359

Yen-shee. *See under* Opiates
Yerington, H. M., 283
Yerington, Nev., 277, 281, 294, 345, 346-47
Yerington Indian Colony, 2, 277, 294-95, 351; Indians moved to, 48-49; and opiates, 247-49, 250-51, 351
Yerington Paiute Tribe, 2, 208-9, 364; first chairman of, 208-9; *Tabooseedokado* 'Grass Nut Eaters', 2, 45, 47-49, 274-75